JAVA Programming

JAVA Programming

K. Rajkumar

Department of Computer Science
Bishop Heber College
Tiruchirappalli, India

Chennai • Delhi

Associate Editor—Acquisitions: R. P. Mathivathani
Editor—Production: M. Balakrishnan

ISBN 978-81-317-9909-3

First Impression

Published by Dorling Kindersley (India) Pvt. Ltd, licensees of Pearson Education in South Asia.

Head Office: 7th Floor, Knowledge Boulevard, A-8(A), Sector 62, Noida 201 309, UP, India.
Registered Office: 11 Community Centre, Panchsheel Park, New Delhi 110 017, India.

Compositor: Map Systems, Bengaluru.
Printer: HT Media Ltd., Noida

In loving memory
of
my grandparents

Brief Contents

Contents

PART II - OBJECT ORIENTED JAVA PROGRAMMING

5. Classes and Objects   129

6. Inheritance and Polymorphism   160

PART III - JAVA CONTAINERS FOR HOLDING OBJECTS

13. Processing Byte and Object Streams   414

16. GUI Development Using JFrame   538

Pedagogical Features

Chapters of this book include the following components for effective teaching:

OBJECTIVES

- To introduce implementations of Set interface
- To check whether Sets allow duplicates
- To introduce the add and remove operations on Sets
- To introduce the union and difference operations on Sets
- To develop counting duplicates application
- To introduce LinkedHashSet's insertion ordering
- To introduce TreeSet's red black tree implementation

● Objectives

List the learning requirements for the chapter, which could be topics, concepts and solved programs.

INTRODUCTION

You are about to start a joyful journey to the world of Java by learning the powerful features of Java and developing exciting Java applications now. In this book, Part 1 containing the first four chapters presents Java language as a **structured programming** language. That is, you will learn how to solve problems based on algorithmic steps and modular programming, very similar to C language. In this chapter, we will introduce you to the development of a Java application, besides highlighting the evolution of Java since 1991.

● Introduction

Gives an overview of the chapter and sets the context for the discussion of concepts.

Example 9.1. LinkedLists as Hashtable Values

```
LinkedList javaUsers = new LinkedList();
LinkedList linuxUsers = new LinkedList();
LinkedList pythonUsers = new LinkedList();

Hashtable users = new Hashtable();
users.put("java", javaUsers);
users.put("linux", linuxUsers);
users.put("python", pythonUsers);
```

● Examples

Give adequate illustrations that improve the understandability of concepts and Java language features.

Listing 4.1. Method to Find Biggest of Two Numbers

```
public static int max(int a, int b)
{
    int big = a > b ? a : b;
    return big;
}
```

● Listing

Depicts solved programs with expected outputs and lots of annotated comments which enhance the readability of the source code.

SUMMARY

1. Arrays store values of the same type
2. Arrays can have unlimited dimensions from one dimension, two dimensions, three-dimensions to *n*-dimensions
3. **Array index** identifies its elements
4. Java needs arrays to be declared and initialized first before accessing array elements
5. For-each statement can be used with arrays

Summary

Presents a concise review of topics covered and concepts introduced along with the points that are to be remembered.

KEY TERMS

Access modifiers, 138	Inheritance, 130	Polymorphism, 130
Aggregation, 130	Object, 130	RTTI, 130
Behaviours, 130	Object-oriented programming, 129	States, 130
Encapsulation, 130	Overriding, 130	Static data, 141
Information hiding, 130	Pass objects, 143	Structured programming, 129

Key Terms

Indicate all important terminologies that are to be clearly and precisely understood.

Multiple-choice Questions

1. Given a list of int values, how will you sort these int values?
   a. Arrays.sort()   b. Collections.sort()
   c. TreeSet class   d. All of the above

2. Given a list of wrapper class values, how will you sort these wrapper class values?
   a. Arrays.sort()   b. Collections.sort()
   c. TreeSet class   d. All of the above

Multiple-choice Questions

Test whether readers learnt the syntax and semantics of Java language APIs.

Short-answer Questions

1. Explain Hashtable and its important methods.
2. Explain the important methods of Map interface.
3. What are the three implementations of Map interface?
4. What is the difference between Hashtable and HashMap?
5. How can you create a HashMap inside another HashMap?
6. What is Multimap?

Short-answer Questions

Test whether readers gained adequate knowledge and skills to develop simple programs based on the concepts learned.

EXERCISES

13.1. Count the nuhber of characters in a given file.
13.2. Count the number of words in a file.
13.3. Print the frequency (i.e. number of times it occurs) of each character from a given file.
13.4. Print the frequency of words in a given file.
13.5. [File Encryption] Caesar cipher (with k=2) replaces A by C, B by D, .., Y by A and Z by B. Now read characters of a file, encrypt and store it in a new file. Just ignore when you encounter lowercase letters or other characters. Display both source and destination files.
13.6. [File Decryption] Read an already encrypted file, perform the reverse replacement of characters and recover the original file.

Exercises

Expect readers to develop programs based on the concepts and skills they have learned throughout the chapter.

Listing 4.10. Fibonacci Series Using Recursion

```
// RecursiveFibonacci.java                          {coderipe}
import java.util.*;

public class RecursiveFibonacci
{
    public static long fib(int n)
    {
        if (n <= 1)
            return n;
        else
            return fib(n-1) + fib(n-2);
    }
}
```

Coderipe

Customized FREE version of Coderipe. Coderipe is a Web-based virtual programming lab on C, C++, Java and others.

Java, since its advent about two decades ago, has been an extremely popular programming language around the world. It is the *Numero Uno* programming language in terms of academic acceptance and the actual number of developers. Further, Java continues to maintain its No.1 rank on *the TIOBE Programming Community Index*. This book aims to introduce Java by unraveling its powerful constructs to develop exciting applications.

AUDIENCE

This book provides concise and simplified introduction to Java programming and is a suitable one-semester text book for B.Sc., BCA, B.E. and B.Tech. students. It also covers major topics of Java syllabus for M.Sc., MCA and other related postgraduate programmes that include a course on Java.

PREREQUISITES

This book does not assume any prior programming knowledge. However, some basic understanding of conditions, iterations, functions and files concepts will help readers to understand the concepts easily. Therefore, a little knowledge of either *C* or *Python* language would be advantageous to learn Java.

READING OUTCOMES

This book is not a reference repository to all Java packages and Application Programming Interfaces (API). As Java is vast, we will touch upon only those classes and methods that are necessary for the presentation of the concepts discussed in this book. So, you are encouraged to refer to online API documentation available from Sun's Web site for further information about Java packages.

In contrast to the idea of a reference text book, this book will teach you the art of programming using Java language. That is, you will learn how to solve problems by leveraging Java features through its wealthy collection of classes and methods. The book also focuses on a few interesting problems from data structures, algorithms and web engineering, besides object-oriented programming.

As Java certification is an added advantage, this book is designed to equip readers to take up *Oracle Certified Associate, Java SE7 Programmer – I* (the erstwhile *Sun Certified Java Programmer*) certification examination, with its unique multiple-choice question collections.

ORGANIZATION OF THE BOOK

This book groups all topics that are related to an introductory course on Java programming into five parts. These five parts of the book are structured around the four Java packages, namely, *java.lang*, *java.util* (including *java.util.concurrent*), *java.io* (including *java.nio*) and *java.swing* (including all necessary *java.awt* classes).

Part I: Java Basics (Chapters 1–4)

The first part of this book introduces Java as a structured programming language. You will learn in Chapter 1 all details about data types, variables, literals and console I/O features. Next, you will learn about conditional and looping statements (Chapter 2), followed by arrays (Chapter 3) and methods (Chapter 4).

Part II: Object Oriented Java Programming (Chapters 5–7)

The second part of the book depicts Java as an object-oriented programming language. You will be exposed to classes and methods in Chapter 5. Then, you will learn inheritance and polymorphism (Chapter 6). Finally, Chapter 7 discusses abstract classes, interfaces, enums, packages and exception handling methods.

Part III: Java Containers for Holding Objects (Chapters 8–11)

Part 3 of this book deals with all data structures to store objects. You will learn all sequence containers including vector, string tokenizer and stack (Chapter 8). The book then elaborates on all map containers including hashtable (Chapter 9) and all set containers (Chapter 10). Finally, all sorting and searching methods are discussed in Chapter 11.

Part IV: Java Threads and IO Streams (Chapters 12–14)

This part of the book is devoted to multithreading and files processing. More specifically, you will learn Java threads and thread synchronization (Chapter 12), byte streams (Chapter 13) and finally, character streams and NIO (Chapter 14).

Part V: Java GUI Programming (Chapters 15–17)

The last part of this book introduces Graphical User Interface (GUI) development in Java. You will learn 2D graphics to generate lines, arcs and other patterns (Chapter 15), create interesting GUI applications using JFrame (Chapter 16) and create GUI based applets using JApplet (Chapter 17). As swing has become a matured technology now and many AWT classes are deprecated, this book focuses on swing-based GUI design.

The appendices include Java-reserved words list, list of selected J2SE 7 packages and the syllabus for OCA, Java Programmer-I (Exam Number 1Z0-803).

COURSE OUTLINE

Although the whole book can be conveniently covered in one semester, instructors can customize the syllabus according to their requirements. The following flow diagram suggests three sample tracks for the Java programming course. The first track outlines the syllabus for the beginners who do not have any prior programming knowledge. The second track is meant for the intermediate level who have a little programming knowledge. The third track specifies the syllabus for the seniors who have complete knowledge of one programming language.

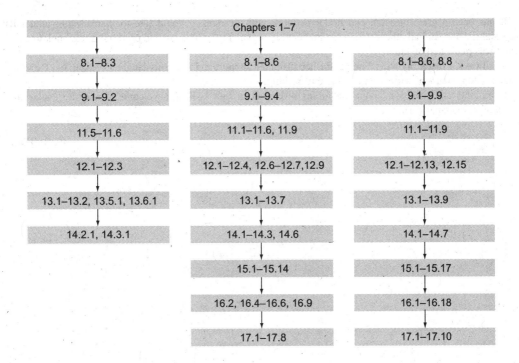

ONLINE RESOURCES

Source code of all examples and exercises, instructor's lecture slides as well as errata can be accessed online from www.pearsoned.co.in/krajkumar

ONLINE PRACTICE

The book comes with a customized FREE version of Coderipe with selected programming exercises and examples from the book (highlighted in the textbook using the Coderipe logo ({coderipe})). Coderipe is a Web-based virtual programming lab on C, C++, Java and others.

ACKNOWLEDGEMENTS

I would like to thank Dr D. Paul Dhayabaran, Principal, Bishop Heber College, and all other staff members of this college for providing me the opportunity to teach Java in this college for over a decade. This experience has served well to make this book a reality. I am grateful to all teachers and students for their comments and suggestions to improve this text.

This book has received a lot of insightful comments, suggestions and reviews from eminent instructors. My heartfelt thanks to Maria Bielikova (Slovak University of Technology, Slovakia), George Ghinea (Brunel University, UK), Frederic Andres (National Institute of Informatics, Japan), Asanee Kawtrakul (Kasetsart University, Thailand), Fernando Ferri (CNR, Italy), Patrizia Grifoni (CNR, Italy), Joemon Jose (University of Glasgow, UK), Krzysztof Michalak (Wroclaw University, Poland), Kalaiarasi Anbananthen (Multimedia University, Malaysia), and Christian Guetl (Graz University of Technology, Austria). Also, I am indebted to all the anonymous reviewers for their constructive comments.

It has been a great pleasure and honor to work with Pearson. I would like to thank Mathivathani RP, M. Balakrishnan, and all others who were involved in organizing, producing and promoting this book to ensure that it was published on time.

As always, I thank my wife, Sheela, for her sustained support and my little daughters Hazel and Beryl who made my long hours of writing cheerful and refreshing.

Comments and feedback about the topics discussed in this book are welcome. I may be contacted at dr.rajkumarkannan@gmail.com

K. Rajkumar

PART I Java Basics

1

Java Data Types, Operators and Console I/O Statements

OBJECTIVES

- To introduce Java and World Wide Web
- To introduce Java Editing Environments
- To explore Java comments, errors and debugging
- To explore Java constants, variables, literals, data types (both primitive and wrapper) and operators
- To initialize data types with binary values
- To write numeric values with underscore
- To understand the ways of type casting such as upcasting, downcasting, auto-boxing and unboxing
- To explain Java console input and output statements
- To implement Command line arguments using SumIt application
- To briefly explain exception handling with try-catch statements
- To explain Scanner class with PrintSum application
- To implement BufferedReader class with CircleArea application
- To develop EllipseArea application with DataInputStream class
- To develop ConsoleTest application with Console class

1.1 INTRODUCTION

You are about to start a joyful journey to the world of Java by learning the powerful features of Java and developing exciting Java applications now. In this book, Part 1 containing the first four chapters presents Java language as a **structured programming** language. That is, you will learn how to solve problems based on algorithmic steps and modular programming, very similar to C language. In this chapter, we will introduce you to the development of a Java application, besides highlighting the evolution of Java since 1991.

1.2 JAVA, WORLD WIDE WEB AND SENSOR DEVICES

Today, it is very hard for us to think of a world without Internet. The present-day Internet and all tools for our daily lives like **web browsers** (such as Firefox, Internet Explorer, Safari and others) are possible as a result of research and technology innovations that started in the early 1990s.

Now Java powers many devices and applications such as computers, printers, routers, cell phones, e-readers, parking meters, vehicle diagnostic systems, ATMs, credit cards, MRIs, VOIP, robots, home security systems, airplane systems, televisions, cable boxes and many more. But, the evolution of Java dates back to 1990.

In 1990, Sun Microsystems gathered some of its top engineers to examine the then-upcoming consumer electronics market such as TV set-top boxes and interactive TVs. The efforts of the research resulted in a new language called *Oak*. Sun engineers Patrick Naughton and Jonathan Payne used the Oak to write WebRunner (later renamed HotJava), the first browser that supported moving objects and dynamic executable content. In 1994, Oak was renamed as Java and James Gosling became the Father of Java. In 1995, Internet wave made Java as an **object-oriented programming** tool. With Java, information and programming made surfing the web a more dynamic experience.

Java language was created with five important goals:

- It should be object oriented.
- It should be platform independent. That is, a single program could be executed on multiple operating systems.
- It should fully support network programming.
- It should execute code from remote sources securely.
- It should be easy to use.

Java addresses traditional concerns like security, reusability and transportability (called **platform independence**). Java has been defined with two entities:

- A platform, namely **Java Runtime Environment** (JRE)
- A language, namely Java Software Development Kit (SDK)

In 1999, Sun announces a redefined architecture for the Java platform for software developers, service providers, and device manufacturers to target specific markets. It introduced free version of the three flavours for Java platform under GPL license:

- Java 2 Platform, Standard Edition **(J2SE)** for desktop and workstation applications
- Java 2 Platform, Enterprise Edition **(J2EE)** for heavy-duty server-side applications and
- Java 2 Platform, Micro Edition **(J2ME)** for consumer and handheld devices

Now, with its current release Java 1.7 (also called Java 7), Java technology has evolved from a simple tool to animated Web sites to the end-to-end Java 2 platform for building rich Web sites, smartcards, small consumer devices and enterprise data center servers.

1.3 JAVA EDITING ENVIRONMENTS

Now we introduce the readers to the development of a Java application by performing the three basics steps that are required to run the program. The Java Platform Standard Edition (J2SE) Application Programming Interfaces **(APIs)** consists of a collection of packages, where each package has a set of

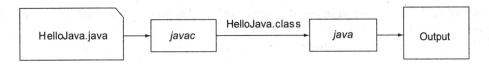

Figure 1.1. Java Programming Steps

classes, abstract classes and interfaces that can be imported and invoked inside the Java program. Some examples of primitive packages we are interested in this book are lang, util, io, awt, applet and swing.

Essentially, developing a Java application is simply designing the algorithm as a collection of sequential steps and translating it into a Java source code. To be precise, the process of Java programming has three steps (see Figure 1.1):

- Creating the program using any **text editor** (such as NetBeans (*www.netbeans.org*), Eclipse (*www.eclipse.org*), JEdit (*www.jedit.org*), IntelliJCommunity Edition (*http://www.jetbrains. com*) and many others and saving it to a file with *.java* extension, say *HelloJava.java*.
- Compiling the file, using *javac* **compiler**, as by typing *javac HelloJava.java* in the command prompt, this produces a platform-independent byte code, with extension *.class*, say *HelloJava.class*.
- Interpreting or running the class file, with Java Virtual Machine (*JVM*), as by typing *java HelloJava* in the command prompt, which produces the desired output, as shown in Listing 1.1.

Listing 1.1. HelloJava

```java
//HelloJava.java
import java.lang.*;

public class HelloJava {
    public static void main(String[] args) {
        System.out.println("Hello Java World");
    }
}
```

```
E:\Rajkumar\javacourse\basics>javac HelloJava.java
E:\Rajkumar\javacourse\basics>java HelloJava
Hello Java World
E:\Rajkumar\javacourse\basics>
```

Java starts executing a program from the first line of the main() method of a public class. This Java program displays the string *HelloJava* onto the monitor of your computer using *println()* method. Here, *System.out* refers to the standard output device, which is a monitor. Note that the source file should be saved by its class name, and each file should have a public class in which main() method should have been defined.

This application includes all classes in the package named *lang*, which is included automatically by default to any application. Generally, we do not have to import it. Remember, Java is case sensitive.

For simplicity, let us skip the meaning of various words of this program such as *public, class, static* and *void*. You will be able to understand them little later.

Java supports three types of **comments**.

- *Single-line comments*: the entire line followed by // will be ignored by *javac* compiler
- *Multiline comments*: *javac* ignores a block of statements that appear between /* and */
- *Java documentation comments*: statements that appear between /** and */. Java uses these comments to generate html pages for classes.

Often, novice Java developers face many errors during their Java application development. However, most of the errors can be easily debugged by carefully examining the program as we create it. Errors can be classified into two types:

- *Syntax errors*: These errors are reported to users during compilation phase and indicate the mistakes in Java syntax.
- *Semantic errors*: These errors are reported to users during run-time phase and indicate errors in the program logic or the program tries to perform illegal Java operation.

1.4 DATA TYPES AND VARIABLES

Generally, **data types** are used to create **variables** where variables will hold values, as defined in the range of values of a data type. Java supports two types of data types:

- Primitive data types and
- Wrapper classes

The eight primitive data types (*boolean, byte, char, double, float, int, long, and short*) will help Java users to create the corresponding variables. Java supports **wrapper classes** for these eight primitive data types.

Example 1.1 depicts some examples for variable declaration and initialization. Note that all variables in Java begin with lowercase letters. Also, a variable with two words is joined together with an uppercase letter. These are general naming conventions that Java developers follow based on software development practices.

Example 1.1. Variable Declaration and Initialization

```
int age;  // only declaration, here age is a variable of the data
type int
double salary; // salary is a variable of data type double
int age = 30;    // declaration and initialization. Here 30 is
called literal
double salary = 100000.00;
char c = 'a';  // enclosed in single quote
String s = "a";  // enclosed in double quote
String employeeId = "1234";  // even, numerals are enclosed in
double quote
float sum = 10.00f;  // suffix f indicates float
long password = 1234567891234567891L;
String s = null; // null is a literal
boolean valid = true; // true is a literal
```

In Java SE 7, byte, short, int, and long variables can also be expressed using the binary number system. To specify a binary value, add the prefix 0b or 0B to the number. Example 1.2 shows variables with binary values

Example 1.2. Variables with Binary Values

```
// Some int values:
int anInt1 = 0b10100101010001011010100101000101;
int anInt2 = 0b1010;
int anInt3 = 0B1010; // The B can be upper or lower case.

// some long value. Note the "L" suffix
long aLong = 0b10100101010001011010011101000101101000010100110110
10000101000101L;
```

In Java SE 7 and later, any number of underscore characters (_) can appear anywhere between digits in numerical values, which can improve the readability of your code. Example 1.3 shows other ways in which the underscore can be used

Example 1.3. Underscores with Values

```
Long accountNumber = 5100_0129_6733;
long uid = 123_456_789_123;
int regno = 12_100_01;
int salary = 10._50;  // invalid: using underscore with dot
```

Table 1.1 depicts wrapper classes of primitive data types along with the size and value ranges for primitives. These wrapper classes are available in the package named *java.lang*, and each class provides a collection of methods to manipulate the wrapped data.

Table 1.1. Primitives and Wrapper Equivalents

Primitive Data Type	Size (bytes)	Range of Values (inclusive)	Equivalent Wrapper Class
int	4	−2,147,483,648 to +2,147,483,647	Integer
long	8	−9,223,372,036,854,775,808 to +9,223,372,036,854,775,807	Long
short	2	−32,768 to −32,767	Short
double	8	Double-precision 64-bit IEEE 754	Double
float	4	Single-precision 32-bit IEEE 754	Float
boolean	1 bit flag	True/false.	Boolean
char	2	0 to 65,535	Character
byte	1	−128 to +127	Byte
No equivalent			String

1.5 CONSTANTS IN JAVA

Constants are created in Java using *public static final* variables. The basic assumption is that once a value is assigned to constant, it cannot be modified inside the application even during compile time. Some examples of constants are shown in Example 1.4:

Example 1.4. Creating Constants

```
public static final int MAX = 100;
public static final boolean isModified = false;
```

1.6 JAVA OPERATORS

Java supports wealth of **operators** that allow a program to manipulate values of variables. Table 1.2–1.7 depicts the group of operator types in Java.

Table 1.2. Assignment Operators

Operator	Example
Assignment(=)	int a = 100;
Addition & assignment (+=)	a + = 100;
Subtraction & assignment (−=)	a − = 100;
Multiplication & assignment (*=)	a * = 100;
Division & assignment (/=)	a / = 100;
Reminder & assignment (%=)	a % = 100;

Table 1.3. Arithmetic Operators

Operator	Example
Addition (+)	a = a + b;
Subtraction (−)	a = a − b;
Multiplication (*)	a = a * b;
Division (/)	a = a / b;
Reminder (%)	a = a % b;

Table 1.4. Unary and Equality Operators

Operator	Example
Unary +	+a;
Unary −	−a;
++	++a & a++; increments a by 1
−−	−−a & a−−; decrements a by 1
!	!y; negates y
==	a == b

Table 1.5. Relational and Logical Operators

Operator	Example
Greater than (>)	a > b
Greater than or equal to (>=)	a >= b
Less than (<)	a < b
Less than or equal to (<=)	a <= b
Not equal to (!=)	a != b
Logical AND (&&)	(a > b) && (a > c)
Logical OR (||)	(a > b) || (a > c)
Logical NOT (!)	complement
Ternary (?:)	Typical C style if-then-else operator

Table 1.6. Bitwise and Shift Operators

Operator	Example
Bitwise AND (&)	a & b
Bitwise OR (|)	a | b
Bitwise NOT (~)	One's complement
Bitwise XOR (^)	a ^ b
Left shift (<<)	One bit left
Right shift (>>)	One bit right
Unsigned right shift (>>>)	Shifts a 0 into left-most position

Table 1.7. Type Comparison Operator

Operator	Example
instanceof, compares object to a specified type	a *instanceof* Integer

Java follows the same operator precedence as C language to evaluate a given Java expression. Further, we will introduce brackets to expressions as and when required in order to avoid the ambiguity during the evaluation of expressions. Example 1.5 illustrates the evaluation of an arithmetic expression. Normally, we would follow type2 with lots of brackets than type1.

Example 1.5. Evaluation of Arithmetic Expressions

```
Type1: result1 = a + b * c;  // you need to remember, * has
higher precedence than +
Type2: result2 = a + (b * c);  // simply use brackets wherever
required to avoid ambiguity
```

1.7 TYPE CASTING AND BOXING

Type casting or type conversion allows Java developers to convert one type of data to another type. Type casting can be automatic or manual. Automatic type conversion carried out by Java itself is called *upcasting* and manual type conversion is known as *downcasting*. Some examples of type casting are shown in Example 1.6.

Example 1.6. Type Casting

```
int x = 100;
long y = x;  // upcasting
int z = (int)y;  // downcasting
100 + "hello" becomes "100hello"  // concatenation
```

Java 1.5 and later versions of it supports automatic conversion of primitive data types to their wrapper classes in assignment statements and method as well as constructor invocations. This conversion is known as *auto-boxing* or simply *boxing*. Java also supports automatic *unboxing*, where wrapper types are automatically converted into their primitive equivalents as shown in Example 1.7.

Example 1.7. Boxing and Unboxing

```
Integer  i = 5;  // auto-boxing
int j = 0;
j = new Integer(5); // unboxing
```

1.8 CONSOLE I/O STATEMENTS

Now we lead you to the understanding of various ways of reading data from keyboard and writing outputs to screen. Unlike other programming languages, Java does not support direct statements that will perform console input and output operations. The reason behind this is that Java has been designed as a Web programming language with complete object-oriented design principles, and interaction between the business logic of a program and users' data has to happen via graphical user interface (GUI) components such as Frames and Applets. However, it will be interesting to learn all possible ways to perform reading and writing data inside a Java application.

A Java application can receive input values from command prompt by any one of the following ways:

- Command line
- Scanner
- BufferedReader
- DataInputstream
- Console

Now, we explore these console reading statements one after the other with suitable examples.

1.8.1 Command Line

The values a user enters in the command prompt while running a Java application can be collected inside main() method of a public class through the arguments of main(). Remember all the collected values are of string type and have to be parsed according to the required data type. For instance, to run the class file WelcomeMe with a name "Rajkumar," the user needs to type the statement as "*java WelcomeMe Rajkumar*." Here, we transmit one string to the class WelcomeMe. Listing 1.2 gives you a complete illustration.

Listing 1.2. WelcomeMe Application

```java
// WelcomeMe.java

public class WelcomeMe
{
    public static void main(String[] args)
    {
        System.out.println("Hello" + args[0]);
    }
}
```

```
E:\Rajkumar\javacourse\basics>javac WelcomeMe.java
E:\Rajkumar\javacourse\basics>java WelcomeMe Rajkumar
Hello Rajkumar
E:\Rajkumar\javacourse\basics>
```

The println() method displays the output by concatenating the string *Hello* with the command line argument value *Rajkumar*. Understand, args is a string array; thereby users can transmit any number of values from the command prompt. The meaning of System.out will be explained to you in Chapter 14.

Similar to reading strings from command line, other primitive data types can also be read using wrapper class methods. For example, other wrapper classes provide parseXXX() methods to parse primitive types such as int, long, float and double. Here, XXX denotes a primitive data type, either *int, float, long* or *double*. Obviously, parseInt() method from Integer wrapper class converts the given string equivalent of integer into int. Listing 1.3 illustrates the use of parseInt() to find the sum of two numbers.

Listing 1.3. SumIt Application

```java
// SumIt.java                                          {coderipe}
import java.io.*;

public class SumIt
{
    public static void main(String[] args) throws IOException
    {
        // Step1: read data from command line parameters and add them
```

```
        int sum = Integer.parseInt(args[0]) + Integer.
        parseInt(args[1]);
        // Step2: show result
        System.out.println("Sum: " + sum);
    }
}
```

```
E:\Rajkumar\javacourse\basics>javac SumIt.java
E:\Rajkumar\javacourse\basics>java SumIt 10 20
Sum: 30
E:\Rajkumar\javacourse\basics>
```

Here, parseInt() method will throw an exception named *NumberFormatException* which is of type *IOException*. That is, parseInt() expects integer, say, "100." Anything else will throw an exception. For instance, giving "12.00" will throw this exception. Exception can be handled using try-catch statements as shown in Listing 1.4.

Listing 1.4. SumIt2 with Exception Handling

```
// SumIt2.java                                              {coderipe}
import java.io.*;

public class SumIt2
{
    public static void main(String[] args) throws IOException
    {
        try
        {
            int sum = Integer.parseInt(args[0]) + Integer.
            parseInt(args[1]);
            System.out.println("Sum: " + sum);
        }
        catch (NumberFormatException e)
            System.out.println("Enter 2 integers in command
            prompt");
        }
    }
}
```

```
E:\Rajkumar\javacourse\basics>javac SumIt2.java
E:\Rajkumar\javacourse\basics>java SumIt2 15 20
Sum: 35
E:\Rajkumar\javacourse\basics>
```

In this application, users are reported with a message, Enter 2 integers, when they fail to supply two integers through command prompt. Try block contains all Java statements that are likely throw exceptions and catch block will define an exception that is likely to happen. Note that a try block can follow one or more catch() blocks handling several exceptions. Exception handling is discussed in detail in Chapter 7.

1.8.2 Scanner

The **Scanner** class from java.util package allows the user to read numerical values from either keyboard (i.e. *System.in* that is a standard input device) or file without having to convert them from strings and determine whether there are more values to be read. Some of the important methods in Scanner class are shown summarized Table 1.8.

Table 1.8. Scanner Methods

Method	Returns
int nextInt()	Returns the next token as an int
long nextLong()	Returns the next token as a long
float nextFloat()	Returns the next token as a float
double nextDouble()	Returns the next token as a long
String next()	Finds and returns the next complete token from this scanner and returns it as a string; a token is usually ended by whitespace such as a blank or \n
String nextLine()	Returns the rest of the current line, excluding any line separator at the end
void close()	Closes the scanner

Note that if the next token read is not of a specific type, Java will throw an exception, *InputMismatchException*. One final word about tokens, a token is a group of characters in the input, which ends with any of the four whitespace characters, blankspace, \r, \t and end of file by default. Tokens can also be parsed based on any user-defined character, by using useDelimiter() method (Listing 1.5).

Listing 1.5. PrintName Application

```
// PrintName.java                                          {coderipe}
import java.io.*;
import java.util.*;

public class PrintName
{
    public static void main(String[] args)
    {
        // Step1: create a Scanner instance to keyboard
        Scanner sc = new Scanner(System.in);
```

```
        // Step2: get first name
        System.out.print("Enter your first name: " );
        String fname = sc.nextLine();
        // Step3: get last name
        System.out.print("Enter your last name: " );
        String lname = sc.nextLine();
        // Step4: show
        System.out.print("Your name is " + lname + " " +fname);
    }
}
```

```
E:\Rajkumar\javacourse\basics>javac PrintName.java
E:\Rajkumar\javacourse\basics>java PrintName
Enter your first name: Rajkumar
Enter your last name: Kannan
Your name is Kannan Rajkumar
E:\Rajkumar\javacourse\basics>
```

The above application begins with importing all classes available in java.util package, as Scanner is defined in util package. Scanner object is instantiated to read from keyboard using System.in stream. The method nextLine() reads a string with new line character from keyboard. Further, this application uses print() method instead of println() to display a string. Here, the cursor will wait on the same line for the user to give input values.

One final note about Scanner, other nextXXX() methods reading primitive data will not read newline character that is appended to input string while typing values in the keyboard. This will return newline character also as a token, which has to be discarded while reading primitive data from keyboard, by simply calling a dummy nextLine() method. Another obvious solution will be to set up a new scanner for primitive data types. The following application calculates the sum of two integers using nextInt() method (Listing 1.6).

Listing 1.6. PrintSum Application

```
// PrintSum.java
import java.util.*;

public class PrintSum
{
    public static void main(String[] args)
    {
        // Step1: create a Scanner instance to keyboard
        Scanner sc = new Scanner(System.in);
        // Step2: get first number
        System.out.print("Enter integer1: " );
```

```
      int a = sc.nextInt();
      // Step3: get second number
      System.out.print("Enter integer2: " );
      int b = sc.nextInt();
      // Step4: discard \n
      sc.nextLine();
      // Step5: get name
      System.out.print("Enter your name: " );
      String name = sc.nextLine();
      // Step6: show
      System.out.println("Hello " + name + " Sum is " + (a+b));
   }
}
```

```
E:\Rajkumar\javacourse\basics>javac PrintSum.java
E:\Rajkumar\javacourse\basics>java PrintSum
Enter integer1: 30
Enter integer2: 20
Enter your name: Rex Peter
Hello Rex Peter Sum is 50
E:\Rajkumar\javacourse\basics>
```

1.8.3 BufferedReader

Before Scanner class was introduced, in earlier Java versions, most of the Java developers were using BufferedReader class from *io* package to read data from keyboard. It provides one important method named nextLine() that reads a string from keyboard, so that the string can be parsed into specific primitive types, using parseXXX() methods of the wrapper classes, as before.

Now, let us develop a simple application that will calculate the area of a circle. First, we need to identify the set of steps (called algorithm) to be carried out to accomplish this task. The steps are written as comments in the following code snippet (Listing 1.7).

Listing 1.7. Pseudo Code for Circle Area Application

```
import java.io.*;
public class CircleArea
{
   public static void main ( String args[] ) throws IOException
   {
      // Step1: get radius of circle
      // Step2: calculate area of circle
      // Step3: print the calculated area
   }
}
```

Now, we must convert each step into the corresponding Java statement, which will result in the required application, as shown in Listing 1.8. Here, InputStreamReader reads characters from command prompt, buffers them and supplies those characters to BufferedReader class. Note that parse-Double() reads radius as a double value.

Listing 1.8. CircleArea Application

```java
// CircleArea.java
import java.io.*;
public class CircleArea
{
    public static void main ( String args[] ) throws IOException
    {
        BufferedReader in = new BufferedReader (
                new InputStreamReader ( System.in ) );
        // Step1: get radius of circle
        System.out.print ( "Enter radius: " );
        double radius = Double.parseDouble (in.readLine());
        // Step2: calculate area of circle
        double area = 3.14159 * radius * radius;
        // Step3: print the calculated area
        System.out.println ( "Area of circle is: " + area );
    }
}
```

```
E:\Rajkumar\javacourse\basics>javac CircleArea.java
E:\Rajkumar\javacourse\basics>java CircleArea
Enter radius: 5.0
Area of circle is: 78.53975
E:\Rajkumar\javacourse\basics>
```

1.8.4 DataInputStream

DataInputStream is yet another class that provides methods to read primitive data types from keyboard. Like BufferedReader, this class supports readLine() method to read a string from keyboard. Then, the string can be parsed into specific primitive types using parseXXX() methods of wrapper classes as before. In Listing 1.9, let us calculate the area of ellipse using DataInputStream class.

Listing 1.9. Calculating the Area of Ellipse

```java
// EllipseArea.java
import java.io.*;
public class EllipseArea
```

```
{
    public static void main ( String args[] ) throws
    IOException
    {
        // Step1: create stream
        DataInputStream in = new DataInputStream
        ( System.in );
        // Step2: get point 1
        System.out.print ( "Enter point 1: " );
        int f = Double.parseInt (in.readLine());
        // Step3: get point 2
        System.out.print ( "Enter point 2: " );
        int g = Double.parseInt (in.readLine());
        // Step4: calculate area
        int area = 3.14159 * f * g;
        // Step5: show result
        System.out.println ( "Area of ellipse is: " +
        area );
    }
}
```

```
E:\Rajkumar\javacourse\basics>javac EllipseArea.java
E:\Rajkumar\javacourse\basics>java EllipseArea
Enter point 1: 4
Enter point 2: 6
Area of ellipse is: 75.39815999999999
E:\Rajkumar\javacourse\basics>
```

Buffering can also be added by using BufferedInputStream between System.in and DataInput-Stream as shown in Example 1.8.

Example 1.8.

```
DataInputStream in = new DataInputStream
( new BufferedInputStream(System.in ) );
```

1.8.5 Console

Finally, Java supports one more advanced alternative to read strings from command prompt. Two important methods **Console** supports are readLine() to read a string and readPassword() that reads a string that is invisible while typing. In this application, valueOf() converts character array into a string (Listing 1.10).

Listing 1.10. ConsoleTest Application

```java
// ConsoleTest.java

import java.io.*;
public class ConsoleTest
{
    public static void main(String[] args) throws IOException
    {
        // get Console object
        Console c = System.console();
        // get name
        System.out.print("Enter user name: " );
        String s = c.readLine();
        // get password
        System.out.print("Enter password: " );
        char[] pwd = c.readPassword();
        System.out.println("You typed: " + s + "," + String.
        valueOf(pwd));
    }
}
```

```
E:\Rajkumar\javacourse\basics>javac ConsoleTest.java
E:\Rajkumar\javacourse\basics>java ConsoleTest
Enter user name: admin
Enter password:********
You typed: admin,helloraj
E:\Rajkumar\javacourse\basics>
```

1.9 SUMMARY

1. Java application can be edited using any editor such as JEdit and even Notepad
2. Java application is compiled with javac compiler and interpreted with Java interpreter
3. Javac generates byte code from source Java file which is a platform-independent code
4. Errors can be syntactic errors or semantic errors
5. Java supports primitive data types and their equivalent wrapper classes
6. Constants can be created using public static final access type
7. Java has a wealth of operators
8. Java supports many type casting features such as upcasting, downcasting, auto-boxing and unboxing
9. Java application can receive input values using command line, Scanner class, BufferedReader class, DataInputStream as well as Console class

KEY TERMS

API, 4

Comments, 6

Constants, 8

Console, 17

Data types, 6

J2EE, 4

J2ME, 4

J2SE, 4

Javac compiler, 5

Java runtime environment, 4

JVM, 5

Object-oriented programming, 4

Operators, 8

Platform independence, 4

Scanner, 13

Structured programming, 3

Text editor, 5

Variables, 6

Web browsers, 4

Wrapper classes, 6

REVIEW QUESTIONS

Multiple-choice Questions

1. Consider the following program:

```
import java.lang.*;
public class ClassA
{
    // code for the class
}
```

What should be the name of the java file containing this program?

a. lang.java

b. ClassA.java

c. ClassA

d. ClassA.class

e. Any file name with the java suffix will do

2. What is the output of this program?

```
public class HelloJava
{
    public static void main(String a)
    {
        System.out.println("Hello Java World");
    }
}
```

a. Hello Java World

b. Compilation error

c. Runtime error

d. Prints the value of *a* as a command line argument

3. What will be the output for the following code?

```
public class Test
{
    public static void main(String[] args)
    {
    public static final int max = 100;
    max++;
    System.out.println(max);
    }
}
```

a. 100	b. Compilation error
c. Runtime error	d. 101

4. What will be the output for the code segment shown below?

```
public class Test
{
    public static void main(String[] args)
    {
        int a =100;
        System.out.println(a + "100");
    }
}
```

a. 100	b. 200
c. 100100	d. Compilation error

5. Choose the correct output for the following code:

```
public class Test
{
    public static void main(String[] args)
    {
    String s = "-100";
    int i = Integer.parseInt(s);
    System.out.println(i);
    }
}
```

It will throw

a. NumberFormatException	b. IOException
c. InputMismatchException	d. None of the above

6. What is the result of the following code?

```java
public class Test
{
    public static void main(String[] args)
    {
        System.out.println((1 | 3) + (4 & 2));
    }
}
```

a. 3   b. 7

c. 1342   d. 10

7. Select the invalid assignment statements from the following:
   (a) boolean b = "false";
   (b) boolean c = "true";
   (c) float f = 200.20;

a. a and b   b. a and c

c. b and c   d. a, b and c

8. What will be the output?

```java
public class Test
{
    public static void main(String[] args)
    {
        int a = -20;
        int b = -3;
        System.out.println(a%b);
    }
}
```

a. –2   b. 2

c. –6   d. 6

9. What is the value of *b*?

```java
public class Test
{
    public static void main(String[] args)
    {
        int x = 10;
```

```
        String b = Integer.toBinaryString(x);
        System.out.println(b);
    }
}
```

a. 10100000

b. 00001010

c. 1010

d. 0101

10. What is the output for the following program?

```
public class Test
{
    public static void main(String[] args)
    {
        int x = 10;
        System.out.println(Integer.toString(x,2));
    }
}
```

a. 10100000

b. 00001010

c. 1010

d. 0101

11. Find out the output:

```
public class Test
{
    public static void main(String[] args)
    {
        int x = 10;
        String o = Integer.toOctalString(x);
        System.out.println(o);
        System.out.println(Integer.toString(x,8));
    }
}
```

a. 10 8

b. 12 12

c. 8 12

d. 8 8

12. What is the output for the code snippet below?

```
public class Test
{
```

```
 public static void main(String[] args)
 {
    int x = 10;
    String h = Integer.toHexString(x);
    System.out.println(h);
    System.out.println(Integer.toString(x,16));
 }
}
```

a. A A   b. h h

c. a a   d. F F

13. Select the invalid assignment statements from the following:
    (a) float x = 238.88;
    (b) double y = 0x443;
    (c) byte b = 128;
    a. a, b   b. b, c
    c. a, c   d. a, b, c

14. What will be the output for the source code below?

```
public class Test
{
   public static void main(String[] args)
   {
      int a = 14, b = -14;
      System.out.println(a>>2);
      System.out.println(b>>1);
      System.out.println(a>>>2);
      System.out.println(b<<1);
   }
}
```

a. 16 –15 18 –13   b. 15 –14 17 –12

c. 14 –14 28 7   d. 3 –7 3 –28

15. Consider the following code: int x, y, z;

```
public class Test
{
   public static void main(String[] args)
   {
```

```
    int a = 10, b = 5;
    int c = 20 - (++b) - a--;
    System.out.println(a + b + c)
}
}
```

a. 19   b. 20

c. 21   d. 22

16. Identify the output displayed for the code below:

```
public class Test
{
   public static void main(String[] args)
   {
      int a = 3000, b;
      short c;
      byte b1 = -50, b2;
      long l;
      b = a * b1; // statement1
      c = a * b1; // statement2
      l = a * 25f; // statement3
      System.out.println(b +"," + c + "," + l);
   }
}
```

a. Compilation error in statement1,2
b. Compilation error in statement2,3
c. Compilation error in statement1,3
d. Compilation error in statement1,2,3

17. Find out the output:

```
public class Test
{
   public static void main(String[] args)
   {
      int a1 = 0b1010;
      int a2 = 0B1010;
      System.out.println(a1+a2);
   }
}
```

a. 20
                                            b. ob1010ob1010

c. oB10101010
                                            d. 40

18. Find out the output:

```
public class Test
{
    public static void main(String[] args)
    {
        long a = 0b10101010L;
        System.out.println(a>>2);
    }
}
```

a. ob101010
                                            b. OB101010

c. 10101000
                                            d. 00101010

19. Find out the output:

```
public class Test
{
    public static void main(String[] args)
    {
        long salary = 100_000;
        System.out.println(salary+200);
    }
}
```

a. Compilation error
                                      b. Runtime exception

c. 100200
                                            d. 300_000

20. Find out the output:

```
public class Test
{
    public static void main(String[] args)
    {
        int i = new Integer(10);
        double d = new Double(20.0);
        System.out.println(i*d);
    }
}
```

a. 200 b. 200.0

c. Compilation error d. Runtime exception

21. Find out the output:

```
public static void main(String[] args)
{
    boolean b;
    System.out.println(b);
}
```

a. True b. False

c. 0 d. Compilation error: b not initialized

Answers

1. b	2. c	3. b	4. c	5. d	6. a	7. b	8. a	9. c	10. c
11. b	12. c	13. c	14. d	15. a	16. b	17. a	18. d	19. c	20. a
21. d									

Short-answer Questions

1. What is internet and WWW?
2. What is JDK and J2SE?
3. Explain JRE.
4. Explain java compiler and interpreter.
5. Explain primitive data types, variables and literals.
6. What is the range of values for each primitive data types?
7. How to define Java constants?
8. Explain upcasting, downcasting, boxing and unboxing.
9. Explain command line arguments with an example.
10. Explain the methods of Scanner class.
11. Explain Console class and its methods.

EXERCISES

1.1 Write a program that will read an integer and display its ASCII equivalent.
1.2. Write a program that will read a character and display its numeric value.
1.3. Write a program to display the size, minimum value and maximum value of all Java data types (Hint: use constants such as Integer.SIZE, Integer.MIN_VAUE and Integer.MAX_VALUE).
1.4. Develop a Java application to display a string *Hello Java* five times.

1.5. Read five integers from command line and calculate the mean, median and mode of the numbers.

1.6. Write a program to display the result of the following expressions (assume int $i = 1$, double $d = 1.0$);

- $a = a + 5 + 35/8$;
- $d = 2.5 + (++a) + 4 * a + d$;

1.7. Write a program to convert Indian rupees into pounds (GBP) and US dollars (USD).

1.8. Write a program for temperature conversion.

1.9. Calculate body mass index (BMI) of a person given height (in cm) and weight (in kg). BMI is weight (in kg) divided by height squared (in meters).

1.10. Write a program to generate a character A and display it.

1.11. Write a program to solve a quadratic equation (Hint: Math.sqrt() gives square root).

1.12. Write a program that reads account balance and interest rate from a customer and calculate the interest earned by him in one year.

1.13. Write a program that reads a number and checks whether it is a two-digit number or not.

1.14. Write a program that converts the given hex number into its octal equivalent.

1.15. Write a program to calculate the electrical resistance of a wire (Hint: The electrical resistance R of a cylindrical wire with length l (in meter) and diameter d (in meter) can be computed from the area A of its diameter (m^2) and the resistivity P of the material (rho, meter times Ohm).

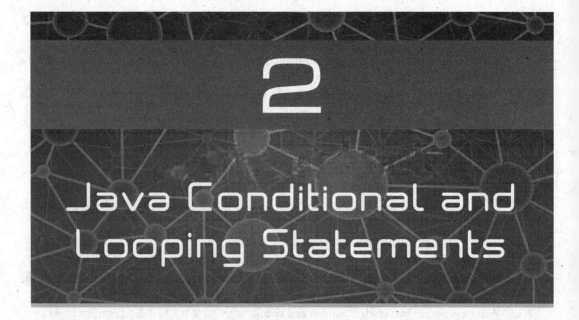

Java Conditional and Looping Statements

OBJECTIVES

- To introduce different conditional statements such as *if, if-else, if-else-if* and *nested if* statements
- To implement the revised *CircleArea* and *Biggest2* application with *if* statement
- To apply *if-else* statement to *Divisible* application
- To implement *CalcGrade* application with *if-else-if* statement
- To explain the importance of conditions and how control flows to different parts of a program
- To explain the relation between *if* statement and logical operators
- To check the given year is leap or not
- To implement switch statement for *ArithCalculator* application
- To introduce switch statement with string case
- To explain looping structures such as *while, do-while* and *for* statements
- To implement nested loops for *MultiplicationTable* application
- To explain *break, continue* and assert statements

2.1 INTRODUCTION

Thus far, all of our programs follow sequential execution. That is, program execution starts at the first statement inside *main()* method and continues till it reaches the end of *main()*, in the order they appear. As a next step, Java supports a variety of control flow statements such that the sequence of execution of statements of a Java application can be altered. The flow of control can be changed based on some decisions or conditions. We can also make a certain block of statements to be executed several times depending on some conditions. This chapter aims to introduce the readers to those features with which a rich collection of Java applications can be developed.

2.2 CONDITIONAL STATEMENTS

Java conditional statements allow a program to execute a certain section of the program only if a particular condition is evaluated to true. Java supports four types of conditional statements. They are:

- *if* statement
- *if-else* statement
- *if-else-if* statement
- Multipoint switch statement

2.2.1 *if* Statement

The *if* **statement** checks a condition first. If the condition is evaluated to true, it executes a block of statements inserted in between curly braces. Then, the execution continues in the next line of the program. The condition can be a simple **boolean condition** or a **complex condition** designed based on relational and/or **logical expressions**. The syntax shown in Figure 2.1 explains the *if* statement.

Figure 2.1. Syntax of the *if* Statement

```
if (condition)
{
    // block of statements
}
```

In Listing 1.8, CircleArea.java application, we have calculated the area of circle by reading the value of radius. Suppose, a user enters a zero or some negative value for radius, the program will show undesired results. So, it is always advisable to check for them first before calculating the area by using the *if* statement, as shown in Listing 2.1.

Listing 2.1. CircleArea Application Using the *if* Statement

```
// CircleArea.java                                    {coderipe}
import java.io.*;

public class CircleArea {
    public static void main ( String args[] ) throws IOException
    {
        // Step1: create reader
        BufferedReader in = new BufferedReader
        ( new InputStreamReader ( System.in ) );
        // Step2: get radius first
        System.out.print ( "Enter radius: " );
        double radius = Double.parseDouble (in.readLine());
        // Step3: check for 0 or -ve number
        if ( radius <= 0)
```

```
        {
                System.out.println("Enter a positive number for
                radius");
                return; // control goes back to command
                prompt
        }
        // Step4: calculate area
        double area = 3.14159 * radius * radius;
        // Step5: print result
        System.out.println ( "Area of circle is: " + area );
    }
}
```

```
Enter radius: 10.0
Area of circle is: 314.159

Enter radius: -5.0
Enter positive number for radius

Enter radius: 0
Enter positive number for radius
```

In this application, if a user enters 0 or a negative number, the application gives a message asking to enter some positive number for radius and terminates execution.

2.2.2 Problem: Finding Biggest of Three Integers

As another illustration, let us calculate the biggest of the given three integers. Here we will assume the first number to be the current *big* and successively compare the second number with the current *big* and update current *big*. We repeat the same process with the third number. Finally current *big* will hold the biggest of all three numbers. The application shown in Listing 2.2 calculates the biggest of three integers using a simple *if* statement.

Listing 2.2. Finding the Biggest of Three Integers

```
// Biggest3.java                                        {coderipe}
import java.io.*;

public class Biggest3
{
    public static void main(String[] args) throws
    IOException
    {
        // Step1: create reader
```

```
        BufferedReader in = new BufferedReader
        (new InputStreamReader(System.in));

        // Step2: read 3 numbers
        System.out.println("Enter numbers one at a time");
        int a1 = Integer.parseInt(in.readLine());
        int a2 = Integer.parseInt(in.readLine());
        int a3 = Integer.parseInt(in.readLine());

        // Step3: assume a1 is biggest first
        int big = a1;

        // Step4: check a2 is bigger than current big
        if(a2 > big)
        big = a2;
        // Step5: check a3 is bigger than current big
        if(a3 > big)
        big = a3;

        // Step6: show biggest
        System.out.println("Biggest: " + big);
    }
}
```

```
Enter numbers one at a time
5
8
2
Biggest: 8
```

Observe in this program that the second *if* statement will be executed irrespective of whether the first *if* statement is evaluated to true or not.

2.2.3 *if-else* Statement

The *if-else* **statement** allows us to define two blocks of statements, one called as true-block and the other else-block. When the condition is evaluated to true, then true-block will be executed, otherwise else-block will be executed as shown in Figure 2.2.

Figure 2.2. Syntax for *if-else* Statement

```
if (condition)
{
    // true-block of statements
```

```
}
else
{
    // else-block of statements
}
```

Listing 2.3 shows an example that checks whether a given integer is divisible by another integer or not, using reminder operator (%) available in Java. A number is divisible by another number if the result of integer division gives reminder zero. The input values have to be entered in the command prompt and are collected from args.

Listing 2.3. Divisibility Testing Application

```
// Divisible.java                                            {coderipe}
import java.io.*;

public class Divisible
{
    public static void main(String[] args) throws IOException
    {
        // Step1: read first number
        int x = Integer.parseInt(args[0]);

        // Step2: read second number
        int y = Integer.parseInt(args[1]);

        // Step3: check whether reminder is zero
        if (x % y == 0)
                System.out.println(x + " is divisible by " + y);
        else
                System.out.println(x + " is NOT divisible by " + y);

        System.out.println("This line will be executed anyway");
    }
}
```

```
C:\jdk> java Divisible 10 2
10 is divisible by 2
This line will be executed anyway

C:\jdk> java Divisible 10 3
10 is NOT divisible by 3
This line will be executed anyway
```

2.2.4 *if-else-if* **Statement**

If-else-if statement allows us to specify a series of *if* statements. So that the corresponding block of statements of *if* block will be executed, depending on the condition. The syntax for *if-else-if* statement is shown in Figure 2.3.

Figure 2.3. Syntax for *if-else-if* Statement

```
if (condition1)
{
    // true-block of statements for condition1
}
else if (condition2)
{
    // true-block of statements for condition2
    // similarly we can have any number of else-if statements
}
else
{
    // else-block of statements.
    // This block will be executed if neither condition1 nor
    condition2 is true
}
```

In order to illustrate *if-else-if* statement, we will develop a Java application that will calculate grade (such as S, A, B, C and F) of a student depending on his/her marks as shown in Listing 2.4.

Listing 2.4. Calculating the Grade of Students

```
// CalcGrade.java                                    {coderipe}
import java.util.*;
import java.io.*;

public class CalcGrade
{
    public static void main(String[] args) throws IOException
    {
        // Step0: create a scanner
        Scanner sc = new Scanner(System.in);

        // Step1: read mark for a subject of a student
        System.out.print("Enter mark: ");
        int marks = sc.nextInt();

        char grade;
```

```
        // Step2: check score and assign a grade
        if (marks >= 90)
        {
             grade = 'S';
        }
        else if (marks >= 80)
        {
             grade = 'A';
        }
        else if (marks >= 70)
        {
             grade = 'B';
        }
        else if (marks >= 60)
        {
             grade = 'C';
        }
        else
        {
             grade = 'F';
        }
        // Step3: print grade
        System.out.println("Grade = " + grade);
    }
}
```

```
Enter mark: 86
Grade = A
```

Here any one of the *if* statements will be executed, depending on the marks of a student. If the given mark does not satisfy any of the *if* statements, then the else part will be executed assigning F to grade.

2.2.5 *Nested if Statement*

Generally, a ***nested if*** **statement** is a *if* statement with another *if* statement. The nesting can be defined at multiple levels such as two-level, three-level and so on. The syntax shown in Figure 2.4 explains *nested if* statement

Figure 2.4. Syntax for *Nested if* Statement

```
if (condition1)
{
    if (condition2)
```

```
    {
        // true block, here condition1 and condition2 are true
    }
    else
    {
        // else block for condition2, here condition1 is true, but
        condition2 is false
    }
}
else
{
    // else block for condition1. Here condition1 is false and we
    don't care for condition2
}
```

Consider the program snippet depicted in Example 2.1. Here a two-level *nested if* statement is used to check whether num is between 80 and 90.

Example 2.1. Two-level Nesting

```
if ( num > 80 )
    if ( num < 90 )
        System.out.println( num + " is between 80 and 90");

Remember, this two-level nested if statement can also be written
using logical AND operator as

if ( num > 80 && num < 90 )
        System.out.println( num + " is between 80 and 90");
```

Similarly, a three-level nesting can be done using three *if* statements as shown in Example 2.2.

Example 2.2. Three-level Nesting

```
If ( num > 80 )
    if ( num < 90 )
        if ( num % 2 == 0 )
            System.out.println( num + " is between 80 and 90 and
                even" );
```

Multilevel *nested if* statement is generally not recommended because of its complex structure. Some of the *nested if* statements can be avoided by using logical operators as discussed above. Also software development practices emphasize us to introduce curly braces as and when required with control structures, to avoid unexpected results during the evaluation of expressions. Let us now rewrite the above example with proper curly braces to enhance readability, as depicted in Example 2.3.

Example 2.3. Three-level Nesting with Curly Braces

```
if ( num > 80 )
{
    if ( num < 90 )
    {
        if( num % 2 == 0 )
        {
            System.out.println( num + " is between 80 and 90 and
            even" );
        }
    }
}
```

2.2.6 Problem: Checking Leap Year

Checking the given year is a leap year or not is another classic example for if statement.
A year is considered to be a leap if

- it is divisible by 400 or
- it is divisible by 4 and not divisible by 100

Here is the complete application depicted in Listing 2.5 that checks whether a given year is leap or not.

Listing 2.5. Leap Year

```
// LeapYear.java                                    {coderipe}
import java.util.*;

public class LeapYear
{
    public static void main(String[] args)
    {
        System.out.print("Enter Year: ");
        Scanner sc = new Scanner(System.in);
        int year = sc.nextInt();

        boolean isLeap = false;
        if( ((year % 4 == 0) && (year % 100 != 0)) ||
        (year % 400 == 0))
                isLeap = true;

        if(isLeap)
```

```
              System.out.println("Year " + year + " is leap year");
        else
              System.out.println("Year " + year + " is NOT leap
              year");
    }
}
```

```
Enter Year: 2004
Year 2004 is leap year

Enter Year: 2010
Year 2010 is NOT leap year

Enter Year: 2000
Year 2000 is leap year

Enter Year: 2012
Year 2012 is leap year
```

2.2.7 Multipoint Switch Statement

If-else-if statement can be effectively converted into a switch statement, where multiple cases or choices can be checked and the corresponding block of statements can be executed. The syntax of switch statement is shown in Figure 2.5.

Figure 2.5. Syntax for Switch Statement

```
switch ( expr )
{
   case literal-1:
      case literal-1 body; break;
   case literal-2:
      case literal-2 body; break;
   case literal-3:
      case literal-3 body; break;
   default:
      default body
}
```

Unlike *if* statements that contain a condition in the parentheses, switch contains an expression.

Here, expression is evaluated first. Then, starting from top to bottom, if the value of the expression matches with a case, then its body of statements will be executed. Since **break statement** is present, control is brought out of **switch statement**. If no case matches, then the body of the default case will be executed.

A switch statement works with the byte, short, char and int primitive data types. It also works with *enumerated types*, the string class (Java 1.7 onwards) and few wrapper classes such as Character, Byte, Short and Integer.

Now, let us design an arithmetic calculator that uses switch statement to check the operation type and calculate accordingly. Listing 2.6 depicts arithmetic calculator application.

Listing 2.6. Arithmetic Calculator Application

```java
// ArithCalculator.java
import java.io.*;

public class ArithCalculator
{
    public static void main(String[] args) throws IOException
    {
        // Step0: create a reader
        BufferedReader in = new BufferedReader
        (new InputStreamReader(System.in));

        // Step1: create variables for operands and operator
        int opd1, opd2;
        char opr;

        // Step2: read operand 1
        System.out.print("Enter operand1: ");
        opd1 = Integer.parseInt(in.readLine());

        // Step3: read operand 2
        System.out.print("Enter operand2: ");
        opd2 = Integer.parseInt(in.readLine());

        // Step4: read operator
        System.out.print("Enter operator: ");
        opr = in.readLine().charAt(0);

        // Step5: initialize result
        int result = 0;

        // Step6: based on operator, branch to any one of the
        choices and find result
        switch (opr)
        {
                case '+' : result = opd1 + opd2; break;
                case '-' : result = opd1 - opd2; break;
                case '*' : result = opd1 * opd2; break;
```

```
            case '/': result = opd1 / opd2; break;
            default : System.out.println("Illegal operator"); return;
        }
        // Step7: show result
        System.out.println("Result: " + result);
    }
}
```

```
Enter operand1: 10
Enter operand2: 20
Enter operator: +
Result: 30

Enter operand1: 10
Enter operand2: 20
Enter operator: &
Illegal Operator
```

In this example, an arithmetic operator has to be read as a character, for that we use *charAt()* method from string class that returns a specific character given a location. Switch statement branches to any of the cases depending on *opr* and performs the necessary operation and comes out of switch, where the result is printed. A word of caution, failure to use break statement will result the control to continue executing subsequent case statements.

2.2.8 String Cases for Switch

Suppose, we want our switch statement to handle **string cases**, the application shown in Listing 2.7 demonstrates this feature.

Listing 2.7. Switch with String Cases

```
// StringSwitch.java                                    {coderipe}
import java.util.*;

public class StringSwitch
{
    public static void main(String[] args)
    {
        Scanner sc = new Scanner(System.in);
        System.out.print("Enter University Programme Name: " );
        String name = sc.next();

        int passMark;

        switch(name.toLowerCase())
```

```
    {
        case "ba" :
        case "bcom" :
        case "bsc" : passMark = 40; break;
        case "ma" :
        case "mcom" :
        case "msc" : passMark = 50; break;
        default : System.out.println("Unavailable
        programme");
    }

    System.out.println("Minimum pass mark for " +
        name + " is " + passMark);
    }
}
```

```
Enter University Programme Name: bsc
Minimum pass mark for bsc is 40

Enter University Programme Name: be
Unavailable programme
```

Here, toLowerCase() method of string class converts the user input into lowercase string and switch branches accordingly. This application calculates the minimum pass marks to be secured by bachelors or masters students. It assigns a passMark to either 40 or 50 depending on whether cases are *ba, bcom and bsc* or *ma, mcom or msc*. Then it displays the pass marks.

2.3 JAVA LOOPING STATEMENTS

There are many situations when we need to execute a block of statements several number of times. This behaviour is known as a **loop**. Java has very flexible three looping mechanisms. You can use one of the following three loops:

- while Loop
- do-while Loop
- for Loop

Looping is basically an iterative process with four steps. They are:

- initialize loop index variable
- check looping condition
- execute loop body
- continue next iteration by incrementing/decrementing index variable

All these three looping structures will follow these steps in their own order.

2.3.1 while Loop

A **while loop** is a control structure that allows you to repeat a task a certain number of times. The syntax for *while* loop is depicted in Figure 2.6.

Figure 2.6. Syntax for *while* Loop

```
while(condition)
{
    // block of statements
}
```

Initially, condition is evaluated in the while loop. If it is true, then the block of statements will be executed. This will continue as long as the expression result is true. If the condition is false, the loop body will be skipped and the first statement after the while loop will be executed.

2.3.2 do-while Loop

The **do-while loop** is very similar to the while loop, except that the body of the loop is guaranteed to execute at least once. The syntax for *do-while* loop is shown in Figure 2.7.

Figure 2.7. Syntax for *do-while* Loop

```
do
{
    // block of statements
}
while (condition);
```

Notice that the condition appears at the end of the loop, so the statements in the loop are executed once before condition is tested. If the condition is true, the control jumps back up to do statement, and the statements in the loop are executed again. This process repeats until the condition is false.

2.3.3 for Loop

A *for* **loop** is a repetition control structure that will execute the body of the loop a specific number of times. A *for* loop is useful when you know how many times a task is to be repeated. Figure 2.8 depicts the syntax for *for* loop.

Figure 2.8. Syntax for *for* Loop

```
for(initialize variables; check condition; increment/decrement
variables)
{
    // block of statements
}
```

Once index variables are initialized and the condition is evaluated to true, then the body of the loop will be executed. The index variables are either incremented or decremented, so that condition can be checked again, and accordingly the body of the loop will be again and again executed.

Listing 2.8 illustrates the working of the three **looping statements** by simply printing values 1 to 10.

Listing 2.8. Printing 1 to 10 Using Loops

```java
// Loops.java
// print 1 to 10 using while, do-while and for loops
public class Loops
{
    public static void main(String[] args)
    {
        // using for loop
        for (int i = 1; i <= 10; i++) // initialize, check &
        increment
        {
            System.out.print(i); // print
        }

        // using while loop
        int i = 10; // initialize
        while (i >= 0) // check
        {
            System.out.print(i); // print
            i--; // decrement i
        }

        // using do-while loop
        i = 1; // initialize
        do
        {
            System.out.print(i); // print
            i++; // increment i
        } while (i <= 10); // check

        /* indefinite loops
        while(true)     // you can use while with true as condition
        {
            System.out.println("Hello"); // displayed until you
            press CNTL-C
        }
```

```
    for(;;)    // you can also use for with 2 semicolons
    {
        System.out.println("Hello");
    }*/
}
}
```

```
12345789101098765432101234 5678910
```

2.3.4 Problem: Generating Multiplication Table

Very similar to if statement inside another if statement, we can create a loop inside another loop, called as nested loop. To appreciate the power of nested loop, let us generate a multiplication table of order 4 by 4 as depicted in Lisiting 2.9.

Listing 2.9. Multiplication Table

```
// MultiplicationTable.java                        {coderipe}
// multiplication table of 4x4
public class MultiplicationTable
{
    public static void main(String[] args)
    {
        // using for loop
        for (int i = 1; i <= 4; i++) // for each row
        {
            for (int j = 1; j <= 4; j++) // for each column
            {
                System.out.print(i * j + "\t"); // multiply row
                and col value
            }

            System.out.println("\n"); // continue in next line
        }
    }
}
```

```
1   2   3   4
2   4   6   8
3   6   9   12
4   8   12  16
```

2.3.5 *break, continue* and *assert* Statements

The *break* **statement** brings control out of a loop either outer loop or inner loop, if there is a nested loop. The ***continue*** statement causes the control immediately jump to the next iteration of the loop. In *for* loop, continue statement transfers control to increment/decrement statement. In a while loop or do-while loop, continue statement transfers control to checking condition.

The assert statement enables you to check whether a condition is true, just like an *if* statement. If it is not true, Java will throw an error named AssertionError. There are two types of assertion as shown in the following Figure 2.9.

Figure 2.9. The Assert Statement

```
Type1: assert boolean-expr;
Type2: assert boolean-expr : expression
```

Type1 just ensures whether the boolean expression is true, otherwise it will throw an error. The second type checks whether the boolean expression is true. If true, it will execute the expression that is mentioned in the second part of the assert statement. The expression should not return void. An example of assert statement is given in Listing 2.10.

Listing 2.10. Assert Example

```java
// AssertEx.java
public class AssertEx
{
    public static void main(String[] args)
    {
        int x = Integer.parseInt(args[0]);
        assert( x > 0);
        System.out.println("You typed a +ve number");
    }
}
```

```
javac AssertEx.java
java -ea AssertEx 10
You typed a +ve number

java -ea AssertEx -10
Exception in thread "main" java.lang.AssertionError
        at AssertEx.main(AssertEx.java:6)
```

Here, assert ensures the command line parameter value is greater than 0. If it is zero, control continues with next statement. If it is not greater than 0, AssertionError will be thrown. Remember you need to run the program with –ea option.

2.4 SUMMARY

1. There are four types of conditional statements – *if, if-else, if-else-if, nested if* statements
2. Conditions for *if* statements can be boolean, relational and logical conditions
3. Java loops allow us to execute a set of statements iteratively several times
4. Every looping statement (such as *while, do-while* and *for*) will define four parts in any order – initialize index variables, check condition, execute body of loop and increment or decrement index variables
5. Nested loops are used to achieve iteration at multiple levels
6. Curly braces should be introduced as and when required with conditional and looping statements to avoid ambiguity
7. Control flow can be manually altered with *break* and *continue* statements
8. Break and continue statements should be used only inside a loop and not inside any block of statements.
9. **Assert statement** checks whether an assumption is true. Otherwise, Java generates Assertion Error. Assert statement can also have an expression that will be executed when the assertion is ture.

KEY TERMS

Assert statement, 45

Boolean condition, 29

Break statement, 37

Complex conditon, 29

Continue statement, 44

do-while loop, 41

for loop, 41

if statement, 29

if-else statement, 31

Logical expressions, 29

Loop, 40

Looping statements, 42

nested if statement, 34

Switch statement, 37

String cases, 39

while loop, 41

REVIEW QUESTIONS

Multiple-choice Questions

1. What will be the output for the program shown below?

```java
public class Test
{
    public static void main(String[] args)
    {
        String s = new String("Hello");
        if(s == "Hello")
            System.out.println( "Hello by ==" );
        if(s.equals("Hello"))
```

```
                System.out.println( "Hello by equals" );
    }
}
```

a. Hello by ==
b. Hello by equals
c. Hello by ==, Hello by equals
d. None of the above

2. Find out the output:

```
public class Test
{
    public static void main(String[] args)
    {

        int i = 10, j = 5;
        if(i == j || i-j == j)
            System.out.println("i is multiple of j");
        else
            System.out.println("i is not multiple of j");
    }
}
```

a. Compilation error
b. i is not multiple of j
c. i is multiple of j
d. Runtime error

3. What will be the output?

```
public class Test
{
    public static void main(String[] args)
    {

        for(int i = 0; i < 5; i++)
            for(int j = 0; j < 5; j++)
                System.out.println("Hello");
    }
}
```

a. Prints Hello 25 times
b. Prints Hello 5 times
c. Prints Hello 10 times
d. Prints Hello indefinitely

4. What is the correct output?

```
public class Test
{
```

```java
   public static void main(String[] args)
   {

        for(int i = 0; i < 3; i++)
             for(int j = 0; j < i*i; j++)
                   System.out.println("Hello");
   }
}
```

a. Prints Hello 5 times

b. Prints Hello 12 times

c. Prints Hello 9 times

d. Prints Hello 25 times

5. Find out the output:

```java
public class Test
{
    public static void main(String[] args)
    {
        for(int i = 0; i < 3; i++)
             for(int j = 0; j < 3; j++)
                   for(int k = 0; k < 3; k++)
                        System.out.println("Hello");
    }
}
```

a. Prints Hello 27 times

b. Prints Hello 25 times

c. Prints Hello 23 times

d. Prints Hello 21 times

6. Find out the output:

```java
public class Test
{
    public static void main(String[] args)
    {
        for(int i = 0; i < 100; i++)
             if(i % 2 == 0)
                   System.out.println(i);
    }
}
```

a. Prints all even numbers from 0 to 100

b. Prints all odd numbers from 0 to 100

c. Compilation error

d. Runtime error

7. Find out the output:

```
public class Test
{
    public static void main(String[] args)
    {
        for(int i = 0; i < 100; i++)
            if(i % 2 != 0)
                System.out.println(i);
    }
}
```

a. Prints all even numbers from 0 to 100
b. Prints all odd numbers from 0 to 100
c. Compilation error
d. Runtime error

8. Find out the output:

```
public class Test
{
    public static void main(String[] args)
    {
        for(int i = 0; i <5; i++)
        {
            for( int j = 0; j < 5; j++)
            {
                if(i == j)
                    break;
                System.out.println("Hello");
            }
        }
    }
}
```

a. Prints Hello 25 times
b. Prints Hello 10 times
c. Prints Hello 5 times
d. None of the above

9. Find out the output:

```
public class Test
{
    public static void main(String[] args)
    {
        for(int i = 0; i < 256; i++)
```

```
            System.out.println(i + ": " + (char)i);
    }
}
```

a. Prints all ASCII characters from 0 to 255   b. Prints binary equivalents from 0 to 255
c. Prints bytes equivalents from 0 to 255   d. Prints binary equivalents from 1 to 255

10. What will the output?

```
public class Test
{
    public static void main(String[] args)
    {
        for(int i = 0; i < 256; i++)
            if(i >= 65 && i <= 90)
                System.out.println((char)i);
    }
}
```

a. Prints all special characters   b. Prints all uppercase alphabets
c. Prints all lowercase alphabets   d. Prints all digits and operators

11. Find out the output:

```
public class Test
{
    public static void main(String[] args)
    {
        for(int i = 0; i < 256; i++)
            if(i >= 97 && i <= 122)
                System.out.println((char)i);
    }
}
```

a. Prints all special characters   b. Prints all uppercase alphabets
c. Prints all lowercase alphabets   d. Prints all digits and operators

12. What will be the output?

```
public class Test
{
    public static void main(String[] args)
    {
```

```
    int val = 10;
    if( val > 4 )
    {
            System.out.println( "Test A" );
    }
    else if( val > 9 )
    {
            System.out.println( "Test B" );
    }
    else
            System.out.println( "Test C" );
    }
}
```

a. Test A
b. Test B
c. Test C
d. None of the above

13. What will be the value of val that will print "Test B"?

```
public class Test
{
    public static void main(String[] args)
    {
        int val;
        if( val > 4 )
        {
                System.out.println( "Test A" );
        }
        else if( val >= 9 )
        {
                System.out.println( "Test B" );
        }
        else
                System.out.println( "Test C" );
    }
}
```

a. 9
b. 10
c. Any number greater than 9
d. Test B can never be printed

14. Find out the output:

```
public class Test
{
```

```
    public static void main(String[] args)
    {
        int n = 0;
        while(n++ < 2)
              System.out.println(n);
    }
}
```

a. 0, 1, 2   b. 0, 1
c. 1, 2   d. 1, 2, 3

15. Find out the output:

```
public class Test
{
    public static void main(String[] args)
    {
        int i = 0, j = 10;
        while( i++ < j--)
              System.out.println(i+j);
    }
}
```

a. Prints 10 five times   b. Prints 5 ten times
c. Prints 0 ten times   d. Prints 10 ten times

16. Find out the output:

```
public class Test
{
    public static void main(String[] args)
    {
        for(int i = 1; i <4; i++)
        {
            for( int j = 1; j < 4; j++)
            {
                if(j==2)
                      continue;
                System.out.println("Hello");
            }
        }
    }
}
```

a. Prints Hello 16 times

b. Prints Hello 8 times

c. Prints Hello 10 times

d. Prints Hello 6 times

17. Find out the output:

```java
public class Test
{
    public static void main(String[] args)
    {
        for(int i = 1; i < 4; i++)
        {
            for( int j = 1; j < 4; j++)
            {
                if(j==3)
                    break;
                System.out.println("Hello");
            }
        }
    }
}
```

a. Prints Hello 16 times

b. Prints Hello 8 times

c. Prints Hello 10 times

d. Prints Hello 6 times

18. Find out the output:

```java
public class Test
{
    public static void main(String[] args)
    {
        for(int i = 0; i <3; i++)
        {
            for( int j = 0; j < 5; j++)
            {
                if(j%2 == 0)
                    continue;
                System.out.println("Hello");
            }
        }
    }
}
```

a. Prints Hello 16 times

b. Prints Hello 8 times

c. Prints Hello 10 times

d. Prints Hello 6 times

19. What will be the output?

```java
public class Test
{
    public static void main(String[] args)
    {
        double x = 45.0;
        x = x % (2 * Math.PI);

        double term = 1.0;
        double sum  = 0.0;

        for (int i = 1; term != 0.0; i++)
        {
            term = term * (x/i);
            if (i % 4 == 1)
                sum = sum + term;
            if (i % 4 == 3)
                sum = sum - term;
        }
        System.out.println(sum);
    }
}
```

a. Prints sin value for 45

b. Prints cos value for 45

c. Prints tan value for 45

d. None of the above

20. What will be the output?

```java
public class Test
{
    public static void main(String[] args)
    {
        int n = 1;
        while (n < 50)
        {
```

```
                for (int i = 0; i < 10; i++)
                {
                        n += 4;
                      if (n > 20)
                              break;
                }
                n++;
        }
      System.out.println(n);
  }
}
```

a. 50

b. 52

c. 54

d. None of the above

21. What will be the output?

```
public class Test
{
   public static void main(String[] args)
   {
      int n = 100;
      double sum = 0.0;
      for(int i = 1; i <= n; i++)
            sum = sum + 1.0 / i;
      System.out.println(sum);
   }
}
```

a. Prints the factorial of n

b. Prints Armstrong number of n

c. Prints harmonic number of n

d. None of the above

22. Find out the output:

```
public class Test
{
   public static void main(String[] args)
   {
      int i=1;
      switch(i)
      {
            case 1: System.out.println("one"); break;
```

```
        case 2: System.out.println("two"); break;
        case 3: System.out.println("three"); break;
        default: System.out.println("not a number");
    }
  }
}
```

a. One

b. Two

c. Three

d. Not a number

23. Find out the output:

```
public class Test
{
    public static void main(String[] args)
    {
        int i=1;
        switch(i)
        {
            case 1: System.out.println("one");
            case 2: System.out.println("two");
            case 3: System.out.println("three");
            default: System.out.println("not a number");
        }
    }
}
```

a. One two three not a number

b. One two three

c. One two

d. One

e. Not a number

24. Find out the output:

```
public class Test
{
    public static void main(String[] args)
    {
        char c = "b";
        switch(c)
        {
            case "a": System.out.println("apple");
            case "b": System.out.println("ball");
            case "c": System.out.println("cat");
```

```
            default: System.out.println("not a character");
    }
  }
}
```

a. Ball

b. Ball cat

c. Ball cat not a character

d. Not a character

25. Find out the output:

```
public class Test
{
    public static void main(String[] args)
    {
        char c = "b";
        switch(c)
        {
            default: System.out.println("not a character");
            case "a": System.out.println("apple");
            case "b": System.out.println("ball");
            case "c": System.out.println("cat");

        }
    }
}
```

a. ball cat

b. ball

c. ball cat not a character

d. Compilation error as default appears in the beginning

26. Find out the output:

```
public class Test
{
    public static void main(String[] args)
    {
        String s = "b";
        switch(s)
        {
            case "a": System.out.println("apple"); break;
```

```
            case "b": System.out.println("ball"); break;
            case "c": System.out.println("cat"); break;
            default: System.out.println("not a string");


        }
    }
}
```

a. apple
b. ball
c. ball cat
d. ball cat not a string
e. not a string
f. Error: String for cases not allowed

27. Find out the output:

```
public class Test
{
    public static void main(String[] args)
    {
        int i = 1;
        do
        {
            System.out.println(i++);
        }
        while(i < 3);
    }
}
```

a. 1, 2, 3   b. 1, 2
c. Prints i indefinitely   d. Runtime exception

28. Find out the output:

```
public class Test3
{
    public static void main(String[] args)
    {
        for(int i=0; i<10; i++)
        {
            /* some code that does not modify i */
```

```
        }
    System.out.println(i);
    }
}
```

a. 9   b. 10
c. 11   d. Exception as scope of i is limited to inside
                                     for loop

29. Find out the output:

```
public class Test2
{
    public static void main(String[] args)
    {
        int j = 1;
        for(; j < 4; j++)
        {
                switch(j)
                {
                        case 1: System.out.println("Line 1");continue;
                        case 2: System.out.println("Line 2");continue;
                        case 3: System.out.println("Line 3");continue;
                        default: System.out.println("Default line");
                }
        }
    }
}
```

a. Line 1
b. Line 1 Line 2 Line 3
c. Line 1 Line 2 Line 3 Default line
d. Compilation error: continue statement inside switch not allowed

30. Find out the output:

```
public class Test2
{
    public static void main(String[] args)
    {
        System.out.println("Line 1");
        break;
```

```
        System.out.println("Line 2");
    }
}
```

a. Line 1   b. Line 1 Line 2
c. Compilation error: break inside main()   d. No output is printed
   not allowed

Answers

1. b   2. c   3. a   4. a   5. b   6. a   7. b   8. b   9. a   10. b
11. c   12. a   13. d   14. c   15. a   16. d   17. d   18. d   19. a   20. b
21. c   22. a   23. a   24. c   25. a   26. b   27. b   28. b   29. b   30. c

Short-answer Questions

1. Explain *if* statement with an example.
2. Explain *if-else* statement with an example.
3. Explain *nested if* statement with an example.
4. Discuss switch statement with an example.
5. Explain *while* loop with an example.
6. Explain *do-while* loop with an example.
7. Explain *for* loop with an example.
8. Discuss assert statement with an example.

EXERCISES

2.1. Count the number of digits in a number.
2.2. Compute the number of days in a month.
2.3. Print numbers from 1 to 1 million.
2.4. Modify the above program so that it exits by using break keyword at value 999. Try using return instead.
2.5. Create a switch statement that prints a message for each case and put the switch inside a *for* loop that tries each case. Put a break after each case and test it. Then remove the breaks and see what happens.
2.6. Print "hello world" *N* times.
2.7. Reverse a given integer.
2.8. Reverse a given string.
2.9. Test whether the given number is Armstrong or not.
2.10. Find the sum of the given digits of a number.
2.11. Check the given character is lowercase or not.

2.12. Check the given character is uppercase or not.

2.13. Find the factorial of a large number (over crores). Print factorial table.

2.14. Find the number and sum of all integers greater than 100 and less than 200 that are divisible by 7.

2.15. Print Floyd's triangle.

2.16. Swap the values of two integers without a temporary variable.

2.17. Generate the first n terms of the sequence 1 2 4 8 16 32... without using multiplication.

2.18. Generate Lucas sequence 1 3 4 7 11 18 29 ...

2.19. Read n individual digits and form an integer.

2.20. Convert decimal to octal number.

2.21. Convert binary number to octal.

2.22. Convert decimal to BCD.

2.23. Given two positive non-zero integers, write a program to find their GCD.

2.24. Find the nth member of the Fibonacci sequence.

3

Arrays in Java

OBJECTIVES

- To explain how to declare one-dimensional, two-dimensional and multidimensional arrays
- To explain different array types
- To make developers learn how to choose arrays
- To illustrate accessing one-dimensional array elements with *StudentMarks* application
- To develop application for sequential search
- To develop application for binary search
- To implement *BiggestN* application with for-each statement
- To develop application for Euclidean distance
- To develop application for reversing an array
- To explain two-dimensional arrays by implementing *TopStudent* application
- To understand three-dimensional arrays by storing semester-wise marks
- To find the transpose of a two-dimensional matrix

3.1 INTRODUCTION

In the CalcGrade application Listing 2.4 of Chapter 2, we have illustrated a method to calculate a grade from the mark of a student in a given course. Suppose a student has obtained marks in four courses in a particular semester. So, a single variable cannot hold all these four marks. To solve this problem, we have a handy static **data structure** that will store a collection of values under a single name, namely *arrays*. In this chapter, we will learn how to create and use arrays to store a collection of values. Apart from studying the basic notion of arrays, the readers will also be introduced to some interesting applications such as sequential search, **binary search**, finding Euclidean distance, reversing arrays without copying and finding the transpose of a given matrix.

3.2 DECLARING AND INITIALIZING ARRAYS

An array is a collection of fixed data storage locations, each of which holds the same type of data. Think of an array as a "box" drawn in memory with a series of subdivisions, called elements, to store the data. There are different types: **one-dimensional** (one row of values), **two-dimensional** (rows and columns of values, like a matrix) and **multidimensional arrays** (where there are three or more dimensions). The typical syntaxes for Java arrays are shown in Figure 3.1.

Figure 3.1. Array Declaration

```
data-type [ ] array-name = new data-type[size];
                                        // one-dimensional array
data-type [ ][ ] array-name = new data-type[size1][size2];
                                        // two-dimensional array
data-type [ ][ ][ ] array-name = new data-type[size1][size2]
[size3];                                // three-dimensional array
```

Before the values are stored in array locations, the array has to be declared by specifying its type and required size as shown in Example 3.1. Each array is identified with its name, also called reference. Once declared, the array can be initialized with values of the specified type. Array values can also be initialized during declaration time using curly braces. Example 3.1 shows different instances of declaring arrays.

Example 3.1. Student Marks Array

```
// stores marks of a student in four courses, as a one-
dimensional array
int[ ] marks = new int[4];  // here, marks is a reference to the
four-element array

// stores marks of 50 students in four courses, as a two-
dimensional array
int[ ][ ] allStudentsMarks = new int[50][4];  // also
allStudentsMarks is a reference

// stores marks of 50 students, in four subjects, for six
semesters, as a three-dimensional array
int[ ][ ][ ] allStudentsMarks6Sem = new int[50][4][6];
```

3.3 ACCESSING ARRAY ELEMENTS

Elements of an array can be accessed by its **index** value. Remember, one-dimensional array will have one index value to identify an element; two-dimensional array will need two index values (row value and column value) to identify one element. In general, an *n*-dimensional array would need *n* index values to identify an element in the array.

The StudentMarks application (shown in Listing 3.1) receives MAX marks from command line and calculates the percentage of those marks.

Listing 3.1. StudentMarks Application

```java
// StudentMarks.java
import java.io.*;

public class StudentMarks
{
    public static void main(String[] args) throws
    IOException
    {
        // max number of courses
        final int MAX = 4;

        // declare array to hold marks
        int[] marks = new int[MAX];

        // check if user supplies 4 marks for a student
        if ( args.length != MAX )
        {
            // display error message
            System.out.println("Enter four marks");
            // return to command prompt
            return;
        }

        // so, we have four marks now, initialize the array
        for(int i = 0; i < MAX; i++)
            marks[i] = Integer.parseInt(args[i]);

        // find sum
        int sum = 0;
        for(int i = 0; i < MAX; i++)
            sum += marks[i];

        // show average
        System.out.println("Average: " + ((double)sum/MAX));
    }
}
```

{coderipe}

```
C:\jdk> java StudentMarks 56 65 86 71
Average: 69.5
```

```
C:\jdk>java StudentMarks 55
Enter four marks
```

Note that, the array is not just declared with the size 4, instead we have defined a constant MAX, which will be used for declaration. Also, before calculating the sum of marks, the *if* statement is used to verify whether the command line argument contains four values, otherwise the control will return to the command prompt.

3.4 PROBLEM: SEQUENTIAL SEARCH FOR A KEY

Sequential search allows us to search for a given key in an array of elements. The search starts by comparing each array element with the key to check whether they are same. Otherwise search is continued with subsequent elements one at a time until the end of array is reached. Though sequential search is simple, in the worst case there might be n comparisons where n represents the size of the array. Listing 3.2 depicts the processing of sequential search.

Listing 3.2. Sequential Search for a Given Key

```
// SequentialSearch.java                          {coderipe}
public class SequentialSearch
{
    public static void main(String[] args)
    {
        // Step1: check command line arguments
        if(args.length < 2)
        {
            System.out.println("Enter list of numbers and key to
            search");
            return;
        }

        // Step2: get size
        int size = args.length;
        // Step3: last element is the key to search
        int key = Integer.parseInt(args[size-1]);
        // Step4: create array to hold elements
        int[] elements = new int[size];

        // Step5: copy all elements
        for(int i = 0; i < size-1; i++)
        {
            int value = Integer.parseInt(args[i]);
            elements[i] = value;
        }
```

```
        // Step6: assume key does not exist
        int loc = -1;
        // Step7: search for the key
        for(int i = 0; i < size; i++)
        {
                // Step8: remember the first occurrence
                if(elements[i] == key)
                {
                        loc = i;
                        break;
                }
        }

        // Step: 8 if loc is -1 then key does not exist
        if(loc == -1)
                System.out.println(key + " does not exist in given
                list");
        else
                System.out.println(key + " exists first at location "
                + loc);
    }
}
```

```
E:\Rajkumar\javacourse\basics>javac SequentialSearch.java

E:\Rajkumar\javacourse\basics>java SequentialSearch 1 2 3 4 5 6 7
8 9 8
8 exists first at location 7

E:\Rajkumar\javacourse\basics>java SequentialSearch 1 2 3 4 5 6 7
8 9 10
10 does not exist in given list
```

Once a set of numbers followed by the key to be searched in the command prompt are entered, the key is compared with every array element to check whether they are same. At the end, the location of the key is returned as output if it exists.

3.5 PROBLEM: BINARY SEARCH FOR A KEY

Binary search reduces the amount of comparisons by $n/2$ where n represents the size of the array, provided the given array elements are pre-sorted. Every time the algorithm divides the array into two half and checks whether the key lies in the left half or the right half of the array. Accordingly, the search is continued with either the left half or right half. Listing 3.3 explains binary search for the given key.

Listing 3.3. Binary Search for a Given Key

```java
// BinarySearch.java                              {coderipe}
public class BinarySearch
{
    public static void main(String[] args)
    {
        if(args.length < 2)
        {
            System.out.println("Enter list of numbers and key to
            search");
            return;
        }

        // last element is the key to search
        int size = args.length;
        int key = Integer.parseInt(args[size-1]);

        int[] elements = new int[size];

        // copy all elements
        for(int i = 0; i < size-1; i++)
        {
            int value = Integer.parseInt(args[i]);
            elements[i] = value;
        }

        // assume key does not exist
        int loc = -1;
        // lower bound for the sorted array
        int lb = 0;
        // upper bound excluding last element
        int ub = size - 2;
        // middle position in the array
        int mid;

        // search for the key
        for(;;)
        {
            // find middle location
            mid = (lb + ub) / 2;
            // search left half
            if (key < elements[mid])
                ub = mid - 1;
            else if (key > elements[mid]) //search right half
```

```
                  lb = mid + 1;
          else
          {
                  // key matches with mid element
                  // so remember mid element's location
                  loc = mid;
                  break;
          }

                  // entire left half searched and key not exists, so
                  break from loop
                  if (lb > ub)
                          break;
          }

          // if loc is -1 then key does not exist
          if(loc == -1)
                  System.out.println(key + " does not exist in given
                  list");
          else
                  System.out.println(key + " exists at location "
                  + loc);
    }
}
```

```
E:\Rajkumar\javacourse\basics>java BinarySearch 1 2 3 4 5 6 7 8 9
4
4 exists at location 3

E:\Rajkumar\javacourse\basics>java BinarySearch 1 2 3 4 5 6 7 8 9
50
50 does not exist in given list

E:\Rajkumar\javacourse\basics>java BinarySearch 1 2 3 4 5 6 7 8 9
-5
-5 does not exist in the given list
```

Binary search assumes the given input array is pre-sorted. The midpoint is calculated between the first element and the last element of the array. If key is less than the midpoint element, it indicates that key might be present in the left half of the array and search is continued only in the left half. This way binary search effectively eliminates searching the right half. Therefore, efficiency in binary search is improved by 50%. On the other hand, if key is greater than the midpoint element, search will be continued only with the right half of the array. This processing is repeated until the midpoint element is the key or the lower bound crosses the upper bound of the reduced array.

3.6 THE FOR-EACH STATEMENT

Java supports a convenient for loop that will traverse the array sequentially without an index variable. The syntax for **for-each statement** is shown in Figure 3.2.

Figure 3.2. Syntax for for-each Statement

```
for (index-variable : array-name)
{
    // statements
}
```

Here, index-variable iterates through the array, specified by array-name, and body of statements will be executed until array has more elements.

For instance, the following program snippet shown in Example 3.2 prints the marks of a student stored in the array marks using for-each statement.

Example 3.2. for-each Example

```
for (int m : marks)
{
    System.out.println(m);
}
```

In this application, let us extend our previous version of Biggest3 application in order to find the biggest number among the given *n* numbers. In Listing 3.4, we have introduced for-each statement to move through the numbers during the calculation.

Listing 3.4. Biggest of *n* Integers Application

```
// BiggestN.java
import java.io.*;
public class BiggestN
{
    public static void main(String[] args) throws IOException
    {
        // Step1: Create buffered reader
        BufferedReader in = new BufferedReader(new
                InputStreamReader(System.in));

        // Step2: read how many numbers to process
        System.out.print("Enter total no. to be processed: ");
        int n = Integer.parseInt(in.readLine());  // to keep total
        number of numbers
```

```
// Step3: declare array of n size
int a[] = new int[n]; // to keep actual numbers

// Step4: initialize array elements by reading
values
System.out.println("Enter actual numbers: ");
for (int i = 0; i < a.length; i++)
        a[i] = Integer.parseInt(in.readLine());

// Step5: assume a[0] is biggest first
int big = a[0];

// Step6: compare second number onwards with big
for (int e : a )   // for each element e in the array a
{
        // Step7: check current number bigger than current
        big
        if(e > big)
        big = e; // Step8: if so, assign this number
}

// Step9: show biggest number
System.out.println("Biggest: " + big);
    }
}
```

```
Enter total no. to be processed: 5
Enter actual numbers:
23
81
5
72
92
Biggest: 92
```

3.7 PROBLEM: FINDING EUCLIDEAN DISTANCE BETWEEN TWO VECTORS

Euclidean distance compares the distance between two one-dimensional arrays (one-dimensional arrays are also called vectors). It is calculated as the square root of the sums of the squares of the differences between corresponding entries in the arrays. It is used to find the similarity between two vectors. If Euclidean distance is zero, then the given two vectors are the same. Listing 3.5 explains the functioning of Euclidean distance.

Listing 3.5. Euclidean Distance

```java
// Euclidean.java
import java.util.*;

public class Euclidean
{
    public static void main(String[] args)
    {
        Scanner sc = new Scanner(System.in);
        // get size for arrays
        System.out.println("Enter size of array");
        int size = sc.nextInt();

        // instantiate arrays
        int[] arr1 = new int[size];
        int[] arr2 = new int[size];

        // get values for arr1
        System.out.println("Enter array 1");
        for(int i = 0; i < size; i++)
            arr1[i] = sc.nextInt();

        // get values for arr2
        System.out.println("Enter array 2");
        for(int i = 0; i < size; i++)
            arr2[i] = sc.nextInt();

        // find square root of the sums of the squares of the
        differences
        // between corresponding entries in the arrays
        double sum = 0;
        for(int i = 0; i < size; i++)
        {
            int diff = arr1[i] - arr2[i];
            sum = sum + Math.pow(diff, 2);
        }

        // show Euclidean distance
        System.out.println("Euclidean distance " + Math.
        sqrt(sum));
    }
}
```

```
Enter size of square array
5
Enter array 1
1 2 5 8 2
Enter array 2
8 3 1 2 6
Euclidean distance 10.862780491200215

Enter size of square array
4
Enter array 1
1 2 3 4
Enter array 2
1 2 3 4
Euclidean distance 0.0
```

Here, Math.pow() method finds the power while Math.sqrt() calculates the square root of the arguments. Rest of the code is self-explanatory.

3.8 PROBLEM: REVERSE AN ARRAY WITHOUT COPYING

In order to reverse a given array, you can simply copy elements to another array backwards. Here is another example where you will see how to reverse an array without copying to another array as depicted in Listing 3.6.

Listing 3.6. Reverse an Array Without Copying

```java
// ReverseArray.java
import java.util.*;

public class ReverseArray
{
   public static void main(String[] args)
   {
      Scanner sc = new Scanner(System.in);
      // Step1: get size
      System.out.println("Enter array size");
      int size = sc.nextInt();

      // Step2: create array
      int[] arr = new int[size];

      // Step3: get values for arr
```

```
        System.out.println("Enter array elements");
        for(int i = 0; i < size; i++)
                arr[i] = sc.nextInt();


        // Step4: reverse without copying
        for (int i = 0; i < size/2; i++)
        {
                int temp = arr[size-i-1];
                arr[size-i-1] = arr[i];
                arr[i] = temp;
        }


        // Step5: show result
        System.out.println("Reversed array elements");
        for(int i = 0; i < size; i++)
                System.out.print(arr[i] + " " );
    }
}
```

```
E:\Rajkumar\javacourse\basics>java ReverseArray
Enter array size
5
Enter array elements
1 2 3 4 5
Reversed array elements
5 4 3 2 1
```

Here, with a temporary variable the first element and last element is interchanged. Then second element and the previous element to the last are interchanged. This swapping is continued half of the size of the input array.

3.9 MULTIDIMENSIONAL ARRAYS

In Listing 3.7, we have created a two-dimensional array that can store marks of several students. Now, let us find out among the students, which student has got the highest percentage of marks, considering all courses in a particular semester.

Listing 3.7. Predicting Top Student Application

```
// TopStudent.java
import java.io.*;
public class TopStudent
{
```

```java
public static void main(String[] args) throws
IOException
{
    BufferedReader in = new BufferedReader(new
        InputStreamReader(System.in));
    // Step1: declare how many students & courses
    int total_students, total_courses;

    // Step2: read how many students
    System.out.print("Enter total no. of students: ");
    total_students = Integer.parseInt(in.readLine());

    // Step3: read how many courses
    System.out.print("Enter how many courses: ");
    total_courses = Integer.parseInt(in.readLine());

    // Step4: declare the array, marks
    int[][] marks = new int[total_students][total_courses];

    // Step5: initialize array elements by reading values
    for (int i = 0; i < marks.length; i++)  // for each
    student
    {
        System.out.println("Enter marks of student: " + i);
        for (int j = 0; j < marks[i].length; j++) // for each
        mark
        {
            System.out.println("Enter mark " + j + " : ");
            marks[i][j] = Integer.parseInt(in.readLine());
        }
    }

    // Step6: array to store average of each student's
    marks
    double[] average = new double[total_students];

    for (int i = 0; i < marks.length; i++)  // length returns
    no. of rows
    {
        double sum = 0.0;

        for (int j = 0; j < marks[i].length; j++)  // length
        holds no. of columns
        {
```

```
                    sum += marks[i][j];
            }


        // update average of this student i
        average[i] = (double)sum / total_courses;
    }


    // Step7: assume first students' average is highest
    double big = average[0];
    // Step8: assume first student is the top student
    int topStudent = 0;


    // Step9: compare second number onwards with big
    for (int i = 0; i < average.length;i++ )
    {
        // Step10: check current number bigger than current
        big
        if(average[i] > big)
        {
                // Step11: if so, assign this number
                big = average[i];
                // Step12: remember this student
                topStudent = i;
        }
    }


    // Step13: show biggest number
    System.out.println("Top student: " + topStudent +
        "\nHis average is : " + big);
    }
}
```

```
Enter total no. of students: 3
Enter how many courses: 2
Enter marks of student 0
Enter mark 0 :
53
Enter mark 1 :
83
Enter marks of student 1
Enter mark 0 :
43
Enter mark 1 :
```

```
73
Enter marks of student 2
Enter mark 0 :
93
Enter mark 1 :
83
Students average marks: 68.0 58.0 88.0
Top student: 2
His average is : 88.0
```

A three-dimensional array can be thought of as a collection of two-dimensional arrays, where each two-dimensional array is just a collection of one-dimensional arrays. Example 3.1 cited an instance of how to declare a three-dimensional array that will store marks of few courses, of many students, in several semesters. In order to populate this three-dimensional array with values of marks, we will have to follow the steps as depicted in Example 3.3.

Example 3.3. Steps to Populate Three-dimensional Array

```
for each semester        // depth of an array
    for each student      // rows
        for each course   // columns
            read a mark // cell value
```

The above algorithmic steps can be converted into a code snippet as shown in Example 3.4.

Example 3.4. Reading Values to Three-dimensional Array

```
Scanner sc = new Scanner(System.in);

// declare variables
int nSemesters = 4;  // assume number of semesters is 4
int nStudents = 50;  // number of students = 50
int nCourses = 5;    // number of courses = 5

// create array marks
int[ ][ ][ ] marks = new int [nSemesters][nStudents]
[nCourses];

// initialize values
for (int i = 0; i < nSemesters; i++)
    for (int j = 0; j < nStudents; j++)
        for (int k = 0; k < nCourses; k++)
            marks[i][j][k] = sc.nextInt();
```

3.10 PROBLEM: TRANSPOSE OF A MATRIX

Given a matrix of any order, transpose can be calculated easily by simply copying an element of the source matrix to another matrix of the required size. For instance, a matrix element A[i][j] can be copied to matrix element B[j][i]. At the end, matrix B will hold the required transpose as illustrated in Listing 3.8.

Listing 3.8. Transpose of a Matrix

```java
// TransposeCopy.java
import java.util.*;

public class TransposeCopy
{
    public static void main(String[] args)
    {
        Scanner sc = new Scanner(System.in);

        // Step1: get row size
        System.out.println("Enter rows");
        int rows = sc.nextInt();

        // Step2: get column size
        System.out.println("Enter cols");
        int cols = sc.nextInt();

        // Step3: create arrays
        int[][] arr = new int[rows][cols];
        int[][] arr2 = new int[cols][rows];

        // Step4: get values for arr
        System.out.println("Enter array elements");
        for(int i = 0; i < rows; i++)
            for(int j = 0; j < cols; j++)
                arr[i][j] = sc.nextInt();

        // Step5: transpose
        for(int i = 0; i < rows; i++)
            for(int j = 0; j < cols; j++)
                arr2[j][i] = arr[i][j];
        // Step6: show result
        System.out.println("Transpose Matrix");
        for(int i = 0; i < cols; i++)
        {
            for(int j = 0; j < rows; j++)
```

```
                    System.out.print(arr2[i][j] + " " );
            System.out.println();
        }
    }
}
```

```
E:\Rajkumar\javacourse\basics>java TransposeCopy
Enter rows
2
Enter cols
3
Enter array elements
1
2
3
4
5
6
Transpose Matrix
1 4
2 5
3 6
```

Suppose you have a larger matrix say order 1 million by 1 million. Then you feel you are wasting memory by allocating space for the destination array. So you just want to eliminate destination array and do not want to reserve space for the target array indeed. Listing 3.9 shows a modified application that will find transpose without copying elements to another array.

Listing 3.9. Transpose Without Copying

```
// Transpose.java
import java.util.*;

public class Transpose
{
    public static void main(String[] args)
    {

        Scanner sc = new Scanner(System.in);
        // Step1: get size
        System.out.println("Enter array size");
        int size = sc.nextInt();
        // Step2: instantiate array
```

```java
    int[][] arr = new int[size][size];

    // Step3: get values for arr
    System.out.println("Enter array elements");
    for(int i = 0; i < size; i++)
         for(int j = 0; j < size; j++)
               arr[i][j] = sc.nextInt();

    // Step4: transpose
    for (int i = 0; i < size; i++)
    {
         for (int j = i+1; j < size; j++)
         {
               int temp = arr[i][j];
               arr[i][j] = arr[j][i];
               arr[j][i] = temp;
         }
    }

    // Step5: show result
    System.out.println("Transpose Matrix");
    for(int i = 0; i < size; i++)
    {
         for (int j = 0; j < size; j++)
               System.out.print(arr[i][j] + " " );
         System.out.println();
    }
  }
}
```

```
E:\Rajkumar\javacourse\basics>java Transpose
Enter array size
3
Enter array elements
1
2
3
4
5
6
7
8
9
```

```
Transpose Matrix
1  4  7
2  5  8
3  6  9
```

Here by keeping the inner loop j to begin with (i+1), we are ignoring diagonal elements as they need not be swapped.

3.11 SUMMARY

1. Arrays store values of the same type
2. Arrays can have unlimited dimensions from one dimension, two dimensions, three-dimensions to *n*-dimensions
3. **Array index** identifies its elements
4. Java needs arrays to be declared and initialized first before accessing array elements
5. For-each statement can be used with arrays

KEY TERMS

Array index, 79
Arrays, 61
Binary search, 61

Data structure, 61
for-each statement, 68
Index, 62

Multidimensional arrays, 62
One-dimensional, 62
Two-dimensional, 62

REVIEW QUESTIONS

Multiple-choice Questions

1. Which of these statements are correct methods to create arrays?

```
public class Test3
{
    public static void main(String[] args)
    {
        int[] a = new int[5];
        System.out.println(a[0]);
        String[] flower = new String[1];
        System.out.println(flower[0]);
    }
}
```

a. \0, null   b. null, null

c. 0, null   d. garbage value

2. Find out the output for the following program:

```java
public class Test3
{
    public static void main(String[] args)
    {
        char[] c = new char[20];
        boolean[] b = new boolean[2];
        System.out.println(c[10], b[0]);
    }
}
```

a. \0, true   b. \u, true

c. \null, true   d. null, false

3. Find out the output for the following program:

```java
public class Test3
{
    public static void main(String[] args)
    {
        char[] name = {'a', 'b', 'c'};
        System.out.println(name);
    }
}
```

a. abc   b. a

c. Compilation error   d. Runtime error

4. Find out the output for the following program:

```java
public class Test3
{
    public static void main(String[] args)
    {
        int[] array = {10,20,30};
        System.out.println(array);
    }
}
```

a. 10 20 30

b. 10

c. Some random value representing the address of the handle array

d. Runtime error

5. Which of the following methods will create strings?

   (a) `String s = "Hello Java";`

   (b) `String s[] = "Hello Java";`

   (c) `new String s = "Hello Java";`

   (d) `String s2 = new String("Hello Java");`

   a. a, b   b. a, c

   c. a, d   d. b, c

6. Which of the following methods will create double numbers?

   (a) `double n[] = new double[20];`

   (b) `double n[20] = new array[20];`

   (c) `double n[20] = new array;`

   (d) `double[] n = new double[20];`

   a. a, b   b. a, c

   c. a, d   d. a, b, c

   e. a, b, d

7. Which of the following methods will create double objects?

   (a) `Double d = new Double(100);`

   (b) `Double d = new Double(100.00f);`

   (c) `Double d = new Double(100.00);`

   a. a   b. a, b

   c. a, b, c   d. a, c

   e. b, c

8. Which of the following methods will create integers?

   (a) `int[5][5]a = new int[][];`

   (b) `int a = new int[5,5];`

   (c) `int[]a[] = new int[5][5];`

   (d) `int[][]a = new[5]int[5];`

   (e) `Integer i = new Integer(5);`

   a. a, b, c

   b. a, b, c, d

   c. a, c, e

   d. a, b, c, d, e

   e. e

9. Find out the output?

```
public class Test3
{
    public static void main(String[] args)
    {
        Integer n = Integer.valueOf("1111", 2);
        System.out.println(n.toString());
    }
}
```

a. 15   b. 2222
c. 1111   d. 3333

10. What will be the output for the following code?

```
public class Test3
{
    public static void main(String[] args)
    {
        String s = Integer.toString(12, 16);
        System.out.println(s);
    }
}
```

a. a   b. b
c. c   d. d

11. Find out the output:

```
public class Test3
{
    public static void main(String[] args)
    {

        int i = Integer.rotateRight(8, 1);
        int i2 = 8>>1;
        System.out.println(i + "," + i2);
    }
}
```

a. 8, 8   b. 4, 4
c. 8, 16   d. 16, 16

12. Find out the output:

```
public class Test3
{
    public static void main(String[] args)
    {

        int i = Integer.rotateLeft(8, 1);
        int i2 = 8<<1;
        System.out.println(i + "," + i2);
    }
}
```

a. 4, 16	b. 8, 32
c. 8, 8	d. 16, 16

13. What is the output?

```
public class Test3
{
    public static void main(String[] args)
    {
        int[] no = new int[10];
        System.out.println(no[5]);
    }
}
```

a. 0	b. '0'
c. null	d. 1

14. You want to initialize all of the elements of a int array arr to the same value equal to 10. What could you write? Assume the array has been correctly instantiated.

```
(a) for(int i=1; i<a.length; i++) a[i] = 10;
(b) for(int i=0; i<=a.length; i++) a[i] = 10;
(c) for(int i=0; i<a.length; i++) a[i] = 10;
(d) for(int i=0; i<a.length+1; i++) a[i] = 10;
```

a. a	b. b
c. c	d. a, c

15. What is the output of the program below?

```
public class Test3
{
    public static void main(String[] args)
```

```
{
    int[] x = {5,6,7,8,9, 10};
    int[] y = x;
    y[2] = 20;
    System.out.println(x[2]);
}
}
```

a. 20   b. 6
c. 7   d. None of the above

16. What is the output?

```
public class Test3
{
    public static void main(String[] args)
    {
        int[] arr = {0,2,4,6};
        for(long i : arr)
            System.out.print(i);
    }
}
```

a. 0 2 4 6
b. Compilation error: int array accessed by long index variable
c. Runtime error
d. 0 2 4 6, but possible loss of precision

17. What is the output for the program below?

```
public class Test3
{
    public static void main(String[] args)
    {
        int[] arr = {0,2,4,6};
        for(int i : arr)
            System.out.print(++i);
    }
}
```

a. 1, 3, 5, 7   b. 0, 2, 4, 6
c. Compilation error: trying to   d. Runtime error
   update index variable

18. What is the output?

```
public class Test3
{
    public static void main(String[] args)
    {
        int[][] arr = {{0,2},{2,5,6},{4,7,8},{6,1,29}};
        for(int i = 0; i < arr.length; i++)
            System.out.println(arr[i][0]);
    }
}
```

a. 0, 2   b. 2, 5, 6
c. 0, 2, 4, 6   d. 5, 6, 7, 8

19. What is the output?

```
public class Test3
{
    public static void main(String[] args)
    {
        int[][] arr = {{0,2},{2,5,6},{4,7,8},{6,1,29}};
        for(int[] a : arr)
            System.out.println(a[0]);
    }
}
```

a. 0, 2   b. 2, 5, 6
c. 0, 2, 4, 6   d. 5, 6, 7, 8

20. Find out the output:

```
public class Test3
{
    public static void main(String[] args)
    {
        int[] a = {0, 4, 5, 1, 3};
        for (int i = 0; i < a.length; i++)
            a[i] = a[(a[i] + 3) % a.length];
        System.out.println(a[2]);
    }
}
```

a. 0   b. 4

c. 5   d. 1

e. 3

21. What will be the values of arr after this for loop?

```
public class Test3
{
    public static void main(String[] args)
    {
        int[] arr = {1, 0, 0, 1, 1};
        for (int i = 2; i < arr.length; i++)
            arr[i] = arr[i-1] + arr[i-2];
    }
}
```

a. 10112   b. 10011

c. 10022   d. 21011

22. Java arrays are static. That means its size cannot be increased during runtime

    a. True   b. False

23. An array A can be declared as

    a. int[] A;   b. int A[];

    c. int[]A = new int[10];   d. Either A or B

    e. All A, B and C

24. An array A that is already declared as int[] A can be constructed or instantiated as

    a. A = new int[10];   b. A = new A[10];

    c. Either A or B   d. Both A and B

25. An array should be initialized before it is used

    a. True   b. False

26. An array declaration, construction and initialization can be combined as

    (a) int[] A = {1,2,3};   (b)   int[] A = new int[] {1,2,3};

    (c) int[] A = new int[3]{1,2,3};   (d)   int A[] = new int[3]{1,2,3};

    a. (a)   b. (b)

    c. Either (a) or (b)   d. Both (a) and (b)

27. Which of the following array declarations are wrong?

    (a) int[] i[] = {{}, new int[] { }};

    (b) int i[][] = { {1,2}, new int[2]};

    (c) int i[] = {1,2,3,};

    (d) int i[] = {{1,2,3}};

a. (a)   b. (b)
c. (c)   d. (d)

28. Find out the output:

```java
public class Test31
{
    public static void main(String[] args)
    {
        int[] array = {1,2,3,4,5};
        int index = 0;
        int a = 3;
        array[index] = index = a++;
        for(int i: array)
            System.out.print(i);
    }
}
```

a. 12345   b. 32345
c. 13345   d. 12445

29. Find out the output:

```java
public class Test3
{
    public static void main(String[] args)
    {
        int i = 1;
        int[][] arr = {{1,2,3}, {4,5,6}, {7,8,9}};
        System.out.println(arr[i++][i++]);
    }
}
```

a. 4   b. 9
c. 6   d. Error

Answers

1. c	2. d	3. a	4. c	5. c	6. c	7. c	8. c	9. a	10. c
11. b	12. a	13. a	14. c	15. a	16. a	17. a	18. c	19. c	20. d
21. a	22. a	23. e	24. a	25. a	26. c	27. d	28. b	29. c	

Short-answer Questions

1. What is an array? How do you access array elements?
2. What is 2D array? How do you access array elements?

3. Explain for-each statement with an example.
4. How will you create 3D array and access array elements?

EXERCISES

3.1. Read a set of values from command line and print them one at a time back to the user.
3.2. Collect integers from command line and store them in an array.
3.3. Read a line of text followed by a word to search from command line. Search for the word and print proper message.
3.4. Find the product of two vectors.
3.5. Reverse the order of 1D array without a temporary array.
3.6. Given an array of n elements, list all duplicate elements. Do not use a temporary array.
3.7. Find the longest consecutive sequence of integers with no primes.
3.8. Develop an application for Sudoku game.
3.9. Given an array A, find its 1D and 2D Haar Wavelet Transform.
3.10. Generate 100 random integers from 0 to 9. If the sum is 300 keep these integers in an array. In this way, generate integer array 100 times. Print a histogram saying how many times each digit occurs.
3.11. Given a 2D, check whether the sums of each row or each column is 1.
3.12. Given a 1D array, find mean, median and mode.
3.13. Find the most frequent element in a given 1D array.
3.14. Find Pascal's triangle.
3.15. Create 125 random numbers and store them in a 3D [5x5x5] array. Search for an element in this array.

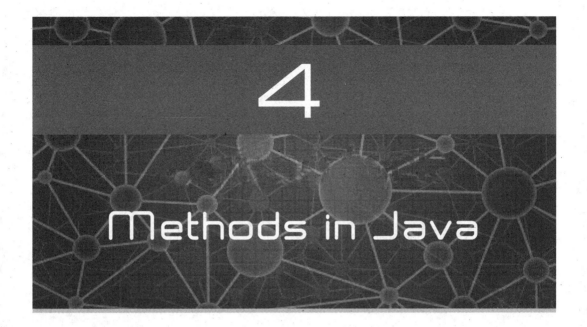

4

Methods in Java

OBJECTIVES

- To introduce Java method definition and method invocation
- To implement *Big2* application to understand methods
- To explain passing primitive data types to methods with *AreaFunction* application
- To generate prime numbers
- To introduce the power of recursion with factorial function
- To explain the pitfalls of recursion with Fibonacci function
- To design overloaded methods
- To explain method overloading with *AdditionCalculator* application
- To illustrate passing one-dimensional arrays to methods using *SortNumbers* applications
- To define *sort()* method with String array as an argument
- To explain passing two-dimensional arrays to methods with *Recipes* application

4.1 INTRODUCTION

A method is a set of Java statements, which is referred to by a name and can be called at any point in an application simply by its name. When method name is encountered in an application, execution of the program branches to the body of the method. After the method is executed, the control returns to the area of the main program code from which it was called, and the program continues at the next statement. Java uses stack to remember the address of Java statement from where the control is transferred to the method, so that it can return to the calling place.

Modular programming applies divide-and-conquer strategy in order to divide the larger program into a set of small pieces so that each piece of a program can be implemented as a method. Therefore, each method can be implemented separately by different developers and integrated later to form a single application. Also, methods support code reusability – that is the same code can be applied to multiple sets of values. Method is also called function by earlier structured languages like C. In this chapter, we lead the readers to the understanding of methods and how to achieve **modular programming** using methods.

4.2 DEFINING A METHOD

A **method** can be defined with syntax as shown in Figure 4.1.

Figure 4.1. Method Definition in Java

```
access-type return-type method-name(arguments) {
  // body;
}
```

As shown in Figure 4.1, each method will have an access-type (right now assume *public static* for simplicity), value to be returned by the method, name of the method and a set of arguments. Note that arguments are optional and a method need not return any value. If a method does not return any value, it is indicated by *void* data type. Now, we shall develop a method *max()* that will read two integers and calculate the biggest and return the result to the calling place. Listing 4.1 depicts the method *max()*.

Listing 4.1. Method to Find Biggest of Two Numbers

```
public static int max(int a, int b)
{
   int big = a > b ? a : b;
   return big;
}
```

Here, the access-type is *public static*, return type is *int*, name of the method is *max*, there are two arguments *a* & *b* and the method returns an *int* value.

4.3 CALLING A METHOD

Once the method is defined, we can call a method by its name with necessary values and collect the result, from the calling place. The syntax for invoking a method is depicted in Figure 4.2.

Figure 4.2. Calling a Method

```
variable = method-name(arguments);
```

Listing 4.2 illustrates the complete application for finding the biggest of the given two integers. The method max2() will find out the biggest.

Listing 4.2. Biggest of Two with Methods

```java
// Big2.java                                              {coderipe}

import java.util.*;

public class Big2
{
    // define method max2(). It receives two integers and returns
    the biggest as an integer
    // here variables a, b and result are visible only inside
    max2() and not outside

    public static int max2(int a, int b)
    {
        int result = a > b ? a : b;
        return result;
    }

    public static void main(String[] args)
    {
        Scanner sc = new Scanner(System.in);

        // read two integers
        System.out.println("Enter two integers one by one");
        int a = sc.nextInt();
        int b = sc.nextInt();

        // now call method with a and b and collect result
        int result = max2(a, b);

        // show result
        System.out.println("Biggest: " + result);
    }
}
```

```
Enter two integers one by one
23
31
Biggest: 31
```

Note that even though the names of variables (a and b) are same in main() and max2(), they are totally different local copies. In other words, the scope of those variables is limited within either main() or max2() where they are defined.

As another illustration for methods, let us develop a method cube() that will return the cube of a number. The complete application shown in Listing 4.3 generates cubes of first 1000 integers.

Listing 4.3. The Cube() Method

```java
//Cubes.java
public class Cubes
{
    public static int cube(int i)
    {
        return (i * i * i);
    }

    public static void main(String[] args)
    {
        for(int i = 0; i < 1000; i++)
            System.out.println(i + ":" + cube(i));
    }
}
```

```
0:0 // only first 10 cubes are shown here
1:1
2:8
3:27
4:64
5:125
6:216
7:343
8:512
9:729
```

Suppose we want to print the reverse of a number. Then you can use reminder operator to extract digits and iteratively create new digits by multiplying the powers of 10 as shown in Listing 4.4.

Listing 4.4. The Reverse() to Find Reverse of a Number

```java
// ReverseNumber.java                              {coderipe}

public class ReverseNumber
{
    public static int reverse(int n)
    {
        int reverse = 0;
        int remainder = 0;
        do
        {
```

```
                remainder = n%10;
                reverse = reverse*10 + remainder;
                n = n/10;
        }
        while(n > 0);
        return reverse;
    }

    public static void main(String[] args)
    {
        int n = 1539;
        System.out.println("Reverse of " + n + ": " + reverse(n));
    }
}
```

```
Reverse of 1539 : 9351
```

4.4 PROBLEM: NESTED METHOD CALLS

The DupGenerator application defines a method duplicate() that returns a concatenated string with itself. Inside main(), this function is invoked as nested calls. The complete application is illustrated in Listing 4.5.

Listing 4.5. Nested Function Calls

```
//DupGenerator.java                                      {coderipe}
public class DupGenerator
{
    public static String duplicate(String s)
    {
        return s + s;
    }

    public static void main(String[] args)
    {
        String s = duplicate("Java");
        System.out.println(s); // prints Java two times

        s = duplicate(duplicate(duplicate("Hello")));
        System.out.println(s); // 8 times
    }
}
```

```
JavaJava
HelloHelloHelloHelloHelloHelloHelloHello
```

4.5 PROBLEM: CALCULATE AREA OF GEOMETRIC OBJECTS

We will discuss another larger application that will calculate the area of geometric objects such as square, rectangle, triangle, circle and cylinder using methods. Listing 4.6 calls appropriate methods by its name from main() method.

Listing 4.6. Calculating the Area of Geometric Objects

```java
// AreaFunction.java

import java.io.*;

public class AreaFunction
{
    // receives side and returns area
    public static int areaSquare(int a)
    {
        return a * a;
    }

    // receives sides a and b, returns area
    public static int areaRectangle(int a, int b)
    {
        return a * b;
    }

    // receives sides a and b, returns area
    public static double areaTriangle(int a, int b)
    {
        return 0.5 * a * b;
    }

    // receives radius and returns area
    public static double areaCircle(int r)
    {
        return 2 * 3.1415 * r;
    }

    // receives radius and height, returns area
    public static double areaCylinder(int r, int h)
    {
        return 2 * 3.1415 * r * r + 2 * 3.1415 * r * h;
    }

    public static void main(String[] args)
```

```
    {
        int area = areaSquare(5);
        System.out.println(area);

        // alternatively println() method can also call a method
        directly
        System.out.println(areaSquare(5));
        System.out.println(areaRectangle(5,3));
        System.out.println(areaTriangle(5,3));
        System.out.println(areaCircle(3));
        System.out.println(areaCylinder(3,4));
    }
}
```

```
25
25
15
7.5
18.849
131.94299
```

4.6 PROBLEM: GENERATE PRIME NUMBERS

A prime number is a natural number that is greater than 1 and is divisible by 1 and itself. For example, 3 is a prime number because 1 and 3 will divide it, whereas 4 is not a prime number because it has the divisor 2 in addition to 1 and 4. Let us generate all prime numbers from 2 to 500 as depicted in Listing 4.7.

Listing 4.7. Generate all Prime Numbers from 2 to 500

```
// PrimeNumber.java

public class PrimeNumber
{
    public static boolean isPrime(int n)
    {
        boolean prime = true;
        int max = (int)Math.sqrt(n);

        for (int i = 2; i <= max; i++)
        {
            if (n % i == 0)
            {
```

```
                prime = false;
                break;
          }
     }

     return prime;
}

public static void main(String[] args)
{
     for(int i = 2; i <= 500; i++)
     {
          if(isPrime(i))
                System.out.print(i + " ");
     }
}
}
```

```
2  3  5  7  11  13  17  19  23  29  31  37  41  43  47  53  59  61  67  71  73  79  83
89  97  101  103  107  109  113  127  131  137  139  149  151  157  163  167  173
179  181  191  193  197  199  211  223  227  229  233  239  241  251  257  263
269  271  277  281  283  293  307  311  313  317  331  337  347  349  353  359
367  373  379  383  389  397  401  409  419  421  431  433  439  443  449  457
461  463  467  479  487  491  499
```

You can even generate millions of prime numbers. Just change the data type from *int* to bigger types such as *BigInteger* and enjoy playing with the code.

4.7 RECURSION: POWER AND PITFALLS

Recursion allows a function to call itself several times. Recursion is a powerful programming technique where iterative computation becomes tedious. **Recursion** is widely applied in combinatorial search and sorting methods. You will be able to appreciate the power of recursion with the calculation of factorial of a number. The factorial function for a positive number N is defined by the equation

$$N! = N \times (N-1) \times (N-2) \times ... \times 2 \times 1$$

The $N!$ can be easily computed iteratively with a *for* loop as shown in the following Listing 4.8.

Listing 4.8. Factorial Using Loops

```
// Factorial.java
import java.util.*;
```

```
public class Factorial
{
   public static int fact(int n)
   {
      int f = 1;

      if( n == 1)
             return f;
      for(int i = 2; i <= n; i++)
             f = f * i;

      return f;
   }
   public static void main(String[] args)
   {
      Scanner sc = new Scanner(System.in);
      System.out.print("Enter a number: ");
      int n = sc.nextInt();

      if (n >= 0)
             System.out.println("Factorial of "+ n + ": "
             + fact(n).);
   }.
}
```

```
Enter a number: 5
Factorial of 5: 120

Enter number: 2
Factorial of 2: 2

Enter number: 0
Factorial of 0: 1
```

Calculating factorial is even easier with recursion. The recursive function that calculates factorial is shown in Figure 4.3.

Figure 4.3. Recursive Function for Factorial

```
int factorial(int n)
{
   if (n == 0)
       return 1;
```

```
        return n * factorial(n-1);
}
```

A recursive function must always have a stop condition with which the execution of the function terminates. For example in the factorial function, the factorial calculation terminates with 0!, which is assumed to be 1. Until this, factorial function will be recursively called (Listing 4.9).

Listing 4.9. Factorial Using Recursion

```java
// RecursiveFactorial.java
import java.util.*;

public class RecursiveFactorial
{
    public static long fact(long n)
    {
        if(n < 0)
                throw new RuntimeException
                    ("Exception: " + n + " is a negative number");

        if (n == 0)
                return 1;
        else
                return n * fact(n-1);
    }

    public static void main(String[] args)
    {
        System.out.print("Enter a number: ");
        Scanner sc = new Scanner(System.in);
        long n = sc.nextLong();
        System.out.println(fact(n));
    }
}
```

```
Enter a number: 5
120
```

```
Enter a number: 10
3628800
```

```
Enter a number: -2
Exception: -2 is a negative number
```

Though recursion is a powerful programming technique, it demands a lot of memory space as the state of every recursive call has to be stored in a runtime stack. Not only excessive space requirements, there is also a lot of re-computation involved. This is evident when you write a recursive function that generates Fibonacci sequence. The sequence of numbers *0 1 1 2 3 5 8 13 21 34 55 89 144 233 ...* represents a Fibonacci sequence. A Fibonacci sequence can be generated with the following equation as shown in Figure 4.4.

Figure 4.4. Fibonacci Sequence

$$F_0 = 0$$
$$F_1 = 1$$
$$F_n = F_{n-1} + F_{n-2} \text{ for } n \geq 2$$

A novice developer will implement this recursive function to generate Fibonacci sequence as depicted in Figure 4.5.

Figure 4.5. Fibonacci Function Using Recursion

```
fibo(int n)
{
    if( n == 0)
        return 0;
    if( n == 1)
        return 1;
    return fibo(n-1) + fibo(n-2);
}
```

The complete application that generates Fibonacci numbers using recursion is illustrated in Listing 4.10.

Listing 4.10. Fibonacci Series Using Recursion

```
// RecursiveFibonacci.java
import java.util.*;

public class RecursiveFibonacci
{
    public static long fib(int n)
    {
        if (n <= 1)
            return n;
        else
            return fib(n-1) + fib(n-2);
    }
```

{coderipe}

```
public static void main(String[] args)
{
    System.out.print("How many numbers?: ");
    Scanner sc = new Scanner(System.in);
    int n = sc.nextInt();

    for (int i = 0; i <= n; i++)
            System.out.print(fib(i) + " ");
}
}
```

```
How many numbers?: 10
0 1 1 2 3 5 8 13 21 34 55
```

Although writing recursive version of Fibonacci sequence is easy, it is inefficient. To understand the reason, consider the calculation fibo(7) which is 13. It is calculated as fibo(6) = 8 and fibo(5) = 5. To calculate fibo(6), it recursively calculates fibo(5) and fibo(4) without bothering fibo(5) which is already computed. So it unnecessarily computes fibo(5) again. The same recomputation will be carried out for lower numbers until the termination condition is reached. Therefore, a better solution for generating Fibonacci sequence is to calculate the terms iteratively using loops as illustrated in Listing 4.11.

Listing 4.11. Fibonacci Sequence Using Loops

```
// Fibonacci.java
import java.util.*;

public class Fibonacci
{
    public static void fibo(int n)
    {
        int f0 = 0, f1 = 1;

        if (n == 0)
        {
            System.out.println(f0);
            return;
        }

        if (n == 1)
        {
            System.out.println(f0 + " " + f1);
            return;
```

```
        }

        // if beyond 1, print f0 and f1 and proceed
        System.out.print(f0 + " " + f1);

        for(int i = 2; i <= n; i++)
        {
            // add previous 2 numbers
            int f2 = f0 + f1;
            System.out.print(" " + f2);
            // update previous 2 numbers
            f0 = f1;
            f1 = f2;
        }
    }

    public static void main(String[] args)
    {
        System.out.print("How many numbers?: ");
        Scanner sc = new Scanner(System.in);
        int n = sc.nextInt();
        // call
        fibo(n);
    }
}
```

```
How many numbers?: 10
0 1 1 2 3 5 8 13 21 34 55

How many numbers?: 1
0 1

How many numbers?: 0
0
```

4.8 METHOD OVERLOADING

In Java, it is possible to define two or more methods with the same name, within the same class. Hence, these methods are called overloaded methods and this process is known as **method over-loading**. Method overloading is one of Java's most exciting and useful features that avoid redundant names for those methods whose behaviour is the same.

Java distinguishes overloaded methods through their arguments. Two overloaded methods can differ by any of the following ways:

- Type of arguments
- Number of arguments
- Order of appearance of the arguments

However, methods should not be overloaded by its return types. Example 4.1 illustrates the concepts of Java method overloading with various method signatures for *add()* method.

Example 4.1. Types of Method Overloading

```
Case 1. Type of arguments
public static int add(int a, int b)
public static double add(double a, double b)

Case 2. Number of arguments
public static int add(int a, int b)
public static int add(int a)

Case 3. Order of appearance of arguments
public static double add(int a, double b)
public static double add(double a, int b)

Case 4. Overloading by return type
public static float add(float a, float b)
public static double add(float a, float b)
This is prohibited in Java
```

Suppose we will extend our earlier Calculator application by providing overloaded methods for adding various primitive data types (i.e. int, double, float and mixed types) as shown in Listing 4.12.

Listing 4.12. Addition Calculator Using Overloading

```java
// AdditionCalculator.java

public class AdditionCalculator
{
    public static int add(int i, int j)
    {
        return i + j;
    }

    public static double add(double i, double j)
    {
        return i + j;
    }
```

```
public static float add(float i, float j)
{
    return i + j;
}

public static double add(int i, double j)
{
    return i + j;
}

public static double add(double i, int j)
{
    return i + j;
}

public static void main(String[] args)
{
    System.out.println(add(10,20));
    System.out.println(add(10.0,20.0));
    System.out.println(add(100.0f,200.0f));
    System.out.println(add(30,20.0));
    System.out.println(add(50.0,20));
}
}
```

```
30
30.0
300.0
50.0
70.0
```

In AdditionCalculator application, the appropriate overloaded method will be called inside main() depending on the input values automatically.

4.9 PASSING ONE-DIMENSIONAL ARRAYS TO METHODS

Similar to passing primitive data types to methods, arrays can also be passed to methods. However, there is a difference between passing primitive data types and **passing arrays**. Remember, every array name behaves as a reference or a pointer to memory locations containing array values. In methods with primitive type arguments, the arguments are just local variables whose scope is restricted to only that method. Any updates happening inside the method will not get reflected outside the method, whereas changes in array values made inside the method will update the source array outside the method in the calling place.

Listing 4.13 shows SortNumbers application that arranges the given integers in ascending order. It defines a method sort() that takes array of numbers and sorts them. The sort() method does not have to return the sorted sequence, as original sequence will get modified directly through the reference in the method.

Listing 4.13. Sorting Numbers Application

```java
// SortNumbers.java

import java.io.*;

public class SortNumbers
{
    public static void sort(int[] numbers) // reference numbers
    will directly modify original array a in main()
    {
      // take ith number
      for (int i = 0; i < numbers.length-1; i++)
      {
       // compare ith number with all other jth numbers
       for (int j = i+1; j < numbers.length; j++)
        {
         // if second number < first
         if(numbers[j] < numbers[i])
         {
            // interchange
            int temp;
            temp = numbers[i];
            numbers[i] = numbers[j];
            numbers[j] = temp;
         }
        }
      }
      // since numbers is a reference to original array, through
      numbers original array gets sorted, so nothing has to be
      returned
    }

    public static void main(String[ ] args) throws IOException
    {
        BufferedReader in = new BufferedReader
                    (new InputStreamReader(System.in));

        // read n
        System.out.print("Enter total no. to be processed: ");
```

```
        int n = Integer.parseInt(in.readLine());

        // create array a of n size
        int[ ] a = new int[n]; // to keep actual numbers

        // read actual numbers
        System.out.println("Enter actual numbers: ");
        for (int i = 0; i < n; i++)
            a[i] = Integer.parseInt(in.readLine());

        // show
        System.out.println("Original numbers before
        sorting ");
        for (int i = 0; i < n; i++)
            System.out.print( a[i] + " ");

        // call sort() method with array a
        sort(a);

        // show sorted sequence
        System.out.println("\nSorted sequence of numbers ");
        for (int i = 0; i < n; i++)
            System.out.print( a[i] + " ");

    }
}
```

```
Enter total no. to be processed: 5
Enter actual numbers:
9
2
5
7
1
Original numbers before sorting
9 2 5 7 1
Sorted sequence of numbers
1 2 5 7 9
```

4.10 PROBLEM: METHOD TO SORT NAMES

Naturally as a next step, we will be interested to arrange the given set of names in alphabetic order. In order to customize the above code, we need a String array that will hold all names. We will make use of *compareTo()* method from String class to compare two Strings. The *compareTo()* will return some negative number, zero or some positive number if the first string is less than, equal to or greater than the second string respectively. Listing 4.14 illustrates the overloaded *sort()* method to perform this alphabetic sorting of names.

Listing 4.14. Sort() to Sort Strings

```java
public static void sort(String[ ] names)
{
    // take ith name
    for (int i = 0; i < names.length-1; i++)
    {
        // compare ith name with all other jth names
        for (int j = i+1; j < names.length; j++)
        {
            // if second number < first
            if(names[j].compareTo(names[i]) < 0)
            {
                // interchange values
                String temp;
                temp = names[i];
                names[i] = names[j];
                names[j] = temp;
            }
        }
    }
}
```

The complete program that arranges the given names in alphanumeric order is depicted in Listing 4.15.

Listing 4.15. Sorting Names

```java
// SortNames.java
import java.io.*;

public class SortNames
{
    public static void sort(String[] names)
    {
        // take ith name
        for (int i = 0; i < names.length-1; i++)
        {
            // compare ith name with all other jth names
            for (int j = i+1; j < names.length; j++)
            {
                // if second number < first
```

```
              if(names[j].compareTo(names[i]) < 0)
              {
                  // interchange values
                  String temp;
                  temp = names[i];
                  names[i] = names[j];
                  names[j] = temp;
              }
          }
      }
  }

  public static void main(String[] args) throws IOException
  {
      BufferedReader in = new BufferedReader
          (new InputStreamReader(System.in));

      // read numbers
      System.out.print("Enter total no. of names to be
      processed: ");
      int n = Integer.parseInt(in.readLine());
      String a[] = new String[n]; // to keep actual names

      System.out.println("Enter actual names: ");
      for (int i = 0; i < n; i++)
          a[i] = in.readLine();

      // sort names
      sort(a);

      // show
      System.out.print("Sorted names: ");
      for (int i = 0; i < n; i++)
          System.out.print( a[i] + " ");
  }
}
```

```
Enter total no. of names to be processed: 5
Enter actual names:
rex
anabel
peter
lavanya
```

```
oviya
Sorted names: anabel lavanya oviya peter rex
```

4.11 PASSING TWO-DIMENSIONAL ARRAYS TO METHODS

You can pass a two-dimensional array as an argument to a method very similar to passing a one-dimensional array to a method. In the same way, a method can return either one-dimensional, two-dimensional or multidimensional arrays back to the calling place.

We will send a two-dimensional array as arguments to a method in a Recipes application. Assume, we have three recipes for evening snacks. Each recipe feeds three people. The required ingredients are as follows:

- Pancakes: 2 cups flour, 2 eggs and 1 cup milk.
- Biscuits: 2.25 cups flour and 0.75 cups milk.
- Waffles: 2 cups flour, 1 egg, 1.35 cups milk and 1 tablespoons oil.

Suppose we want to feed six people. How much ingredients do we need for the recipes? Further, If we want to feed 3 people pancakes, 12 people biscuits and 9 people waffles, how much flour, will we need?

To calculate ingredients, first let us tabulate the ingredients required to prepare recipes (see Table 4.1).

This table of values can be represented as a two-dimensional array, say A(3,4), where rows indicate recipes and columns indicate the required ingredients.

$$
\text{Recipe R} = \begin{matrix} 2 & 2 & 1 & 0 \\ 3 & 0 & 1 & 0 \\ 2 & 1 & 2 & 1 \end{matrix}
$$

Now, let us calculate how much ingredients we need in order to serve six people. Note that A will serve three people. So, we need 2 × A ingredients that will serve six people, as illustrated below.

$$
\text{Recipe R1} = 2 \times \begin{matrix} 2 & 2 & 1 & 0 \\ 3 & 0 & 1 & 0 \\ 2 & 1 & 2 & 1 \end{matrix}
$$

Now let us consider the second case. Here, we will have to calculate ingredients to feed 3 people pancakes, 12 people biscuits and 9 people waffles. Remember, our earlier recipe A will already serve

Table 4.1. Ingredients

Serving Size = Three People			
	Flour	Eggs	Milk	Oil
Pancake	2	2	1	0
Biscuits	3	0	1	0
Waffles	2	1	2	1

three people. We need to make one batch of pancakes, four batches of biscuits, and three batches of waffles. Let's represent this with the row vector as

	Pancake	Biscuits	Waffles
s =	1	4	3

The vector describing how much flour is needed is the first column of R. Let us represent it as a column vector v

$$v = \begin{matrix} 2 \\ 3 \\ 2 \end{matrix}$$

Therefore, total number of cups of flour required can be calculated by taking *dot product* between s and v as $1 \times 2 + 4 \times 3 + 3 \times 2 = 20$ cups. Similarly, by taking dot products with other columns we can calculate the required ingredients such as eggs, milk and oil. These set of dot product with all columns of the matrix is called matrix multiplication. So, we can multiply vector s with A to calculate the required ingredients.

	Flour	Eggs	Milk	Oil
R2 = s * R =	20	5	11	3

Therefore, to serve 3 people pancake, 12 people biscuits and 9 people waffles, we need 20 cups of flour, 8 eggs, 11 cups of milk and 3 tablespoons of oil as shown above.

Listing 4.16 depicts calcIngredient() method that takes a vector of serving requirement and a recipe matrix and then calculates the required number ingredients such as flour, eggs, milk and oil.

Listing 4.16. Recipes Application

```java
// Recipes.java

public class Recipes
{
    public static int calcIngredient( int[] serv, int[][] flour,
    int column )
    {
        int total = 0, i, j;

        for( i = 0, j = 0; i < serv.length; i++, j++)
            total = total + serv[i] * flour[j][column];   // only one
            column in flour required

        return total;
```

```
        }

    public static void main(String[] args)
    {
        int[ ][ ] recipe = { {2,2,1,0}, {3,0,1,0}, {2,1,2,1}};
        int[ ] serving = {1, 4, 3};

        // call to calculate flour
        int cups = calcIngredient(serving, recipe, 0);   // only oth
        column required
        System.out.println("No. of cups of flour required: " + cups);

        // call to calculate eggs
        int eggs = calcIngredient(serving, recipe, 1);   // only 1st
        column required
        System.out.println("No. of eggs required: " + eggs);

        // call to calculate milk
        int milk = calcIngredient(serving, recipe, 2);   // only 2nd
        column required
        System.out.println("No. of cups of milk required: " + milk);

        // call to calculate oil
        int oil = calcIngredient(serving, recipe, 3);   // only 3rd
        column required
        System.out.println("No. of tablespoons of oil required:
        " + oil);

    }
}
```

```
No. of cups of flour required: 20
No. of eggs required: 5
No. of cups of milk required: 11
No. of tablespoons of oil required: 3
```

Another notable feature of this application is the power of code reusability, an important trait of modular programming. The calcIngredient() is invoked by main() four times with different sets of values. Otherwise, we should have defined four different methods to handle the four cases.

4.12 VARIABLE LENGTH ARGUMENT LISTS

Java supports variable length arguments of the same type in a method. The argument in the method declaration is defined as depicted in Figure 4.6.

Figure 4.6. Syntax for Variable Length Arguments

```
data-type... argument
```

In the method declaration, you need to specify the type followed by an ellipsis. Only one variable length argument can be specified in a method, and this argument must be the last argument. Any regular arguments must precede it.

Java treats a variable-length argument as an array and creates it. Arrays can also be passed to **variable length arguments**. Listing 4.17 depicts a method show() that prints an integer and list of strings.

Listing 4.17. ShowNames Using Varargs

```java
// ShowNames.java

public class ShowNames
{
    public static void show(int id, String... names)
    {
        System.out.println("id: " + id);
        for(int i = 0; i < names.length; i++)
          System.out.println("Name " + i + " : " + names[i]);
    }

    public static void main(String[] args)
    {
        // call show() with varargs
        show(100, "C", "C++", "Java", ".NET", "PhP", "Python"); //
        just some value 100

        // call show() with an array too
        String[] names = {"C", "C++", "Java", ".NET", "PhP",
        "Python"};
        show(100, names);   // assume 100 for id
    }
}
```

```
id: 100
Name 0 : C
Name 1 : C++
Name 2 : Java
Name 3 : .NET
Name 4 : PhP
Name 5 : Python
id: 100
```

```
Name 0 : C
Name 1 : C++
Name 2 : Java
Name 3 : .NET
Name 4 : PhP
Name 5 : Python
```

4.13 SUMMARY

1. Methods help to achieve modular programming
2. Each method is identified and called by its name
3. Methods can receive arguments. The arguments can be primitive data types, strings and arrays
4. Method overloading allows a method name to be shared by several methods
5. Overloaded methods should differ by its arguments
6. Methods should not be overloaded by their return types
7. Array names behave as references, so a method need not return the array back to calling place
8. Method can call other methods
9. Methods can be defined with variable length arguments list

KEY TERMS

Method, 90   Modular programming, 90   Recursion, 96
Method overloading, 101   Passing arrays, 103   Variable length arguments, 111

REVIEW QUESTIONS

Multiple-choice Questions

1. Find out the output:

```java
public class Test4
{
    public static int[] incr(int[] a)
    {
        int[] c = new int[a.length];

        for(int i = 0; i < a.length; i++)
        {
```

```
            a[i] = a[i] + 1;
            c[i] = a[i];
        }

    return c;
    }

public static void main(String[] args)
    {
        int[] n = {1,2,3,4,5};
        int[] t = incr(n);
        for(int i : t)
            System.out.print(i);
        for(int i : n)
            System.out.print(i);
    }
}
```

a. 1234512345   b. 2345612345
c. 1234523456   d. 2345623456

2. Find out the output:

```
public class Test4
{
    public static int[] sum(int[] a, int[] b)
    {
        int[] c = new int[a.length];
        for(int i = 0; i < a.length; i++)
            c[i] = a[i] + b[i];
        return c;
    }
    public static void main(String[] args)
    {
        int[] n = {1,2,3,4,5};
        int[] t = sum(n, n);
        for(int i : t)
            System.out.println(i);
    }
}
```

a. 1 2 3 4 5   b. 2 4 6 8 10
c. Compilation error   d. Runtime error

3. Find out the output:

```
public class Test4
{
    public static void sum2(int[] a, int[]b)
    {
        int[] c = new int[a.length];
        for(int i = 0; i < a.length; i++)
            a[i] = a[i] + b[i];
    }
    public static void main(String[] args)
    {
        int[] n = {1,2,3,4,5};
        int[] n2 = {1,2,3,4,5};
        sum2(n, n2);
        for(int i : n)
            System.out.println(i);
    }
}
```

a. 1 2 3 4 5

b. 2 4 6 8 10

c. Some garbage value will be displayed

d. Compilation error

4. Find out the output:

```
public class Test4
{
    public static double sqrt(double x)
    {
        return Math.sqrt(x);
    }
    public static void main(String[] args)
    {
        double y = 4.0;
        double x = sqrt(double y);
    }
}
```

a. Compilation error

b. 2

c. 2.0

d. Runtime error

5. Find out the output:

```
public class Test4
{
    public static void f1(int i)
    {
        System.out.println(i * i);
    }

    public void f1(double i)
    {
        System.out.println(i * i + 100);
    }
    public static void main(String[] args)
    {
        f1(10);
    }
}
```

a. 100

b. 200

c. Overloading static and non-static versions of f1() not allowed

d. Throws runtime exception

6. Find out the output:

```
public class Test4
{
    public static void f1(int i)
    {
        System.out.println(i * i);
    }

    public static void f1(double i)
    {
        System.out.println(i * i);
    }
    public static void main(String[] args)
    {
        f1(10);
    }
}
```

a. 100

b. 200

c. Overloading static versions of f1() not allowed

d. RTTI encountered during run time

7. Find out the output:

```
public class Test4
{
    public void sqr(int i)
    {
        System.out.println(i * i);
        return;
        System.out.println(i * i);
    }
    public static void main(String[] args)
    {
        sqr(10);
    }
}
```

    a. 100

    b. 100 100

    c. Recursively prints 100

    d. Compilation error as statements after return occurs

8. What will be the output for the program below?

```
public class Test4
{
    public static void swap(int a, int b)
    {
        int t = a;
        a = b;
        b = t;
    }
    public static void main(String[] args)
    {
        int a = 10, b = 20;
        swap(a, b);
        System.out.println(a + "," + b);
    }
}
```

    a. 20, 10

    b. 10, 20

    c. 10, 10

    d. 20, 20

9. Find out the output:

```
public class Test4
{
    public static void f1()
    {
        f2();
    }

    public static void f2()
    {
        System.out.println("Hello");
    }
    public static void main(String[] args)
    {
        f1();
    }
}
```

a. Hello
b. Compilation error
c. Static method cannot call another static method
d. Hello Hello

10. Find out the output:

```
public class Test4
{
    public static void f1()
    {
        f2();
    }

    public void f2()
    {
        System.out.println("Hello");
    }
    public static void main(String[] args)
    {
        f1();
    }
}
```

a. Hello
b. Compilation error
c. Static method cannot call nonstatic method
d. Hello Hello

11. Consider the following functions:

```
public static int f1() { }
public static void f1() { }
```

    a. Methods will compile, but will not run

    b. Methods will compile and run

    c. Methods will not compile as overloading with return type not allowed

    d. None of the above

12. Find out the output:

```
public class Test4
{
   public static String test(int a)
   {
      String s;
      if(a < 0)
           s = "-ve";
      return s;
   }
   public static void main(String[] args)
   {
      System.out.println(test(-10));
   }
}
```

    a. –ve   b. Will not compile as s not initialized

    c. Null   d. \0

13. Find out the output:

```
public class Test4
{
   public static void main(String[] args)
   {
      int[][] a = new int[4][5];
      System.out.println(a.length);
   }
}
```

    a. 4   b. 5

    c. Array not initialized   d. Syntax error in length()

14. Find out the output:

```
public class Test4
{
    public static void main(String[] args)
    {
        int[][] a = new int[4][5];
        System.out.println(a[0].length);
        System.out.println(a[1].length);
        System.out.println(a[2].length);
        System.out.println(a[3].length);
    }
}
```

a. 5 5 5 5   b. 4 4 4 4

c. 0 0 0 0   d. null null null null

15. Find out the output:

```
public class Test4
{
    public static int[][] transform(int[][] a)
    {
        int rows = a[0].length;
        int cols = a.length;
        int[][] b = new int[rows][cols];

        for (int r = 0; r < rows; r++)
            for (int c = 0; c < cols; c++)
                b[r][c] = a[cols - 1 - c][r];   // STATEMENT-1
        return b;
    }
    public static void main(String[] args)
    {
        int[][] m = {{1,2,3},{4,5,6}};
        m = transform(m);

        for(int i = 0; i < m.length; i++)
        {
            for(int j = 0; j < m[0].length; j++)
            System.out.print(m[i][j] + " ");
            System.out.println();
        }
    }
}
```

a. 4 1   5 2   6 3   b. 1 2   3 4   5 6

c. 1 4   2 5   3 6   d. 3 6   2 5   1 4

16. How will you modify STATEMENT-1 of the above example to print the following matrix:

3 6

2 5

1 4

a. b[r][c] = a[c][r];   b. b[r][c] = a[c][rows - 1 - r];

c. b[r][c] = a[cols - 1 - c][r];   d. b[r][c] = a[cols - 1 - c][rows - 1 - r];

17. Find out the output:

```
public class Test31
{
    public enum Colors {RED, GREEN, BLUE};
    public static void main(String[] args)
    {
        for(Colors c : Colors.values())
            System.out.print(c);
    }
}
```

a. RED GREEN BLUE   b. BLUE GREEN RED

c. Compilation error   d. Runtime error

18. Find out the output:

```
public class Test31
{
    public enum Colors {RED, GREEN, BLUE};

    public static void main(String[] args)
    {
        for(Colors c : Colors.values())
        {
            switch(c)
            {
                case RED:
                    System.out.print("Red colour");
                    break;
                case GREEN:
                    System.out.print("Green colour");
                    break;
```

```
                    case BLUE:
                        System.out.print("Blue colour");
                        break;
            }
        }
    }
}
```

 a. Red colour Green Colour Blue Colour b. Red Colour

 c. Green Colour   d. Blue Colour

19. What will be the output for the following program?

```
public class Test41
{
    public static void f1(int a, double d, char c)
    {
        System.out.println("Primitive type arguments");
    }

    public static void f1(Integer a, Double d, Character c)
    {
        System.out.println("Wrapper type arguments");
    }
    public static void main(String[] args)
    {
        f1(new Integer(1), new Double(1.0), new Character('1'));
    }
}
```

 a. Wrapper type arguments

 b. Primitive type arguments

 c. Compilation error: references of wrappers cannot be passed to f1

 d. Compilation error: ambiguity occurs between primitives and wrappers

20. How will you call these overloaded functions?

```
public class Test41
{
    public void exchange(int i, int j) { }
    public void exchange(double d1, double d2) { }

    public static void main(String[] args)
```

```
    {
        // call these functions
    }
}
```

    a. exchange(10,20); exchange(10.0,20.0);

    b. exchange("10","20"); exchange("10.0","20.0");

    c. exchange(10l,20f); exchange(10.0f,20.0l);

    d. None of the above

21. Find out the output:

```
public class Test41
{
    public void show(int c)
    {
        System.out.println((char)c);
    }
    public void show(String s)
    {
        System.out.println(s);
    }

    public static void main(String[] args)
    {
        Test41 t = new Test41();
        t.show('h');
    }
}
```

    a. h

    b. 104

    c. Compilation error: No char version of show() exists

    d. Runtime error: Unable to find char version of show()

22. What will be the output?

```
public class Test41
{
    public void show(int c)
    {
        System.out.println(c);
```

```
    }
    public void show(float f)
    {
        System.out.println(f);
    }

    public static void main(String[] args)
    {
        Test41 t = new Test41();
        t.show(10.0);
    }
}.
```

a. 10
b. 10.0
c. Compilation error: No double version of show() exists
d. Runtime error: Unable to find double version of show()

23. What will be the output?

```
public class Test41
{
    public void show(int c)
    {
        System.out.println(c);
    }
    public void show(double d)
    {
        System.out.println(d);
    }

    public static void main(String[] args)
    {
        Test41 t = new Test41();
        t.show(10.0f);
    }
}
```

a. 10.0f
b. 10.0
c. 10
d. Runtime error: Unable to find float version of show()

24. What does the following method do?

```
public static String cat(String[] s)
{
    if(s == null)
        return null;
    String t = "";
    for(String s1 : s)
        t = t + s1;
    return t;
}
```

a. Concatenates the given string array
b. Concatenates the given string array into a string
c. Concatenates the given string array into a string and returns the string
d. Concatenates the given string array into a string and returns the string, if the given string is non-null
e. All of the above

Answers

1. d	2. b	3. b	4. a	5. a	6. a	7. a	8. b	9. a	10. c
11. c	12. b	13. a	14. a	15. a	16. b	17. a	18. a	19. a	20. a
21. a	22. c	23. b	24. e						

Short-answer Questions

1. How do you define methods? How do you call methods in Java?
2. What is recursion? Explain recursion with an example.
3. What are the benefits and pitfalls of recursion?
4. Explain method overloading with an example.
5. Explain passing 1D arrays to methods.
6. Explain passing 2D arrays to methods.
7. Explain variable length arguments with an example.

EXERCISES

4.1. Develop a method squeeze() that will take an array of integers and returns an array without duplicates.
4.2. Develop a method crypt() that will take a char array and return a modified array of chars. Replace each character as *a by c, b by d, c by e* and so on.
4.3. Develop a method oddparity() that will return a boolean if the given binary array (0's and 1's) has odd number of 1's.

4.4. Develop a method nonagram() to print Nonagram.

4.5. Develop a method to plot Neckar cube.

4.6. Develop a method that takes a 2D array representing a graph and calculates a page rank of a node.

4.7. Develop a method that calculates the square root of a number (use Newton–Raphson method).

4.8. Develop a method that returns the given number odd or not.

4.9. Develop a method that reads a boolean array of opinion values and returns a boolean indicating an opinion is true or false.

4.10. Develop a method that takes two vectors and check whether they are equal or not.

4.11. Develop overloaded methods for add(), sub(), mul() and div() for Arithmetic calculator application. Overload int, float, double and long data types.

4.12. Develop a method that counts, blanks, tabs and new lines in a given string.

4.13. Develop a method that will replace one or more blank spaces by a single space.

4.14. Develop a method that will read an array of strings and display the occurrences of each word in a decreasing order.

4.15. Develop a method currencyConverter() that will convert numerical value of rupees into words.

PART II OBJECT ORIENTED JAVA PROGRAMMING

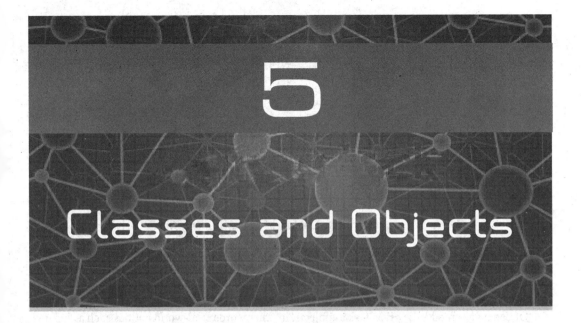

5

Classes and Objects

OBJECTIVES

- To explain object-oriented paradigm with encapsulation, information hiding, aggregation, inheritance and polymorphism features
- To cultivate object-oriented thinking to design applications
- To create classes with data members and member functions
- To illustrate classes with *Laptop* application
- To write different access types for classes, data members and member functions
- To implement aggregation with *OOCollege* application
- To explain static variables and static methods
- To implement array of objects for *Student* application
- To implement methods with objects as arguments for *BookStore* application
- To understand the scope with *this* reference

5.1 INTRODUCTION

In chapters 1–4, the readers were exposed to Java as a **structured programming** language. Java language was used to develop applications based on algorithmic steps and modular programming paradigm. Although, Java can be used as a structured programming language, the power of Java is its object-oriented features. Chapters 5–7 present Java as a language for **object-oriented programming** (OOP) paradigm.

5.2 OBJECT-ORIENTED PROGRAMMING PARADIGM

In chapters 1–4, we had used Java to solve problems as a structured programming language. This programming paradigm emphasizes separating a program's *data* from its *functionality*. This separation

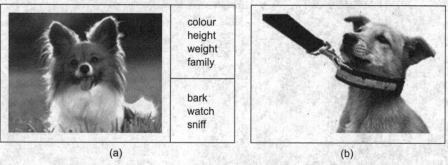

Figure 5.1. (a) Dog as a Real-world Entity (b) Dog with a Belt

of data from program leads to a software that is difficult to maintain and understand. Later, a new software development methodology evolved, which allowed developers to bind data and functionality together, and it is known as OOP methodology. Java is one of the important OOP languages, with a wealth of features for object-oriented system development (OOSD).

OOP languages model the given task as objects, in other words, real-world entities such as laptops, cars, bank accounts, cats and dogs. Structured programming languages specify conditions that every **object** has to adhere while creating object, whereas OOP emphasizes the language to support objects' conditions. For instance, in structured programming, a dog is represented by a set of functions such as *bark, watch, sniff* and so on. A separate set of variables will define the dog's *colour, height, weight, family* and so on. So, you initialize dog's variables and call some functions that operate on those variables and my goodness, you have a dog!

In contrast, OOP language sees dog as a real-world entity or object with **behaviours** (i.e. functions) and **states** (i.e. variables that hold data values) as shown in Figure 5.1(a). So, OOP thinks in terms of objects and not in terms of separate functions and variables. The integration of state variables and behaviours into objects is called **encapsulation**. Encapsulation promotes **information hiding**. Information hiding makes state variables and behaviour inaccessible to the external world. **Aggregation** is another property of OOP language, which characterizes that an entity is composed of other entities. For instance, a *car* is composed of *engine, wheels, doors* and so on, each of which is known as entities.

Aggregation expresses HAS-A relationship between entities. Consider a dog wears a belt in its neck as in Figure 5.1(b). In this case, we say Dog HAS-A Belt. So Dog and Belt are two entities where Dog contains Belt.

In OOP, we encounter **inheritance** – the ability to derive something specific from something generic. For example, the entities cat and dog, both are classified as animals. Cats and dogs inherit states and behaviours from generic entity animals. There are two types of inheritance – *single inheritance* and *multiple inheritance*. In single inheritance, an entity inherits from just one generic entity, whereas in *multiple inheritance*, an entity inherits from more than one generic entity. Here, entities in inheritance express IS-A behaviour. For example, Dog IS-A animal. Java supports only single inheritance. **Polymorphism** or runtime **overriding** is another unique feature of Java. Java uses runtime type identification (**RTTI**) in order to identify the correct behaviour of a child class.

5.3 CREATING A CLASS

A *class* is a source code blueprint for objects. That blueprint specifies each object's state variables (we call data members) and behaviours (we call member functions or methods). Use the Java syntax shown in Figure 5.2 to create a class in an application.

Figure 5.2. Syntax for Creating a Class

```
[public | private | protected] [abstract | final] class class-name
{
    // data members (both primitive and objects) and member functions
}
```

This syntax creates a class that can be a public class, private class, protected class or default class without any of these three keywords. Also, it can be an abstract class or final class. A public class is accessible to all class in all packages. A package is a collection of classes bundled together and identified by a common name. Assume a package to be a directory with a collection of files. We will discuss packages in Chapter 7.

A private class cannot be accessed by any other class in any package. Only member functions can access its data members. A private class may allow other classes to access data members through its member functions. A protected class is either accessible to its subclasses in any package or any class within the current package.

An abstract class is an incomplete class, where objects cannot be created from abstract class. It is a first step towards interfaces which is identified as a pure abstract class. These abstract classes and interfaces tell those related classes that all of them should implement abstract methods and interface methods with necessary method body. The final class cannot be subclassed. Suppose, we want to restrict access to all subclasses, then the final class is more useful to achieve this functionality.

Finally, a class can be defined without any of these keywords that we can call default class. Default classes are accessible to all classes defined in the current package. A class can contain data members (variables of primitive type or objects of a class) and member functions (methods).

We have so far learnt enough theory about OOP concepts. Now, it is time to start developing applications using OOP concepts. Let us consider the following real-world entity, Laptop (shown in Figure 5.3). Laptop has many states such as *monitorSize, colour, processor, ram* and *hardDisk* and many behaviours such as *turnOn, turnOff, idle* and *running*.

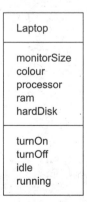

Figure 5.3. Laptop Real-world Object

We can convert this entity into a Java class as a class diagram with data members and member functions and is represented in Figure 5.4.

```
            class Laptop

      int monitorSize
      String colour
      String processor
      int ram
      int hardDisk

      void turnOn
      void turnOff
      void idle()
      void running()
```

Figure 5.4. Laptop Class

Let us now convert this Java class diagram into a Java class that is accessible to any class in the current package (i.e. in the current directory) as shown in Listing 5.1.

Listing 5.1. Laptop Class

```java
// Laptop.java

public class Laptop
{
    int monitorSize;
    String colour;
    String processor;
    int ram;
    int hardDisk;

    void turnOn()
    {
        System.out.println(" Laptop switched on now…");
    }
    void turnoff()
    {
        System.out.println(" Laptop switched off now…");
    }
    void idle()
    {
        System.out.println(" Laptop is in idle
        mode now…");
    }
    void running()
    {
        System.out.println(" Laptop is currently running …");
    }
}
```

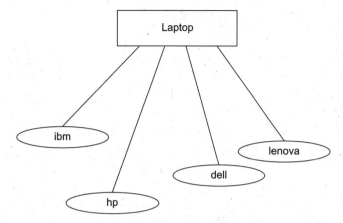

Figure 5.5. Laptop Class with Objects

Once Laptop class is defined, we can then create objects of Laptop such as *ibm, hp, dell* and *lenova* as shown in Figure 5.5. Further, Listing 5.2 depicts the public class that creates objects of Laptop.

Listing 5.2. LaptopTest Application

```java
// LaptopTest.java
public class LaptopTest
{
    public static void main(String[] args)
    {
        // create object ibm
        Laptop ibm = new Laptop();

        // set object properties with
        values
        ibm.monitorSize = 14;
        ibm.colour = "Black";
        ibm.processor = "Core2";
        ibm.ram = 32;
        ibm.hardDisk = 500;
        // now, do operations
        // turn on laptop
        ibm.turnOn();

        // set it is currently running
        ibm.running();

        // switch off now
```

{coderipe}

```
        ibm.turnOff();

        // similarly, you can create other laptops, initialize
        values to data members and perform operations
        Laptop hp = new Laptop();
        Laptop dell = new Laptop();
        Laptop lenova = new Laptop();
    }
}
```

```
Laptop switched on now
Laptop is currently running
Laptop switched off now
```

When you compile *LaptopTest.java*, it will automatically compile *Laptop.java*, provided *Laptop.java* is available in the same directory where *LaptopTest.java* is saved. For brevity, many novice Java users would prefer to save both classes in the same file. In such cases, you must keep Laptop class as a default class without public keyword and save files with the name of the public class which is now *LaptopTest.java*. Here, object names (also called instance) such as ibm, hp, dell and lenova are references that hold the address of memory locations where Laptop objects are available respectively. This process is known as creation or instantiation of objects. Also remember when program execution stopped, objects will be automatically destroyed by Java Virtual Machine (JVM).

5.4 PROBLEM: DESIGNING OBJECT-ORIENTED COLLEGE APPLICATION

Now, for example, we want to extend our understanding of classes to view some larger software application with more classes. Suppose, we want to design an object-oriented college that has many entities interacting with each other such as students, courses, professors, department and many others. Figure 5.6 depicts the class diagram for this college.

Here, college aggregates many courses, many students, many professors and many departments. Listing 5.3 depicts the simple application defining all these classes.

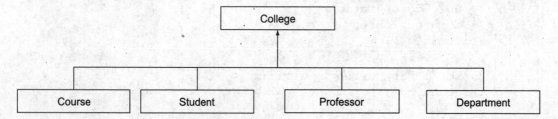

Figure 5.6. Object-oriented College

Listing 5.3. Object-Oriented College

```java
// OOCollege.java

class Course
{
    String cid;      // course id
}

class Department
{
    String did;      // department id
}

class Student
{
    String sid;      // student id
}

class Professor
{
    String pid;      // professor id
}

public class OOCollege
{
    Course c = new Course();           // here, only one course
                                       // available
    Department d = new Department();   // only one department
    Student s = new Student();         // only one student
    Professor p = new Professor();     // only one professor
                                       // but array of objects can
                                       // be created

    public void startCollege()
    {
        c.cid = "CS001";   // use dot operator to access variables
        d.did = "CS";
        s.sid = "UCS001";
        p.pid = "FCS001";

        System.out.println("College Started");
    }

    public static void main(String[] args)
```

```
    {
        OOCollege c = new OOCollege();
        c.startCollege();
    }
}
```

```
College Started
```

5.5 CREATING DATA MEMBERS

Data members can hold object's state (by instance variable) or class's state (by static variables) values as depicted in Figure 5.7.

Figure 5.7. Syntax for Creating Data Members

```
[ public | private | protected ] [ final | volatile ] [static ]
[transient ]
    data-type variable-name;
```

In the above syntax, data members can be declared optionally as public, private and protected, very similar to access types of classes as discussed in section 5.3. If any of these three access types is not present, then default package access will be assumed. So any class not declared in the same package cannot access default variables.

Further, final data member does not allow its value to be modified once it is assigned. It is a way to create constants as discussed in Chapter 1. Volatile variable allows its values to be accessed by multiple threads and prevents certain compiler optimizations.

If a variable is declared as static, all objects share one copy of the variable. Therefore, if one object changes the value, all other objects can see this new value. Hence, if a variable is not static, then it is assumed to be instance variable and every object will have a separate copy. Finally, the value of the transient variable will not be saved during object serialization.

Listing 5.4 illustrates the concepts of data members that are public, private, package access members, static and final.

Listing 5.4. DataMembersTest Application

```
// DataMembersTest.java                              {coderipe}

class DataMembers
{
    public int i = 100;
    private float f = 200f;
    double d = 300;
```

```
   public static int si = 10;
   public final int MAX = 1000;
}

public class DataMembersTest
{
   public static void main(String[] args)
   {
      // create object
      DataMembers d1 = new DataMembers();
      DataMembers d2 = new DataMembers();

      // access data members, instance variables by dot operator

      System.out.println("d1.i " + d1.i); // 100
      System.out.println("d2.i " + d2.i); // 100

      // error: f has private access in DataMembers
      //System.out.println("d1.f " + d1.f); // error
      //System.out.println("d1.f " + d1.f); // error

      System.out.println("d1.d " + d1.d); // 300.0
      System.out.println("d1.d " + d1.d); // 300.0

      System.out.println("d1.si " + d1.si); // 10
      System.out.println("d2.si " + d2.si); // 10
      System.out.println("DataMembers.si " + DataMembers.si);
      // 10

      // increment si using class name
      DataMembers.si++;
      System.out.println("d1.si " + d1.si); // 11
      System.out.println("d2.si " + d2.si); // 11
      System.out.println("DataMembers.si " + DataMembers.si);
      // 11

      // increment si using instance variable d1
      d1.si++;
      System.out.println("d1.si " + d1.si); // 12
      System.out.println("d2.si " + d2.si); // 12
      System.out.println("DataMembers.si " + DataMembers.si);
      // 12

      System.out.println("d1.max " + d1.MAX); // 1000
      System.out.println("d2.max " + d2.MAX); // 1000
```

```
        // error: cannot assign value to final variable max
        //d1.MAX++;  // error
        //d2.MAX++;  // error
    }
}
```

```
d1.i  100
d2.i  100
d1.d  300.0
d1.d  300.0
d1.si  10
d2.si  10
DataMembers.si  10
d1.si  11
d2.si  11
DataMembers.si  11
d1.si  12
d2.si  12
DataMembers.si  12
d1.si  12
d2.si  12
DataMembers.si  12
d1.max  1000
d2.max  1000
```

5.6 CREATING MEMBER FUNCTIONS

Java methods describe the behaviours of either an object or a class. Also, methods of a class are completely defined inside the class. To declare a method inside a class, use the Java syntax shown in Figure 5.8.

Figure 5.8. Syntax for Creating Member Functions

```
[ public | private | protected ] [ abstract ] | [ final ] [ static ]
[ native ] [ synchronized ]
    return_type method_name (arguments)
{
    // body
}
```

A method declaration consists of a method signature followed by method body. The method signature specifies the method's name, return type, arguments list, access-types such as public, private or protected, **access modifiers** such as abstract or final, static, native and synchronized. Also a method can throw an exception (exceptions will be discussed in Chapter 7.). The method body will be executed when the caller invokes this method by its name.

If a method is declared as abstract, it only consists of a method signature; there is no block of statements. Furthermore, the class in which the abstract method is declared must also be declared abstract. Finally, an abstract method cannot be declared final, static, native, synchronized or private at the same time.

If a method is declared as final, the compiler ensures that the method cannot be overridden by subclasses.

If a method is declared as static, that method is known as a class method because it can only access class fields. However, if static is not specified, the method is known as an instance method because it can access instance fields as well as class fields.

If a method is declared as native, only a method signature is present. The method body is written in C language and stored in a platform-specific library. Finally, if a method is declared as synchronized, only one thread at a time can execute method code. We will discuss method overriding in Chapter 6, abstract and final concepts in Chapter 7 and native and synchronized methods in Chapter 12.

Listing 5.5 illustrates Student object that has data members rollno, name, year, m1, m2, m3, m4 and member functions getdata() to collect values from console, display() to show the values and calc_result() to calculate result from the marks of a student.

Listing 5.5. Student Class with Members

```
// StudentTest.java

import java.io.*;

class Student
{
    BufferedReader in = new BufferedReader (new InputStreamReader
    (System.in));

    public int rollno;
    String name;
    String year;
    float m1;
    float m2;
    float m3;
    float m4;

    // get data
    public void getdata() throws IOException
    {
        rollno = Integer.parseInt(in.readLine());
        name = in.readLine();
        year = in.readLine();
        m1 = Float.parseFloat(in.readLine());
```

```
      m2 = Float.parseFloat(in.readLine());
      m3 = Float.parseFloat(in.readLine());
      m4 = Float.parseFloat(in.readLine());
   }


   // define method
   public void display()
   {
      System.out.println("Rollno = " + rollno);
      System.out.println("Name = " + name);
      System.out.println("Year = " + year);
      System.out.println("Marks = " + m1 + ", " + m2 + ", " + m3
      + ", " + m4);
   }


   public void calc_result()
   {
      String result = "fail";

      if (m1 >= 40 && m2 >= 40 && m3 >= 40 && m4 >= 40)
          result = "pass";

      System.out.println( "Result = " + result);
   }
}

public class StudentTest
{
   public static void main(String[] args) throws
   IOException
   {
      Student s  = new Student();
      s.getdata();
      s.display();
      s.calc_result();
   }
}
```

```
Rollno = 12001
Name = Rex
Year = 2012
Marks = 57.0, 7.0, 87.0, 98.0
Result = fail
```

5.7 STATIC DATA AND METHODS

Static method belongs to the class and not to the instance. It can access only **static data** and cannot access nonstatic data (through instance variables). A static method can call only other static methods and cannot call a nonstatic method from it. It can be accessed directly by the class name (using dot operator) and doesn't need any instance or object name. A static method cannot refer to "this" or "super" keywords in anyway. We explain static methods with an example shown in Listing 5.6.

Listing 5.6. Example for Static Data and Methods

```
// StaticMethodDemoTest.java

class StaticMethodDemo
{
    public static int i = 100;  // here i is a class variable, so
    only one copy exists
    public int j = 200; // j is an instance variable

    public static void incr()
    {
        i++;
        // j++; error: static method can access only static var
    }
}

public class StaticMethodDemoTest
{
    public static void main(String[] args)
    {
        StaticMethodDemo s1 = new StaticMethodDemo();
        StaticMethodDemo s2 = new StaticMethodDemo();

        System.out.println(s1.i);
        s1.incr();
        System.out.println("s1.i : " + s1.i);
        System.out.println("s2.i : " + s2.i);

        s2.incr();
        System.out.println("s1.i : " + s1.i);
        System.out.println("s2.i : " + s2.i);

        // Remember main() is also static method.
        // It can also call another static method incr()
        StaticMethodDemo.incr();
        System.out.println("main() calls incr() : " +
        StaticMethodDemo.i);
```

```
        System.out.println("s1.i :  " + s1.i);
        System.out.println("s2.i :  " + s2.i);
    }
}
```

```
100
s1.i : 101
s2.i : 101
s1.i : 102
s2.i : 102
main() calls incr() : 103
s1.i : 103
s2.i : 103
```

5.8 ARRAY OF OBJECTS

Very similar to arrays with primitive data type values, Java supports arrays where elements are objects. Listing 5.7 shows a revised StudentTest class that creates array of Student objects and calculates result.

Listing 5.7. Student Array of Objects

```java
// StudentTest2.java
import java.io.*;

public class StudentTest2
{
    public static void main(String[] args) throws
    IOException
    {
        BufferedReader in = new BufferedReader
        (new InputStreamReader (System.in));
        System.out.print("How many students? :  " );
        int max = Integer.parseInt(in.readLine());

        // declare array of objects
        Student s[]  = new Student[max];

        // initialize objects
        for(int i = 0; i < max; i++)
            s[i] = new Student();

        // get details
```

```
        for(int i = 0; i < max; i++)
        {
                System.out.println("Enter details of student" + i);
                s[i].getdata();
        }

        // process
        for(int i = 0; i < max; i++)
        {
                System.out.println("Result of student" + i);
                s[i].display();
                s[i].calc_result();
        }
    }
}
```

```
How many students? : 1
Enter details of student0
5001
Rex
2012
67
87
98
71
Result of student0
Rollno = 5001
Name = Rex
Year = 2012
Marks = 67.0, 87.0, 98.0, 71.0
Result = pass
```

5.9 OBJECTS AS ARGUMENTS TO METHODS

Java allows us to **pass objects** as arguments to methods. Like passing an array, passing an object is actually passing the reference of the object. Listing 5.8 depicts BookStore application. The show-Book() method receives a book object as an argument and displays isbn, author and title of the book.

Listing 5.8. BookStore Application

```
// BookStore.java
class Book
{
```

{coderipe}

```
    int isbn;
    String author;
    String title;

    public void init(int isbn, String author, String title)
    {
        this.isbn = isbn;  // this.isbn refers to instance
        variable,
                           // isbn refers to local variable
        this.author = author;
        this.title = title;
    }
}

public class BookStore
{
    public static void showBook(Book b)
    {
        System.out.println("ISBN: " + b.isbn + "\nTitle: " +
        b.title + "\nAuthor: " + b.author);
    }

    public static void main(String[] args)
    {
        Book b = new Book();
        b.init(1234, "Peter", "Java");
        showBook(b);
    }
}
```

```
ISBN: 1234
Title: Java
Author: Peter
```

Here init() method has a local variable namely isbn, apart from the instance variable isbn of Book class. Java resolves this scope of variables through *this* reference. Therefore, this.isbn refers to instance variable, whereas isbn refers to the local variable inside the method init().

5.10 SUMMARY

1. Object-oriented paradigm binds data and code together, in contrast to structured programming paradigm
2. Abstraction, encapsulation, information hiding, aggregation, inheritance and polymorphism are powerful features of OOP

3. Java is a pure OOP language

4. Real-world entity is called object and the template for objects is known as class

5. Instance variable and method are unique with each object. Therefore, each object will have a separate copy of its variables and methods

6. Static data members and methods belong to class. Therefore, only one copy will exist for all objects and all objects will share the data members and methods of the same copy

7. Static data can be accessed by its class name

5. Very similar to primitive type arrays, object arrays can be created

6. Object arrays can also be passed to methods as arguments

KEY TERMS

Access modifiers, 138	Inheritance, 130	Polymorphism, 130
Aggregation, 130	Object, 130	RTTI, 130
Behaviours, 130	Object-oriented programming, 129	States, 130
Encapsulation, 130	Overriding, 130	Static data, 141
Information hiding, 130	Pass objects, 143	Structured programming, 129

REVIEW QUESTIONS

Multiple-choice Questions

1. Find out the output:

```
class Number
{
    public int i = 15;
}

public class Test5
{
    public static void main(String[] args)
    {
        Test5 t = new Test5();
        t.change();
    }

    public void change()
    {
        int i = 0;
        Number n = new Number();
```

```
      n.i = 25;

      Number n2. = new Number();
      n2 = n;

      Number n3 = new Number();
      n = n3;

      System.out.println(n.i + "," + n2.i + "," + n3.i);
   }
}
```

a. 25 15 15   b. 15 25 15

c. 15 15 25   d. 25 15 25

2. Find out the output:

```
class Number
{
   public int i = 15;
}

public class Test5
{
   public static void main(String[] args)
   {
      Test5 t = new Test5();
      Number n = new Number();
      t.change(n);
   }

   public void change(Number n)
   {
      int i = 0;
      Number n2 = new Number();
      n2.i = 20;
      n2 = n;

      System.out.println(n.i + "," + n2.i);
   }
}
```

a. 15, 15   b. 20 20

c. 20 15   d. 15 20

3. Find out the error statement in the following program:

```
class Data
{
   public int i = 15;
   public static String s = "hello";
}

public class Test5
{
   public static void main(String[] args)
   {
      Data d = new Data();
      System.out.println(d.i);    // statement-1
      System.out.println(d.s);  // statement-2
      System.out.println(Data.s); // statement-3
   }
}
```

   a. Error in statement-1   b. Error in statement-2

   c. Error in statement-3   d. No error

4. Find out the output:

```
class Data
{
   public static int i = 0;
}

public class Test5
{
   public int increment()
   {
      return Data.i++;
   }
   public static void main(String[] args)
   {
      Test5 t1 = new Test5();
      Test5 t2 = new Test5();

      System.out.println(t1.increment());
      System.out.println(t2.increment());
      System.out.println(Data.i);   // statement-3
   }
}
```

a. 0 0 1

b. 0 1 2

c. 1 2 3

d. 1 1 2

5. Find out the output:

```
class Data
{
    int i = 10;
    int j = 20;
}

public class Test5
{
    public void swap(Data d)
    {
        int t = d.i;
        d.i = d.j;
        d.j = t;
    }
    public static void main(String[] args)
    {
        Test5 t = new Test5();
        Data d = new Data();
        t.swap(d);
        System.out.println(d.i + "," + d.j);
    }
}
```

a. 20, 10

b. 10 20

c. 10 10

d. 20 20

6. Find out the output:

```
class Data
{
    static int i = 10;
    int j = 20;

    public void incr()
    {
        i++; j++;
    }
}

public class Test5
```

```
{
    public static void main(String[] args)
    {
        Data d1 = new Data();
        Data d2 = new Data();

        d1.incr(); d2.incr();
        System.out.println(
        d1.i + "," + d1.j + "," + d2.i + "," + d2.j);
    }
}
```

a. 12 21 12 21
b. 10 20 11 21
c. 11 20 12 21
d. 11 21 12 21

7. Find out the output:

```
class Data
{
    public int[] a = new int[5];
}

public class Test5
{
    public void change(Data d)
    {
        for(int i : d.a)
        i++;
    }

    public static void main(String[] args)
    {
        Test5 t5 = new Test5();
        Data d1 = new Data();
        t5.change(d1);
        for(int i : d1.a)
            System.out.println(i);
    }
}
```

a. 0 0 0 0 0   b. 1 1 1 1 1
c. null null null null null   d. Runtime error

8. Find out the output:

```java
class Data
{
    public int[] a = new int[5];
}

public class Test5
{
    public void change(Data d)
    {
        for(int i = 0; i < d.a.length; i++)
            d.a[i]++;

    }

    public static void main(String[] args)
    {
        Test5 t5 = new Test5();
        Data d1 = new Data();
        t5.change(d1);
        for(int i : d1.a)
            System.out.println(i);
    }
}
```

a. 0 0 0 0 0

b. 1 1 1 1 1

c. null null null null null

d. Runtime error

9. Find out the output:

```java
public class Test5
{
    public void change(int[] i)
    {
        i[i.length - 1]++;
    }

    public static void main(String[] args)
    {
        int[] a = {0,1};
        Test5 t = new Test5();
        t.change(a);
        System.out.println(a[a.length - 1]);
    }
}
```

a. 0   b. 1

c. 2   d. Runtime error

10. Find out the output:

```
public class Test5
{
    static int i = 7;

    public void go(int i)
    {
        i++;
        for(; i < 10; i++)
        System.out.print(" " + i);
    }

    public static void main(String[] args)
    {
        new Test5().go(i);
        System.out.print(" " + i);
    }
}
```

a. 8 9 7   b. 8 9 9

c. 8 9 8   d. 7 8 9

11. Find out the output:

```
public class Mango
{
    int n = 5;

    static Mango transfer(Mango m1, Mango m2)
    {
        Mango m = m1;
        m.n = 10;
        return m;
    }

    public static void main(String[] args)
    {
        Mango m1 = new Mango();
        Mango m2 = new Mango();

        Mango m3 = transfer(m1, m2);
```

```
        System.out.println(m1 == m3);
        System.out.println(m1.n == m2.n);
    }
}
```

   a. true false   b. true true

   c. false true   d. false false

12. Find out the output:

```
class A
{
    public static int call(int i)
    {
        return ++i;
    }
}

class B
{
    public static int call(int i)
    {
        System.out.println(A.call(i--));
        return 1;
    }
}

public class Test5
{
    public static void main(String[] args)
    {
        B.call(100);
    }
}
```

   a. 99   b. 100

   c. 101   d. 1

13. What is the type of relationship that exists between the following classes?

```
class Wheel
{
    public int no;
```

```
}
class Bike
{
   Wheel[] wheels = new Wheel[2];
   public enum color{RED, WHITE, BLUE, YELLOW};
}
```

a. is-a   b. has-a

c. Abstract class relationship   d. Interface relationship

14. Find out the output:

```
public class Test5
{
   public int square(int i)
   {
      return i * i;
   }
   public static void main(String[] args)
   {
      for(int i = 5; i < 11; i++)
            System.out.println(square(i));
   }
}
```

a. Prints the square from 5 to 10   b. Prints the square from 5 to 11

c. Prints the square from 0 to 10   d. Compilation error

15. Find out the output:

```
class A { }
public class Test5 extends A
{
   public void check()
   {
      boolean test = true;
      if(test & Test5.this instanceof Test5)
            System.out.println("yes");
      else
            System.out.println("no");
   }
   public static void main(String[] args)
   {
```

```
        Test5 t = new Test5();
        t.check();
    }
}
```

a. yes   b. no
c. If statement is not at all executed   d. Error in calling check()

16. Find out the output:

```
class A { }
public class Test5 extends A
{
    public static void main(String[] args)
    {
        Test5 t = new Test5();
        boolean test = true;
        if(test && t instanceof Test5)
            System.out.println("yes");
        else
            System.out.println("no");
    }
}
```

a. yes   b. no
c. If statement is not at all executed   d. Error in calling check()

17. Find out the output:

```
class A { }
public class Test5 extends A
{
    public static void main(String[] args)
    {
        boolean test = true;
        if(test && this instanceof Test5)
            System.out.println("yes");
        else
            System.out.println("no");
    }
}
```

a. yes   b. no
c. Compilation error   d. Runtime error

18. Find out the output:

```
class A { }
public class Test5 extends A
{
    public static void main(String[] args)
    {
        if(Integer.valueOf(10) instanceof Number)
            System.out.println("yes");
        else
            System.out.println("no");
    }
}
```

a. yes   b. no

c. Compilation error   d. Runtime error

19. Consider three entities Dog, PetDog and Belt. What are the possible relationships which can be expressed between these classes?

   1. Dog, PetDog and Belt can be expressed as three independent classes
   2. PetDog class can inherit from Dog class through is-a relationship
   3. Dog class can inherit from PetDog class through is-a relationship
   4. PetDog class can contain Belt class through has-a relationship
   5. Dog class can contain Belt class through has-a relationship

   a. 2, 4, 5   b. 2, 3, 4

   c. 1, 3, 5   d. 1, 4, 5

20. Find out the output:

```
class Belt
{
    int size = 20;
}
class Dog
{
    Belt belt = new Belt();
    String color = "red";
}
public class Test5
{
    public static void main(String[] args)
    {
        Dog d = new Dog();
```

```
    d.color = "white";
    d.belt.size = 40;
    System.out.println(d.color + "," + d.belt.size);
  }
}
```

a. white, 40   b. red 20
c. white 20   d. red 40

21. What is the output?

```
public class Test5
{
  public static void main(String[] args)
  {
    go:
    for(int i = 0; i < 3; i++)
        for(int j = 0; j < 3; j++)
        {
            System.out.print(j);
            if(i == 2 && j == 2) break go;
            if(j == 1) break;
        }
  }
}
```

a. 010101   b. 011011
c. 001101   d. 011101

22. What is the output?

```
public class Test5
{
  int x = 1;
  public static void main(String[] args)
  {
    for(int i = x; i < 5; i++)
        System.out.print(i);
  }
}
```

a. 1234   b. 01234
c. Compilation error   d. Runtime error

23. What is the output?

```
class Pen
{
   public static void write()
   {
      System.out.println("Pen");
   }
}
class InkPen extends Pen
{
   public static void write()
   {
      System.out.println("InkPen");
   }
}

public class Test5
{
   public static void main(String[] args)
   {
      Pen[] p = new Pen[2];
      p[0] = new Pen();
      p[1] = new InkPen();
      p[0].write();
      p[1].write();
   }
}
```

a. Pen Pen   b. Pen InkPen

b. InkPen Pen   d. InkPen InkPen

Answers

1. b	2. a	3. d	4. b	5. a	6. a	7. a	8. b	9. c	10. a
11. a	12. c	13. b	14. d	15. a	16. a	17. c	18. c	19. a	20. a
21. a	22. c	23. a							

Short-answer Questions

1. Explain the terminologies object, state, behaviour and class.
2. What is abstraction? Explain with an example.
3. Explain encapsulation and information hiding with an example.
4. Explain HAS-A and IS-A relationships with an example.

5. What is aggregation? Give an example.
6. What is inheritance? Give an example.
7. Explain final data, methods and classes with an example.
8. Explain native and volatile methods with an example.

EXERCISES

5.1. Modify OOCollege application with additional private data members and member public functions.

- Class Course: private String cid, String courseName, int credit, String pid (i.e. prerequisite course id), getCourse() that returns Course and setCourse() that receives values through arguments and assigns them to data members
- Class Department: private String did, String name, String location, getDepartment() and setDepartment() public methods
- Class Student: String sid, String name, String address, String degree, String year, getStudent() and setStudent() public methods
- Test objects of these classes inside main() with values

5.2. Design a class *Cylinder* to represent a cylinder.

- private data members: private double radius (r), private double height(h)
- public void setCylinder(): to assign values to data members
- public double volume(): calculates and returns volume of the cylinder as PI*r*r*h
- public double areaSide(): returns area of side only without top and bottom sides as 2*PI*r*h
- public double area(): returns area of top, bottom and side as 2*PI*r (r+h)
- Develop a public class *TestCylinder* to test all these methods

5.3. Design a class *Prism* to represent a prism.

- Data members: private double length(l), width(w), height(h)
- public void setPrism(): to assign values to l, w and h
- public double topArea(): returns top area of the prism as l*w
- public double bottomArea(): returns bottom area of the prism as l*w
- public double leftArea(): returns left area of the prism as h*w
- public double rightArea(): returns right area of the prism as h*w
- public double frontArea(): returns front area of the prism as h*l
- public double backArea(): returns back area of the prism as h*l
- pubic double area(): returns a sum of the areas of all six sides as 2(l*w + h*w + h*l)
- Develop a public class *TestPrism* that tests all these methods

5.4. Design a class *Fan* to represent a fan.

- private data members: String fanType, String manufacturer, String model, boolean isOn
- public data members: enum Speed with 5 levels from 1 to 5
- public void setFan() and getFan() methods
- public void on(): switch on the fan
- public void off(): switch off the fan
- public void speedUp(): to increase current speed, if not maximum 5
- public void speedDown(): to reduce current speed, if not minimum 1

6

Inheritance and Polymorphism

OBJECTIVES

- To introduce constructor, its importance and functionality
- To explain default constructor
- To explain constructor with parameters or arguments
- To define overloaded constructors
- To introduce Math class from java.lang package
- To explain different methods of Character class
- To create immutable strings with String class
- To manipulate strings with StringBuffer class
- To manipulate strings using StringBuilder class
- To explain inheritance and its types
- To call base class constructor, data members and member functions
- To implement *Object-Oriented Dog* application
- To introduce polymorphism with *Instrument* class
- To differentiate aggregation from inheritance
- To introduce java.lang.Object class
- To check object's class type with *instanceof* operator
- To clone an object
- To prevent inheritance and overriding
- To allow restricted access to subclasses with protected type
- To explore visibility of classes and its members
- To create an inner class inside a class

6.1 INTRODUCTION

In Chapter 5, the readers were introduced to solve a real-world problem object-oriented way by thinking everything in terms of objects. For each object, states and behaviours of the object can be identified and represented by means of Java class. The difference between object instances and class members is also known. In this chapter, we build on the traits of objects and classes. First, the reader is exposed to object initialization using **constructors**. Further, some of the important Java Wrapper classes along with their methods are introduced. This is followed by **inheritance**, another powerful feature of Java. Finally, we make the reader to understand the **visibility** of data members and member functions across classes within a package or across packages.

6.2 CONSTRUCTORS

A constructor is a special kind of method that has class name as its name and can be used to initialize objects. It is called just after the memory is allocated for the object. Constructor is always public and does not return any value including void. Just like any other method, a constructor can call any other method.

A constructor without any argument is called default constructor and it will be automatically called. In contrast, a **parameterized constructor** has arguments and so it should be called manually during object creation. Constructors can also be overloaded, very similar to overloading other methods. Constructors are called starting from the root class down the class hierarchy. The reader is introduced to class hierarchy and inheritance in section 6.7.

6.3 DEFAULT CONSTRUCTOR

Whenever a class is instantiated, its **default constructor** will be automatically invoked; thereby its body will be executed. Listing 6.1 depicts HelloConstructor() displaying a string.

Listing 6.1. Default Constructor

```
// HelloConstructor                                    {coderipe}

class HelloConstructor
{
    public HelloConstructor()
    {
        System.out.println("Hello Java");
    }
}
public class HelloConstructorTest
{
    public static void main(String[] args)
    {
        HelloConstructor h = new HelloConstructor();
    }
}
```

```
Hello Java
```

6.4 PARAMETERIZED CONSTRUCTOR

A constructor can be represented with arguments. Therefore, when a class is instantiated, parameterized constructor needs argument values, failing which JVM will complain error. Listing 6.2 shows a parameterized constructor version of the above application.

Listing 6.2. Parameterized Constructor

```java
// HelloConstructor2Test.java                          {coderipe}

class HelloConstructor2
{
   public HelloConstructor2(String name)
   {
     System.out.println("Hello " + name);
   }
}
public class HelloConstructor2Test
{
   public static void main(String[] args)
   {
     HelloConstructor2 h = new HelloConstructor2("Rex");

     // error: JVM cannot identify default constructor
     // HelloConstructor2 h2 = new HelloConstructor();
   }
}
```

```
Hello Rex
```

6.5 CONSTRUCTOR OVERLOADING

Constructor overloading is another feature of Java object-oriented programming (OOP). Like method overloading, constructors can also be overloaded. This allows object values to be initialized in many ways. Accordingly, any one of the constructors will be called.

Listing 6.3. Overloading Constructors

```java
// HelloConstructor3Test.java                          {coderipe}

class HelloConstructor3
```

```
{
    public HelloConstructor3()
    {
        System.out.println("Hello Java");
    }
    public HelloConstructor3(String name)
    {
        System.out.println("Hello " + name);
    }
    public HelloConstructor3(int empId)
    {
        System.out.println("Hello " + empId);
    }
}
public class HelloConstructor3Test
{
    public static void main(String[] args)
    {
        new HelloConstructor3();
        new HelloConstructor3("Rex");
        new HelloConstructor3(2725);
    }
}
```

```
Hello Java
Hello Rex
Hello 2725
```

Java application does not have to destroy the allocated memory manually through destructors. Rather, memory space allocated to objects will be automatically cleaned up by JVM itself.

6.6 ESSENTIAL JAVA.LANG CLASSES

Before moving on to other OOP concepts of Java, let us pause for a while and revisit some of the important classes from java.lang package. Though lang package has a variety of classes for different application requirements, we focus on few classes that are required for further understanding of the text.

6.6.1 Math

The class Math provides many class methods for performing basic scientific operations. It supports methods to calculate absolute values using abs(), sin(), cos(), tan(), min(x,y), max(x,y), ceiling using ceil(x,y), floor(x,y), pow(x,y) to find power, random() to generate random number and sqrt(x) methods. Listing 6.4 explains some representative methods of Math class.

Listing 6.4. Math Class Example

```java
// MathTest.java

public class MathTest
{
    public static void main(String[] args)
    {
        System.out.println("abs(-100.0) : " + Math.abs(-100.0));
        System.out.println("sin(90): " + Math.sin(90));
        System.out.println("min(10,20): " + Math.min(10,20));
        System.out.println("pow(10,2): " + Math.pow(10,2));
        System.out.println("sqrt(25) : " + Math.sqrt(25));

        for(int i = 0; i < 3; i++)
                System.out.println("Random number " + i +
                    " : " + Math.random());
    }
}
```

```
abs(-100.0) : 100.0
sin(90): 0.8939966636005579
min(10,20): 10
pow(10,2): 100.0
sqrt(25) : 5.0
Random number 0 : 0.44320911613762604
Random number 1 : 0.7391733959979383
Random number 2 : 0.7082800388148885
```

6.6.2 Character

The **Character** class supports many static and instance methods to manipulate a character. There are important methods such as isDigit(), isLetter(), isLowerCase(), isUpperCase(), compare() to compare two characters, compareTo() to compare two character objects, isWhiteSpace(), valueOf() to convert char to Character wrapper and charValue() to convert Character wrapper to char primitive type. Listing 6.5 depicts important methods of Character class.

Listing 6.5. Character Class Example

```java
// CharacterTest.java
public class CharacterTest
{
    public static void main(String[] args)
    {
```

```
        Character c = new Character('c');
        System.out.println(c.charValue());
        System.out.println("Character.isDigit('a'): " +
            Character.isDigit('a'));
        System.out.println("Character.isLetter('a'): " +
            Character.isLetter('a'));
        System.out.println("Character.toLowerCase('A'): " +
            Character.toLowerCase('A'));
        System.out.println("compare c and b: " +
            c.compareTo('b'));
    }
}
```

```
c
Character.isDigit('a'): false
Character.isLetter('a'): true
Character.toLowerCase('A'): a
compare c and b: 1
```

6.6.3 String

The **String** class includes methods to perform many operations on strings. Strings in Java are immutable, which means, the original content of the string cannot be modified. Any operation on string will create a new string.

String object can be created from char[], byte[] and String through various overloaded constructors. Some important instance methods are charAt() to return a char at location, compare(str), length(), toUpperCase(), toLowerCase(), trim(), concat(str) to concatenate two strings, substring(), getBytes() to convert string to byte[] and a class method valueOf() that converts primitive data types to string. For instance, Listing 6.6 explains the various string methods in detail.

Listing 6.6. String Class Example

```
//StringTest.java

public class StringTest
{
    public static void main(String[] args)
    {
        String s1 = new String("HELLO");
        char[] c = {'h','e','l','l','o'};
        String s2 = new String(c);

        System.out.println("s1.charAt(2): " + s1.charAt(2));
        // compareTo() returns -ve, 0, or +ve number if <, ==, or >
```

```
        System.out.println("s1.compareTo(s2): "
        + s1.compareTo(s2));
        System.out.println("s1.toLowerCase(): "
        + s1.toLowerCase());
        System.out.println("s2.toUpperCase(): "
        + s2.toUpperCase());
        System.out.println("s1.length(): " + s1.length());
    }
}
```

```
s1.charAt(2): L
s1.compareTo(s2): -32
s1.toLowerCase(): hello
s2.toUpperCase(): HELLO
s1.length(): 5
```

6.6.4 StringBuffer

The **StringBuffer** class allows a string's original contents to be modified, that is the string is mutable. It is safe for threads. StringBuffer can be created from String. There are two important methods: append() to append any primitive data types, String or even StringBuffer as well as insert(loc, value) to insert a primitive data type or String to the specified location. The length() returns the length of string buffer, while reverse() reverses its contents. Listing 6.7 appends 100 random characters to string buffer.

Listing 6.7. String Buffer Example

```java
//StringBufferTest.java

public class StringBufferTest
{
    public static void main(String[] args)
    {
        StringBuffer sb = new StringBuffer("Welcome Admin");
        System.out.println(sb.toString());

        System.out.println("sb length: " + sb.length());
        sb.reverse();
        sb.insert(0, "Hello");
        System.out.println(sb.toString());

        for(int i = 0; i < 10; i++)
            sb.append((char)(Math.random() * 100));
        System.out.println(sb.toString());
    }
}
```

```
Welcome Admin
sb length: 13
HellonimdA emocleW
HellonimdA emocleW.&H9T\Q.
```

6.6.5 StringBuilder

The **StringBuilder** class also supports string processing features as StringBuffer. However, String-Builder is very fast in computation, but not thread safe as StringBuffer. All methods of StringBuffer are also available in StringBuilder. Listing 6.8 explains few StringBuilder instance methods.

Listing 6.8. StringBuilder Example

```java
//StringBuilderTest.java

public class StringBuilderTest
{
    public static void main(String[] args)
    {
    StringBuilder sb = new StringBuilder("Hello Java");

        sb.append("How are you?");
        System.out.println("sb length: " + sb.length());
        System.out.println("sb reverse: " + sb.reverse());
        System.out.println("sb.insert: " + sb.insert(0,
        "Hello"));
        System.out.println(sb.toString());
    }
}
```

```
sb length: 22
sb reverse: ?uoy era woHavaJ olleH
sb.insert: Hello?uoy era woHavaJ olleH
Hello?uoy era woHavaJ olleH
```

So, we have three options to handle strings – String class, StringBuffer and StringBuilder. Our natural question is which one to use? Apply the following rule of thumb.

- If your text is not going to change, use a String class because a String object is immutable.
- If your text can change and will only be accessed from a single thread, use a StringBuilder because StringBuilder is unsafe for threads.
- If your text can change and will be accessed by multiple threads, use a StringBuffer because StringBuffer is synchronous and thread safe.

6.7 INHERITANCE

Inheritance is the ability of a class to derive something specific from a generic class. The generic class is called super class or base class or parent class and the specific class is known as child class or subclass or derived class. There are two types of inheritance:

- *Single-level inheritance*, where a child class inherits from its parent class
- *Multilevel inheritance*, where a class inherits from its parent, this parent in turn inherits from its parent and so on (see Figure 6.1)

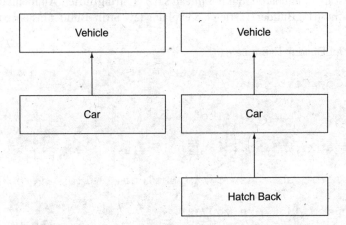

Figure 6.1. Single-level and Multilevel Inheritance

For example as shown in Figure 6.2, class LibraryBook is a child class of a super class Book (that we developed in Chapter 5). Here, we say LibraryBook inherits states and behaviours of objects of Book class such as isbn, author, title and many others. Apart from deriving from Base class, Library-Book can have its own data members such as number of copies and member functions representing states and behaviours of objects (Listing 6.9).

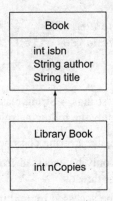

Figure 6.2. LibraryBook

Listing 6.9. LibraryBook Class

```java
public class LibraryBook extends Book                    {coderipe}
{
    int nCopies = 10; // number of copies of the book

    public void show()
    {
        System.out.println("isbn = " + isbn + "\nauthor = " +
        author +
                "\ntitle = " + title + "\ncopies = " + nCopies);
    }

    public static void main(String[] args)
    {
        LibraryBook lb = new LibraryBook();
        lb.show();
    }
}
```

```
isbn = 1234
author = Rex
title = Hello Java
copies = 10
```

The *extends* keyword causes a subclass to inherit all data members and member functions declared in a nonfinal super class (including the super class's super classes). The subclass can access all inherited nonprivate data members and member functions; it cannot access any inherited private data members and member functions. In inheritance, objects are instantiated starting from base class down in the class hierarchy.

6.8 CALLING BASE CLASS CONSTRUCTOR

You already know that parameterized constructors have to be called manually by your program. This is also applicable to inheritance. Suppose, a super class has a parameterized constructor, then it is the duty of the child class constructor to call the super class's constructor first before executing any other Java statements inside its constructor, otherwise JVM will generate a compile time error.

Child class constructor will use **super()** method along with the required argument values to call super class constructor. Finally, keep in mind that any other member functions apart from constructor cannot call super class's constructor.

It is obvious that super class's object will be constructed first before child class's object construction. Also, single inheritance can be extended to multiple levels of classes, one class above another and is called multilevel inheritance.

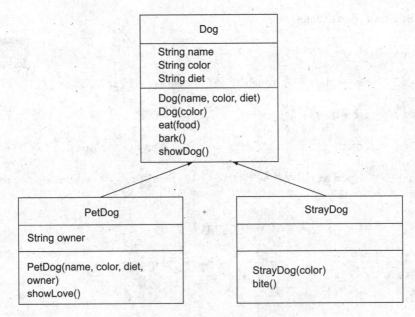

Figure 6.3. Class Hierarchy of Dog

Figure 6.3 depicts the class hierarchy of Dog. Here, PetDog and StrayDog are child classes of the base class Dog. The OODog class aggregates PetDog and StrayDog objects. Listing 6.10 depicts the object-oriented design of Dog.

Listing 6.10. Object-Oriented Dog

```java
//OODog.java
class Dog
{
    String name;
    String colour;
    String diet;

    public Dog(String name1, String colour1, String diet1)
    {
        name = name1;
        colour = colour1;
        diet = diet1;
    }

    public Dog(String colour1)
    {
        colour = colour1;
    }
```

```java
   public void eat(String food)
   {
      diet = food;
   }

   public void bark()
   {
      System.out.println("Dog " + name + " can bark: Lol Lol
      Lol");
   }

   public void showDog()
   {
      System.out.println("Dog name: " + name);
      System.out.println("Dog colour: " + colour);
      System.out.println("Dog can eat food: " + diet);
   }
}

class PetDog extends Dog
{
   String owner;

   public PetDog(String name, String colour, String diet, String
   owner1)
   {
      // super() should be the first statement
      super(name, colour, diet);
      owner = owner1;
   }

   public void showLove()
   {
      System.out.println("Dog " + name + " can express love: Ich
      Ich Ich");
   }
}

class StrayDog extends Dog
{
   public StrayDog(String colour)
   {
      // super() should be the first statement
      // stray dog has only colour, and call overloaded
      constructor
```

```
        super(colour);
    }

    public void bite()
    {
        System.out.println("Beware: This stray Dog will
        bite");
    }
}

public class OODog
{
    public static void main(String[] args)
    {
        PetDog petDog = new PetDog("Tommy", "white", "meat",
        "Rajkumar");
        petDog.showDog();
        petDog.showLove();

        StrayDog strayDog = new StrayDog("black");
        strayDog.showDog();
        strayDog.bite();
    }
}
```

```
Dog name: Tommy
Dog colour: white
Dog can eat food: meat
Dog Tommy can express love
Dog name: null
Dog colour: black
Dog can eat food: null
Beware: This stray Dog will bite
```

6.9 CALLING BASE CLASS DATA MEMBER WITH SUPER

Suppose we have a data member whose name is same in base class and child class. In this case, the child class can access the base class data member by using the keyword super as shown in Figure 6.4.

Figure 6.4. Using Super

```
super.i; // assume i appears both in base class and child class
```

6.10 OVERRIDING AND POLYMORPHISM

A child class member function can override or redefine a base class member function with same signature of the base class member function. That is, same name, same return type and same argument list can be given to both methods. Remember always that child class method can override, only if base class method is not private, static and final (Listing 6.11).

Listing 6.11. Polymorphism for Instrument Application

```java
class Instrument
{
    String colour;
    public void tune() { };
}

class Guitar extends Instrument
{
    public void tune()
    {
        System.out.println("Guitar sound: Ting Ting Ting...");
    }
}

class Keyboard extends Instrument
{
    public void tune()
    {
        System.out.println("Keyboard sound: Pam Pam Pam...");
    }
}

class Sax extends Instrument
{
    public void tune()
    {
        System.out.println("Sax sound: Bham Bham Bham...");
    }
}
public class InstrumentTest
{
    public static void main(String[] args)
    {
        Instrument[] instrument = new Instrument[3];

        instrument[0] = new Guitar();    // normal up casting
```

{coderipe}

```
        instrument[1] = new Keyboard();
        instrument[2] = new Sax();

        for(int i = 0; i < 3; i++)
                instrument[i].tune(); // JVM identifies without down
                casting correctly by RTTI
    }
}
```

```
Guitar sound: Ting Ting Ting...
Keyboard sound: Pam Pam Pam...
Sax sound: Bham Bham Bham...
```

In this application, child class objects are assigned to base class reference by normal upcasting which is something JVM will identify at compile time. During runtime, JVM correctly identifies the appropriate child class version of the tune() method and invokes it. It does not complain to us that we did not downcast.

Rather with a feature named runtime type identification (RTTI), it invokes appropriate tune() method from any of the child class. This behaviour is known as **polymorphism**. Suppose if there is a variation in the signature, say for instance, different arguments list, then JVM will consider these two methods as overloaded instead of overridden methods. So, as overloading it will invoke either a base class method or child class method depending on the input values.

One final note about **overriding**. A child class method, defined in another package other than the package where base class is defined, can override the base class method which is only public or protected. It cannot override private or default access methods. Before leaving this topic, let us consider the keyword `protected`. If you declare a super class field or method as `protected`, any method, declared in any class that subclasses the class that declares the protected field or method, can access that field or method.

6.11 AGGREGATION VERSUS INHERITANCE

There is always a doubt of when to apply **aggregation** and inheritance. A general rule of thumb would be to apply aggregation when you want to represent containment relationship, that is, *part-of* relationship (also called *has-a* relationship). On the other hand, if there is a natural hierarchical ordering present among classes, such as, *is-a* relationship, then inheritance is a preferred way of modelling objects and their associated classes. One trivial example, keypad is *part of* a laptop, whereas laptop *is a* computer.

6.12 OBJECT AND OBJECT CLONING

The object is the root of the Java class hierarchy. Every class has object as a super class. Some important instance methods are explained in Table 6.1 and illustrated in Listing 6.12.

Listing 6.12 explains the different methods that are available in Object class.

Table 6.1. Object Methods

toString()	Returns String representation of the object
equals(obj)	Returns object is equals to obj
getClass()	Returns class name of the object
hashCode()	Returns the hash code of the object
clone()	Returns a copy of the object

Listing 6.12. Cat Class

```java
// ObjectTest.java

class Cat
{
    String name;
    public Cat(String name1)
    {
        name = name1;
    }
}

public class ObjectTest
{
    public static void main(String[] args)
    {
        Cat cat1 = new Cat("Lily");
        Cat cat2 = new Cat("Pussy");

        System.out.println(cat1.toString() + " , " + cat2.
        toString());
        System.out.println("cat1.equals(cat2) : " + cat1.
        equals(cat2));
        System.out.println("cat1 class: " + cat1.getClass());
        System.out.println("cat1's hashcode : " + cat1.hashCode());
    }
}
```

```
Cat@19821f , Cat@addbf1
cat1.equals(cat2) : false
cat1 class: class Cat
cat1's hashcode : 1671711
```

Cloning allows a Java application to create a copy of an object. For that, the class should be declared as **cloneable** as illustrated in Listing 6.13.

Listing 6.13. Cloneable Dog Class

```java
// Dog.java, it is a cloneable dog
public class Dog implements Cloneable
{
    String name;

    public Dog(String name1)
    {
        name = name1;
    }

    public static void main(String[] args) throws
    CloneNotSupportedException
    {
        Dog oDog = new Dog("Dane");
        Dog cDog = (Dog) oDog.clone();
        // cloning is faster than new
        // no constructor calling for cloned object
        System.out.println("Original dog's name: " + oDog.name);
        System.out.println("Cloned dog's name: " + cDog.name);
    }
}
```

```
Original dog's name: Dane
Cloned dog's name: Dane
```

6.13 CHECKING OBJECT'S CLASS TYPE

There is another important operator that is useful when we store objects of different types in data structures such as vectors. Vector is one of the important data structures that stores objects using add() method. Further details about vector will be given to you in Part III. This operator is called **instanceof** and it checks whether an object is an instance of a particular class. In Listing 6.14, a book shelf contains different items such as books, dictionaries, CD, DVD and note books. It identifies the type during runtime correctly using instanceof operator.

Listing 6.14. BookShelf Application

```java
// BookShelf.java

import java.util.*;

class Book
{
```

```
  int isbn = 1234;
}
class Dictionary
{
  String title = "Tamil-English dictionary";
}
class CD
{
  String title = "TOEFL examination";
}
class DVD
{
  String title = "Java Tutorial";
}
class NoteBook
{
  String name = "Writing pad";
}
public class BookShelf
{
  public static void main(String[] args)
  {
    Vector shelf = new Vector();
    // add all items to shelf as Objects
    shelf.add( new Book());
    shelf.add( new Dictionary());
    shelf.add( new CD());
    shelf.add( new DVD());
    shelf.add( new NoteBook());

    // now, display all details.
    for(Object o : shelf)
    {
        if (o instanceof Book )
            System.out.println("Book iSBN: " +
            ((Book)o).isbn);
        else if (o instanceof Dictionary )
            System.out.println("Dictionary title: " +
                ((Dictionary)o).title);
        else if (o instanceof CD )
            System.out.println("CD title: " +
            ((CD)o).title);
        else if (o instanceof DVD )
            System.out.println("DVD title: " +
            ((DVD)o).title);
```

```
            else if (o instanceof NoteBook )
                    System.out.println("Rough note book title: " +
                            ((NoteBook)o).name);
        }
    }.
}
```

```
Book iSBN: 1234
Dictionary title: Tamil-English dictionary
CD title: TOEFL examination
DVD title: Java Tutorial
Rough note book title: Writing pad
```

6.14 PREVENTING INHERITANCE AND OVERRIDING

A class can restrict its subclasses to inherit data members and member functions by declaring final. In other words, final classes cannot be subclassed. Similarly, a base class can restrict its subclass method to override its base class counterpart by declaring it final method. In other words, a final method cannot be overridden inside child class. Further, if a class is final, then all of its methods are also final implicitly.

A compile time error will be thrown when an attempt is made to subclass a base class or override a base class method. Recollect, earlier we have defined final variables, which allows us to create Java constants.

6.15 VISIBILITY OF MEMBERS OF A CLASS

Finally, we close this chapter by consolidating the visibility or accessibility of data members and member functions in a class as depicted in Table 6.2.

The question now is, what to use when? Suppose data members and member functions of a class to be accessible within the class, within the package in which it is defined, to its subclasses and from a different package, then define it as public. In contrast, if you want to hide everything to all, define it as private.

Suppose data members and member functions are to be available only to its subclasses in any package or to all classes within the same package, then you need to declare them as protected. If no access

Table 6.2. Visibility Types

Access Type	Accessed by the Same Class	Accessed by Another Class within Same Package	Accessed by a SubClass (Within Same Package or Different Package)	Accessed by a Class from Different Package
Public	Yes	Yes	Yes	Yes
Protected	Yes	Yes	Yes	No
Default	Yes	Yes	No	No
Private	Yes	No	No	No

type appears, then those data members and member functions are available to all classes within the same package. Packages are discussed in detail in Chapter 7.

6.16 INNER CLASSES

Inner classes nest within other outer classes. The outer class is a direct member of a package, whereas inner class is a member of an outer class. Inner classes behave like a normal class. It improves object-oriented design of an application by separating functionality from the object. That is, operations can be separately defined using inner class. Inner class can access all data members and member functions, just like any other member of the class. There are typically four flavours:

- Member inner class
- Static inner class
- Local inner class
- Anonymous inner class

A *member inner class* is an instance member of a class. The instance of an inner class can exist only within the instance of outer class and has direct access to all methods and data members of the outer class's instance. Figure 6.5 illustrates member inner class.

Figure 6.5. Member Inner Class

```
// Member inner class
class OuterClass
{
    .......
    class InnerClass
    {
        .......// can access all instance members of outer class
    }
}
```

A *static inner class* is a static member of a class. Like any other static method, a static inner class has access to all static methods of the outer class. Figure 6.6 depicts static inner class.

Figure 6.6. Static Inner Class

```
// Static inner class
Class OuterClass
{
    .......
    static class StaticInnerClass
    {
        ....... // can access all static data and members
    }
}
```

Local inner classes are declared within a block of code (say between curly braces) and are visible only within that block. Finally, an *anonymous inner* class is a local class without name. Local inner class is illustrated in Figure 6.7.

Figure 6.7. Local Inner Class

```
class OuterClass
{
    public void method1()
    {
        .......
        class InnerClass
        {
            .......
        }
    }
}
```

The member inner classes are instantiated with the instance of the outer class as shown in Example 6.1.

Example 6.1. Instantiating Member Inner Object

```
OuterClass oc = new OuterClass();
OuterClass.InnerClass ic = oc.new InnerClass();
```

Similarly, static inner classes are instantiated with the syntax shown in Example 6.2.

Example 6.2. Instantiating Static Inner Class

```
OuterClass.StaticInnerClass ic = new OuterClass.
StaticInnerClass();
```

Listing 6.15 depicts a member inner class OverTime, which is a member of outer class Employee. The count() method of OverTime calculates the number of overtime days of an employee by accessing its data member.

Listing 6.15. OverTime Inner Class

```
// Employee.java
public class Employee
{
    // employee worked overtime these days
    int[] overtimeDays = {1, 5, 18, 25, 31};

    class OverTime
```

```
{
    public void count()
    {
        System.out.println("No. of overtime days: " +
        overtimeDays.length);
    }
}

public static void main(String[] args)
{
    Employee emp = new Employee();
    Employee.OverTime ot = emp.new OverTime();
    ot.count();
}
}
```

```
No. of overtime days: 5
```

You will learn more about inner classes when you design graphical user interface (GUI) applications using Frames and Applets. Inner classes are highly useful to handle events generated by various Abstract Windowing Toolkit (AWT) and Swing components. So you will appreciate the power of inner classes while you learn GUI programming in Chapter 16.

6.17 SUMMARY

1. Constructor is a special method used for initialization of objects
2. Default constructor is automatically called
3. Constructors can have arguments or parameters
4. Parameterized constructors should be manually called
5. Constructors can also be overloaded
6. **Math** class provides many methods for mathematic and trigonometric operations
7. Character class has methods to manipulate single character
8. String class supports many methods to create and manipulate strings
9. Strings are immutable in Java. That is, original string cannot be modified
10. StringBuffer allows a string's original content to be modified
11. StringBuilder also supports string manipulation and is faster than StringBuffer
12. StringBuffer is thread safe, but not StringBuilder
13. Inheritance allows a child class to reuse data members and methods of super class
14. The keyword *super* is used to call base class constructor and data member
15. The keyword *this* refers to current object
16. A child class can override a base class method

17. Polymorphism is an RTTI of child class method
18. The relationship *part-of* or *has-a* represents aggregation whereas *is-a* relationship represents inheritance
19. Overloading is achieved at compile time, but polymorphism is achieved at runtime
20. A class can give restricted access only to its subclasses by declaring those members as protected
21. Object is the root of all Java classes
22. You can create a copy of an object using clone() method if that object is cloneable
23. You can check an object's class type using *instanceof* operator
24. Inner classes improve encapsulation of an object and can access the members of the outer class

KEY TERMS

Aggregation, 174
Character, 164
Cloneable, 175
Constructor overloading, 162
Constructors, 161
Default constructor, 161
Inheritance, 161

Inner classes, 179
instanceof, 176
Math, 181
Overriding, 174
Parameterized constructor, 161
Polymorphism, 174
String, 165

StringBuffer, 166
StringBuilder, 167
super, 181
super(), 169
Visibility, 161

REVIEW QUESTIONS

Multiple-choice Questions

1. Find out the output:

```
class B extends A
{
    short i = 10;
    int j = 20;

    public B()
    {
        System.out.println(add(i, j));
    }
}
class A
{
    int add(int i, int j)
    {
        return i + j;
    }
}
```

a. 30

b. Compilation error: arguments do not match

c. Compilation error: adding int with short not permitted

d. Runtime exception

2. Find out the output:

```
class A extends B
{
   A() { System.out.println("A"); }
}
class B
{
   B() { System.out.println("B"); }
}

public class Test6
{
   public static void main(String[] args)
   {
      new A();
   }
}
```

a. B A

b. A B

c. No output

d. Compilation error during object creation for A

3. Find out the output:

```
class A extends B
{
   A() { System.out.println("A"); }
}
class B
{
   B() { System.out.println("B"); }
}

public class Test6
{
   public static void main(String[] args)
   {
```

```
        new B();
    }
}
```

a. A   b. A B

c. B   d. B A

4. What is the output?

```
class A extends B
{
    A() { System.out.println("A"); }
}
class B
{
    B(String s) { System.out.println(s); }
}

public class Test6
{
    public static void main(String[] args)
    {
        new A();
    }
}
```

a. Compilation error   b. A

c. A null   d. null A

5. What is the output?

```
class A
{
    void show() { System.out.println("A"); }
}
class B extends A
{
    public B() { System.out.println("C"); }
    void show() { System.out.println("B"); }
}

public class Test6
{
    public static void main(String[] args)
```

```
    {
        A a = new A();
        a.show();
        a = new B();
        a.show();
    }
}
```

a. A C B

b. A B

c. A B C

d. None of the above

6. What is the output?

```
class Building
{
    public Building()
    {
        System.out.println("Building");
    }
    public Building(int n)
    {
        this();
        System.out.println("Building" + n);
    }
}
class Office extends Building
{
    public Office()
    {
        System.out.println("Office");
    }
    public Office(int n)
    {
        this();
        System.out.println("Office" + n);
    }
}

public class Test6
{
    public static void main(String[] args)
    {
        new Office(100);
    }
}
```

a. Building 100 Office Office
b. Building Office Office 100
c. 100 Office Building Office
d. Office Building 100 Office

7. Find out the output:

```java
class Flower
{
   public void smell()
   {
      System.out.println(
            "Flower smells");
   }
}
class WinterFlower extends Flower
{
   public void smell()
   {
      System.out.println(
            "winter Flower smells");
   }
   public void color()
   {
      System.out.println(
            "winter Flowers color");
   }
}
public class Test7
{
   public static void main(String[] args)
   {
      Flower f = new Flower();
      f.smell();
      f.color(); // statement-1
      f = new WinterFlower();
      f.smell();
      f.color(); // statement-2
   }
}
```

a. Error at statement 1 and 2
b. Error at statement 1
c. Error at statement 2
d. Prints output as expected

8. What is the output?

```
class Flower
{
   public static void smell()
   {
      System.out.println(
"Flower smells");
   }
}
class WinterFlower extends Flower
{
   public static void smell()
   {
      System.out.println(
"winter Flower smells");
   }
}
public class Test7
{
   public static void main(String[] args)
   {
      Flower f = new Flower();
      WinterFlower wf = new WinterFlower();
      f.smell();
      wf.smell();
   }
}
```

a. Flower smells Winter Flower smells   b. Flower smells

c. Winter Flower smells   d. Winter Flower smells Flower smells

9. What is the output?

```
class Flower
{
   String color = "red";
   public String smell()
   {
      return "Flower smells";
   }
}
class WinterFlower extends Flower
{
```

```
    String color = "white";
    public String smell()
    {
        return "winter Flower smells";
    }
}
public class Test7
{
    public static void main(String[] args)
    {
        Flower f = new WinterFlower();
        System.out.println(f.color);
        System.out.println(f.smell());
    }
}
```

a. red flower smells
b. red winter flower smells
c. white flower smells
d. white winter flower smells

10. Which object is eligible for garbage collection?

```
class Cat
{
    public Cat del(Cat c)
    {
        c = null;
        return c;
    }
}

public class Test6
{
    public static void main(String[] args)
    {
        Cat c1 = new Cat();
        Cat c2 = new Cat();
        Cat c3 = c2.del(c1);
    }
}
```

a. c1, c2   b. c2, c3
c. c1, c3   d. None of the above

11. What is the output?

```
class Calculator
{
   public int add(int i)
   {
      return 10 + i;
   }
   public int add(int... a)
   {
      int s = 0;
      for(int j=0; j < a.length; j++)
            s += a[j];
      return s;
   }
}

public class Test6
{
   public static void main(String[] args)
   {
      Calculator c = new Calculator();
      short i = 1, j = 2;
      System.out.println(c.add(i, j));
   }
}
```

a. 3

b. 11

c. No output

d. Compilation error

12. Find out the output:

```
class Concatenator
{
   Object s = "";
   public void concat(Object o)
   {
      s = s + "A";
   }
   public void concat(Object... o)
   {
      s = s + "B";
   }
   public void concat(Float... f)
```

```
    {
        s = s + "C";
    }
}

public class Test6
{
    public static void main(String[] args)
    {
        Concatenator c = new Concatenator();
        c.concat(10, true);
        c.concat("Hello");
        c.concat(10.0f, 20.0f);
        System.out.println(c.s);
    }
}
```

a. ABC   b. BAC

c. CAB   d. BCA

13. Find out the output:

```
class Vowel
{
    char[] v = {'a', 'e', 'i', 'o', 'u'};
}

public class Test6
{
    public static void main(String[] args)
    {
        Vowel[] vowels = new Vowel[5];
        vowels[0] = new Vowel();
        Vowel v = new Vowel();
        vowels[1] = v;
        for(char c : vowels[0].v)
            System.out.print(c);
    }
}
```

a. a e i o u   b. No output

c. Compilation error   d. Runtime exception

14. Choose statements so as the program will compile:

```
class A
{
    void show(int i) { System.out.println("A"); }
}
class B extends A
{
    // insert a statement here
}
```

    1. public void show(int i) { System.out.println("B"); }

    2. protected void show(int i) { System.out.println("B"); }

    3. public void show(Integer i) { System.out.println("B"); }

    a. 1   b. 2

    c. 3   d. Any 1, 2, or 3

15. Find out the output:

```
class A
{
    public A() { System.out.println("default constructor"); }
    public A(int a) { System.out.println("int constructor"); }
    public A(char c) { System.out.println("char constructor"); }
}
public class Test6
{
    public static void main(String[] args)
    {
        new A();
    }
}
```

    a. Default constructor   b. Int constructor

    c. Char constructor   d. None of the above

16. Find out the output:

```
class A
{
    String s = "A";
}
```

```
class B extends A
{
    String s = "B";
}
class C extends B
{
    String s = "C";

    public C()
    {
        A a1 = new A();
        B b1 = new B();
        System.out.println(this.s + "," +
        super.s + "," + b1.s + "," + a1.s);
    }
}

public class Test7
{
    public static void main(String[] args)
    {
        new C();
    }
}
```

a. A, B, B, C

b. C, B, B, A

c. B, B, A, C

d. B, B, C, A

17. Find out the output:

```
class A
{
    public A()
    {
        System.out.println("A");
    }
}
class B extends A
{
    private B()
    {
        System.out.println("B");
    }

    public static void main(String[] args)
```

```
    {
        new B();
    }
}
```

a. A B   b. B A

c. A   d. B

18. Find out the output:

```
class A
{
    public void show()
    {
        System.out.println("A");
    }
}
class B extends A
{
    public void show()
    {
        System.out.println("B");
    }
}
class C extends B {}

public class Test6
{
    public static void main(String[] args)
    {
        new C().show();
    }
}
```

a. A   b. B

c. A B   d. B A

e. No output

19. Find out the output:

```
class A
{
    static int i = 1;
```

```
    public void show()
    {
        System.out.println(i);
    }
}
class B extends A
{
    static int i = 2;
    public void show()
    {
        System.out.println(i);
    }
}

public class Test6
{
    public static void main(String[] args)
    {
        A a = new B();
        a.show();
        System.out.println(a.i);
    }
}
```

a. 2 1   b. 2 2
c. 1 1   d. 1 2

20. Find out the output:

```
public class Test6
{
    public static void main(String[] args)
    {
        String s1 = "hello";
        s1.concat("java");
        System.out.println(s1);
    }
}
```

a. hello
b. hellojava
c. javahello
d. java

21. What is the relationship that exists between the following classes?

```
class B extends A { }
class A   { }
```

    a. Is-a relationship   b. Has-a relationship

    c. Abstract relationship   d. Interface relationship

22. What is the output?

```
class Furniture
{
   public Furniture(String s)
   {
      System.out.println(s);
   }
}
class Chair extends Furniture
{
   public Chair(String s)
   {
      super("office furniture");
      System.out.println(s);
   }
}

public class Test6
{
   public static void main(String[] args)
   {
      new Chair("office chair");
   }
}
```

    a. Office furniture office chair   b. Office chair office furniture

    c. Furniture office chair office   d. Furniture chair office office

23. What is the output?

```
class Furniture
{
   public Furniture(String s)
   {
```

```
        System.out.print(s);
    }
}
class Chair extends Furniture
{
    public Chair(String s)
    {
        System.out.print(s);
        super("office furniture");
    }
}

public class Test6
{
    public static void main(String[] args)
    {
        new Chair("office chair");
    }
}
```

a. Office chair office chair

b. Office chair followed by exception

c. Compilation error

d. None of the above

24. What is the output?

```
class A
{
    public final void a()
    {
        System.out.println("A");
    }
}
class B extends A
{
    public void a()
    {
        System.out.println("B");
    }
}

public class Test6
{
    public static void main(String[] args)
    {
```

```
        A a1 = new B();
        a1.a();
    }
}
```

a. A B

b. B A

c. A A

d. B B

e. Compilation error

25. What is the output?

```
class DoIt
{
    void go(int... x) { System.out.print("1");}
    void go(int d, char...x) { System.out.print("2");}
}

public class Test6
{
    public static void main(String[] args)
    {
        DoIt d = new DoIt();
        d.go(1,2);
        d.go(3, 'b', 'c');
    }
}
```

a. 1 2

b. 3 b c

c. 1 2 3 b c

d. Compilation error

26. What is the output?

```
class Ball
{
    public Ball() { System.out.println("1"); }
    public void Ball() { System.out.println("2"); }
}

public class Test6
{
    public static void main(String[] args)
    {
```

```
      new Ball().Ball();
   }
}
```

    a. 1 2   b. 1
    c. 2   d. 1 1
    e. Compilation error

27. Which of the following are true?
    a. Final class cannot be sub-classed   b. Final methods cannot be overridden
    c. Final variables cannot be modified   d. All of the above

28. Which of the following are true?
    a. Interfaces cannot be declared as static   b. Local variables cannot be declared as static
    c. Constructors cannot be made static   d. All of the above

29. What is the output?

```
public class Test6
{
   public static void main(String[] args)
   {
      Integer a = 10;
      Integer b = 10;

      if(a == b)
            System.out.print("same1");
      if(a.equals(b))
            System.out.print("same2");
   }
}
```

    a. same1   b. same2
    c. same1 same2   d. No output

30. What is the output?

```
public class Test6
{
   public static void main(String[] args)
   {
      Integer c = 128;
      Integer d = 128;
```

```
        if(c == d)
              System.out.println("same3");
        if(c.equals(d))
              System.out.println("same4");
    }
}
```

a. same3

b. same4

c. same3 same4

d. No output

31. What is the output?

```
public class Test6
{
    static void m(int i)
    {
        System.out.println(++i);
    }
    public static void main(String[] args)
    {
        Integer a = new Integer(10);
        m(a);
    }
}
```

a. 11

b. m() with Integer argument not found

c. Unable to convert Integer object with value 10 to int inside m()

d. Runtime exception

32. What is the output?

```
public class Test6
{
    public static void main(String[] args)
    {
        String s = "ABCDEFGHIJ";
        System.out.println(s.length());
    }
}
```

a. Method length() does not exist

b. 10

c. 9

d. 11

33. What is the output?

```java
public class Test6
{
    public static void main(String[] args)
    {
        String s = "ABCDEFGHIJ";
        System.out.println(s.substring(7));
        System.out.println(s.substring(3,7));
    }
}
```

a. ABCDEFGH, DEFG   b. HIJ, DEFG

c. GHIJ, CDEFG   d. ABCDEFGH, CDEFGHIJ

34. What is the output?

```java
public class Test6
{
    public static void main(String[] args)
    {
        StringBuffer sb = new StringBuffer("123");
        sb.append("456");
        System.out.println(sb);
    }
}
```

a. 123456   b. 456123

c. 456 as 123 will be overwritten   d. Some garbage value will be displayed

35. What is the output?

```java
public class Test6
{
    public static void main(String[] args)
    {
        StringBuilder sbr = new StringBuilder("123");
        sbr.append("456");
        System.out.println(sbr);
    }
}
```

a. 123456   b. 456123

c. 456 as 123 will be overwritten   d. Some garbage value will be displayed

36. What is the output?

```
public class Test6
{
    public static void main(String[] args)
    {

        StringBuffer sb = new StringBuffer("abc");
        sb.append("def").reverse();
        System.out.println(sb);
    }
}
```

a. cbafed

b. fedcba

c. fed

d. Some garbage value will be displayed

37. What is the output?

```
public class Test6
{
    public static void main(String[] args)
    {
        String s = "ab";
        s = s.concat("cd").toUpperCase().replace('A','a');
        System.out.println(s);
    }
}
```

a. aBCD

b. aBcd

c. abCD

d. CDBa

38. Choose the incorrect statement:

```
class A
{
    public A() { }
    public A(int i) { }
}
class B extends A
{
    public B() { }
    public B(int i)
    {
        super(i);
```

```
    }
}
public class Test61
{
    public static void main(String[] args)
    {
        A a1 = new A();   // Line-1
        B b1 = new B();  // Line-2
        B b2 = new B(10); // Line-3
        B b3 = new B(10.0); // Line-4
    }
}
```

a. Line-1   b. Line-2

c. Line-3   d. Line-4

39. Which of the following are valid overloaded methods for the method add()
    int add(int a, int b) { }?

    a. int add(int a) { }   b. float add(float a, float b) { }

    c. float add(int a, float f) { }   d. All of the above

40. What is the output?

```
class A
{
    public A() {System.out.print("A"); }
}
class B extends A
{
    public B()  {System.out.print("B"); }
}
public class Test61
{
    public static void main(String[] args)
    {
        A a1 = new A();
        B b1 = new B();
        A a2 = new B();
    }
}
```

a. ABBAB   b. BABAA

c. AABAB   d. AABBA

Answers

1. a	2. a	3. c	4. a	5. a	6. b	7. a	8. a	9. b	10. c
11. a	12. b	13. a	14. d	15. a	16. b	17. a	18. b	19. a	20. a
21. a	22. a	23. c	24. e	25. d	26. a	27. d	28. d	29. c	30. b
31. a	32. b	33. b	34. a	35. a	36. b	37. a	38. d	39. d	40. c

Short-answer Questions

1. What is a constructor? Explain with an example.
2. Explain default constructor with an example.
3. Explain parameterized constructor with an example.
4. Explain constructor overloading with an example.
5. Explain important methods of Math class.
6. Discuss important methods of Character class.
7. Discuss important methods of String class.
8. Explain StringBuffer and its important methods.
9. Explain StringBuilder and its important methods.
10. What is the difference between StringBuffer and StringBuilder?
11. Explain inheritance and multilevel inheritance with suitable examples.
12. How will you call base class constructor? Give an example.
13. Explain overriding with an example.
14. Explain polymorphism with an example.
15. What is object cloning?
16. How to identify object's class type?
17. How will you prevent inheritance?
18. How will you prevent overriding?
19. What is inner class? Explain all 4 types of inner class.

EXERCISES

6.1. Replace setCourse() method of Exercise 5.1 with a constructor to initialize the data members of Course class.
6.2. Replace setCylinder() method of Exercise 5.2 with a constructor to initialize the data members of Cylinder class.
6.3. Replace setPrism() method of Exercise 5.3 with a constructor to initialize the data members of Prism class.
6.4. Replace setFan() method of Exercise 5.4 with a constructor to initialize the data members of Fan class.
6.5. Develop a class MyString with your member functions for string processing.
6.6. Develop a class hierarchy for Food as shown in Figure 6.8.

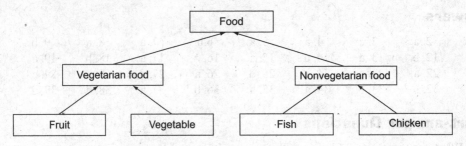

Figure 6.8. Food Class Hierarchy

Data members and member functions for these classes

Food	int Calories, int Fat, int Protein, int Carb, int Sugar	Getcalories() Getfood() Returns Fat+Protein+Carb
VegetarianFood	int iron	getIron() isLeafy() isWatery()
NonvegetarianFood		
Vegetable	String type; //leafy, water	
Fruit	String type;//dry, water	isDry() isWatery()

Create a class Lunch that has Fruit, Vegetable, Fish and Chicken. Create objects for Fruit, Vegetable, Fish and Chicken. For example,

```
Fruit apple = new Fruit();
apple.calories = 50; apple.fat = 5;
apple.protein = 10; apple.carb = 20;
System.out.println(apple.getCalories());
System.out.println(apple.getFood());

Vegetable carrot = new Vegetable();
Fish salmon = new Fish();
```

Assign values for data members and test getCalories() and getFood() methods. Design new methods for other classes too and test them.

More on Objects and Exceptions

OBJECTIVES

- To explain the need for abstract class and abstract methods
- To define abstract class, abstract methods and non abstract methods
- To implement an abstract class *Flower*
- To explain interfaces and its method definitions
- To explain the difference between interfaces and abstract classes
- To create *Wearable* and *Flyable* interfaces
- To explain enum and its applications
- To create packages and subpackages for class taxonomy
- To add classes to packages
- To import packages containing classes and interfaces
- To explain how packages help to avoid name collision
- To illustrate protected data members with package
- To define compile time errors and runtime exceptions
- To explain Java built-in exception class hierarchy with root class Throwable
- To introduce all runtime exceptions and IO exceptions
- To handle exceptions with try-catch-finally statements
- To pipe exceptions using multicatch statement
- To introduce checked exception that allows users to create their own exceptions by extending Exception class
- To explain *throw* and *throws* statements

- To design *UnderAgeException* class to check kid's age for school admission
- To introduce unchecked exception that allows users to create their own exceptions by extending *RuntimeException* class

7.1 INTRODUCTION

In chapters 5 and 6, the readers were introduced to few of the powerful object-oriented features of Java. For instance, object-oriented development involves designing classes with encapsulation, with which we would bind data representing states and code representing behaviours of objects together. Aggregation and inheritance help us to organize class based on whether classes exhibit *part-of* (or *has-a*) relationship or *is-a* relationship. Member visibility allows us to specify access rights to other classes depending on whether those classes access from within the same package or other packages or are subclasses. Once classes are designed, we can create objects, initialize objects using constructors, overload constructors and identify objects' methods at runtime using polymorphism.

In this chapter, the readers are introduced to the remaining two important object-oriented features of Java, namely *abstract classes* and *interfaces*. The readers learn how abstract classes allow us to define some behaviours that we might think are common to several subclasses (in a single-class hierarchy). They force all subclasses to perform actions for the behaviours. Abstract classes will also behave as a normal class with its own states and behaviours. Then readers learn interfaces that are like only managers; they will define some behaviours and expect all implementing classes (from multiple-**class hierarchies**) to perform action for those behaviours. This will be followed by **enum**, which is a feature to group a set of static final constants as a list.

The later part of this chapter introduces you to the concepts of **code reusability**. You can group those common classes that may be used by many others into a package. **Packages** can also be organized hierarchically. The final part of this chapter is devoted to handling exceptions which are runtime errors that are thrown to users indicating some unexpected interruption in the execution of your application. So, you handle those errors so that the execution of your program does not terminate.

7.2 ABSTRACT CLASSES

In a class hierarchy, the root class will always represent generic concepts that are common to all subclasses. Mostly, we create objects from child classes and do not need to create objects from the root class. As a developer, we know what objects are to be created from those classes. However, other developers do not know that objects should not be created from this root class.

7.2.1 Defining Abstract Classes

Fortunately, Java provides a way to prevent object creation from generic classes, and these generic classes are known as abstract classes. Any attempt to create an object from an abstract class will cause a compiler error. The syntax for abstract class is shown in Figure 7.1.

Figure 7.1. Syntax for Abstract Class

```
[public][abstract] class class-name
{
    // variables and methods to be accessible to subclasses
```

```
    // can declare static variables and static methods
    // abstract method declarations
}
```

7.2.2 Defining Abstract Methods

An abstract class can include **abstract methods**. Abstract classes cannot be instantiated, but they can be subclassed. An *abstract method* is a method that is only declared without an implementation (that is, without method body, and followed by a semicolon). If there is an abstract method in a class, then the class must be declared abstract. When an abstract class is subclassed, the subclass usually provides implementations for all of the abstract methods in its parent class. However, if it does not, the subclass must also be declared abstract. The syntax for abstract method is depicted in Figure 7.2.

Figure 7.2. Syntax for Abstract Method

```
[public] [abstract] return-type method-name(arguments);
```

Listing 7.1 illustrates the abstract class Flower which defines a non abstract data member and member function, besides an abstract method declaration, namely *smell()*. Therefore all subclasses will provide implementation to the abstract method.

Listing 7.1. Abstract Class Flower

```
//FlowerObject.java                                      {coderipe}

abstract class Flower
{
    public String colour;

    public void getColour()
    {
        System.out.println(colour);
    }

    public abstract void smell();   // abstract method
}

class Rose extends Flower
{
    public void smell()
    {
        System.out.println("Wow, this " + colour +
            " rose spreads romantic fragrance...");
    }
}
```

```
class Jasmine extends Flower
{
   public void smell()
   {
      System.out.println("Wow, this " + colour +
            " jasmine spreads something different fragrance...");
   }
}

public class FlowerObject
{
   public static void main(String[] args)
   {
      Rose rose = new Rose();
      rose.colour = "Red";
      rose.smell();

      Jasmine jasmine = new Jasmine();
      jasmine.colour = "White";
      jasmine.smell();
   }
}
```

```
Wow, this Red rose spreads romantic fragrance...
Wow, this White jasmine spreads something different fragrance...
```

7.3 INTERFACES

Interface is called pure abstract class. The reason is that interfaces can contain only data members and abstract methods. In contrast, abstract classes can contain abstract and nonabstract methods. Whether you declare or not, all data members in an interface are *public final*. That means, they will be identified as constants and you can even assign values. Similarly, all method declarations are *public abstract* by default. Interface can also extend another interface.

7.3.1 Declaring Interfaces

Interfaces are declared with the syntax shown in Figure 7.3.

Figure 7.3. Syntax for Interface Declaration

```
[ public ] [ abstract ] interface interface-name
{
   // constants and method declarations
}
```

As an example, let us define an interface *Wearable* so that we can say flowers such as rose and jasmine are flowers as well as wearable as shown in Listing 7.2.

Listing 7.2. Wearable Interface

```
interface Wearable
{
    public void canWear();
}
```

7.3.2 Implementing Interfaces

Once an interface is defined, the class can implement this interface by providing behaviours to interface methods as shown in Figure 7.4. Note that a class can implement any number of interfaces.

Figure 7.4. Syntax for Implementing Interface

```
class class-name [extends superclass] [implements interface-
name1, interface-name2,...]
```

Now let us say flowers such as rose and jasmine are flowers as well as wearables. So we create class Rose and Jasmine by extending class Flower and implementing wearable as shown in Listing 7.3.

Listing 7.3. WearableFlower

```
// WearableFlower.java                                          {coderipe}
import java.util.*;

interface Wearable
{
    public void canWear();
}

class Flower
{
    public String colour;

    public void getColour()
    {
        Scanner sc = new Scanner(System.in);
        System.out.print("Enter colour: " );
        colour = sc.nextLine();
    }
}

class Rose extends Flower implements Wearable
{
```

```
    public void smell()
    {
       System.out.println("Wow, this " + colour +
             " rose spreads romantic fragrance...");
    }

    public void canWear()
    {
       System.out.println("Girls can wear this " + colour +
             " rose ");
    }
}

public class WearableFlower
{
    public static void main(String[] args)
    {
       Rose rose = new Rose();
       rose.getColour();
       rose.smell();
       rose.canWear();
    }
}
```

```
Enter colour:  red
Wow, this red rose spreads romantic fragrance...
Girls can wear this red rose
```

Here, the object rose invokes getcolor() which is a method available in the base class Flower. The other two methods are implementations of interface.

7.3.3 Problem: Flyable Interface

We will now define the interface *Flyable* by specifying a constant *wings* and interface method *fly()*. Further we will define classes such as *Aircraft* and *Crow* so that they can fly. Figure 7.5 depicts two class hierarchies for Aircraft and Bird and Flyable interface represents common behaviour namely fly(). Listing 7.4 explains this Flyable interface.

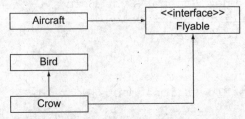

Figure 7.5. Flyable with Multiple-class Hierarchies

Listing 7.4. Flyable Object

```java
//FlyableObject.java                            {coderipe}

interface Flyable
{
   public int wings = 2;   // by default, public final
   public void fly();   // public abstract, by default
}

class Aircraft implements Flyable
{
   public void fly()
   {
      System.out.println("Aircrafts can fly 40000 feets with " +
          wings + " wings");
   }
}

class Bird
{
   int leg;   // number of legs
}

class Crow extends Bird implements Flyable
{
   public void fly()
   {
      System.out.println("Crows can fly 1000 feets with " +
          wings + " wings" + " and without using its " + legs +
          " legs");
   }
}

public class FlyableObject
{
   public static void main(String[] args)
   {
      Aircraft a = new Aircraft();
      a.fly();

      Crow c = new Crow();
      c.legs = 2;
      c.fly();
   }
}
```

```
Aircrafts can fly 40000 feets with 2 wings
Crows can fly 1000 feets with 2 wings and without using its 2 legs
```

The interesting part in this application is the ability of the interface Flyable that represents common behaviours across multiple-class hierarchies. For instance, the class Aircraft belongs to one class hierarchy, whereas the class Crow belongs to another class hierarchy namely Bird. Thus, interfaces are something like bridges that represent the commonalities in multiple-class hierarchies, whereas abstract classes capture generalization in a single-class hierarchy.

7.4 JAVA ENUMS

Enum, introduced in Java 1.5, is one of the important features of Java like *boxing* and *varargs*. Enumeration (or enum) was not originally available before Java 1.5 though it was supported in C and C++. Readers from C or C++ background would be able to appreciate the power of enum. Java realized its importance and Java enum emerged as a powerful feature to define a set of static values.

7.4.1 Basics of Enum

An enum is used to represent a list of static final values. There are several applications where you need to keep such a list such as colours, states, font-styles and others. In earlier Java, constants were used to replicate enum like static values. For example, you can define many states for a machine such as *idle, running* and *stopped*, so that you can set the current state of your machine with any of these states as shown in Listing 7.5.

Listing 7.5. Machine

```java
//Machine.java
class State
{
    public static final int IDLE = 1;
    public static final int RUNNING = 2;
    public static final int STOPPED = 3;
}

public class Machine
{
    private int state;
    public static void main(String[] args)
    {
        Machine weldingMachine = new Machine();
        weldingMachine.state = State.IDLE;
        System.out.println(weldingMachine.state);
    }
}
```

```
1
```

Here, the state of your welding machine is set to IDLE; So far so good. It prints its state value 1. But it is not type-safe in the sense that you might set the state of your welding machine to any value (that does not exist, of course) besides these three states such as

```
weldingMachine.state = 100;
System.out.println(weldingMachine.state);
```

So you set a state with value 100 that does not exist and JVM will not generate compilation error. It does not prevent this setting and displays a value 100. So absolutely no type-safety!

Apart from type-safe problem, you cannot print string labels. The state prints 1 which is the numerical value of its state, but not its string label IDLE. In fact, string labels are more meaningful than its numerical counterparts. Further, there is no namespace. You need to access it by its class name prefix such as State.IDLE but not simply IDLE.

So the solution for all these three limitations is *enum*. Java enum is a type-safe list of static final constants, providing meaningful string labels and has its own namespace. Enum is created with the syntax shown in Figure 7.6.

Figure 7.6. Enum Syntax

```
public enum enum-name {enum-constants};
```

There can be several enum constants which are comma separated, and all these constants are by default static and final. This implies you are not allowed to change its value. Trying to change enum constants will generate compilation error. For instance, let us create enum State with three states as shown in Example 7.1.

Example 7.1 Enum State

```
public enum State {IDLE, RUNNING, STOPPED};
```

Then our Machine can be set with any of these three states from State enum as illustrated in Listing 7.6.

Listing 7.6. Type-safe Machine

```
//Machine1.java
public class Machine1
{
    public enum State {IDLE, RUNNING, STOPPED};
```

```
    State state;

    public static void main(String[] args)
    {
        Machine1 weldingMachine = new Machine1();
        weldingMachine.state = State.RUNNING;
        System.out.println(weldingMachine.state);

        //weldingMachine.state = 4; // ERROR
        //System.out.println(weldingMachine.state);
    }
}
```

```
RUNNING
```

If the state of the welding machine is assigned to any other value (such as 4) besides its constants, JVM will generate compilation error. Also there are times that you might need to display the constants in enum. Then *values()* method will display them for you as shown in Listing 7.7.

Listing 7.7. The Values() Method

```
//Machine2.java
public class Machine2
{
    public enum State {IDLE, RUNNING, STOPPED};
    State state;

    public static void main(String[] args)
    {
        Machine2 weldingMachine = new Machine2();
        weldingMachine.state = State.RUNNING;
        System.out.println(weldingMachine.state);

        State[] states = State.values();
        for(State s : states)
            System.out.println(s);
    }
}
```

```
IDLE
RUNNING
STOPPED
```

7.4.2 Advanced Features of Enum

In Java, enums are implemented as a full-featured class so that they can have variables, methods and constructors. This is how Java enums are powerful than C and C++ languages.

Enum constants can have attributes. In order to access these attributes, you need to define a constructor and a private variable which will hold attribute of the enum constant. Now let us assign some character codes for enum constants such as I, R and S for State enum as shown below:

```java
// State.java
public enum State
{
    IDLE('I'), RUNNING('R'), STOPPED('S');
    char code;
    State(char c)
    {
        code = c;
    }
};
```

Note that here State is considered to be an independent class. It need not be just a Java statement. So you can save it as a Java file and compile it without any problem. Now it is easy to refine our Machine application so that it will display enum constants along with their attribute values as depicted in Listing 7.8.

Listing 7.8. Machine3 Application

```java
//Machine3.java
public class Machine3
{
    public static void main(String[] args)
    {
        // show all enum constants with its attributes
        State[] states = State.values();
        for(State s : states)
            System.out.println(s.code + "-" + s);
    }
}
```

```
I-IDLE
R-RUNNING
S-STOPPED
```

Enum constants can be sent to switch statement as an argument so that enum constants will act like case options for the switch as illustrated in Listing 7.9.

Listing 7.9. Enum Inside Switch Statement

```java
//Machine4.java
enum State
{
    IDLE('I'), RUNNING('R'), STOPPED('S');
    char code;
    State(char c)
    {
        code = c;
    }
};

public class Machine4
{
    State state;

    public static void main(String[] args)
    {
        Machine4 weldingMachine = new Machine4();
        weldingMachine.state = State.STOPPED;

        switch(weldingMachine.state)
        {
        case IDLE:
                System.out.println
                    ("Currently machine is idle"); break;
        case RUNNING:
                System.out.println
                    ("Currently machine is running"); break;
        case STOPPED:
                System.out.println
                    ("Currently machine is stopped");
        }
    }
}
```

```
Currently machine is stopped
```

Apart from constructors, any other method can be added to enum just like normal members of a class. Now let us develop an enum Age that will define three age groups namely NEW, HALFNEW and OLD with some age ranges for each type; define a method that will return the age range of age group and develop a static method that will return age group for the given age value. Listing 7.10 explains the complete application for this Age enum.

Listing 7.10. Age of a Machine

```java
//Machine5.java
enum Age
{
   NEW(0,2), HALFNEW(3,5), OLD(6,10);

   private int minAge;
   private int maxAge;

   private Age(int min, int max)
   {
      minAge = min;
      maxAge = max;
   }

   public void getRange()
   {
      System.out.println(minAge + "," + maxAge);
   }

   public static Age getAge(int n)
   {
      for(Age age : Age.values())
      {
         if(n >= age.minAge && n <= age.maxAge)
               return age;
      }
      return null;
   }
};

public class Machine5
{
   Age age;

   public static void main(String[] args)
   {
      Machine5 weldingMachine = new Machine5();
      weldingMachine.age = Age.NEW;
      System.out.print("Age range: ");
      weldingMachine.age.getRange();

      // what is the age group of 4-year-old machine?
      System.out.println(Age.getAge(4));
   }
}
```

```
Age range: 0,2
HALFNEW
```

Here, getRange() displays 0 and 2 as the minimum and maximum age of the weldingMachine whose age group is NEW. In the second part, we want to find out the age group of a machine whose age is 4 years. The getAge() returns HALFNEW as the age group for the 4-year-old machine.

In summary, enums are good for representing predefined list of values. Use it selectively. If you want to add new values when the application is running, do not use enums.

7.5 PACKAGES

Many times our Java applications consist of few classes; thereby we keep all such classes inside a single directory. However it will be more difficult if our applications grow into several classes and files. In such cases, we are grouping them into many categories according to their usability and functionality and keeping them into multiple directories for effective taxonomy.

Java APIs are centred on packages. Some of the packages are already introduced such as *java.lang* and *java.io*. Here, *java* is a package and *lang* is a subpackage within java package. Some more packages such as *java.util, java.awt, java.applet* and *javax.swing* will be introduced in Chapter 7 and 16. Readers are advised to refer to Java API documentation for accessing a complete set of packages available from Oracle (http://docs.oracle.com/javase/7/docs/api/overview-summary.html).

7.5.1 Creating a Package

To organize user-defined files into groups, Java supports package statement to bundle all classes and interfaces together. Once package is created, all items in the package can be imported to other classes. Packages can be created with the syntax as depicted in Figure 7.7.

Figure 7.7. Package Declaration

```
package package-name;
```

All those classes we want to bundle together should be saved under the subdirectory with the package-name. Now, let us create a package *tools* with a class Pr as in Listing 7.11. The class Pr provides overloaded print() and println() methods that will display string and integers. Pr also includes another method get() that will read an integer from user.

Listing 7.11. Pr Class Inside Tools

```
package tools;
import java.io.*;

public class Pr
{
    public static void print(String s)
```

```
{
    System.out.print(s);
}

public static void print(int i)
{
    System.out.print(i);
}

public static void println(String s)
{
    System.out.println(s);
}

public static void println(int i)
{
    System.out.println(i);
}

static BufferedReader in = new BufferedReader
( new InputStreamReader( System.in));

public static int get() throws IOException
{
    return Integer.parseInt(in.readLine());
}
}
```

Here, we create a package named *tools* and bundle the class Pr into *tools*. We create a subdirectory namely *tools* (see Figure 7.8) from the current directory (assume our current directory is *basics*) and save Pr.java in *tools* directory and compile it.

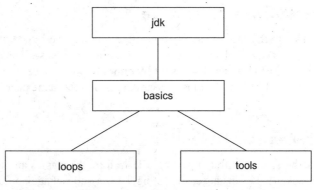

Figure 7.8. Package Tools

7.5.2 Importing Packages

Now we can import all classes of *tools* package from the current directory using the normal import statement so that we can access all classes and interfaces as we like. Listing 7.12 illustrates importing package classes.

Listing 7.12. Biggest Using Package

```
// PaBiggest2.java

import tools.*;
import java.io.*;

public class PaBiggest2
{
    public static void main(String[] args) throws IOException
    {
        Pr.println("Hello 2BE day! ");
        int i = Pr.get();
        Pr.print(i);
    }
}
```

```
Hello 2BE day!
100
100
```

The class *Biggest2.java* should be saved in the current directory, that is, *basics*. In this example, we access the class Pr and utilize two of its methods namely print() and get(). Packages are also useful to avoid name collisions and to support code reusability. We can create a package *io* as a subpackage of tools (see Figure 7.9), so that *tools.io* package will be different from *java.io* package.

7.5.3 Including Classes to Package

New classes can be added to the package at any time after it has been created with the package statement along with the name of the package to which we want to tag a class. Package access would be public always; however we can restrict if we want by omitting public access. In this case, it will be identified as default access; thereby only those classes defined in the same package can access package classes.

7.5.4 Subpackages

Subpackages can also be created within a package. Therefore, the classes and interfaces have to be bundled inside a subpackage. For instance, in Listing 7.13, a subpackage *console* has been created within *tools* package. We add a class Scan to console package.

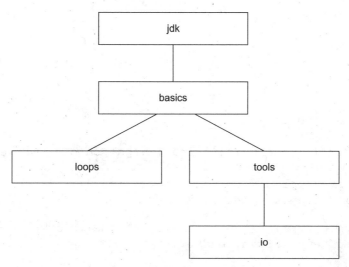

Figure 7.9. Packages Avoid Name Collision

Listing 7.13. Scan Class Inside Subpackage

```java
package tools.console;

import java.io.*;
import java.util.*;

public class Scan
{
    static Scanner sc = new Scanner(System.in);

    public static int readInt() throws IOException
    {
        int no = 0;
        no = sc.nextInt(); sc.nextLine();
        return no;
    }
    public static String readStr() throws IOException
    {
        return sc.nextLine();
    }
}
```

Once subpackage (i.e. subdirectory *console* within the current directory *tools*) has been created, then it can be imported into a class where we access the classes and interfaces defined in the sub-package. We can access subpackage items anywhere before this subdirectory, that is, in any parent directory. Listing 7.14 shows a class ScanTest that imports all classes of the package console.

Listing 7.14. ScanTest Using Subpackage

```
import tools.console.*;

import java.util.*;
import java.io.*;

public class ScanTest
{
    public static void main(String[] args) throws IOException
    {
        System.out.print("Enter employee id: ");
        int i = Scan.readInt();

        System.out.print("Enter employee name: ");
        String name = Scan.readStr();

        System.out.println("Employee id: " + i + "\nEmployee
        name: " + name);
    }
}
```

```
Enter employee id: 1001
Enter employee name: Rex
Employee id: 1001
Employee name: Rex
```

7.5.5 Protected Members Revisited

In Chapter 6, the readers were introduced to the visibility of protected data members and member functions. Protected members are accessible to the class they are defined, to any class within the same package and to its subclasses within the same package or from any other package. Figure 7.10 illustrates the visibility of protected data members.

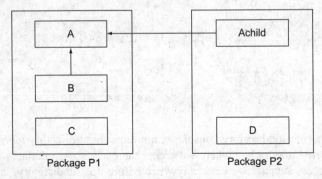

Figure 7.10. Visibility of Protected Data Members of Class A

Here, protected data members of class A are visible inside class A, inside class B as B is child class of A, inside class C as class A and class C belong to the same package P1 and inside the child class of A namely Achild (though Achild is defined in another package P2). However, class D cannot access protected members of A as it is defined in P2.

7.6 EXCEPTION HANDLING

During editing our Java program, we might encounter a lot of errors. Basically errors are classified into two types:

- **Syntax errors** such as spelling mistakes, which will be reported to users while compiling the program using *javac* compiler.
- **Semantic errors** such as *dividing an integer by zero*, which will be reported to users while executing the program using *java* interpreter. They are also called runtime errors.

In Java, semantic errors are represented as exceptions. Exception is an abnormal situation that halts the execution of a program abruptly if it is not handled. If all possible exceptions are handled inside the program, then program will not terminate in the middle of execution.

7.6.1 Try-catch-finally Statements

Before learning the different constructs available in Java to handle exceptions, we will first look at an example that will highlight the problem as shown in Listing 7.15.

Listing 7.15. SimpleException Example

```
// SimpleException.java
public class SimpleException {
    public static void main(String args[])
    {
        int a = 20;
        int b = 0;
        int value = a/b;
        System.out.println("value: " + value);
    }
}
```

```
Exception in thread "main" java.lang.ArithmeticException: / by
zero
at SimpleException.main(SimpleException.java:7)
```

In this application, the println() statement displaying *value* will not be executed because in the previous line, the integer division by zero is not allowed and it will raise an exception, thereby the program terminates. So, we need to instruct the application what is to be done when division by zero occurs. This process is known as exception handling.

Exception handling is a process of identifying possible runtime errors that are likely to happen and handle or solve this exception so that normal execution will continue. Java supports three constructs for handling exceptions. They are

- **try-catch-finally** statements, as shown in Figure 7.11
- try-resource statement; it will be introduced to the readers in Chapter 14.
- Multicatch statement

Figure 7.11. Try-catch-finally Syntax

```
Try
{
    // statements that will possibly throw one or more exceptions
}
catch(exception-type 1)
{
    // handling code for exception-type1
}
catch(exception-type n)
{
    // handling code for exception-type n.
}
finally
{
    // statements to be executed after try block or catch block
}
```

Try block will contain statements that are likely to **throw** exceptions. If an exception has occurred, control is transferred to any one of the catch blocks. Catch block will contain statements that can solve this exception. Then execution will continue with finally block. Remember, finally block will be executed irrespective of exceptions. Also, there can be any number of catch blocks for the given single try block.

The application depicted in Listing 7.16 checks three types of runtime errors. A user may enter something other than int that causes parseInt() method unable to convert string into int, may supply a zero for second number that causes division by zero and intentionally we try to access an array location outside its size.

Listing 7.16. ExceptionTest

```
// ExceptionTest.java                                    {coderipe}
import java.io.*;
import java.util.*;

public class ExceptionTest
{
    public static void main(String[] args)
    {
```

```
        try
        {
                int a = Integer.parseInt(args[0]);   // user may enter
                other than int
                int b = Integer.parseInt(args[1]);   // user may enter
                other than int

                int sum = a / b;   // infinity may happen if b is zero

                int[] array = new int[2];
                array[0] = a;
                array[1] = b;
                // beware, you try to access outside array size
                array[2] = array[0] + array[1];
        }
        catch(NumberFormatException n)
        {
                System.out.println("Please type only integers for a
                and b");
        }
        catch(ArithmeticException n)
        {
                System.out.println("Trying to divide by zero, ensure
                nonzero for b");
        }
        catch(ArrayIndexOutOfBoundsException n)
        {
                System.out.println("Trying to access outside array
                index");
        }
        finally
        {
                System.out.println
                        ("Think of all possible exceptions while
                        designing your code");
        }
    }
}
```

```
C:\jdk>java ExceptionTest 10 20.o
Please type only integers for a and b
Think of all possible exceptions while designing your code

C:\jdk>java ExceptionTest 10 o
```

```
Trying to divide by zero, ensure nonzero for b
Think of all possible exceptions while designing your code

C:\jdk>java ExceptionTest 10 20
Trying to access outside array index
Think of all possible exceptions while designing your code
```

When parseInt() is unable to convert, then control is transferred to catch block of NumberFormat Exception. When division by zero occurs, then control goes to catch block with ArithmeticException. Also, when array[2] is accessed, then control goes to the third catch block where ArrayIndexOut ofBoundsException is handled. Finally block will be executed anyway irrespective of exceptions. **Exception class** hierarchy should be followed when defining exception objects for catch blocks.

7.6.2 Multicatch Statement

In Java 7, it is possible to catch multiple different exceptions in the same catch block. This is also known as multicatch statement and is created using pipe character. Listing 7.17 illustrates multicatch statement catching NumberFormatException and ArithmeticException.

Listing 7.17. MultiCatch Class

```java
// MultiCatch.java
import java.io.*;
public class MultiCatch
{
    public static void main(String[] args)
    {
        try
        {
            int a = Integer.parseInt(args[0]);
            int b = Integer.parseInt(args[1]);
            int sum = a / b;
        }
        catch(NumberFormatException | ArithmeticException e )
        {
            System.out.println("Enter only nonzero integers for a
            and b");
        }
    }
}
```

```
C:\jdk>java MultiCatch 10 20

C:\jdk>java MultiCatch 10 20.0
```

```
Enter only nonzero integers for a and b

C:\jdk>java MultiCatch 10 0
Enter only nonzero integers for a and b
```

7.6.3 Exception Hierarchy

All exception classes are subclasses of the java.lang.Exception class, which is a subclass of the Throwable class. There is another subclass called Error which is derived from the Throwable class. The Exception class has two main subclasses, IOException class and RuntimeException class, as shown in Figure 7.12.

Errors are not handled in the Java programs. These conditions normally happen in case of severe failures. Errors are generated to indicate that the errors are generated by the runtime environment. For example, JVM is out of memory. Normally programs cannot recover from errors.

7.6.4 User-defined Exceptions with *throw* and *throws*

Java developer can create their own exception class by extending **Exception** or RuntimeException class. In order to display meaningful information about the exception, toString() method can be overridden inside the user-defined exception class.

Throw Statement

The *throw* statement can be used to create an object of user-defined exception and used inside try-catch block. For example, a school wants to check the age of a kid for possible admission to its kinder garden programme. Listing 7.18 explains this application.

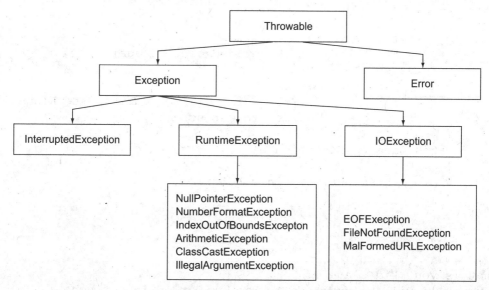

Figure 7.12. Portion of Exception Hierarchy

Listing 7.18. UnderAgeException Using Throw

```java
//UnderAgeExceptionTest.java
import java.util.*;

class UnderAgeException extends Exception
{
    private int age;
    public UnderAgeException(int a)
    {
      age = a;
    }
    public String toString()
    {
        return age + " year is under age for Kinder Garden" +
        "\nPlease come next year for admission! ";
    }
}
public class UnderAgeExceptionTest
{
    public static void main(String[] args)
    {
        Scanner sc = new Scanner(System.in);

        System.out.print("What is your kid's age ?: ");
        int age = sc.nextInt();

        try
        {
            if (age < 2)
                throw new UnderAgeException(age);
            else
                System.out.print
                    ("Your child will be admitted to Kinder
                    Garden in our school");
        }
        catch(UnderAgeException e)
        {
            System.out.println(e.toString());
        }
    }
}
```

```
What is your kid's age ?: 2
Your child will be admitted to Kinder Garden in our school
```

```
What is your kid's age ?: 1
1 year is under age for admission to Kinder Garden
Please come next year for admission!
```

Throws Statement

A method can use *throws* statement to indicate that it might throw the exception back to the caller, so that the caller can catch this exception and take appropriate action. Listing 7.19 is a revised school admission application where checkAge() method may throw UnderAgeException exception.

Listing 7.19. UnderAgeException Using Throws

```java
//UnderAgeExceptionTest1.java
import java.util.*;

public class UnderAgeExceptionTest1
{
    public void checkAge(int age) throws UnderAgeException
    {
        if (age < 2)
                throw new UnderAgeException(age);
        else
                System.out.print
                        ("Your child will be admitted to Kinder Garden
                        in our school");
    }

    public static void main(String[] args)
    {
        UnderAgeExceptionTest1 u = new UnderAgeExceptionTest1();
        Scanner sc = new Scanner(System.in);

        System.out.print("What is your kid's age ?: ");
        int age = sc.nextInt();

        try
        {
                u.checkAge(age);
        }
        catch(UnderAgeException e)
        {
                System.out.println(e.toString());
        }
    }
}
```

```
What is your kid's age ?: 2
Your child will be admitted to Kinder Garden in our school

What is your kid's age ?: 1
1 year is under age for admission to Kinder Garden
Please come next year for admission!
```

7.6.5 Extending *RuntimeException* Class

A class can also extend **RuntimeException class** instead of Exception class. This feature will be useful when we do not wish to use try-catch statements and just we would like to signal the presence of this exception to the caller. This extending class is called *unchecked exception*. In contrast, when a class extends Exception class, then this class is called *checked exception*.

7.7 SUMMARY

1. Abstract class is a generic root class which defines some behaviours that are to be performed by subclasses
2. Abstract classes prevent others to instantiate objects, but can have its own members accessible for its child classes
3. If a method in a class is abstract, then this class must be abstract
4. The subclass of an abstract class must perform the behaviour defined by abstract method. That is it should provide implementation for abstract method. Otherwise, the subclass should also be declared as abstract
5. Interfaces are called pure abstract classes
6. Interfaces can define constants and methods that are by default public abstract
7. All implementing classes of an interface must provide implementation to interface methods, failing which compilation error will be generated
8. Interface can also extend another interface
9. Interfaces represent the commonalities in multiple-class hierarchies, whereas abstract classes capture generalization in a single-class hierarchy
10. Enum allows us to represent a type-safe predefined set of static values
11. Enum behaves like a public class or interface with its members
12. Packages group classes into taxonomy; thereby classes can import classes and interfaces from a package
13. Packages can define subpackages
14. Errors can be compile time errors or runtime exceptions
15. Runtime exceptions are handled using try-catch-finally statements
16. Try block includes those Java statements that are likely throw an exception
17. Catch block defines statements that will handle a possible exception type if generated
18. Finally block will be executed irrespective of exceptions whether thrown or not
19. Exception can be piped using multicatch statement

20. Users can create checked exception by extending Exception class
21. The *throw* statement can be used to create an object of user defined exception
22. A method can use *throws* statement to indicate that it might throw the exception back to the caller
23. Users can also create unchecked exception by extending RuntimeException class

KEY TERMS

Abstract classes, 206
Abstract methods, 207
Class hierarchies, 206
Code resuability, 206
Enum, 206

Exception class, 226
Interfaces, 206
Packages, 206
RuntimeException class, 230
Subpackages, 220

Throw, 224
Throws, 229
Try-catch-finally, 224

REVIEW QUESTIONS

Multiple-choice Questions

1. Choose all incorrect statements:
   1. Static variables can be serialized
   2. Transient variables can be serialized
   3. To serialize object, you need to implement writeObject() method
   4. Objects are deserialized in first-in-first out order

   a. 1, 2   b. 2, 3
   c. 3, 4   d. 1, 4

2. What is the output?

```
public class Test7
{
    public static void main(String[] args)
    {
        try
        {
            System.out.print("Hello Java");
        }
        finally
        {
            System.out.print("finally Hello Java");
        }
    }
}
```

a. Hello Java
b. finally Hello Java
c. Hello Java finally Hello Java
d. Compilation error

3. Which of the following are not exceptions?
   a. ArrayIndexOutOfBoundsException
   b. NumberFormatException
   c. ArithmeticException
   d. NullPointerException
   e. None of the above

4. What is wrong in the following code?

```
abstract class Greeting
{
    public abstract greet();
}
class  MorningGreeting extends Greeting
{}
```

a. Correct code
b. greet() does not have return type
c. MorningGreeting does not implement greet()
d. greet() does not have method body

5. Find out the error in the following code:

```
abstract class Greeting
{
    public abstract void greet(String s){};
}
class MorningGreeting extends Greeting
{}
```

a. greet() should not have method body
b. MorningGreeting does not override greet()
c. Both 1 and 2
d. None of the above

6. Which of the following are true?
   a. Abstract classes should not be instantiated
   b. Abstract methods should be overridden inside its subclass
   c. Constructors cannot be created for abstract classes
   d. Static methods cannot be created inside abstract class
   e. All of the above

7. How will you make member of a class visible to all subclasses of any package?
   a. By declaring it private
   b. By declaring it protected
   c. By declaring it public
   d. Any of the above

8. Choose the correct abstract classes:

   a.
```
class Pen
{
    abstract void write();
}
```
   b.
```
abstract Pen
{
    abstract void write();
}
```
   c.
```
abstract class Pen
{
    abstract void write();
}
```
   d.
```
abstract class Pen
{
    abstract void write(){}
}
```
   e. None of the above

9. What is the output?

```
interface Device
{
    public void volume();
}
class Phone implements Device
{
    public void volume(){}
}

abstract class MobilePhone extends Phone{}

abstract class WiredPhone extends Phone
{
    public void volumeHigh(int n){}
}

abstract class MobilePhone2 extends Phone implements Device
{
    public void volume(int n){}
}
```

   a. Compilation error   b. Runtime error
   c. Runtime exception   d. No error

10. Which of the following statements will not compile?
    1. abstract class A1 { public abstract void a(); }
    2. abstract class A2 { public void a(){}}
    3. class A3 { public abstract void a(); }

    a. 1   b. 2
    c. 3   d. No error

11. Find out the output for the command line: java Test7 hello java:

```
public class Test7
{
    public static void main(String... args)
    {
        System.out.println(args[1]);
    }
}
```

    a. Test7
    b. Hello
    c. Java
    d. Error: varargs cannot be applied to main()

12. Find out the output:

```
public class Test7
{
    public static void callIt()
    {
        throw new RuntimeException();
    }

    public static void main(String[] args)
    {
        System.out.println("Hello");
        callIt();
        System.out.println("Java");
    }
}
```

    a. Hello followed by RuntimeException message
    b. Hello
    c. Hello Java
    d. Compilation error

13. Find out the output:

```
public class Test7
{
   public static void callIt()
   {
      throw new RuntimeException();
   }

      public static void main(String[] args)
   {
      try
      {
            System.out.println("Hello");
            callIt();
            System.out.println("Java");
      }
      finally
      {
            System.out.println("Finally");
      }
   }
}
```

   a. Hello   b. Finally

   c. Hello Finally   d. RuntimeException message

   e. Hello Finally RuntimeException message

14. Find out the output:

```
public class Test7
{
   public static void callIt()
   {
      throw new RuntimeException();
   }

   public static void main(String[] args)
   {
      try
      {
            System.out.println("Hello");
            callIt();
            System.out.println("Java");
      }
```

```
        catch(Exception e)
        {
                System.out.println("inside catch");
        }
        finally
        {
                System.out.println("Finally");
        }
    }
}
```

a. Hello   b. Hello Java
c. Hello Java inside catch   d. Hello inside catch Finally

15. What is the output?

```
interface A
{
   public void a();
}
abstract class B implements A
{
   public void a(){};
}
class C extends B
{
   public void a()
   {
      System.out.println("C");
   }
}
class Test7
{
   public static void main(String[] args)
   {
      new C().a();
   }
}
```

a. C
b. Compilation error
c. Runtime error
d. Runtime Exception

16. What is the output?

```
interface A
{
    public void a(String s);
}
abstract class B implements A
{}
class C extends B
{
    public void a()
    {
        System.out.println("A");
    }
    public void a(String s)
    {
        System.out.println("C");
    }
}
class Test7
{
    public static void main(String[] args)
    {
        new C().a();
    }
}
```

    a. A   b. A C

    c. C A   d. Runtime exception

17. What is the output?

```
interface A
{
    void a(String s);
}
interface B extends A
{
    void b(int i);
}
class C implements B
{
    public void a()
    {
```

```
        a("B");
        System.out.println("A");
    }
    public void a(String s)
    {
        b(100);
        System.out.println(s);
    }
    public void b(int i)
    {
        System.out.println("D");
    }
}
class Test7
{
    public static void main(String[] args)
    {
        new C().a();
    }
}
```

    a. B A D   b. D B A
    c. A B D   d. Runtime exception

18. Find out the output?

```
final class A { }
class B extends A {}
public class Test6
{
    public static void main(String[] args)
    {
        new B();
    }
}
```

    a. Compilation error   b. Compilation successful
    c. No output   d. Runtime exception

19. What is the output?

```
public class Test7
{
    public static void main(String[] args)
```

```
{
    try
    {
        int x = Integer.parseInt("ten");
    }
    catch (Exception e)
    {
        System.out.println("Exception: " + e.toString());
    }
}
}
```

a. ten   b. 10
c. NumberFormatException   d. Compilation error

20. Choose the correct statement?

```
public class Test7
{
    public static void main(String[] args)
    {
        String s = "+ve number";
        int x = Integer.parseInt(args[0]);
        assert( x < 0): s = "-ve number";
        System.out.println(s);
    }
}
```

a. +ve number   b. −ve number
c. +ve number, if args[0] is +ve number   d. −ve number if args[0] is −ve number

21. What is the output?

```
package tools;
public abstract class Furniture
{
    public abstract void size();
}

import tools.Furniture;
class Chair extends Furniture
{
    public void size()
```

```
    {
        System.out.println("Kid's size");
    }
    public static void main(String[] args)
    {
        new Chair().size();
    }
}
```

a. Kid's size

b. Error in import statement

c. Error in package declaration

d. None of the above

22. What is the output?

```
interface Furniture
{
    int size = 3;
    void setSize(int n);
}

class Chair implements Furniture
{
    public void setSize(int i)
    {
        size = n;
        System.out.println(size);
    }
}
public class Test7
{
    public static void main(String[] args)
    {
        new Chair().setSize(4);
    }
}
```

a. Compilation error

b. No output

c. 4

d. Runtime exception

23. Choose all correct statements inside interface declarations:

```
interface Furniture
{
    int size = 3;    // statement-1
```

```
    static int size = 3; // statement-2
    public int size = 3;  // statement-3
    final int size = 3; // statement-4
}
```

    a. 1, 2, 3   b. 2, 3

    c. 2, 3, 4   d. 1, 2, 3, 4

24. Choose all correct declarations inside an interface:

```
interface Furniture
{
    public static int size = 3; // statement-1
    static final int size = 3; // statement-2
    public final int size = 3; // statement-3
    public static final int size = 3; // statement-4
}
```

    a. 1, 2, 3   b. 2, 3

    c. 2, 3, 4   d. 1, 2, 3, 4

25. What is the output?

```
public class Test7
{
    static enum TeaSize {SMALL, MEDIUM, LARGE};

    public static void main(String[] args)
    {
        TeaSize size = TeaSize.SMALL;
        System.out.println(size);
    }
}
```

    a. SMALL   b. 0

    c. 1   d. Compilation error

26. Find out the output?

```
public class Test7
{
    public static void main(String[] args)
```

```
{
    enum TeaSize {SMALL, MEDIUM, LARGE};
    TeaSize size = TeaSize.SMALL;
    System.out.println(size);
}
}
```

a. SMALL　　　　　　　　　　　　b. 0

c. 1　　　　　　　　　　　　　　d. Compilation error

27. Assume tools and tools2 are packages available inside a directory. What is the output?

```
package tools;
public class Furniture
{
    int i = 10;
    protected int j = 20;
}

package tools2;
import tools.*;
public class Chair extends Furniture
{
    public static void main(String[] args)
    {
        Furniture f = new Furniture();
        System.out.println(f.i + "," + f.j);
    }
}
```

a. 10 20　　　　　　　　　　　　b. 10 followed by exception

c. 20 followed by exception　　　　d. Compilation error

28. Assume *tools* is a subpackage of *tools2*. Then which of the following statements is correct?

```
package tools;
public class Furniture
{
    int i = 10;
    protected int j = 20;
}

package tools2;
```

```
import tools.Furniture;
public class Chair extends Furniture
{
    public static void main(String[] args)
    {
        Furniture f = new Furniture();
        System.out.println(f.i); // statement-1
        System.out.println(f.j); // statement-2

        Chair c = new Chair();
        System.out.println(c.i); // statement-3
        System.out.println(c.j); // statement-4
    }
}
```

    a. Statement-1   b. Statement-2

    c. Statement-3   d. Statement-4

29. What is the output?

```
public class Test7
{
    public static void main(String[] args)
    {
        char c = 'a';
        try
        {
            System.out.println((int)c);
        }
    }
}
```

    a. a   b. 97

    c. Error: try without catch   d. Error: try without finally

30. Find out the output:

```
public class Test7
{
    public static void main(String[] args)
    {
        char c = 'a';
        try
```

```
    {
          System.out.println((int)c);
    }
    c = (char) ((int)c + 2);
    finally
    {
          System.out.println(c);
    }
  }
}
```

a. Compilation error   b. 97, c

c. 97   d. 97, a

31. What is the output?

```
public class Test7
{
   public static void main(String[] args)
   {
      int x = 10;
      char c = 'a';
      try
      {
          x = x / 0;
          System.out.println((int)c);
      }
      catch (Exception e){}
      finally
      {
          System.out.println(c);
      }
   }
}
```

a. a   b. 97

c. 97 a   d. 97 a followsing by exception message

32. What is the output?

```
public class Test7
{
   public static void main(String[] args)
```

```
    {
        int[] a = {1,2,3};
        System.out.println(a[3]);
    }
}
```

    a. throws ArrayIndexOutOfBoundsException b. throws RuntimeException
    c. throws ArrayOutOfBoundsException   d. None of the above

33. What is the output?

```
public class Test7
{
    public static void main(String[] args) throws Exception
    {
        int x = 10, y = 0;
        System.out.println(x/y);
    }
}
```

    a. throws ArrayIndexOutOfBoundsException b. throws RuntimeException
    c. throws ArrayOutOfBoundsException   d. throws ArithmeticException

34. What is the output?

```
class A
{
    int x = 10;
}
public class Test7
{
    public static void main(String[] args)
    {
        A a = new A();
        A b = new A();
        a = null; b.x = 100;
        System.out.println(a.x + "," + b.x);
    }
}
```

    a. throws ArrayIndexOutOfBoundsException b. throws RuntimeException
    c. throws throws NullPointerException   d. throws ArithmeticException

35. What is the output?

```
class A
{
    int x = 10;
}
class B extends A
{
    int y = 20;
}
public class Test7
{
    public static void main(String[] args)
    {
        A a = new A();
        B b = (B)a;
        System.out.println(b.y);
    }
}
```

    a. throws ArrayIndexOutOfBoundsException b. throws throws NullPointerException

    c. throws ArithmeticException   d. throws ClassCastException

36. What is the output?

```
public class Test7
{
    static int x = 1;
    public static void m1() throws Exception
    {
        try
        {
            m2();
            m2();
            m2();
        }
        catch (Exception e) {System.out.println(x++); }
    }
    public static void m2() throws Exception
    {
        throw new Exception();
    }

    public static void main(String[] args) throws Exception
```

```
    {
        m1();
    }
}
```

a. 1 b. 1 2

c. 1 2 3 d. 1 1 1

37. What is the output?

```
public class Test7
{
    static int x = 1;

    public static void m1() throws Exception
    {
        x = x / 0;
    }

    public static void main(String[] args) throws Exception
    {
        try
        {
            m1();
        }
        catch(Exception e)
        {
            x++;
            throw new Exception();
        }
        System.out.println(x);
    }
}
```

a. 1 b. 2

c. Throws Exception d. Displays 1 indefinitely

38. Which of the following are true?

a. Enum constructors are not invoked directly

b. More than one argument is possible with enum constructor

c. Enum constructors can be overloaded

d. Enums are not strings or ints; they are instances

e. All of the above

39. What is the output?

```
class A
{
    public void m1() {System.out.print("A"); }
}
class B extends A
{
    public void m1() {System.out.print("B"); }
    public void m2() {System.out.print("C"); }
}
public class Test61
{
    public static void main(String[] args)
    {
        A a = new A();
        a.m1();
        a = new B();
        a.m1();
        a.m2();
    }
}
```

a. Compilation error   b. A B C

c. A A C   d. B B C

e. A followed by exception

40. What is the output?

```
class A {}
public class B extends A
{
    public void m1() {System.out.print("B"); }
    public static void main(String[] args)
    {
        A a = new B();
        B b = (B)a;
        b.m1();
    }
}
```

a. B   b. No output

c. Compilation error   d. throws ClassCastException

Answers

1. a	2. c	3. e	4. b	5. c	6. e	7. b	8. c	9. d	10. c
11. c	12. a	13. e	14. d	15. c	16. a	17. b	18. a	19. c	20. c, d
21. a	22. a	23. d	24. d	25. a	26. d	27. d	28. d	29. c, d	30. a
31. a	32. a	33. d	34. c	35. d	36. a	37. c	38. e	39. a	40. a

Short-answer Questions

1. What is an abstract class? Why do we need abstract classes?
2. Explain abstract class and abstract methods with an example.
3. What is an interface? Explain interfaces with an example.
4. Compare abstract classes and interfaces.
5. What is enum? Why do we need enums?
6. Explain advanced features of enum such as variables, methods and constructors of enum class.
7. Explain java package concepts with an example.
8. What is an exception? Explain exception handling concepts with an example.
9. Explain multi catch statement with an example.
10. Discuss exception hierarchy.
11. How to create user-defined exceptions?
12. Explain RuntimeException class with an example.

EXERCISES

7.1. Create an abstract class *Breakfast* with two abstract methods checkCarb(), and checkNutri-ents(). If carb count is less than 200, breakfast is healthy. If it contains all nutrients such as vitamins, minerals etc, breakfast is healthy. Create three sub classes *Indian, Mediterranean* and *Chinese* and all subclasses should override the two abstract methods by providing appropriate implementations. Create a public class that will create objects of these three breakfast imple-mentations, and call implementation methods.

7.2. Consider Exercise 6.6, create interface *Healthy* with a method *eat()* indicating this is eatable food. Class *Food* should implement *Healthy* and override eat() method. Let eat() display a mes-sage *You can eat this food.*

7.3. Consider Exercise 6.6, create interface *Juicy* with methods *squeeze()* to prepare juice and *drink()* to indicate it is a drinkable juice. Class *Fruit* should implement *Juicy* and override squeeze() and drink() methods. Let squeeze() display a message *Juice ready* and drink() display a message *Have a nice drink.* Test these classes and methods accordingly inside class *Lunch.*

7.4. Create enum *TrafficLight* with three constants RED, YELLOW and GREEN. Each constant has a string attribute, "stop", "wait" and "go" respectively. Define a method show() that displays the attribute values of each light. Create a public class that displays these three lights and their attribute values.

7.5. Create enum *Snacks* with three constants CHOCHOLATE(200), COOKIES(50), ICECREAM (100), where attribute values indicate calories of the snack. Define a method setCalories(int) that can change the attribute values of enum constants. Create a public class that will call setCalories() with a new value. Also display enum constants and their calories.

7.6. Create a package *tools* in the current directory and a subpackage *io* inside *tools* package. Create a class *Print* with a method s(String s) that prints a given string. Save Print onto *io* package. Create a class *PrintTest* in the current directory, import Print class and call s("hello") and check hello is printed onto the command window.

7.7. Provide overloaded methods for s() that will take variety of other types such as int, float, double, long and char. Test these overloaded methods.

7.8. Create an exception *NegativeBalanceException* with a data member private double *balance* and override *toString()* to print appropriate message. Create a public class *Account* with a data member *balance*. Assign values to *balance* and accordingly throw this exception.

PART III Java Containers for Holding Objects

8

Sequence Containers

OBJECTIVES

- To introduce *java.util* class hierarchy
- To create Vector object; add primitives, wrappers and objects to vector; and retrieve elements from vector
- To create Enumeration iterator to vectors and explain how to iterate over vector objects
- To implement type-specific vectors that will hold specific types only
- To create StringTokenizer with default delimiter and user-defined delimiters
- To create Stack and explain stack operation such as push and pop
- To implement type-safe stack
- To solve brackets matching problem using stacks
- To introduce Iterator interface and its methods
- To introduce Queue interface and queue implementations using PriorityQueue and LinkedList-based queue
- To explain creating ArrayList and type-safe ArrayList
- To solve shopping cart problem using array list
- To search a key in an array using ArrayList
- To merge two arrays using ArrayList
- To remove duplicates from an array using ArrayList
- To create LinkedList and explain all its methods
- To implement type-safe LinkedList

- To implement stack using linked list
- To create type-safe linked list-based stack using Generics

8.1 INTRODUCTION

Holding data inside an application is the fundamental requirement for solving any problem. Java has several ways to hold primitive data type values and objects (or rather, references to objects). In the previous chapters, the readers were introduced to some of the methods to store a single value or a collection of values. To hold a single value, variables were used and to store a set of values arrays were used.

The array is the most efficient container to store values and object references in a linear sequence. Also, array elements can be randomly accessed with the index. Apart from efficiency of random access, arrays are type specific. That means, arrays will store elements of the same type. For example, an *int* array will hold only integers and a *Dog* array will hold only dogs. Storing an inappropriate element to array will result into a compile time error. Java will notify all mistakes during compilation itself.

Though arrays are faster, they are static data structure which means array's size is fixed and cannot be changed once created, during runtime. For dynamic data structures, Java utilities library named **Collections** has a reasonably complete set of classes in *java.util* package that provide sophisticated ways to store objects and manipulate them. Whatever may be the container type such as **Lists, Maps** and Sets, all containers will store objects (wrapper types or user-defined types) as java.lang.Object, the root of all classes in Java. Since user objects are upcasted to Object type, you have lost the type information of your object. In other words, container classes will not bother about type checking at compile time. So you need to downcast into a specific type you want when you retrieve objects from the container. This is where arrays are better than containers.

Part 3 of this book containing four chapters focuses on Java's built-in support for data structures and algorithms. For the sake of simplicity, we refer to all collection classes and interfaces available in *java.util* package as containers. This chapter deals with all List containers. The Map and set containers are discussed in Chapters 9 and 10 respectively. Chapter 11 is devoted to the discussion on sorting and searching support available in java.util package. In this chapter, we will lead you to the understanding of all List and Queue types such as **Vector, StringTokenizer, Stack, PriorityQueue, ArrayList** and **LinkedList.** We will see the features of each container, its advantages and how to apply them to different problems.

8.2 COLLECTION TAXONOMY

Figure 8.1 depicts some important classes and interfaces of java.util package that we focus in this book. Readers are advised to refer to JDK documentation for complete list of class hierarchy. Here the coloured boxes indicate interfaces and others are classes. The List, Set and Map are top-level interfaces, along with their implementing classes we will be using very often. These classes and interfaces will be introduced to you gradually in this book.

8.3 VECTORS

The Vector class is one of the important classes for application development in Java. The Vector is a growable array of objects. Similar to arrays, it contains objects that can be accessed using an integer index. The size of the Vector can expand or shrink in order to accommodate adding and removing objects after the Vector has been created. Vector can be created as shown in Figure 8.2.

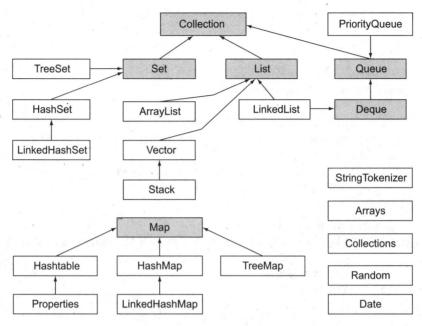

Figure 8.1. Collection and Map Taxonomy

Figure 8.2. Vector Instantiation

```
Vector v = new Vector();
Vector v = new Vector(Collection c);
```

Vectors can be created with a default constructor or it can also take any of the collection types such as List types, Set types or Map types. Remember Vector is also part of a Collection. So a vector can contain even another vector.

Once Vector is created, then objects can be added, removed and retrieved from it as and when required. Objects can be added to vector using **add()** and **addElement()** methods and retrieved using **get(index)** and **elementAt(index)** by the given index position. The size() method returns its size. The remove(index) and removeElementAt(index) methods remove an element at index and removeElement(o) removes object o.

Listing 8.1 depicts a course vector that will hold list of courses and manipulate its contents using various methods.

Listing 8.1. CourseVector

```
// CourseVector.java

import java.util.*;

public class CourseVector
```
{coderipe}

```java
{
    public static void main(String[] args)
    {
        // create a vector
        Vector v = new Vector();

        // courses hold strings
        String[] courses = {"BA", "BSc", "MCA", "BCA", "BE"};
        // add to v
        for(int i = 0; i < courses.length; i++)
            v.addElement(courses[i]);

        // retrieve second element
        System.out.println("Element 2: " + (String)v.elementAt(2));

        // add BArch to end of v
        v.add("BArch");

        // insert at 1
        v.add(1, "BCOM");

        // remove BCA
        v.removeElement("BCA");

        // remove at 0
        v.remove(0);

        // show elements using get()
        for(int i = 0; i < v.size(); i++)
            System.out.println((String)v.get(i));
    }
}
```

```
Element 2: MCA
BCOM
BSc
MCA
BE
BArch
```

Recall that Vector can hold object of any type in contrast to arrays. So, it is the responsibility of the developer to downcast into appropriate type while retrieving elements. In the above example, we downcast elements to String type while retrieving them from vector. Listing 8.2 illustrates type-specific problem of a vector.

Listing 8.2. Animals Vector

```java
//AnimalsVector.java
import java.util.*;

class Cat
{
    int i;
    public Cat(int j) { i = j; }
}

class Dog
{
    int i;
    public Dog(int j) { i = j; }
}

class Fish
{
    int i;
    public Fish(int j) { i = j; }
}

public class AnimalsVector
{
    public static void main(String[] args)
    {
        // create a vector object
        Vector animals = new Vector();

        // add animals
        animals.add(new Cat(2));
        animals.add(new Dog(5));
        animals.add(new Fish(9));

        // retrieve and downcast
        System.out.println("Displaying Animals");
        System.out.println("Cat number: " + ((Cat)animals.
        get(0)).i);
        System.out.println("Dog number: " + ((Dog)animals.
        get(1)).i);
        System.out.println("Fish number: " + ((Fish)animals.
get(2)).i);
```

```
    }
}
```

```
Displaying Animals
Cat number: 2
Dog number: 5
Fish number: 9
```

Here, animals vector contains objects of different types such as Dog, Cat and Fish. Therefore, objects have to be appropriately downcasted while retrieving using get() method.

8.3.1 Enumeration

Enumeration is the iteration interface that enables us to loop through the vector. With hasMoreElements() and nextElement() methods, you can check for elements and extract the next object. Listing 8.3 explains adding Cat objects to a vector and retrieving elements using enumeration.

Listing 8.3. Cats Using Enumeration

```
// CatEnumerator.java
import java.util.*;

class Cat
{
    int number;

    public Cat(int i) { number = i; }
}

public class CatEnumerator
{
    public static void main(String[] args)
    {
        Vector cats = new Vector();

        // add cats
        for (int i = 0; i < 5; i++)
                cats.add(new Cat(i));

        // show all cats
        Enumeration e = cats.elements();
        while (e.hasMoreElements())
                System.out.println("Cat number: " + ((Cat)
                e.nextElement()).number);
    }
}
```

```
Cat number: 0
Cat number: 1
Cat number: 2
Cat number: 3
Cat number: 4
```

8.3.2 Type-specific Vectors

Type-specific vectors can be created with Java generics. The type of the vector should be specified within < and > symbols while creating the vector as shown in Figure 8.3.

Figure 8.3. Type-specific Vector

```
Vector<object-type> name = new Vector<object-type>();
```

For example, let us create an Integer vector (see Listing 8.4) that will hold only Integers. Any attempt to add objects of any other type other than Integer will generate a compile time error.

Listing 8.4. Integer Vector

```java
// IntVector.java
import java.util.*;

public class IntVector
{
    public static void main(String[] args)
    {
        // create integer vector
        Vector<Integer> iv = new Vector<Integer>();

        // add elements to end of vector
        iv.addElement(new Integer(200))
        iv.add(new Integer(100));
        iv.addElement(500); // auto-boxing

        for(int i = 0; i < iv.size(); i++)
                System.out.println(iv.get(i)); // unboxing
    }
}
```

```
200
100
500
```

8.4 STRINGTOKENIZER

The StringTokenizer class splits a string into a number of tokens that are delimited by \s, \t, \n, \r and \f, by default. Delimiters can also be specified during initialization as a string. Figure 8.4 shows the syntax for StringTokenizer.

Figure 8.4. Syntax for StringTokenizer Class

```
StringTokenizer name = new StringTokenizer(string);
StringTokenizer name = new StringTokenizer(string, delimiter);
```

Once StringTokenizer is initialized, hasMoreTokens() and nextToken() methods can be used to check and return the tokens as strings as shown in Listing 8.5.

Listing 8.5. StringTokenizer for Address

```
// StringTokenizerTest.java                          {coderipe}
import java.io.*;
import java.util.*;

public class StringTokenizerTest
{
    public static void main(String[] args)
    {
        String s = "I am a bad boy";
        // create string tokenizer
        StringTokenizer st = new StringTokenizer(s);

        // show one token at a time
        while (st.hasMoreTokens())
            System.out.println(st.nextToken());

        String s2 = "Anita Trichy*Beryl Chennai*Cathy Bangalore";
        // create string tokenizer with delimiter *
        StringTokenizer st2 = new StringTokenizer(s2, "*");
        // show one token at a time
        while (st2.hasMoreTokens())
            System.out.println(st2.nextToken());

        // nested st
        StringTokenizer st3 = new StringTokenizer(s2, "*");
        while (st3.hasMoreTokens())
        {
            String str = st3.nextToken();
            // tokenize again
```

```
                    StringTokenizer st4 = new StringTokenizer(str);
                    while (st4.hasMoreTokens())
                            System.out.println(st4.nextToken());
            }
        }
}
```

```
I
am
a
bad
boy
Anita Trichy
Beryl Chennai
Cathy Bangalore
Anita
Trichy
Beryl
Chennai
Cathy
Bangalore
```

As StringTokenizer implements Enumeration, it can also be iterated using enumeration methods.

8.5 STACK

The Stack class supports a last-in-first-out (LIFO) behaviour of objects. The push() and pop() methods insert and remove objects, whereas peek() returns the top item on the stack. The empty() method tests whether the stack is empty or not and search(o) method returns the position of o from top. Stack will also behave as a vector as it inherits from Vector, and so usual Vector operations can be performed on Stack too.

Listing 8.6 creates a Stack to push names of months in the reverse order and pops them one at a time from the stack until the stack is empty.

Listing 8.6. Stack of Months

```
// MonthStack.java                                          {coderipe}

import java.io.*;
import java.util.*;


public class MonthStack
{
```

```java
    public static void main(String[] args)
    {
        Stack stk = new Stack();

        String[] months = {"Jan","Feb","Mar","Apr","May","Jun",
        "Jul","Aug","Sep","Oct","Nov","Dec"};

        // push months elements to stk
        for(int i = 0; i < months.length; i++)
                stk.push(months[i]);

        // pop until stack is not empty
        while (!stk.empty())
                System.out.println(stk.pop());
    }
}
```

```
Dec
Nov
Oct
Sep
Aug
Jul
Jun
May
Apr
Mar
Feb
Jan
```

8.5.1 Character Stack

As another example, let us generate random characters and hold them in a stack. Note that the application uses Random class' nextInt() to get a random number between 0 and 100.

Listing 8.7. Character Stack

```java
// CharStack.java
import java.util.*;

public class CharStack
{
```

```
public static void main(String[] args)
{
    // this stack can store only either char or Character
    object
    Stack<Character> stk = new Stack<Character>();

    // generate a random character and push
    Random r = new Random();

    for(int i = 0; i < 50; i++)
        stk.push((char)r.nextInt(100)); // chars between
            0 to 100

    // pop them all
    while(!stk.empty())
        System.out.print(stk.pop() + " ");
}
}
```

```
F & < X # \ A ? 5 ,   .   0   S N K . \ Z Q 5 c H   ] a - N < M 2
^ , > X C = ) +
```

8.5.2 Problem: Brackets Matching

Now, let us solve slightly big problem of brackets matching. Suppose we are given a long expression containing all three types of brackets (brackets, curly braces and square brackets). Our application has to check whether the expression has exact brackets or not. That is, for every open bracket there should be a closing bracket. Listing 8.8 shows the source code of this application.

Listing 8.8. Brackets Checking Application

```
// BracketChecker.java
import java.io.*;
import java.util.*;

public class BracketChecker
{
    public void match()
    {
        // create stack
        Stack<Character> stk = new Stack<Character>();

        // get an expression as a string
```

```
        Scanner sc = new Scanner(System.in);
        String expr = sc.nextLine();

        // take one char at a time
        for (int i = 0; i < expr.length(); i++)
        {
                // take one character at a time
                char c = expr.charAt(i);
                // check all three open bracket types
                if (c == '{' || c == '(' || c == '[' )
                        stk.push(c);
                else
                if (c == '}' || c == ')' || c == ']' )
                        stk.pop();
        }

        // if stk is empty, given expr is perfectly balanced
        if(stk.empty())
                System.out.println("The given expression " + expr +
                " is perfectly balanced");
        else
                System.out.println("The given expression" + expr +
                " is NOT perfectly balanced");
    }

    public static void main(String[] args)
    {
        BracketChecker m = new BracketChecker();
        m.match();
    }
}
```

```
The given expression a*(b+c)/d*{f-r} is perfectly
balanced
The given expression a*[b+c is NOT perfectly balanced
```

In this application, match() first receives an expression with all three bracket types from user as a string. Then, it takes one character at a time from the string and checks if it is any of the three open bracket types. If so, the character is pushed onto stack. If the character is of closing bracket types, then stack is popped once. Otherwise, the next character will be read and processed. This process will be repeated for all characters. The given expression is perfectly balanced if stack is empty.

8.6 ITERATORS

An **iterator** is, like a cursor, an object, similar to enumeration that is used to move through the objects and select each object from the container. The Iterator interface has two methods hasNext() and next() to check whether container has some more elements to be read and to retrieve the actual element.

8.7 PRIORITYQUEUE

PriorityQueue is the implementation of the Queue interface. PriorityQueue stores elements in first-in-first-out (FIFO) order, but not necessarily in this order. The offer() inserts an object to tail of queue. The remove() and poll() delete elements from head of queue. The element() and peek() return the head of queue without deleting it. If you want to preserve the order of insertion, then create a queue with LinkedList.

As an illustration, assume a supermarket has one billing counter where each user's shopping basket will be billed. There are many customers waiting for billing in the queue. New customers will also join the queue. Listing 8.9 simulates this supermarket scenario.

Listing 8.9. Supermarket Queue

```java
// SupermarketQueue.java
import java.util.*;

public class SuperMarketQueue
{
    Queue billingCounter;

    public SuperMarketQueue(Queue q)
    {
        billingCounter = q;
    }

    public void addCustomer(int c)
    {
        // add customer to counter
        billingCounter.offer(c);
    }

    public void service()
    {
        // complete billing for a customer at front
        if(!billingCounter.isEmpty())
            System.out.println("Customer " + billingCounter.
            poll() + " serviced");
    }
```

```java
    public void show()
    {
        System.out.println("Current Queue: " + billingCounter);
    }

    public static void main(String[] args)
    {
        // create 5 customers
        int max = 5;

        Random r = new Random();

        // create q with PriorityQueue
        SuperMarketQueue q = new SuperMarketQueue(new
        PriorityQueue());

        System.out.println("Priority queue based queue");
        // process customers
        q.addCustomer(r.nextInt(100));q.show();
        q.addCustomer(r.nextInt(100));q.show();
        q.service();q.show();
        q.addCustomer(r.nextInt(100));q.show();
        q.service();q.show();

        // create q with LinkedList
        q = new SuperMarketQueue(new LinkedList());
        System.out.println("Linkedlist-based queue");

        // process customers
        q.addCustomer(r.nextInt(100));q.show();
        q.addCustomer(r.nextInt(100));q.show();
        q.service();q.show();
        q.addCustomer(r.nextInt(100));q.show();
        q.service();q.show();
    }
}
```

```
Priority queue based queue
Current Queue: [36]
Current Queue: [36, 89]
Customer 36 serviced
Current Queue: [89]
Current Queue: [83, 89]
Customer 83 serviced
```

```
Current Queue: [89]
Linkedlist-based queue
Current Queue: [21]
Current Queue: [21, 9]
Customer 21 serviced
Current Queue: [9]
Current Queue: [9, 58]
Customer 9 serviced
Current Queue: [58]
```

In this program, queue is created with PriorityQueue and LinkedList. As discussed earlier, PriorityQueue need not maintain the queue's FIFO behaviour. But, LinkedList-based queue maintains FIFO ordering of customers. The readers will learn more about LinkedList in section 8.9. The rest of the program is trivial. You add customers to queue with offer() and service them one at a time from head of the queue using poll(). You service customers if queue is not empty. The isEmpty() checks whether queue is empty or not.

8.8 ARRAYLIST

Both ArrayList and LinkedList are two types of List interface. The List interface defines add() method to insert objects, get() to retrieve objects and remove() to delete an object or an object by index and size() returns size of the List. The List returns both iterator() and the sophisticated listIterator() that are useful for ArrayList and LinkedList. One important point about List, it allows duplicate elements.

ArrayList is the resizable array implementation for the list. ArrayLists support faster random access to elements, but relatively slow for insertion and deletion of elements. ArrayList is an exact equivalent of Vector class but it is unsynchronized. Listing 8.10 explains various methods of ArrayList class.

Listing 8.10. ArrayList Operations

```java
// ArrayList1.java                                    {coderipe}
import java.util.*;

public class ArrayList1
{
    public static void main(String[] args)
    {
        // create array list
        ArrayList list = new ArrayList();

        String[] breakfast = {"Cake", "Bread", "Omelet", "Juice",
        "Coke"};

        // add to list at the end
        for(int i = 0; i < breakfast.length; i++)
```

```
            list.add(breakfast[i]);

    list.add(1, "Coffee"); // at location 1

    String s = (String)list.get(2);  // returns 2nd element
    list.remove(0);  // oth element removed
    list.remove("Coke");  // this object removed

    // iterate throught list
    Iterator it = list.iterator();
    while(it.hasNext())
            System.out.println(it.next());

    list.add("French Fries");

    // also supports list iterator
    ListIterator lit = list.listIterator();
    while(lit.hasNext())
            System.out.println(lit.next());

    // also you can up cast to List
    List lt = new ArrayList();
    }
}
```

```
Coffee
Bread
Omlet
Juice
Coffee
Bread
Omlet
Juice
French Fries
```

8.8.1 Type-Safe ArrayLists

You can create a type-safe array list using generics very similar to type-safe Vector that you have created in section 8.3.2. The syntax for creating type-safe array list is shown in Figure 8.5.

Figure 8.5. Type-safe Array List

```
ArrayList<object-type> name = new ArrayList<object-type>();
```

Here, object-type can be any of the wrapper class types or any Java object including user-defined object types. Example 8.1 depicts the creation of array list which can hold objects of type, class Item.

Example 8.1. Array List of Items

```
class Item { }
ArrayList<Item> items = new ArrayList<Item>();
```

In this example, items will hold an array of objects of type Item class.

8.8.2 Problem: Shopping Cart

Listing 8.11 illustrates shopping cart application. Here, shopping list is a collection of items in which each item has its name. Items are added to array list first and all names of items are retrieved and displayed from the list.

Listing 8.11. Shopping Cart Application

```java
// ShoppingCart.java
import java.util.*;

class Item
{
    String name;
    public Item(String s) { name = s; }
}

public class ShoppingCart
{
    public static void main(String[] args)
    {
        // create list of items
        String[] purchase = {"Laptop", "Pen", "Notebook"};

        // type-specific arraylist
        ArrayList<Item> list = new ArrayList<Item>();

        // add to list
        for(int i = 0; i < purchase.length; i++)
            list.add(new Item(purchase[i]));

        // show
        ListIterator it = list.listIterator();
```

```
        while(it.hasNext())
              System.out.println(((Item)it.next()).name);
    }
}
```

```
Laptop
Pen
Notebook
```

8.8.3 Problem: Search an Element Inside Array

In Chapter 3, the readers were introduced to how to perform sequential search for a key in a given array. You can easily check for an element in ArrayList using contains() method. The reader can also use indexOf() that returns the first occurrence of the key. Here is an example depicted in Listing 8.12 that will check for a vowel.

Listing 8.12. Vowel Test

```
//SearchArrayList.java
import java.util.*;

public class SearchArrayList
{
    public static void main(String[] args)
    {
        Scanner sc = new Scanner(System.in);

        String[] vowels = {"a", "e", "i", "o", "u"};

        // create array list from array
        List list = new ArrayList(Arrays.asList(vowels));

        // get a character
        System.out.println("Enter a character");
        String key = sc.next();
        // check if exists in list
        if(list.contains(key))
              System.out.println(key + " is a vowel");
        else
              System.out.println(key + " is NOT a vowel");
    }
}
```

```
Enter a character
u
u is a vowel

Enter a character
U
U is NOT a vowel
```

Here, Arrays.asList() converts the given array into a list with which ArrayList object is instantiated.

8.8.4 Problem: Merge Two Arrays

Assume you have two arrays of same type and you just want to merge these two arrays. Once you convert the given arrays into array lists, you can easily merge using addAll() method that merges the given argument list to the instance list as illustrated in Listing 8.13.

Listing 8.13. Case-insensitive Vowel Test

```java
//MergeArrays.java
import java.util.*;

public class MergeArrays
{
    public static void main(String[] args)
    {
        Scanner sc = new Scanner(System.in);

        String[] vowel1 = {"a", "e", "i", "o", "u"};
        String[] vowel2 = {"A", "E", "I", "O", "U"};

        // create array list from array
        List list1 = new ArrayList(Arrays.asList(vowel1));
        List list2 = new ArrayList(Arrays.asList(vowel2));

        //merge
        list1.addAll(list2);

        // get a character
        System.out.println("Enter a character");
        String key = sc.next();

        if(list1.contains(key))
                System.out.println(key + " is a vowel");
```

```
        else
            System.out.println(key + " is NOT a vowel");
    }
}
```

```
Enter a character
e
e is a vowel

Enter a character
E
E is a vowel
```

In this application, both lowercase and uppercase vowels are merged into a single list. Thereby this application recognizes vowels case insensitively.

8.8.5 Problem: Remove All Duplicates in an Array

Another interesting array processing is the removal of duplicates in a given array. The remove() deletes the first occurrence of the element from the array list. Here the idea is to remove all occurrences of an element in an array and insert back the first occurrence to the list as illustrated in Listing 8.14.

Listing 8.14. Remove Duplicate Objects

```
//RemoveDuplicates.java
import java.util.*;

public class RemoveDuplicates
{
    public static void main(String[] args)
    {
        Scanner sc = new Scanner(System.in);
        String[] alphabet = {"z", "a", "b", "c", "a", "d",
        "e", "a", "f", "a", "g", "a"};

        // create array list from array
        List list = new ArrayList(Arrays.asList(alphabet));

        // get a character
        System.out.println("Enter a duplicate char to
        remove");
        String key = sc.next();
```

```
        System.out.println("Given array: " + list.
        toString());
        // loc keeps location of first occurrence of key
        int loc = 0;

        // remove all occurrences of key
        for(int i = 0; i < list.size(); i++)
        {
                list.remove(key);
                // keep first occurrence in loc, ignore otherwise
                if(loc == 0)
                        loc = i;
        }

        // keep first occurrence back in list
        list.add(loc, key);

        // show list
        System.out.println("After duplicates removed: "
        + list.toString());
    }
}
```

```
Enter a duplicate char to remove
a
Given array: [z, a, b, c, a, d, e, a, f, a, g, a]
After duplicates removed: [z, a, b, c, d, e, f, g]
```

There is another interesting collection that will not allow you to add duplicates. So you need not have to worry about eliminating duplicate elements. It is called *set* and will be introduced in Chapter 10.

8.9 LINKEDLIST

The LinkedList is another container that will store elements in a sequence. LinkedLists are highly inexpensive for insertion and deletion operations, but relatively slow for random access. ArrayList scores better for random access.

LinkedList supports several methods with which we can design other containers such as stack, queue and deque. The add(), addFirst() and addLast() methods allow us to add elements to linked list. The get(), getFirst() and getLast() methods retrieve elements from linked list. Similarly, remove(), removeFirst() and removeLast() methods delete elements. Contains() checks for an element and size() returns the size. Listing 8.15 explains the various methods of LinkedList class.

Listing 8.15. LinkedList Illustration

```java
// LinkedList1.java
import java.util.*;

public class LinkedList1
{
    public static void main(String[] args)
    {
        LinkedList list = new LinkedList();

        // add 10 integers
        for(int i = 0; i < 10; i++)
            list.add(i);

        list.addFirst(20);  // add 20 first
        list.add(50);  // add 50 to end
        list.addLast(100); // add 100 at last
        list.add(11, 30); // add 30 as 11th element
        System.out.println(list);  // show list

        System.out.println("5: " + list.get(5)); // retrieve 5th element
        System.out.println("get first: " + list.getFirst()); // get first
        System.out.println("get last: " + list.getLast()); // get last

        list.remove(); // deletess first element
        list.remove(1); // deletes element at 1
        list.removeFirst();  // delete first
        list.removeLast();  // delete last
        System.out.println(list); // show list

        System.out.println("contains 50: " + list.contains(50)); //
        checks for 50
        // iterate from 3rd element
        ListIterator lt = list.listIterator(3);
        while (lt.hasNext())
            System.out.println(lt.next());

        // insert few characters
        Random r = new Random();
        for(int i = 0; i < 5; i++)
            list.add((char)r.nextInt(130));
        System.out.println(list);
    }
}
```

```
[20, 0, 1, 2, 3, 4, 5, 6, 7, 8, 9, 30, 50, 100]
5: 4
get first: 20
get last: 100
[2, 3, 4, 5, 6, 7, 8, 9, 30, 50]
contains 50: true
5
6
7
8
9
30
50
[2, 3, 4, 5, 6, 7, 8, 9, 30, 50, , T, m, /, "]
```

In the above example, we add integers as primitives and characters to LinkedList using automatic boxing and unboxing methods. Using generics, we can create type-safe linked list that holds only the specific values like arrays.

8.9.1 Problem: Designing Stack Using LinkedList

Stack can also be created using LinkList class. LinkedList supports methods such as AddFirst() and getFirst() that will allow us to create our stack. Listing 8.16 depicts a linked list-oriented stack.

Listing 8.16. LLStack

```java
// LLStack.java
package tools;
import java.util.*;

class LLStack
{
    // create LinkedList
    private LinkedList list = new LinkedList();

    // push object to list
    public void push(Object o)
    {
        list.addFirst(o);
    }

    // pop from list
    public Object pop()
    {
```

```
        if(!list.isEmpty())
            return list.removeFirst();
        return "Stack empty, cannot pop";
    }

    // check stack top without removing
    public Object peek()
    {
        return list.getFirst();
    }

    // check stack is empty or not
    public boolean empty()
    {
        return list.isEmpty();
    }
}
```

So it is time for us to try our stack LLStack instead of java.util's legacy Stack class for the brackets checking application. Assume LLStack is stored in tools package, so that our application will import tools package. Listing 8.17 illustrates our new BracketChecker application.

Listing 8.17. Brackets Checking Using LLStack

```
// BracketCheckerLLStack.java
import java.io.*;
import java.util.*;
import tools.*;

public class BracketCheckerLLStack
{
    public void match()
    {
        // Create LLStack object
        LLStack stk = new LLStack();
        // rest of code is same as BracketChecker
    }

    public static void main(String[] args)
    {
        BracketCheckerLLStack m = new BracketCheckerLLStack();
        m.match();
    }
}
```

```
The given expression 1*(2+3)/{5-8} is perfectly balanced
The given expression 1*(2+3/{5-8} is NOT perfectly balanced
```

The above application uses our linked list-based LLStack to check proper nesting of parenthesis in a given expression. However, there is one issue with our LLStack. Our LLStack is not type-safe. In other words, it has been designed to push and pop elements as java.lang.Object. So now we need to design our LLStack as generic one such that it will hold only type-safe elements.

8.9.2 Type-safe LLStack Using Generics

We have designed our stack named LLStack as depicted in Listing 8.17. However our LLStack suffers from one important issue that is it is not type-safe. You can push any object to LLStack, it will not bother. But, this will not be preferred. We want to design our LLStack as type-safe stack. Java Generics allows us to create a class as a generic class. A class can be created as a generic class by parameterizing it with a type T.

Listing 8.18 shows a type-safe stack based on linkedlist. It allows you to push only integers and no other primitives or object type is allowed.

Listing 8.18. Generic LL-based Stack

```java
// GenericLLStack.java
import java.util.*;

class GenericLLStack<T>
{
    private LinkedList<T> list = new LinkedList<T>();

    public void push(T o)
    {
        list.addFirst(o);
    }

    public T pop()
    {
        return list.removeFirst();
    }

    public T peek()
    {
        return list.getFirst();
    }

    public boolean empty()
```

```
    {
        return list.isEmpty();
    }
    public void show()
    {
        ListIterator it = list.listIterator();
        while (it.hasNext())
                System.out.print(it.next() + " " );
    }

    public static void main(String[] args)
    {
        GenericLLStack<Integer> stk = new
        GenericLLStack<Integer>();
        System.out.println("Integer stack");
        stk.push(2);
        stk.push(3);
        System.out.println("pop: " + stk.pop());
        stk.push(9);
        stk.push(99);
        stk.show();

        //stk.push("Hello"); Error

        GenericLLStack<Character> cstk = new
        GenericLLStack<Character>();
        System.out.println("\ncharacter stack");
        cstk.push('A');
        cstk.push('X');
        System.out.println("pop: " + cstk.pop());
        cstk.push('D');
        cstk.push('W');
        cstk.show();
    }
}
```

```
Integer stack
pop: 3
99 9 2
character stack
pop: X
W D A
```

8.10 SUMMARY

1. The java.util package includes few important interfaces such as Collection, Set, List, Queue and Map. It also includes their corresponding implementations
2. It contains some important classes Collections, Arrays, Random, Date and StringTokenizer
3. The Vector is a growable array that can hold any primitives or objects of any type
4. The Vector can be created type-safe using generics
5. Enumeration is an iterator that can move through a vector
6. StringTokenizer will split a string into series of tokens
7. The split() method of String class can also split string into an array of strings
8. The Stack supports LIFO behaviour. Stack can also be used as vector as it extends Vector
9. Stack can be made type-safe
10. Java 1.2 supports Iterator interface, besides Enumeration interface
11. PriorityQueue is the implementation for Queue interface. It simulates FIFO behaviour, but not necessarily
12. Design LinkedList-based Queue to obtain exact FIFO behaviour
13. ArrayList and LinkedList are the two List implementations
14. ArrayList is the resizable array implementation for the list. ArrayLists support faster random access to elements, but relatively slow for insertion and deletion of elements
15. LinkedLists are fast for insertion and deletion of elements
16. ArrayList and LinkedList can be created type-safe
17. Data structures such as stack, queue, trees and doubly linked lists can be created using LinkedList class
18. Generics can be applied to classes so that type-safe classes can be created

KEY TERMS

ArrayList, 254	LinkedList, 254	Stack, 254
Collections, 254	Lists, 254	StringTokenizer, 254
Enumeration, 258	Maps, 254	Vector, 254
Iterator, 265	PriorityQueue, 254	

REVIEW QUESTIONS

Multiple-choice Questions

1. What is the output?

```
class Train
{
    public boolean equals(Object o)
```

```
    {
        boolean b = false;
        if (o instanceof Train)
            b = true;
        return b;
    }
}
    public class Test8
    {
        public static void main(String[] args)
        {
            Train t1 = new Train();
            Train t2 = new Train();

            if(t1.equals(t2))
                System.out.println("same");
            else
                System.out.println("not same");
        }
}
```

a. Same

b. Not same

c. Compilation error

d. Runtime exception

2. Which of the following is an overridden method?

```
class Train
{
    public boolean equals(Train o)  {} // method1
    public boolean equals(Object o) {} // method2
    boolean equals(Object o) { } // method3
    boolean equals(Train o) {  } // method4
}
```

a. method1

b. method2

c. method3

d. method4

3. For a given identical objects o1 and o2, if o1.equals(o2) returns true, then o2.equals(o1) will be

a. True

b. False

c. May be true

d. May be false

4. Which of the following in an interface?

a. Collection

b. Collection

c. Collections

d. None of the above

5. Which of the following is not an ordered collection?
   - a. Hashtable
   - b. ArrayList
   - c. LinkedHashSet
   - d. All of the above

6. Which of the following allows us to access elements by its index?
   - a. ArrayList
   - b. Vector
   - c. LinkedList
   - d. All of the above

7. Which of the following collection supports fast iteration and fast random access?
   - a. ArrayList
   - b. Vector
   - c. LinkedList
   - d. None of the above

8. Which of the following supports fast insertion and deletion?
   - a. ArrayList
   - b. Vector
   - c. LinkedList
   - d. None of the above

9. Which of the following implements RandomAccess interface?
   - a. ArrayList
   - b. Vector
   - c. LinkedList
   - d. None of the above

10. Which of the following implements Queue interface?
   - a. ArrayList
   - b. Vector
   - c. LinkedList
   - d. None of the above

11. When will you use Vector over ArrayList?
   - a. To override hashcode()
   - b. To support thread safety
   - c. To override equals()
   - d. ArrayList is always the best

12. Which of the following interfaces does not allow duplicates?
   - a. List
   - b. Map
   - c. Set
   - d. All of the above

13. I need a collection which does not allow duplicates, preserve insertion order and natural sorted order. Which of the following is the best for me?
   - a. ArrayList
   - b. HashSet
   - c. LinkedHashSet
   - d. TreeSet

14. I need a collection which does not allow duplicates, but maintains the insertion order. Which of the following is the best for me?
   - a. ArrayList
   - b. HashSet
   - c. LinkedHashSet
   - d. TreeSet

15. I need a collection which does not allow duplicates, but maintains the natural order. Which of the following is the best for me?
   - a. ArrayList
   - b. HashSet
   - c. LinkedHashSet
   - d. TreeSet

16. Which of the following interfaces define methods to store key-value pairs?
    a. List
    b. Map
    c. Set
    d. None of the above

17. I need a collection that stores key-value pairs. I do not worry about the insertion order or natural order. Which of the following is the best for me?
    a. HashSet
    b. HashMap
    c. LinkedHashMap
    d. None of the above

18. Which of the following is a thread-safe collection?
    a. Hashtable
    b. HashTable
    c. HashMap
    d. Hashmap
    e. None of the above

19. Which of the following stores key-value pairs and supports faster iteration?
    a. HashMap
    b. LinkedHashMap
    c. TreeMap
    d. None of the above

20. Which of the following stores key-value pairs and supports faster insertion and deletion?
    a. HashMap
    b. LinkedHashMap
    c. TreeMap
    d. None of the above

21. Which of the following stores key-value pairs and maintains natural sorted order?
    a. HashMap
    b. LinkedHashMap
    c. TreeMap
    d. None of the above

22. Which of the following is used to store key-value pairs?
    a. Set
    b. Map
    c. HashMap
    d. List

23. What is the correct way of creating ArrayList?

    1. ArrayList list1 = new ArrayList();
    2. List list2 = new ArrayList();
    3. List<String> list3 = new ArrayList<String>();
    4. List<String> list3 = new ArrayList<>();

    a. 1 and 2
    b. 3 and 4
    c. 2 and 3
    d. All of the above

24. What is the output?

```
ArrayList l = new ArrayList();
l.add(100);
l.add('a');
l.add("hello");
l.add(10.25);
System.out.println(l);
```

a. 100 10.25

b. 100 10.25 a

c. hello

d. Displays all

25. What is the output?

```
ArrayList l = new ArrayList();
l.add(100); l.add('a'); l.add("hello"); l.add(10.25);
Collections.sort(l);
System.out.println(l);
```

a. Compilation error
b. ClassCastException
c. Displays 100 and throws NullPointerException
d. None of the above

26. Find out the output?

```
ArrayList l = new ArrayList();
l.add(100); l.add("hello"); l.add(10.25);
System.out.println(l.contains(100));
```

a. True

b. False

c. Compilation error

d. Runtime exception

27. What is the output?

```
ArrayList l = new ArrayList();
l.add('r'); l.add('a'); l.add('x'); l.add('d');
Collections.sort(l);
System.out.println(l);
```

a. [a,d,r,x]

b. [r,a,x,d]

c. [x,r,d,a]

d. random order because of unique hash code

28. What is the output?

```
ArrayList<Integer> l = new ArrayList<Integer>();
l.add(2);
l.add(20.0);
System.out.println(l);
```

a. [2, 20.0]

b. 2 followed by NullPointerException

c. Compilation error

d. ClassCastException

29. What is the output?

```
ArrayList<Integer, String> l = new ArrayList<Integer, String>();
l.add(1, "A");
l.add(2, "B");
l.add(1, "C");
System.out.println(l);
```

    a. [1A, 2B, 1C]   b. [2B, 1C]

    c. [1A, 2B]   d. Compilation error

30. What is the output?

```
class Ball
{
    static int i = 1;
    public String toString()
    { return "Ball" + (i++); }
}
public class Test8
{
    public static void main(String[] args)
    {
        ArrayList<Ball> l = new ArrayList<Ball>();
        l.add(new Ball());
        l.add(new Ball());
        l.add(new Ball());
        System.out.println(l);
    }
}
```

    a. Ball0 Ball0 Ball0   b. Ball1 Ball1 Ball1

    c. Ball0 Ball1 Ball2   d. Ball1 Ball2 Ball3

31. What is the output?

```
Vector v = new Vector();
for(int i = 0; i < 3; i++)
    v.add(0);
System.out.println(v);
```

    a. 000   b. 012

    c. 123   d. None of the above

32. Find out the output?

```
Vector v = new Vector();
for(int i = 0; i < 3; i++)
    v.add(i);
for(int i = 0; i < 3; i++)
    System.out.print(v.get(i));
```

    a. 012   b. 123

    c. 000   d. 111

33. Choose the incorrect array list declaration:

```
class Ball{}
1. List<Ball> l1 = new ArrayList<Ball>();
2. ArrayList<List<Ball>> l2 = new ArrayList<List<Ball>>();
3. List<List<Ball>> l3 = new ArrayList<ArrayList<Ball>>();
4. ArrayList<List<Ball>> l4 = new ArrayList<List<Ball>>();
```

    a. 1   b. 2

    c. 3   d. 4

34. What is the output?

```
class Ball
{
    static int i = 1;
    public String toString()
    { return "Ball" + (i++); }
}
public class Test8
{
    public static void main(String[] args)
    {
        Vector<Ball> v = new Vector<Ball>();
        for(int i = 0; i < 3; i++)
            v.add(new Ball());
        for(int i = 0; i < 3; i++)
            System.out.print(v.get(i));
    }
}
```

    a. Ball0 Ball0 Ball0   b. Ball1 Ball1 Ball1

    c. Ball0 Ball1 Ball2   d. Ball1 Ball2 Ball3

35. How many tokens in the following string?

```
String s = "I am bad you are good";
StringTokenizer st = new StringTokenizer(s, "*");
```

    a. 6   b. 4

    c. 1   d. None of the above

36. What is the output?

```
String s = "I*am*bad//you//are**bad";
StringTokenizer st = new StringTokenizer(s, "*/");
while(st.hasMoreTokens())
    System.out.print(st.nextToken() +" ");
```

    a. I am bad you are bad   b. I am bad/you/are*bad

    c. I am bad//you//are bad   d. I*am*bad you are**bad

    e. None of the above

37. What is the output?

```
public class Test8
{
    public static void main(String[] args)
    {
        Stack stk = new Stack();
        String s = "a b c d";
        StringTokenizer st = new StringTokenizer(s);
        while(st.hasMoreTokens())
            stk.push(st.nextToken());
        while(!stk.empty())
            System.out.print(stk.pop());
    }
}
```

    a. a b c d   b. d c b a

    c. abcd   d. dcba

38. What is the output?

```
Stack stk = new Stack();
stk.push("1");
```

```
stk.add("2");
System.out.print(stk.get(1));
stk.pop();
stk.push("1");
System.out.print(stk.push("2") + "" + stk.pop());
```

    a. 122   b. 222

    c. 212   d. 211

39. What is the output?

```
String s = "I am bad you are good";
StringTokenizer st = new StringTokenizer(s, "*");
while(st.hasNext())
   System.out.print(st.next +" ");
```

    a. I am bad you are good

    b. Iambadyouaregood

    c. Compilation error

    d. No output

40. What is the output?

```
PriorityQueue pq = new PriorityQueue();
pq.offer("1");
pq.add("2");
System.out.print(pq.peek());
System.out.print(pq.poll());
pq.offer("2");
pq.add("1");
pq.remove();
System.out.print(pq.peek());
```

    a. 122   b. 121

    c. 112   d. 221

41. What is the output?

```
String[] a = {"1", "2", "3", "4"};
List l = new ArrayList(Arrays.asList(a));
if(l.contains(2) && !l.isEmpty())
   System.out.println(l);
```

a. [1,2,3,4]   b. 1234

c. Compilation error   d. No output

42. What is the output?

```
String[] a = {"1", "2"};
String[] b = {"1", "2"};
List l1 = new ArrayList(Arrays.asList(a));
List l2 = new ArrayList(Arrays.asList(b));
l1.addAll(l2);
System.out.println(l1 + "," + l2);
```

a. [1,2], [1,2]   b. [1,1,2,2], [2,1]

c. [1,2,1,2], [1,2]   d. None of the above

43. What is the output?

```
LinkedList l = new LinkedList();
l.add("1");
l.addFirst("2");
l.addLast("3");
l.remove(1);
System.out.print(l.getFirst());
System.out.print(l.add("1") + "" + l.removeFirst());
```

a. 12   b. 123

c. 1231   d. 2true2

44. What is the output?

```
public class Test8
{
    public static void main(String[] args)
    {
        Test8 t = new Test8();
        System.out.println(t);
    }
}
```

a. Prints hashcode   b. Prints t

c. Prints true   d. None of the above

45. What is the output?

```
class Car
{
   public String toString()
   {
      return "Benz";
   }
}
public class Test8
{
   public static void main(String[] args)
   {
      Car car = new Car();
      System.out.println(car);
   }
}
```

a. Benz   b. Car

c. Car   d. Null

46. For a given two objects o1 and o2, if o1.equals(o2) is true, then the hashcode of these objects will be

a. Same

b. Different

c. Hashcode will not be generated for identical objects

d. None of the above

47. What is the output?

```
class A {}
public class Test8
{
   public static void main(String[] args)
   {
      A a1 = new A();
      System.out.println(a1.hashCode());
   }
}
```

a. Prints hash code   b. Prints some random number

c. Prints garbage value given by GC   d. None of the above

Answers

1. a	2. b	3. a	4. b	5. a	6. d	7. a	8. c	9. a, b	10. c
11. b	12. c	13. b	14. c	15. d	16. b	17. a	18. a	19. a	20. b
21. c	22. c	23. d	24. d	25. b	26. a	27. a	28. c	29. d	30. d
31. a	32. a	33. c	34. d	35. c	36. a	37. b	38. a	39. c	40. c
41. d	42. c	43. d	44. a	45. a	46. a	47. a			

Short-answer Questions

1. Explain the important java.util classes and interfaces hierarchy.
2. Explain important methods of Vector class.
3. What are the advantages of Enumeration interface?
4. How Enumeration differs from Iterator interface?
5. What are the default delimiters for StringTokenizer?
6. Explain Stack with suitable example.
7. Can Stack behave like a Vector?
8. Explain important methods of PriorityQueue.
9. Differentiate Vector and ArrayList.
10. Explain important methods of LinkedList.
11. Create a doubly linked list using only LinkedList methods.
12. Create a circular linked list using only LinkedList methods.

EXERCISES

8.1. Design a class *BookShop* with the following details

- private Vector bookShelf that will store only *Book* objects
- addBook(Book b) inserts a book to bookShelf
- addBook(Book b, int i) inserts book *b* at location *i* to bookShelf
- removeBook(Book b) removes a book from bookShelf
- removeBook(int i) removes book *i* from bookShelf
- show() displays all books in the bookShelf
- sort() sorts all books according to the title
- Make use of the Book class from chapter 6

8.2. Modify the above exercise so that bookShelf is a LinkedList instead of a Vector.
8.3. Evaluate the given arithmetic expression using stack. The expression can have one or more of the bracket types.
8.4. Convert the given infix expression to postfix form using stack.
8.5. Create a String vector with few strings and clone it.
8.6. Create a string vector with few strings and linked list with few Strings. Add elements of vector and linked list together.
8.7. Develop an application to solve Josephus problem.

9

Map Containers

OBJECTIVES

- To introduce Map interface with an overview of its three implementation types
- To create Hashtable and store key-value pairs to Hashtable
- To add collections such as LinkedList and iterators to Hashtable
- To solve word counting of a text problem
- To check bracket pairs and brackets nesting in an expression
- To introduce HashMap and explain its methods
- To explain multimaps and nested HashMaps
- To explain LinkedHashMap to store pairs of elements
- To introduce TreeMaps and explain its natural ordering of its pairs
- To solve random number generation problem
- To explain how to create a property file
- To populate Hashtable pairs from a file using Properties class

9.1 INTRODUCTION

In Chapter 8, the readers were introduced to containers that will hold elements in sequence. List containers such as arrays and linked lists hold elements in a sequence. Each list type has some merits. ArrayList is efficient like arrays. LinkedList is quick for insertion and deletion operations. **Map** is an interface that will associate keys and their values, similar to dictionaries keeping words and their meanings. In this chapter, the readers will be introduced to three flavours of Map implementations namely **HashMap**, **LinkedHashMap** and **TreeMap**. All these maps have the same basic map interface, but they differ in behaviours including efficiency and the order in which key-value pairs are held.

Performance of Maps is relatively better than Lists. Searching through ArrayList is slower, compared to searching for a key in HashMap. Maps use hash code for efficient search. This results in dramatic improvements in performance. LinkedHashMap makes insertion and deletion much faster, whereas TreeMap maintains natural ordering of its pairs. Apart from these maps, you will also be introduced to **Hashtable**, an old legacy class in earlier JDK versions and Properties which will load pairs from files.

9.2 HASHTABLE

Hashtable is an another interesting container that maps keys to values. Any non-null object can be used as key or value. Hashtable is thread-safe and cloneable. Hashtable is a legacy class in util package. The put() inserts key and value to Hashtable, whereas get() retrieves value for the given key. The keys() and elements() return an Enumeration. The containsValue() and containsKey() check the value and key. The equals() checks the given object and remove() deletes a pair given key.

Listing 9.1 creates a Hashtable that will store user login details such as user name and his password.

Listing 9.1. Login Hashtable

```java
import java.io.*;
import java.util.*;

public class HashtableTest
{
    public static void main(String[] args)
    {
        Hashtable login = new Hashtable(); // stores key-value
        pairs
        login.put("alex", "12ff");
        login.put("rex", "123ff");
        login.put("john", "235ff");

        System.out.println("login.get(alex):" + login.get("alex"));
        System.out.println("login.contains(123ff): " + login.
        contains("123ff"));
        System.out.println("login.containsKey(rex): " + login.
        containsKey("rex"));

        System.out.println("All keys");
        Enumeration ekeys = login.keys(); // all keys
        while(ekeys.hasMoreElements())
                System.out.println(ekeys.nextElement());

        System.out.println("All values");
        Enumeration evalues = login.elements(); // all values
        while(evalues.hasMoreElements())
                System.out.println(evalues.nextElement());
    }
}
```

```
login.get(alex):12ff
login.contains(123ff): true
login.containsKey(rex): true
All keys
john
alex
rex
All values
235ff
12ff
123ff
```

Recall, Hashtable can store any key-value pairs as objects, which includes any container. Suppose we want to map a set of linked lists as values for given keys. This can be easily done with Hashtables as shown in Example 9.1.

Example 9.1. LinkedLists as Hashtable Values

```
LinkedList javaUsers = new LinkedList();
LinkedList linuxUsers = new LinkedList();
LinkedList pythonUsers = new LinkedList();

Hashtable users = new Hashtable();
users.put("java", javaUsers);
users.put("linux", linuxUsers);
users.put("python", pythonUsers);
```

The values() returns all values as a Collection, so you can create Iterator to your Hashtable too as shown in Example 9.2.

Example 9.2. Iterators for Values

```
Hashtable login = new Hashtable();
Iterator it = login.values().iterator();
while (it.hasNext())
      System.out.println(it.next());
```

Like other containers, Hashtable can also be created as a type-safe data structure. Therefore keys and values can use generics for type-safety. For example, let us create a type-safe Hashtable where key is a String and value an Integer as shown in Figure 9.1.

Figure 9.1. Type-safe Hashtable

```
Hashtable<String,Integer> ht = new Hashtable<String,Integer>();
```

9.3 PROBLEM: WORD COUNTING IN A TEXT

Word counter application receives a line of text from users and stores the occurrences of each word in a Hashtable. Listing 9.2 depicts this counting words application.

Listing 9.2. Word Counter

```
// WordCounter.java                                    {coderipe}

import java.io.*;
import java.util.*;

public class WordCounter
{
    public static void main(String[] args) throws IOException
    {
        Scanner sc = new Scanner(System.in);

        // read a line of text
        System.out.println("Enter a line of text: ");
        String s1 = sc.nextLine();

        // Hashtable to hold words as string and their counts
        as int
        Hashtable<String,Integer> ht = new
        Hashtable<String,Integer>();

        // parse file for different words by stringTokenizer
        StringTokenizer st = new StringTokenizer(s1);

        while (st.hasMoreTokens())
        {
            // get next token
            String word = st.nextToken();

            // check if word already present in ht
            if( ht.containsKey(word))
            {
                // get its count
                int count = ht.get(word);

                // increment
                count++;

                // put this new count
                ht.put(word, count);
```

```
            }
            else
            {
              // else new key, so initialize with count 1
              ht.put(word, 1);
            }
        }

    // display ht
    System.out.println(ht.toString());

    }
}
```

```
Enter a line of text: I am a bad boy i speak i walk too i dance
too a dance as bad as you
{dance=2, bad=2, as=2, speak=1, boy=1, i=3, am=1, you=1, too=2,
a=2, I=1, walk=1}
```

9.4 PROBLEM: COUPLES-SENSITIVE BRACKETS CHECKER

In Chapter 8, we had designed BracketChecker application that will nicely check whether the bracket types are proper. It will check whether for each open bracket type there is a closing bracket type and will also take into account of nested brackets. But, there is an issue. The application will not check whether the bracket types are proper pairs. It will also accept improper pairs such as { and]. So, our application has to check apart from number of brackets, whether the opening and closing types are proper couples. Listing 9.3 shows our modified brackets matching application.

Listing 9.3. Couples-sensitive Brackets Checker

```
// SensitiveBrackerChecker.java
import java.io.*;
import java.util.*;

class SensitiveChecker
{
    // create stack
    Stack<Character> stk = new Stack<Character>();

    // create scanner
    Scanner sc = new Scanner(System.in);

    // hashtable to hold proper matching bracket types
```

```java
Hashtable<Character, Character> ht =
    new Hashtable<Character, Character>();

public void match()
{
    // get arithmetic expression as a string
    String expr = sc.nextLine();

    // take one char at a time
    for (int i = 0; i < expr.length(); i++)
    {
        char c = expr.charAt(i);

        // check all three open bracket types
        if (c == '{' || c == '(' || c == '[' )
        {
        stk.push(c);
        }
        else // if closing bracket
        if (c == '}' || c == ')' || c == ']' )
        {
                // if it is a proper closing bracket to stk top
                if (properClosing(c))
                        stk.pop();
                else
                {
                        System.out.println("Open and close
                        bracket do not match");
                        break;
                }
        }
    }

    // if stk is empty, given expr is perfectly balanced
    if(stk.empty())
      System.out.println
          ("The given expression is perfectly balanced");
    else
      System.out.println
          ("The given expression is NOT perfectly balanced");
}

public boolean properClosing(char c)
{
    // assume false initially
```

```
        boolean isProper = false;

        // retrieve stack top
        char top = stk.peek();

        // ht has a key top and its value is c
        if(ht.containsKey(top) && ht.get(top) == c)
             isProper = true; // now it is true

        // return
        return isProper;
    }

    public void initHT()
    {
        ht.put('(', ')');
        ht.put('{', '}');
        ht.put('[', ']');
    }
}

public class SensitiveBracketChecker
{
    public static void main(String[] args)
    {
        SensitiveChecker m = new SensitiveChecker();
        m.initHT();
        m.match();
    }
}
```

```
3+2*(5+8)
The given expression is perfectly balanced
3+2*(5+6*{2+1}+3)
The given expression is perfectly balanced
3+2*[1+1}+1
Open and close bracket do not match
The given expression is NOT perfectly balanced
```

In this Sensitive bracket checker application, we keep brackets in a Hashtable. All open bracket types will be keys and corresponding closing types are values. Whenever a closing bracket type is encountered in the input string, our application will check whether stack top and this closing bracket type are proper pairs by consulting Hashtable. If there is an entry in the Hashtable with these two values, then they are couples.

9.5 HASHMAP

The HashMap is a container implemented with Hashtable. HashMap performs insertion and retrieval in constant time. Performance can be tuned with *capacity* and *load factor* of the Hashtable. One notable difference between HashMap and Hashtable is that HashMap allows null values for keys and values. But HashMap is not thread-safe like Hashtable. Similar to Hashtable, HashMap provides put(), get(), containsKey(), containsValue(), size() and values() methods for basic operations. There are some differences between Hashtable and HashMap:

- Hashtable supports Enumeration, but not HashMap
- HashMap allows us to iterate over key-value pairs, but not Hashtable
- Removing elements during iteration is safe with HashMap, but not with Hashtable

Listing 9.4 depicts a type-specific HashMap that maintains country codes as keys and names of countries as values. Both keys and values are stored as Strings. Apart from various Map methods, this application explains different ways of iterating maps using Iterators and for-each statement.

Listing 9.4. CountryMap

```java
// CountryMap.java

import java.util.*;

public class CountryMap
{
    public static void main(String[] args)
    {
        String[] code = {"IN", "US", "UK", "JP", "DE"};
        String[] names = {"India", "United States", "United
        Kingdom",
            "Japan", "Germany"};
        // add to map
        HashMap<String, String> map = new HashMap<String,
        String>();

        for(int i = 0; i < code.length; i++)
            map.put(code[i], names[i]);

        System.out.println("IN: " + map.get("IN"));
        System.out.println("Contains key UK: " + map.
        containsKey("UK"));
        System.out.println("Contains Value Germany: " +
            map.containsValue("Germany"));

        // show all keys
        System.out.println("All keys");
```

```
      Set keys = map.keySet();
      System.out.println(keys);

      // show all values
      System.out.println("All values");
      Iterator it = map.values().iterator();
      while(it.hasNext())
            System.out.println(it.next());

      // show all key-value pairs
      System.out.println("All keys and values using
      Iterator");
      Iterator ite = map.entrySet().iterator();
      while(ite.hasNext())
      {
            Map.Entry pair = (Map.Entry)ite.next();
            System.out.println(pair.getKey() + "," +
                  pair.getValue());
      }
      // show all key-value pairs using for-each
      System.out.println("All keys and values using
      for-each");
      for(Map.Entry<String, String> e : map.entrySet())
            System.out.println(e.getKey() + "," + e.getValue());
   }
}
```

```
IN: India
Contains key UK: true
Contains Value Germany: true
All keys
[JP, US, IN, DE, UK]
All values
Japan
United States
India
Germany
United Kingdom
All keys and values using Iterator
JP,Japan
US,United States
IN,India
DE,Germany
UK,United Kingdom
```

```
All keys and values using for-each
JP,Japan
US,United States
IN,India
DE,Germany
UK,United Kingdom
```

9.6 MULTIMAPS

A **multimap** is a map (such as HashMap or Tree Map) but it can map each key to multiple values. Multiple values can be specified using any of the Lists such as array list or linked list. Figure 9.2 depicts an example that creates a multimap.

Figure 9.2. Multimaps

```
HashMap<String, ArrayList<String>> m = new HashMap<String,
ArrayList<String>>();
```

Here, values are stored as an Array List, where each list holds a set of strings.

9.7 NESTED HASHMAPS

So far we have created HashMap that holds key and value pairs. Suppose we want to know the list of all supermarkets available given a state and a city code. So you should define a two-level HashMap; for every state and for every city, our HashMap will hold a list of supermarkets. Listing 9.5 depicts this supermarket HashMap.

Listing 9.5. Hashmap of Supermarkets

```
// SuperMarketHMap.java                              {coderipe}
import java.util.*;

public class SuperMarketHMap
{
    Scanner sc = new Scanner(System.in);
    String state, city;

    String[] states = { "TN", "KL", "KA", "MH", "DL" };
    String[] citiesTN = { "chennai", "coimbatore", "trichy",
    "madurai" };
    String[] smChennai = { "Reliance", "Spensors", "More", "Big
    Bazaar" };
    String[] smCoimbatore = { "More", "Spensor" };
    String[] smTrichy = { "More", "Spensor", "Walmart", "Tesco" };
```

```java
    String[] smMadurai = { "More", "Spensor" };

HashMap stateCity = new HashMap();
HashMap citySMarket = new HashMap();

public void init()
{
    // init cities
    int i = 0;
    citySMarket.put(citiesTN[i++], Arrays.asList(smChennai));
    citySMarket.put(citiesTN[i++], Arrays.
    asList(smCoimbatore));
    citySMarket.put(citiesTN[i++], Arrays.
    asList(smTrichy));
    citySMarket.put(citiesTN[i++], Arrays.asList(smMadurai));

    // init states
    int j = 0;
    stateCity.put(states[j++], citySMarket);
    stateCity.put(states[j++], new HashMap());
    stateCity.put(states[j++], new HashMap());
    stateCity.put(states[j++], new HashMap());
}

public void get()
{
    System.out.print("Enter state code : " );
    state = sc.nextLine();
    System.out.print("Enter city : " );
    city = sc.nextLine();

    List supermarkets = (List)((HashMap)stateCity.get(state)).
    get(city);
    System.out.println("Super Markets in " + city + ": " +
    supermarkets);
}

public static void main(String[] args)
{
    SuperMarketHMap map = new SuperMarketHMap();
    map.init();
    map.get();
}
}
```

```
Enter state code : TN
Enter city : trichy
Super Markets in trichy: [More, Spensor, Walmart, Tesco]
Enter state code : TN
Enter city : chennai
Super Markets in chennai: [Reliance, Spensors, More,
Big Bazaar]
```

In this program, the two-level hashmap is first initialized with state, city and supermarket information. Then users are asked to supply state code and city name as inputs, and accordingly both hashmaps are searched and the corresponding list of supermarkets are retrieved. Furthermore, asList() from Arrays class is used to create a list from an array. The readers will learn more about Arrays at the end of this chapter.

9.8 LINKEDHASHMAP

LinkedHashMap, a subclass of HashMap, contains the behaviours of both Hashtable and LinkedList. Since it uses a doubly linked list, it maintains the insertion order of elements with Least Recently Used (**LRU**) method. It permits null values for its keys and values, insertions and deletions can be done at constant time and iteration is slightly costly, compared to HashMaps.

LinkedHashMaps differ from HashMaps in few ways as shown below:

- LinkedHashMap preserves the order of elements insertion
- HashMap does not require the expense of maintaining the linked list. However, both are not thread-safe

Listing 9.6 explains LinkedHashMap methods for retrieving language name given its code.

Listing 9.6. LanguageLHMap

```java
// LanguageLHMap.java
import java.util.*;

public class LanguageLHMap
{
    LinkedHashMap map = new LinkedHashMap();

    public void init()
    {
        map.put("en", "english");
        map.put("ta", "tamil");
        map.put("de", "german");
        map.put("fr", "french");
        System.out.println(map.toString());
```

```
    }

    public static void main(String[] args)
    {
        LanguageLHMap r = new LanguageLHMap();
        r.init();
    }
}
```

```
{en=english, ta=tamil, de=german, fr=french}
```

Listing 9.7 explains how linked hashmap preserves the order of insertion of elements. In contrast hashmap just maintains its elements according to its hashcode.

Listing 9.7. Rhymes Map

```
// RhymesLHMap.java
import java.util.*;

public class RhymesLHMap
{
    public void init(Map map)
    {
        map.put("b", "banana");
        map.put("a", "apple");
        map.put("d", "dog");
        map.put("c", "cat");
        System.out.println(map.toString());
    }

    public static void main(String[] args)
    {
        RhymesLHMap r = new RhymesLHMap();
        r.init(new LinkedHashMap());
        r.init(new HashMap());
    }
}
```

```
{b=banana, a=apple, d=dog, c=cat}
{d=dog, b=banana, c=cat, a=apple}
```

Since Map is an interface, any of its implementations can be assigned to Map. So init() can receive any of Map type such as HashMap and LinkedHashMap as arguments.

9.9 TREEMAP

TreeMap is a red black tree-based implementation of maps. TreeMap maintains keys or key-value pairs in sorted order automatically. The subMap() method returns a portion of TreeMap. TreeMap provides log time performance for checking, retrieval and removal. As others, tree maps are not thread-safe. A TreeMap can be simply created and put() and get() methods insert pairs and retrieve value for a given key as usual. Example 9.3 depicts a tree map.

Example 9.3. Tree Map

```
TreeMap map1 = new TreeMap();
TreeMap<String, Map<String, List<String>>> map2 = new
TreeMap<String, Map<String, List<String>>>();
```

The first example simply creates an instance of TreeMap. The second example creates a tree map whose value is again a tree map (you can call nested tree map of course). The inner tree map has List as values.

Listing 9.8 illustrates the important methods of tree map. It also compares the output of hashmap, tree map and linked hashmaps.

Listing 9.8. Rhymes Tree Map

```java
// RhymesTMap.java
import java.util.*;

public class RhymesTMap
{
    public void init(Map map)
    {
        map.put("b", "banana");
        map.put("a", "apple");
        map.put("d", "dog");
        map.put("c", "cat");
        System.out.println(map.toString());
    }

    public static void main(String[] args)
    {
        RhymesTMap r = new RhymesTMap();
        r.init(new LinkedHashMap());
        r.init(new HashMap());
        r.init(new TreeMap());
    }
}
```

```
{b=banana, a=apple, d=dog, c=cat}
{d=dog, b=banana, c=cat, a=apple}
{a=apple, b=banana, c=cat, d=dog}
```

From the output, you can easily understand that hashmaps hold pairs according to their hash code; linked hashmap maintains the order of insertion of pairs and tree map maintains sorted sequence of its pairs.

9.10 PROBLEM: RANDOM NUMBER GENERATOR

Now let us generate 1,00,000 random numbers and count how many times each random number is generated again and again. Let us keep each random number and its counts as a pair in tree map. Tree map is most suitable for this application as it keeps its random numbers in sorted sequence as shown in Listing 9.9.

Listing 9.9. Tree Map of Random Numbers

```java
//RandomNumberMap.java
import java.util.*;

class Counter
{
    int i;
    public Counter(int j) { i = j; }
    public String toString() { return Integer.toString(i);}
}

public class RandomNumberMap
{
    // create Random instance
    Random random = new Random();

    // type-safe TreeMap
    TreeMap<Integer, Counter> map = new TreeMap<Integer, Counter>();

    public void count()
    {
        // generate 100,000 random numbers
        for(int i = 0; i < 100000; i++)
        {
            // produce
            int rno = random.nextInt(20);

            // check if it exists
            if(map.containsKey(rno))
                ((Counter)map.get(rno)).i++; // get its value
            else    // new count
                map.put(rno, new Counter(1));
```

```
      }
      // show all numbers
      System.out.println(map);
  }

  public static void main(String[] args)
  {
      RandomNumberMap r = new RandomNumberMap();
      r.count();
  }
}
```

```
{0=4958, 1=4930, 2=5034, 3=5036, 4=5015, 5=4839, 6=4954, 7=4995,
8=4905, 9=4995, 10=5005, 11=5042, 12=5047, 13=5025, 14=5187,
15=5110, 16=4956, 17=5007, 18=4952, 19=5008}
```

We can observe from the output of this application that random numbers (between 0 and 19) are generated almost equally around 5000 times.

So, having seen three types of maps, which type scores better? This is a natural question we all have in mind. You could follow a general rule of thumb to select any of the maps as below:

- Hashtable is suitable for threads
- HashMap is slightly better than Hashtable, but not thread-safe
- TreeMap is slower than HashMap, but suitable if you need the map in sorted order
- Linked HashMap is slower than HashMap, but it is preferred if more number of insertions and deletions happen

9.11 PROPERTIES

Properties class, a subclass of Hashtable, manages key-value pairs as persistent objects in a file. In each pair, key and values are String types. Before Properties class is instantiated, a property file should be first created (using any text editor) as shown in Figure 9.3. Each property pair will use a delimiter in between key and value. Some of the delimiters are =, : and \t characters. The characters # and ! represent a comment statement in the property file.

Figure 9.3. Property List Country.Prop

```
# country.prop
lang=ta
currency=inr
capital=newdelhi
```

Once property list is created with a set of key-value pairs as a file, then we can call this list and populate our Properties class using load() method. The getProperty() returns the value for the given property key. Listing 9.10 illustrates how to populate Properties object using property list.

Listing 9.10. Country Properties

```java
// PropertiesCountry.java

import java.util.*;
import java.io.*;

public class PropertiesCountry
{
    public static void main(String[] args) throws
    IOException
    {
        Properties p = new Properties();
        p.load(new FileReader("country.prop"));

        // show all pairs
        System.out.println(p);

        // get value
        System.out.println("lang: " + p.getProperty("lang"));

        // get keys as enumeration
        Enumeration keys = p.keys();
        while (keys.hasMoreElements())
            System.out.println(keys.nextElement());

        Enumeration values = p.elements();
        while (values.hasMoreElements())
            System.out.println(values.nextElement());

        Set s = p.stringPropertyNames();
        System.out.println("All values: " + s);
    }
}
```

```
{currency=inr, capital=newdelhi, lang=ta}
lang: ta
currency
capital
lang
inr
newdelhi
ta
All values: [currency, lang, capital]
```

Here, load() populates properties object with property file using FileReader. FileReader is a Reader available in java.io package. It opens the file for reading by load(). The readers will be introduced to more about files in Part 4 of this book.

9.12 SUMMARY

1. Map is another important interface that provides methods to add and retrieve key-value pairs of objects
2. HashMap, LinkedHashMap and TreeMap are the three important map implementations
3. Hashtable is a popular legacy class of Java 1.0 and Java 1.1 for holding key-value pairs
4. Hashtable can be populated with property list from files
5. Hashtable can hold any collection types
6. For counting different words in a given text, Hashtable can keep words as keys and its count as values
7. HashMap is an implementation of Map and it is same as Hashtable
8. HashMap is not thread-safe, but Hashtable is thread-safe
9. HashMap supports Iterator, whereas Hashtable supports only Enumeration
10. Lists can be added as values for HashMap, and this type of HashMap is called multimap
11. HashMap can contain other HashMaps and is known as nested HashMaps
12. LinkedHashMap is efficient for insertion and deletion of elements
13. TreeMap is a red black tree-based implementation of HashMap
14. Properties class manages key-value pairs as persistent objects in a file
15. The load() and store() methods open and save Property lists. Property list can be queried using getProperty() method

KEY TERMS

HashMap, 291	LinkedHashMap, 291	Map, 291	Properties class, 306
Hashtable, 292	LRU, 302	Multimap, 300	TreeMap, 291

REVIEW QUESTIONS

Multiple-choice Questions

1. What is the output?

```
Hashtable ht = new Hashtable();
ht.put("1", "1");
ht.put("2", "2");
```

```
System.out.print(ht.get("2"));
ht.put("1", "11");
ht.put("2", "21");
System.out.print(ht.get("1"));
```

    a. 2 1   b. 2 11

    c. 21 11   d. None of the above

2. What is the output?

```
Hashtable<Integer,String> ht =
    new Hashtable<Integer,String>();
ht.put(1, "one");
ht.put(2, "two");
System.out.println(ht.get(1));
```

    a. One   b. Two

    c. Null   d. No output

3. What is the output?

```
Hashtable<Integer,String> ht =
    new Hashtable<Integer,String>();
ht.put(1, "1");
ht.put(2, "2");
ht.put(new Integer(1), "11");
System.out.println(ht.get(1));
```

    a. Null   b. Hashcode displayed

    c. 1   d. 11

4. What is the output?

```
HashMap map = new HashMap();
map.put(2, "b");
map.put(1, "a");
map2.put(2, "b");
```

    a. Compilation error   b. Runtime exception when duplicates are added

    c. Duplicates can be added   d. Added duplicates will not be stored

5. What is the output?

```
HashMap map = new HashMap();
map.put(1, 1);
map.put(2, 2);
map.put("3", "3");
map.put(null, null);
System.out.println(map.size());
```

a. 3
b. 4
c. 2
d. Undefined value

6. Find out the output:

```
HashMap map = new HashMap();
map.put(1, 1);
map.put(2, 2);
map.put("1", "11");
map.put(1,12);
System.out.println(map.size());
```

a. 4
b. 3
c. 2
d. NullPointerException

7. What is the output?

```
HashMap map = new HashMap();
map.put(1, 1);
map.put(2, 2);
HashMap map2 = new HashMap();
map2.put(2, 2);
map2.put(3, 3);
map2.putAll(map);
System.out.println(map2.size());
```

a. 4
b. 3
c. 2
d. None of the above

8. What is the output?

```
HashMap map = new HashMap();
map.put(2, "b");
map.put(1, "a");
```

```
HashMap map2 = new HashMap();
map2.put(3, "c");
map2.put(2,"b");
map2.putAll(map);
System.out.println(map2.keySet());
```

    a. [1, 2, 2, 3]   b. [2, 1, 3, 2]

    c. [1, 2, 3]   d. [3, 2, 1]

9. What is the output?

```
HashMap map = new HashMap();
map.put(2, "b");
map.put(1, "a");
HashMap map2 = new HashMap();
map2.put(3, "c");
map2.put(2, "b");
map2.putAll(map);
System.out.println(map2.values());
```

    a. [a, b, c]   b. [b, a, c]

    c. [b, a, c, b]   d. [a, b, b, c]

10. What is the output?

```
import java.util.*;
public class Test9
{
    public static void main(String[] args)
    {
        HashMap<Integer,Details> map =
            new HashMap<Integer,Details>();
        Details d1 = new Details("Rex", "Pune");
        Details d2 = new Details("Helen", "Bangalore");
        map.put(5001, d1);
        map.put(5002, d2);
        map.put(5001, d1);
        System.out.println(map.keySet());
    }
}
class Details
{
    String name, addr;
```

```
    public Details(String name1, String addr1)
    {
        name = name1;
        addr = addr1;
    }
}
```

a. [5001, 5002, 5001]   b. [5001, 5001, 5002]

c. [5001, 5002]   d. [5002, 5001]

11. Find out the output:

```
import java.util.*;
public class Test9
{
    public static void main(String[] args)
    {
        HashMap<Integer,Details> map =
                new HashMap<Integer,Details>();
        Details d1 = new Details("Rex", "Pune");
        map.put(5001, d1);
        map.put(5002, d1);
        map.put(5003, d1);
        Iterator it = map.values().iterator();
        while(it.hasNext())
                System.out.println(it.next() + " ");
    }
}
class Details
{
    String name, addr;
    public Details(String name1, String addr1)
    {
        name = name1;
        addr = addr1;
    }
    public String toString()
    {
        return name + " " + addr;
    }
}
```

a. Prints Rex Pune   b. Prints Rex Pune 3 times

c. Compilation error   d. Runtime exception

12. What is the output?

```java
import java.util.*;
public class Test9
{
    public static void main(String[] args)
    {
        HashMap<StudentID,Details> map =
                new. HashMap<StudentID,Details>();

        StudentID id1 = new StudentID(5001);
        StudentID id2 = new StudentID(5001);

        map.put(id1, new Details("Rex", "Pune"));
        map.put(id2, new Details("Rita", "Pune"));

        System.out.print(map.size());
        Iterator it = map.keySet().iterator();
        while(it.hasNext())
                System.out.print(
                " " + ((StudentID)it.next()).rollNo);
        it = map.values().iterator();
        while(it.hasNext())
                System.out.print(
                " " + ((Details)it.next()).name);
    }
}

class Details
{
    String name, addr;
    public Details(String name1, String addr1)
    {
        name = name1;
        addr = addr1;
    }
}
class StudentID
{
    int rollNo;
    public StudentID(int n)
    {
        rollNo = n;

    }
```

```
   public boolean equals(Object o)
   {
      return rollNo == ((StudentID)o).rollNo;
   }
   public int hashCode() { return 1;}
}
```

a. 1 5001 Rita

b. 1 5001 Rex

c. 2 5001 5002 Rita Rita

d. 2 5001 5001 Rex Rex

13. What is the output?

```
LinkedHashMap map = new LinkedHashMap();
map.put(2, 21);
map.put(1, 11);
map.put(3, 31);
System.out.println(map.keySet());
```

a. [2, 1, 3]

b. [1, 2, 3]

c. [21, 11, 31]

d. [11.21.31]

14. What is the output?

```
TreeMap map = new TreeMap();
map.put(2, 21);
map.put(1, 11);
map.put(3, 31);
System.out.println(map.keySet());
```

a. [2, 1, 3]

b. [1, 2, 3]

c. [3, 1, 2]

d. [3, 2, 1]

15. What is the output?

```
HashMap map = new HashMap();
map.put(2, "two");
map.put(1, "one");
map.put(3, "three");
System.out.println(map.values());
```

a. [one, two, three]

b. [two, one, three]

c. [2, 1, 3]

d. [1, 2, 3]

16. Which of the following TreeMap method returns the least key greater than or equal to the given key?

 a. ceilingKey() b. floorKey()
 c. lowerKey() d. higherKey()

17. Which of the following TreeMap method returns the greatest key less than or equal to the given key?

 a. ceilingKey() b. floorKey()
 c. lowerKey() d. higherKey()

18. Which of the following TreeMap method returns a view of the portion of the hashmap whose keys are less than the given key?

 a. headMap() b. tailMap()
 c. floorMap() d. ceilingMap()

19. Which of the following TreeMap method returns a view of the portion of the hashmap whose keys are greater than the given key?

 a. headMap() b. tailMap()
 c. floorMap() d. ceilingMap()

20. What is the output?

```
TreeMap map = new TreeMap();
map.put(2, "two");
map.put(1, "one");
map.put(3, "three");
System.out.println(map.descendingMap().keySet());
```

 a. [1, 2, 3] b. [3, 2, 1]
 c. [2, 1, 3] d. [one, two, three]

Answers

1. b	2. a	3. d	4. d	5. b	6. b	7. b	8. c	9. a	10. d
11. b	12. a	13. a	14. b	15. a	16. a	17. b	18. a	19. b	20. b

Short-answer Questions

1. Explain Hashtable and its important methods.
2. Explain the important methods of Map interface.
3. What are the three implementations of Map interface?
4. What is the difference between Hashtable and HashMap?
5. How can you create a HashMap inside another HashMap?
6. What is Multimap?

7. Explain LinkedHashMap with an example.
8. Explain TreeMap with an example.
9. Explain properties class with an example.
10. Load properties file data into a hash table.

EXERCISES

9.1. [*Spelling Checker*] Create a hash table containing 10 spelling errors and their correct words as keys and values. For example, key *appel* and its value *apple*. Then read a string from user with spelling errors and correct them by consulting the hash table.

9.2. Modify spell checking exercise by replacing hash table with hash map.

9.3. [*Dictionary Lookup*] Create a hash table to store a simple dictionary containing 10 words and their list of synonyms. Read a word from the user and display list of its synonyms if that word exists. Note: you may need a vector or linked list to store synonyms.

9.4. Modify dictionary lookup exercise by replacing hash table with hash map.

9.5. [*Language Translator*] Create a property file containing 10 entries of English words and their possible Tamil/Hindi translations. Populate Hashtable with the property file data. Read an English string of words and print its Tamil/Hindi equivalent by hash table lookup.

9.6. Modify language translator exercise by replacing hash table with hash map.

9.7. [*Login Manager*] Create a hash table containing a list of usernames and their passwords. Read a username and a password of a user from keyboard and display appropriate message whether username and password matches with an entry in the hash table. If username does not exist, get new username and password from user and add an entry to hash table.

9.8. [*Spam Detector*] Create a hash table containing spam words and their risk probability values. Read a line of text as email message from user. Print appropriate message as below:

   ■ If email has no spam words, print *Spam Free*
   ■ Otherwise, calculate the average of probability values of all spam words that appear in the email. Print a message *Less Spam* if the value is in between 0.01 to 0.3, *Moderate spam* if the value is in between 0.31 to 0.7 and *High spam*, if more than 0.7

10

Set Containers

OBJECTIVES

- To introduce implementations of Set interface
- To check whether Sets allow duplicates
- To introduce the add and remove operations on Sets
- To introduce the union and difference operations on Sets
- To develop counting duplicates application
- To introduce LinkedHashSet's insertion ordering
- To introduce TreeSet's red black tree implementation

10.1 INTRODUCTION

Sets are the third type of Java containers we are going to deal with in this book. Having seen Lists and Map types, we might have observed that lists and maps allow duplicate values. However there are many situations where we need to hold only unique elements. This is where sets score better. In this chapter, the readers will be introduced to Set interface and its three implementations. Analogous to Map types, sets also have **HashSet**, **LinkedHashSet** and **TreeSet** types.

10.2 SET INTERFACE

Set interface has exactly the same set of features like other collection interfaces such as List and Map. One notable feature of set is that it will not allow duplicate objects. Sets model the mathematical set concept. Set interface inherits only methods from Collection interface.

The set interface has some interesting methods. The add() method adds an object to the set if it is not a duplicate and returns a boolean indicating whether the object is added or not. Similarly, remove() deletes an element from the set. The equals() checks for an element in the set.

The standard **set algebraic operations** can be performed on to sets. Assume there are two sets s1 and s2.

- s1.containsAll(s2) returns true if s2 is a subset of s1
- s1.addAll(s2) returns s1 as a union of s1 and s2
- s1.retainAll(s2) returns s1 as an intersection of s1 and s2
- s1.removeAll(s2) returns s1 as the set difference of s1 and s2

Example 10.1 illustrates the set algebraic operations.

Example 10.1. Set Algebraic Operations

```
s1 = [10, 20, 30, 40, 50]
s2 = [30, 40, 50, 60, 70]
s1.containsAll(s2) = false
s1.addAll(s2): s1 = [10, 20, 30, 40, 50, 60, 70]
s1.retainAll(s2): s1 = [30, 40, 50]
s1.removeAll(s2): s1 = [10, 20]
s2.removeAll(s1): s2 = [60, 70]
```

There are basically three types of set implementations: HashSet, LinkedHashSet and TreeSet. The readers will be introduced to these three types in sections 10.3, 10.5 and 10.6 in more detail.

10.3 HASHSET

HashSet stores its elements in a Hashtable and is considered to be the best set implementation as its lookup time is short. However, the elements are stored according to its hashcode randomly. HashSet can be created as shown in Figure 10.1.

Figure 10.1. HashSet Examples

```
HashSet set = new HashSet();
HashSet<Integer> set = new HashSet<Integer>();
// assume Counter is already exists
HashSet<Counter> set = new HashSet<Counter>();
```

Suppose we have an array list with a set of integers. We want to remove all duplicates that exist in the list. It can be easily done with the set as shown in Listing 10.1.

Listing 10.1. Remove Duplicates in a List

```java
import java.util.*;                                    {coderipe}
public class SetTest
{
   public static void main(String[] args)
   {
      int[] numbers = {60,20,20,40,30,50,50,10};
      ArrayList<Integer> list = new ArrayList<Integer>();
      // add numbers to list
      for(int i = 0; i < numbers.length; i++)
            list.add(numbers[i]);

      HashSet<Integer> set = new HashSet<Integer>(list);
      System.out.println(set);

   }
}
```

```
[50, 20, 10, 40, 30, 60]
```

If a HashSet is type-unsafe, then it will store objects of any type as there is no restriction on HashSet. In Listing 10.2, let us create an unsafe hashset to store any object or collection.

Listing 10.2. Unsafe Set

```java
import java.util.*;

class Cat
{
   int i = 777;
}

public class UnsafeSet
{
   public static void main(String[] args)
   {
      HashSet set = new HashSet();
      // add int
      set.add(10);
      set.add('c');   // add char
      set.add(123456789L);   // add long
      set.add("Hello"); // these 2 hello are same
      set.add("Hello");
      set.add(new Cat()); // these two cats are different
```

```
      set.add(new Cat());
      set.add(new HashMap());
      set.add(new Vector());

      System.out.println(set);
    }
}
```

```
[{}, 123456789, [], c, Cat@addbf1, Cat@19821f, 10, Hello]
```

To appreciate the power of inheritance and polymorphism, it is a programming practice not to create object of individual implementation. Rather, you need to upcast to the appropriate interfaces. For example, let us create a hash set by upcasting to Set interface as shown in Figure 10.2.

Figure 10.2. Set Upcasting

```
Set set = new HashSet();
```

The functionality of Set will remain the same even if we change HashSet by other set implementations; thereby we will get different results depending on set implementations.

10.4 PROBLEM: COUNTING DUPLICATES IN A TEXT

Duplicates are big problems in many applications. Many times in text and web retrieval, we will be interested to count and eliminate duplicates in a text document. The application shown in Listing 10.3 counts duplicate elements in a given list and maintains only unique elements in HashMap.

Listing 10.3. Counting Duplicates in a Given Text

```
import java.util.*;                                    {coderipe}

class Counter
{
   int i;
   public Counter(int j) { i = j; }
   public String toString() { return Integer.toString(i); }
}

public class CountDuplicates
{
   Scanner sc = new Scanner(System.in);
   String line;
```

```
Set set = new HashSet<String>();
Map map = new HashMap<String, Counter>();

public void get()
{
   System.out.print("Enter a line of text: " );
   line = sc.nextLine();
}

public void count()
{
   String[] tokens = line.split(" ");   // by \s

   // check each token and add
   for(int i = 0; i < tokens.length; i++)
   {
        String token = tokens[i];

        // if token is duplicate
        if(!set.add(token))
        {
             // it is a duplicate, so add to HM
             if(!map.containsKey(token))
                   map.put(token, new Counter(1));
             else   // already exists, just incr
                   ((Counter)map.get(token)).i++;
        }
   }
}

public void show()
{
   System.out.println(map);
}

public static void main(String[] args)
{
   CountDuplicates dup = new CountDuplicates();
   dup.get();
   dup.count();
   dup.show();
}
}
```

```
Enter a line of text: i speak i walk too drink too you drink a
drink
{drink=2, too=1, i=1}
```

10.5 LINKEDHASHSET

LinkedHashSet is a linked list-backed hash set which preserves the order of insertion of elements. Though it is slightly slower than hash set, it is very efficient for insertion and deletion of elements. Like other implementations, it is also not thread-safe. LinkedHashSet can be created as shown in Figure 10.3.

Figure 10.3. LinkedHashSet

```
LinkedHashSet set = new LinkedHashSet();
LinkedHashSet<object-type> = new LinkedHashSet
<object-type>();
Set set = LinkedHashSet();
Set set = LinkedHashSet<object-type>();
```

Now let us remove duplicate numbers in a given list with linked hash set as shown in Listing 10.4.

Listing 10.4. Remove Duplicates

```
import java.util.*;
public class SetTest2
{
    public static void main(String[] args)
    {
        int[] numbers = { 60,20,20,40,30,50,50,10};
        ArrayList<Integer> list = new ArrayList
        <Integer>();
        // add numbers to list
        for(int i = 0; i < numbers.length; i++)
                list.add(numbers[i]);

        LinkedHashSet<Integer> set = new
        LinkedHashSet<Integer>(list);
        System.out.println(set);
    }
}
```

```
[60, 20, 40, 30, 50, 10]
```

In section 10.4, the readers were introduced to counting duplicate elements in a line of text using HashMap. In Listing 10.5, let us rewrite the same application using LinkedHashMap. LinkedHash-Map enjoys the feature of constant time performance in insertion and deletion of elements.

Listing 10.5. Counting Duplicates with Linked Hashset

```java
public class CountDuplicates
{
    Scanner sc = new Scanner(System.in);
    String line;

    Set set = new LinkedHashSet<String>();
    Map map = new HashMap<String, Counter>();

    // rest of the code is same
}
```

10.6 TREESET

TreeSet is backed by red black tree similar to tree map and tree list. So tree set maintains sorted order of its elements. Like others, tree set is also not thread-safe. It is substantially slower than hash set. Now let us rewrite removing duplicate application (Listing 10.4) with tree set as shown in Listing 10.6.

Listing 10.6. Removing Duplicates Using Tree Set

```java
// SetTest3.java
import java.util.*;
public class SetTest3
{
    public static void main(String[] args)
    {
        int[] numbers = {60,20,20,40,30,50,50,10};
        ArrayList<Integer> list = new ArrayList<Integer>();
        // add numbers to list
        for(int i = 0; i < numbers.length; i++)
            list.add(numbers[i]);

        HashSet<Integer> set = new HashSet<Integer>(list);
        System.out.println(set);
    }
}
```

```
[10, 20, 30, 40, 50, 60]
```

Listing 10.7 compares all three set implementations of a set. You can observe how each set maintains elements in their own order.

Listing 10.7. Compare Set Implementations

```
import java.util.*;
public class CompareSet
{
   public void add(Set s)
   {
      s.add("apple");
      s.add("orange");
      s.add("kiwi");
      s.addAll(s);  // trying to add duplicates, cannot be added
      s.add("aeiou");
      System.out.println(s);
      System.out.println("s contains apple: " +
      s.contains("apple"));
   }

   public static void main(String[] args)
   {
      CompareSet c = new CompareSet();
      c.add(new HashSet());
      c.add(new LinkedHashSet());
      c.add(new TreeSet());
   }
}
```

```
[orange, aeiou, kiwi, apple]
s contains apple: true
[apple, orange, kiwi, aeiou]
s contains apple: true
[aeiou, apple, kiwi, orange]
s contains apple: true
```

10.7 SUMMARY

1. HashSet, LinkedHashSet and TreeSet are the three set implementations
2. Sets do not allow duplicate elements
3. Each set implementation differs from its functionality and performance
4. HashSet is faster that other implementations but slower for insertion
5. LinkedHashSet is based on linked list and faster for insertion and deletion of elements
6. TreeSet maintains natural ordering of elements, so elements will be automatically sorted

KEY TERMS

HashSet, 317
LinkedHashSet, 317

Set algebraic operations, 318
Set interface, 317

TreeSet, 317

REVIEW QUESTIONS

Multiple-choice Questions

1. What is the output?

```
HashSet set = new HashSet();
set.add(1);
set.add(2);
set.add(1);
System.out.println(set);
```

a. [1,2,1]

b. [1,2]

c. [1]

d. IllegalArgumentException

2. What is the output?

```
HashSet set1 = new HashSet();
set1.add(1);
set1.add(2);
set1.add(1);
HashSet set2 = new HashSet();
set2.add(4);
set2.add(3);
set1.addAll(set2);
System.out.println(set1);
```

a. [1,2,3,4]

b. [1,2,1,4,3]

c. [1,2,4,3]

d. [2,1,4,3]

3. What is the output?

```
HashSet set1 = new HashSet();
set1.add(1);
set1.add(3);
```

```
set1.add(2);
HashSet set2 = new HashSet();
set2.add(2);
set2.add(3);
System.out.println(set1.containsAll(set2));
```

a. True
b. False
c. Compilation error
d. Runtime exception

4. What is the output?

```
HashSet set1 = new HashSet();
set1.add(1);
set1.add(3);
set1.add(2);
HashSet set2 = new HashSet();
set2.add(2);
set1.retainAll(set2);
System.out.println(set1);
```

a. [2]
b. [1,3]
c. [1,3,2]
d. [1,2,3]

5. What is the output?

```
HashSet set1 = new HashSet();
set1.add(1);
set1.add(3);
set1.add(2);
HashSet set2 = new HashSet();
set2.add(2);
set1.removeAll(set2);
System.out.println(set1);
```

a. [2]
b. [1,3]
c. [1,3,2]
d. [1,2,3]

6. What is the output?

```
LinkedHashSet set1 = new LinkedHashSet();
set1.add(1);
set1.add(3);
```

```
set1.add(2);
LinkedHashSet set2 = new LinkedHashSet();
set2.add("four");
set1.addAll(set2);
System.out.println(set1);
```

    a. [1,3,2] followed by exception   b. [1,3,2,four]

    c. [four] followed by exception   d. [1,2,3,four]

7. Find out the output:

```
TreeSet set1 = new TreeSet();
set1.add(1);
set1.add(3);
set1.add("2");
System.out.println(set1);
```

    a. ClassCastException   b. Compilation error

    c. NullPointerException   d. RuntimeException

8. What is the output?

```
public class Test10
{
    public static void insert(Set s)
    {
        s.add(1);s.add("2");
        System.out.println(s);
    }
    public static void main(String[] args)
    {
        insert(new HashSet());
        insert(new LinkedHashSet());
        insert(new TreeSet());
    }
}
```

    a. [1,2], [2.1] and then ClassCastException

    b. [2,1], [1,2] and then ClassCastException

    c. Compilation error

    d. None of the above

9. What is the output?

```
TreeSet set1 = new TreeSet();
set1.add(1); set1.add(3); set1.add(5);
set1.add(4); set1.add(7);
System.out.print(set1.floor(4));
System.out.print(set1.ceiling(4));
```

a. 3 5   b. 1 3
c. 4 4   d. 5 7

10. What is the output?

```
TreeSet set1 = new TreeSet();
set1.add(1); set1.add(3); set1.add(5);
set1.add(4); set1.add(7);
System.out.print(set1.descendingSet());
```

a. Descending order of elements   b. Compilation error
c. Runtime exception   d. No output

11. What is the output?

```
TreeSet set1 = new TreeSet();
set1.add(1); set1.add(3); set1.add(5);
set1.add(4); set1.add(7);
System.out.print(set1.higher(4));
System.out.print(set1.lower(4));
```

a. 5 7   b. 1 3
c. 5 3   d. None of the above

12. What is the output?

```
TreeSet set1 = new TreeSet();
set1.add(1); set1.add(3); set1.add(5);
set1.add(4); set1.add(7);
System.out.print(set1.pollFirst());
System.out.print(set1.pollLast());
```

a. 1 7   b. 34
c. 35   d. 47

13. What is the output?

```
int[] marks = {73,55,96,69,86};
Set set = new TreeSet();
for(int i : marks)
    set.add(i);
System.out.println(set);
```

    a. Prints marks in ascending order   b. Prints marks according to hashcode values
    c. Prints marks in insertion order   d. None of the above

14. Find out the output:

```
int[] marks = {73,55,96,69,86};
Set set = new TreeSet();
for(int i : marks)
    set.add(i);
System.out.println(set.descendingSet());
```

    a. [73,55,96,69,86]   b. [96,86,73,69,55]
    c. Compilation error   d. Runtime exception

15. What is the output?

```
class Cat
{
    int id;
    public Cat(int id1) {id = id1;}
}
public class Test10
{
    public static void main(String[] args)
    {
        TreeSet<Cat> set = new TreeSet<Cat>();
        set.add(new Cat(1));
        set.add(new Cat(1));
        System.out.println(set.size());
    }
}
```

    a. 1   b. 2
    c. Compilation error   d. ClassCastException

16. What is the output?

```
public class Test10
{
   public static void main(String[] args)
   {
      TreeSet set = new TreeSet();
      set.add(1);
      set.add(null);
      set.add(2);
      set.add(2);
      System.out.println(set);
   }
}
```

a. [1,2]

b. [1,2,2]

c. [null,1,2,2]

d. NullPointerException

17. What is the output?

```
HashSet set = new HashSet();
set.add("b"); set.add("d");
set.add("a"); set.add("b");
System.out.println(set);
```

a. [b, d, a]

b. [d, b, a]

c. [a, b, d]

d. [a, b, b, d]

18. A duplicate element is added to a set. Then which of the following about add() is true?

a. The add() generates compilation error
b. The add() throws runtime exception
c. The add() rejects duplicate element
d. The add() returns false when duplicate is added

Answers

1. b	2. a	3. a	4. a	5. b	6. b	7. a	8. b	9. c	10. a
11. c	12. a	13. a	14. c	15. d	16. d	17. b	18. d		

Short-answer Questions

1. Explain all methods for set algebraic operations.
2. Explain HashSet with a suitable example.

3. Explain LinkedHashSet with a suitable example.

4. Explain TreeSet with a suitable example.

5. Compare all three Set implementations.

EXERCISES

10.1. Create three sets namely *business, sports* and *technology* containing news articles business news, sport news and technology news respectively. Populate each set with three to four news articles.

- Now print all articles that discuss a company, InfoSys
- Print all articles related to cricket
- Print all articles related to cricket and stump camera

10.2. Create three sets representing studentID of various courses namely UCS1, UCS2 and UCS3. Populate each of these sets with few student roll numbers. Now

- Print all students who are enrolled in all these courses
- Print all students who are enrolled in UCS2
- Print all students who are enrolled in UCS2 and UCS3

11

Sorting and Searching

OBJECTIVES

- To introduce sorting and searching support available in java.util package
- To introduce all static methods of Arrays and Collections classes for array and list processing
- To copy an array and fill array with an object using Arrays class
- To convert an array into a list using Arrays.asList() method
- To compare two array objects and iterate array elements
- To sort primitive arrays using Arrays.sort() method
- To sort primitive object arrays using Arrays.sort() method
- To sort user-defined object array using Comparable interface with Arrays
- To sort user-defined object array using Comparator interface with Arrays
- To explain why do we need both comparable and comparator types
- To search sorted arrays for a key using Arrays.binarySearch() method
- To introduce max(), min(), reverse(), swap() and shuffle() methods of Collections class
- To perform sorting using Collections.sort() class
- To perform binary search using Collections.binarySearch() class
- To sort user-defined object List using Comparable interface and Collections
- To sort user-defined object List using Comparator interface and Collections

11.1 INTRODUCTION

The *java.util* package provides two ways to sort the given collections automatically. You can either use **Arrays class** or **Collections class**. The Arrays and Collections classes provide methods to perform **sorting** and also searching for a key. Also a lot of features for **comparison**, checking, **filling** and **copying** are provided in these two classes. The sort() available in these two classes performs the necessary sorting. The wrapper objects can be sorted automatically by its built-in natural ordering. On the other hand, user-defined objects can be sorted using **Comparable** and **Comparator** interfaces. This chapter introduces you to sorting and searching methods available in java.util package.

11.2 SORTING AND SEARCHING USING ARRAYS CLASS

The java.util.Arrays class provides a set of *static* methods for sorting, searching, **comparison** and **filling** operation. The sort() sorts a given array (of primitive data types or objects) or a portion of an array, binarySearch() finds an element in the array, equal() compares the given two array for equality and fill() fills an array with a value.

11.3 FILLING AND COPYING ARRAYS

The fill() copies a single value in each location of the array or copies the object reference to each location of the array. The filling can be done to entire array or a portion of an array. There is another interesting method available from System class named arraycopy() that copies values of an array to another much faster. The fill() and arraycopy() support all overloaded methods to handle various primitive types. Listing 11.1 explains fill() and arraycopy() methods. Furthermore, asList() converts an array into a List.

Listing 11.1. Filling and Copying Illustration

```java
// FillCopy.java
import java.util.*;

public class FillCopy
{
    public static void main(String[] args)
    {
        int max = 5;

        int[] ai = new int[max];
        String[] as = new String[max];

        // fill int array with 10
        Arrays.fill(ai, 10);
        System.out.println("\nFill int array");
        for( int i : ai)
            System.out.print(i + " ");
        // fill string array with Java
        Arrays.fill(as, "Java");
        System.out.println("\nFill string array");
        for( String s : as)
            System.out.print(s + " ");
```

```
      // copy int array
      int[] aicopy = new int[max];
      System.arraycopy(ai, 0, aicopy, 0, ai.length);
      System.out.println("\nCopy int array");
      for( int i : aicopy)
            System.out.print(i + " ");

      // copy string array
      String[] ascopy = new String[max];
      System.arraycopy(as, 0, ascopy, 0, as.length);
      System.out.println("\nCopy string array");
      for(String s : ascopy)
            System.out.print(s + " ");

      // convert array into a list
      System.out.println("\nString Array is converted as list");
      System.out.println(Arrays.asList(ascopy));
   }
}
```

```
Fill int array
10 10 10 10 10
Fill string array
Java Java Java Java Java
Copy int array
10 10 10 10 10
Copy string array
Java Java Java Java Java
String Array is converted as list
[Java, Java, Java, Java, Java]
```

11.4 COMPARING ARRAYS

The equals() method compares two arrays of equal size and same type. The arrays that are compared can be of primitive types or objects of same type. Listing 11.2 explains methods for filling and array comparison.

Listing 11.2. Array Comparison and Filling Operations

```
// ArrayCompare.java
import java.util.*;
public class ArrayCompare
{
```

```java
    public static void main(String[] args)
    {
        int max = 5;

        int[] a1 = new int[max];
        int[] a2 = new int[max];
        String[] s1 = new String[max];
        String[] s2 = new String[max];

        Arrays.fill(a1, 10);
        Arrays.fill(a2, 10);
        System.out.println("\n array 1");
        for(int i : a1)
            System.out.print(i + " ");
        System.out.println("\n array 2");
        for(int i : a2)
            System.out.print(i + " ");
        System.out.println("\na1 and a2 are : " + Arrays.
        equals(a1,a2));

        Arrays.fill(s1, "Hello");
        Arrays.fill(s2, "Hello");
        System.out.println("\n array 1");
        for(String s : s1)
            System.out.print(s + " ");
        System.out.println("\n array 2");
        for(String s : s2)
            System.out.print(s + " ");
        System.out.println("\ns1 and s2 are : " + Arrays.
        equals(a1,a2));
    }
}
```

```
array 1
10 10 10 10 10
array 2
10 10 10 10 10
a1 and a2 are : true

array 1
Hello Hello Hello Hello Hello
array 2
Hello Hello Hello Hello Hello
s1 and s2 are : true
```

11.5 SORTING PRIMITIVE ARRAYS

Until Java 1.1, there was no support for sorting primitive type or objects. Java eliminates this deficiency from Java 1.2 onwards with *sort()* method. The sort() performs natural ordering of arrays of any primitive types and objects. Here is a Listing 11.3 that sorts a set of integers.

Listing 11.3. Sorting Integers

```java
// SortIntegers.java
import java.util.*;
public class SortIntegers
{
    public static void main(String[] args)
    {
        if (args.length == 0)
        {
            System.out.println("Enter numbers for
            sorting...");
            return;
        }

        int[] numbers = new int[args.length];

        for(int i = 0; i < args.length; i++)
            numbers[i] = Integer.parseInt(args[i]);

        System.out.println("Before sorting");
        for(int i = 0; i < numbers.length; i++)
            System.out.println(numbers[i]);

        Arrays.sort(numbers);

        System.out.println("After sorting");
        for(int i = 0; i < numbers.length; i++)
            System.out.println(numbers[i]);
    }
}
```

```
Before sorting
9
2
3
6
1
```

```
After sorting
1
2
3
6
9
```

11.6 SORTING STRING OBJECTS

Having seen the ways to sort list of integers, now let us see how to **sort String** objects. Sorting wrapper classes and user-defined objects using sort() method is also straightforward. Listing 11.4 illustrates sorting of string objects.

Listing 11.4. Sorting Strings

```java
// SortStrings.java                                      {coderipe}

import java.util.*;

public class SortStrings
{
    public static void main(String[] args)
    {
        String[] names = { "rita", "alex", "peter", "xavier",
        "benita"};

        System.out.println("Given names");
        for( String s : names)
            System.out.println(s);

        Arrays.sort(names);

        System.out.println("After sorting");
        for( String s : names)
            System.out.println(s);
    }
}
```

```
Given names
rita
alex
peter
xavier
```

```
benita
After sorting
alex
benita
peter
rita
Xavier
```

11.7 ARRAY SORTING USING COMPARABLE

In the previous section, the readers were introduced to how to use Arrays.sort() to sort primitive types and wrapper classes. Suppose we have a set of user-defined objects, say the details about students such as rollno, name and marks. Then, the question before us is how to sort these student objects. In order to sort user-defined objects, we have two ways:

- use java.lang.Comparable interface
- use java.util.Comparator interface

Now, let us use Comparable and Comparator interfaces to sort user-defined objects using Arrays.sort() method. Listing 11.5 explains how to use Arrays.sort() method and Comparable interface to sort students.

Listing 11.5. Sorting Student Objects Using Comparable

```java
// SortStudents.java                                    {coderipe}

import java.util.*;

class Student implements Comparable<Student>
{
    int rollno;
    String name;
    double marks;
    public Student(int rno, String s, double m)
    {
        rollno = rno;
        name = s;
        marks = m;
    }

    public int compareTo(Student o)
    {
        return this.rollno - o.rollno; // sort based on roll no
        // for descending order change as: o.rollno - this.rollno
    }
}
```

```java
public class SortStudents
{
    int max = 5;
    Student[] students = new Student[max];

    public void init()
    {
        int i = 0;
        students[i++] = new Student(5005, "Rex", 85.00);
        students[i++] = new Student(5003, "Peter", 75.00);
        students[i++] = new Student(5001, "Aarthi", 65.00);
        students[i++] = new Student(5002, "Divya", 55.00);
        students[i++] = new Student(5004, "Sam", 95.00);
    }

    public void dosort()
    {
        // sort
        Arrays.sort(students);
    }

    public void show()
    {
        for(Student s : students)
            System.out.println(s.rollno + "\t" + s.name + "\t" +
            s.marks);
    }

    public static void main(String[] args)
    {
        SortStudents st = new SortStudents();
        st.init();

        System.out.println("Given names before sorting");
        st.show();
        st.dosort();
        System.out.println("After sorting");
        st.show();
    }
}
```

```
Given names before sorting
5005    Rex     85.0
5003    Peter 75.0
```

```
5001  Aarthi 65.0
5002  Divya  55.0
5004  Sam    95.0
After sorting
5001  Aarthi 65.0
5002  Divya  55.0
5003  Peter  75.0
5004  Sam    95.0
5005  Rex    85.0
```

In this application, Student class implements Comparable and overrides compareTo() method. The *compareTo()* method compares this object with the argument object (say o). It returns a

- positive integer if this object is greater than o
- zero, if this object equals to o
- negative integer, if this object is less than o

The public class just creates an array of student objects, initializes them with values, performs sorting using sort() and displays students using for-each statement.

11.8 ARRAY SORTING USING COMPARATOR

If we need to sort based on other data members of Student, we will have to change Student's compareTo() method to use those fields. But then, we would lose this rollno-based sorting functionality. This will not be a good choice if we have to sort using additional data members too. Therefore to preserve natural ordering (using rollno) and to perform sorting using other data members, we have a choice; that is Comparator interface.

We create a class that implements Comparator interface and overrides compare() method with two student objects as arguments for compare(). This way, we do not have to touch the Student class; also Student class need not implement either Comparable or Comparator interfaces. For instance, Figure 11.1 depicts a comparator namely StudComparator that implements Comparator and overrides compare(). The compare() takes two student objects and returns an int. Also note that Comparator should be defined type-safe with the class name.

Figure 11.1. StudComparator Interface

```
class StudComparator implements Comparator<Student>
{
    public int compare(Student o1, Student o2)
    {
        return o1.name.compareTo(o2.name);
    }
}
```

Now let us use StudComparator class to sort student objects. The overloaded Arrays.sort() will do the trick as depicted in Listing 11.6.

Listing 11.6. Sorting Using StudComparator

```java
// SortStudents2.java
import java.util.*;                                    {coderipe}

class Student
{
    int rollno;
    String name;
    double marks;

    public Student(int rno, String s, double m)
    {
        rollno = rno;
        name = s;
        marks = m;
    }
}

class StudComparator implements Comparator<Student>
{
    public int compare(Student o1, Student o2)
    {
        return o1.name.compareTo(o2.name);   // sort based on name
    }
}

public class SortStudents2
{
    int max = 5;
    Student[] students = new Student[max];

    public void init()
    {
        int i = 0;
        students[i++] = new Student(5005, "Rex", 85.00);
        students[i++] = new Student(5003, "Peter", 75.00);
        students[i++] = new Student(5001, "Aarthi", 65.00);
        students[i++] = new Student(5002, "Divya", 55.00);
        students[i++] = new Student(5004, "Sam", 95.00);
    }

    public void dosort()
    {
```

```
        // sort using comparator
        Arrays.sort(students, new StudComparator());
    }

    public void show()
    {
        for(Student s : students)
            System.out.println(s.rollno + "," + s.name + "," +
            s.marks);
    }

    public static void main(String[] args)
    {
        SortStudents2 st = new SortStudents2();
        st.init();

        System.out.println("Given names before sorting");
        st.show();
        st.dosort();
        System.out.println("After sorting");
        st.show();
    }
}
```

```
Given names before sorting
5005,Rex,85.0
5003,Peter,75.0
5001,Aarthi,65.0
5002,Divya,55.0
5004,Sam,95.0
After sorting
5001,Aarthi,65.0
5002,Divya,55.0
5003,Peter,75.0
5005,Rex,85.0
5004,Sam,95.0
```

11.9 SEARCHING SORTED ARRAYS

Arrays class supports *binarySearch()* to search for an item from the list. Remember, searching can be accomplished using binarySearch() only with sorted array. Otherwise you might receive unpredictable results from searching an unsorted array. Listing 11.7 illustrates binary search with an integer array.

Listing 11.7. Binary Search of Integer Array

```java
// ArraySearch.java
import java.util.*;

public class ArraySearch
{
    public static void main(String[] args)
    {
        int[] marks = {10,55,93,85,38,72};

        System.out.println("\nGiven array");
        for(int mark : marks)
                System.out.print(mark + " " );

        // sort array first
        Arrays.sort(marks);

        System.out.println("\nSorted array");
        for(int mark : marks)
                System.out.print(mark + " " );

        int item = 55;
        // search for item
        int loc = Arrays.binarySearch(marks, item);

        // display the location
        if(loc >= 0)
                System.out.println("\nLocation of " + item + " is : "
                + loc);
        else
                System.out.println(item + " not found in array");
    }
}
```

```
Given array
10 55 93 85 38 72
Sorted array
10 38 55 72 85 93
Location of 55 is : 2
```

Here binarySearch() takes the sorted array and key to be searched as arguments and searches for the key. It returns the location of the key if it is available in the array. If not found, it will return the next available location where this key can be inserted. If there are some duplicate elements in the array, searching for a duplicate element may return any location not necessarily the first duplicate's location.

11.10 SORTING AND SEARCHING USING COLLECTIONS CLASS

In the previous sections 11.3 to 11.9, the readers were introduced to sorting and search operations using Arrays class. Now the readers will learn Collections class, which is another interesting class in java. util package. Collections class contains a set of static methods that operate on collections. The **max()** and **min()** return the maximum and minimum of the collection. The **reverse()** reverses the order of the given list. The **rotate()** rotates the given list by the specified distance. The **shuffle()** shuffles the given list with default randomness. The overloaded shuffle() shuffles the given list based on the randomness.

The **sort()** sorts the given list by default natural ordering and overloaded sort() will sort the given list based on comparator. The **swap()** swaps two elements in a given list. The binarySearch() searches for the given key in a list and also with a comparator default natural ordering can be altered. Listing 11.8 explains the important methods of Collections class.

Listing 11.8. Simple Illustration of Collections Class

```java
// CollectionsTest.java
import java.util.*;

public class CollectionsTest
{
    public static void main(String[] args)
    {
        List<Integer> list = new ArrayList<Integer>();

        // populate list with random numbers
        Random r = new Random();
        for(int i = 0; i < 10; i++)
            list.add(r.nextInt(50));

        System.out.println("Given array");
        System.out.println(list);

        System.out.println("max: " + Collections.max(list));
        System.out.println("min: " + Collections.min(list));

        Collections.reverse(list);
        System.out.println("After reverse: " + list);

        Collections.shuffle(list);
        System.out.println("After shuffle: " + list);

        Collections.shuffle(list, new Random());
        System.out.println("After shuffle with user-defined
        randomness: " + list);

        Collections.swap(list, 1,2);
```

```
        System.out.println("After swapping 1 and 2: " + list);

    Collections.sort(list);
    System.out.println("After sorting: " + list);

    int loc = Collections.binarySearch(list, list.get(2));
    if(loc >= 0)
        System.out.println("The element " + list.get(2) + "
        exists at " + loc);
    else
        System.out.println("The element " + list.get(2) + "
        not found");

    }
}
```

```
Given array
[39, 43, 24, 45, 15, 16, 23, 37, 37, 37]
max: 45
min: 15
After reverse: [37, 37, 37, 23, 16, 15, 45, 24, 43, 39]
After shuffle: [37, 37, 23, 16, 43, 24, 37, 39, 15, 45]
After shuffle with user-defined randomness: [45, 16, 24, 43, 39,
15, 37, 37, 23, 37]
After swapping 1 and 2: [45, 24, 16, 43, 39, 15, 37, 37, 23, 37]
After sorting: [15, 16, 23, 24, 37, 37, 37, 39, 43, 45]
The element 23 exists at 2
```

11.11 SORTING LISTS USING COMPARABLE

The Comparable and Comparator interfaces can also be used with Lists to sort the given objects. The Collections.sort() is very similar to Arrays.sort() method. However, the difference is Collections. sort() sorts the given list, whereas Arrays.sort() sorts a given object array. Now, let us revisit the sorting application for student objects that we discussed in section 11.7. Listing 11.9 explains sorting student objects using Collections.sort() method.

Listing 11.9. Collections-based Sorting of Student Objects

```
// CSortStudents.java

import java.util.*;

class Student implements Comparable<Student>
```

```java
{
    int rollno;
    String name;
    double marks;
    public Student(int rno, String s, double m)
    {
        rollno = rno;
        name = s;
        marks = m;
    }

    public int compareTo(Student o)
    {
        return this.rollno - o.rollno;   // sort based on roll no
    }
}

public class CSortStudents
{
    int max = 5;
    List<Student> students = new ArrayList<Student>();

    public void init()
    {
        students.add(new Student(5005, "Rex", 85.00));
        students.add(new Student(5003, "Peter", 75.00));
        students.add(new Student(5001, "Aarthi", 65.00));
        students.add(new Student(5002, "Divya", 55.00));
        students.add(new Student(5004, "Sam", 95.00));
    }

    public void dosort()
    {
        // sort
        Collections.sort(students);
    }

    public void show()
    {
        for(Student s : students)
            System.out.println(s.rollno + "," + s.name + "," +
            s.marks);
    }

    public static void main(String[] args)
```

```
    {
        CSortStudents st = new CSortStudents();
        st.init();

        System.out.println("Given students before sorting");
        st.show();
        st.dosort();
        System.out.println("Students details after sorting");
        st.show();
    }
}
```

```
Given students before sorting
5005,Rex,85.0
5003,Peter,75.0
5001,Aarthi,65.0
5002,Divya,55.0
5004,Sam,95.0
Students details after sorting
5001,Aarthi,65.0
5002,Divya,55.0
5003,Peter,75.0
5004,Sam,95.0
5005,Rex,85.0
```

11.12 SORTING LISTS USING COMPARATOR

Comparator interface is capable of comparing two different objects. We have already applied Comparator interface to sorting student array of objects in section 11.8. Once comparator class is defined by implementing Comparator interface and overriding compare(), then we can apply Collections. sort() to sort the given list of objects with the comparator object. Listing 11.10 explains sorting the list student objects with comparator object.

Listing 11.10. Comparator-based Sorting of List of Objects

```
// CSortStudents2.java
import java.util.*;

class Student
{
    int rollno;
    String name;
    double marks;
```

```java
    public Student(int rno, String s, double m)
    {
        rollno = rno;
        name = s;
        marks = m;
    }
}

class StudComparator implements Comparator<Student>
{
    public int compare(Student o1, Student o2)
    {
        return o1.name.compareTo(o2.name);   // sort based on name
    }
}

public class CSortStudents2
{
    int max = 5;
    List<Student> students = new ArrayList<Student>();

    public void init()
    {
        students.add(new Student(5005, "Rex", 85.00));
        students.add(new Student(5003, "Peter", 75.00));
        students.add(new Student(5001, "Aarthi", 65.00));
        students.add(new Student(5002, "Divya", 55.00));
        students.add(new Student(5004, "Sam", 95.00));
    }

    public void dosort()
    {
        // sort
        Collections.sort(students, new StudComparator());
    }

    public void show()
    {
        for(Student s : students)
            System.out.println(s.rollno + "," + s.name + "," +
            s.marks);
    }

    public static void main(String[] args)
```

```
    {
        CSortStudents2 st = new CSortStudents2();
        st.init();

        System.out.println("Given students before sorting");
        st.show();
        st.dosort();
        System.out.println("Students details after sorting");
        st.show();
    }
}
```

```
Given students before sorting
5005,Rex,85.0
5003,Peter,75.0
5001,Aarthi,65.0
5002,Divya,55.0
5004,Sam,95.0
Students details after sorting
5001,Aarthi,65.0
5002,Divya,55.0
5003,Peter,75.0
5005,Rex,85.0
5004,Sam,95.0
```

11.13 SUMMARY

1. The java.util.Arrays class provides a set of *static* methods for sorting, searching, comparison, copying and filling operations
2. The Arrays.sort() performs sorting of primitive arrays and wrapper object arrays
3. The comparable interfaces define user-defined object that is comparable with another object
4. An object is comparable if it extends Comparable interface and overrides compareTo() method
5. The comparator interface compares two user-defined objects via its arguments without touching its own object
6. An object can compare two objects if it extends Comparator interface and overrides compare() method
7. Two arrays can be compared to check whether contents are same or not
8. Collections class supports a set of static methods such as Collections.max(), Collections.min(), Collections.shuffle() and Collections.reverse() to find maximum, minimum and reverse of the given List
9. The Collections.shuffle() shuffles the contents of the given list based on some position
10. The Collections.swap() interchanges two elements of a list
11. The sort() and binarySearch() methods performs the required sorting and searching operations

12. The binarySearch() needs presorted array or List in order to be able to perform binary search
13. The binarySearch() will return unpredictable results if the given input is not sorted
14. Similar to Arrays class, Collections class can sort list of primitive types, wrapper types and user-defined type of objects
15. The Comparable and Comparator interfaces define the required sorting strategy to sort the user-defined objects

KEY TERMS

Arrays class, 332
BinarySearch, 342
Collections class, 332
Comparable, 333
Comparator, 333
Comparison, 332

Copying, 333
Filling, 332
Max, 344
Min, 344
Reverse, 344
Rotate, 344

Shuffle, 344
Sort, 344
Sort String, 337
Sorting, 332
Swap, 344

REVIEW QUESTIONS

Multiple-choice Questions

1. Given a list of int values, how will you sort these int values?
   a. Arrays.sort()
   b. Collections.sort()
   c. TreeSet class
   d. All of the above

2. Given a list of wrapper class values, how will you sort these wrapper class values?
   a. Arrays.sort()
   b. Collections.sort()
   c. TreeSet class
   d. All of the above

3. Given an array of objects, how will you sort this object array?
   a. Arrays.sort()
   b. Collections.sort()
   c. TreeSet along with Comparator or Comparable
   d. All of the above

4. How will you initialize an array with a value?
   a. Arrays.fill()
   b. Arrays.init()
   c. Arrays.fillArray()
   d. None of the above

5. How will you copy one array into another array?
   a. Arrays.copy()
   b. Arrays.copyArray()
   c. System.arraycopy()
   d. System.copy()

6. What is the output?

```
int[] a = {1,2,3,4,5};
a = Arrays.copyOf(a, 4);
for(int i :a)
   System.out.print(i);
```

a. 12345

b. 1234

c. 2345

d. 23451

7. What is the output?

```
int[] a = {1,2,3};
a = Arrays.copyOf(a, 4);
for(int i :a)
   System.out.print(i);
```

a. 0123

b. 2310

c. 3120

d. 1230

8. How will you compare two arrays?

a. Arrays.equals()

b. Arrays.equal()

c. System.equals()

d. System.equal()

e. None of the above

9. What is the output?

```
String[] s1 = {"a","b"};
String[] s2 = {"a","b"};
System.out.println(Arrays.equals(s1, s2));
```

a. True

b. False

c. Compilation error

d. Runtime exception

10. What is the output?

```
public class Test11
{
   public static void main(String[] args)
   {
      Cat[] c1 = {new Cat(1), new Cat(2)};
      Cat[] c2 = {new Cat(1), new Cat(2)};
```

```
      System.out.println(Arrays.equals(c1, c2));
  }
}
class Cat
{
   int a;
   public Cat(int i) { a = i;}
}
```

a. True
b. False
c. Compilation error
d. Runtime exception

11. What is the output?

```
public class Test11
{
   public static void main(String[] args)
   {
       Cat c1 = new Cat(1);
       Cat c2 = new Cat(2);

       Cat[] cat1 = {c1, c2};
       Cat[] cat2 = {c1, c2};
       System.out.println(Arrays.equals(cat1, cat2));
   }
}
class Cat
{
   int a;
   public Cat(int i) { a = i;}
}
```

a. True
b. False
c. Compilation error
d. Runtime exception

12. What is the output?

```
int[] arr = {2,5,1,7,9,4};
Arrays.sort(arr,1,4);
for(int i: arr)
   System.out.print(i);
```

a. 215794
b. 124579
c. 291954
d. None of the above

13. What is the output?

```
String[] s1 = {"a","d", "b"};
Arrays.sort(s1);
for(String s: s1)
   System.out.print(s + " ");
```

a. adb

b. dab

c. bad

d. abd

14. What is the output?

```
int[] a = {1,2,3};
System.out.print(Arrays.binarySearch(a, 2));
String[] s = {"a","b", "c"};
System.out.print(Arrays.binarySearch(s, "c"));
```

a. 12

b. 23

c. 31

d. 13

15. What is the output?

```
int[] a = {1,2,3};
System.out.print(Arrays.binarySearch(a, 4));
String[] s1 = {"a","d", "b"};
System.out.print(Arrays.binarySearch(s1, "b"));
```

a. −3 −2

b. −4 −2

c. −5 −2

d. None of the above

16. What is the output?

```
int[] a = {1,3,2};
Arrays.sort(a);
System.out.print(Arrays.binarySearch(a, 3));
String[] s1 = {"a","d", "b"};
Arrays.sort(s1);
System.out.print(Arrays.binarySearch(s1, "b"));
```

a. 21

b. 31

c. 32

d. 12

17. What is the output?

```
int[] a = {1,3,2,5,6};
Arrays.sort(a);
System.out.print(Arrays.binarySearch(a, 3, 1, 2));
```

    a. Compilation error   b. IllegalArgumentException

    c. ArrayIndexOutOfBoundsException   d. None of the above

18. What is the output?

```
String[] a = {"b", "c", "a", "d"};
List list = Arrays.asList(a);
Collections.sort(list);
System.out.print(list);
```

    a. [a, b, c, d]   b. [b, c, a, d]

    c. [b, c, d, a]   d. [c, b, d, a]

19. What is the output?

```
String[] a = {"b", "c", "a", "d"};
List list = Arrays.asList(a);
Collections.sort(list, Collections.reverseOrder());
System.out.print(list);
```

    a. [a, b, c, d]   b. [b, c, a, d]

    c. [d, c, b, a]   d. [c, b, d, a]

20. Find out the output:

```
Integer[] a = {1,3,2,5};
List list = Arrays.asList(a);
Collections.sort(list, Collections.reverseOrder());
System.out.print(list);
```

    a. [5, 3, 2, 1]   b. [1, 2, 3, 5]

    c. Compilation error   d. Runtime exception

21. What is the output?

```
String[] a = {"b", "c", "a", "d"};
List list = Arrays.asList(a);
```

```
Collections.sort(list);
Collections.rotate(list,2);
System.out.print(list);
```

a. [a, b, c, d]   b. [b, c, a, d]
c. [b, c, d, a]   d. [c, d, a, b]

22. What is the output?

```
String[] a = {"b", "c", "a", "d"};
List list = Arrays.asList(a);
System.out.print(Collections.max(list));
System.out.print(Collections.min(list));
```

a. da   b. ad
c. bc   d. cb

23. What is the output?

```
String[] a = {"b", "c", "a", "d"};
List list = Arrays.asList(a);
System.out.print(Collections.binarySearch(list, "d"));
```

a. True   b. d
c. 3   d. None of the above

24. What is the output?

```
String[] a = {"b", "c", "a", "d", "a"};
List list = Arrays.asList(a);
System.out.print(Collections.frequency(list, "a"));
```

a. 2   b. 24
c. 4   d. 42

Answers

1. a, c   2. b   3. c   4. a   5. c   6. b   7. d   8. a   9. a   10. b
11. a   12. a   13. d   14. a   15. b   16. a   17. b   18. a   19. a, c   20. a
21. d   22. a   23. c   24. a

Short-answer Questions

1. Explain fill, arraycopy and equals methods of Arrays class with an example.
2. How will you sort primitive data types and string using Arrays class?
3. Explain the sorting of array of user-defined objects with Comparable.
4. Explain the sorting of array of user-defined objects with Comparator.
5. Explain binarySearch method with an example.
6. Discuss five static methods of Collections class.
7. What is the difference between Arrays.sort() and Collections.sort()?
8. Explain the sorting of list of user-defined objects with Comparable.
9. Explain the sorting of list of user-defined objects with Comparator.

EXERCISES

11.1. Sort a string array using Arrays.sort() method.

11.2. Sort a string array using Collections.sort() method (you need to convert array into a List first).

11.3. For Exercise 8.2, modify Book so that it implements Comparable interface and overrides compareTo() method. Then sort all books in the bookShelf using Arrays.sort(bookShelf) method.

11.4. Modify the above exercise, so that BookShop implements Comparator interface and sort bookShelf objects using Arrays.sort(bookShelf, BookShop) method.

11.5. Modify Exercise 11.3 so that books are sorted using Collections.sort() method.

11.6. Modify Exercise 11.4 so that books are sorted using Collections.sort() method.

11.7. For Exercise 11.3, instantiate a Book object and perform Arrays.binarySearch() over the array of Books in the bookShelf. Assume now bookShelf is an array of Books instead of a LinkedList.

11.8. For Exercise 11.3, instantiate Book object and perform Collections.binarySearch() over the list of Books in the bookShelf.

11.9. [Super Market Application] Supermarket sells many items every day. For each item sold, item code, quantity sold out and date of sales are represented in a class Sales with the following details:

- int itemCode, int quantity, Date sdate;

    Create a class SuperMarket with the members

- ArrayList<Sales> sales;
- public void sales(Date d) displays total sales on this date
- public void sales(int item) displays total sales based on itemCode
- public void sales() displays sorted list of all sales items based on sdate

    Design a public class that will create few sales details for this supermarket. Read a date from user and get the total sales on this particular date. Also, display total sales for the given itemCode. Finally, display complete sales details sorted datewise.

PART IV Java Threads and IO Streams

12

Concurrency Using Threads

OBJECTIVES

- To explain process, multitasking, thread and multithreading
- To differentiate sequential execution and threaded execution
- To introduce thread creation ways: *Thread* and *Runnable*
- To explain variables inside local cache and master copy at main memory for threads
- To instantiate thread and start a thread
- To make thread to sleep
- To make thread to yield control to another threads
- To find the sum of an array using two threads
- To suspend calling thread using join
- To create daemon threads and explain its life
- To introduce thread priority and also its three constants
- To explain the importance of *Runnable* interface
- To synchronize threads for resource sharing using synchronized methods
- To introduce synchronized block for resource sharing
- To design ThreadedBank application
- To coordinate multiple threads using *wait, notify* and *notifyall*
- To define life cycle of a thread
- To introduce *java.concurrent* package
- To create ConcurrentHashMap and test it with multiple threads
- To introduce *java.concurrent.atomic* package

- To generate random strings using AtomicIntegerArray object
- To introduce *java.concurrent.locks* package and create ReentrantLock for threads

12.1 INTRODUCTION

Generally computer software performs several tasks simultaneously. For example, a word processor responds to our mouse click and key press while performing page alignment of a document. Each of these independent tasks is accomplished using a **thread**. Multitasking operating systems will run more than one program (also called **process**) at a time with a single CPU.

A process is a program in execution and will have its own address space. Sometimes a thread is called lightweight process and is a single sequential flow of control within a process. Therefore a single process will have many concurrently executing threads. Multithreading is a compelling feature of Java language. Every application you create will start with one thread called *main thread* and Java allows an application to create other threads.

Multithreading is highly essential when you develop an application that has several user interface (UI) components such as *buttons, combo boxes* and *text fields*. Apart from performing your main task, your application should listen to the events happening on these UI components. These events include users clicking buttons, selecting items from combo boxes, pressing keys and others. Each of these activities or events will be handled by a separate thread, and all these threads will concurrently execute indefinitely.

Multithreading has many more applications besides handling UI components. **Resource sharing** is another important application of multithreading. Suppose when there is a common resource that needs to be concurrently accessed and updated by many threads, then all threads must cooperatively perform tasks on this resource.

Concurrent programming requires a different understanding of the flow of execution. In sequential execution, a control flows from the start to the end of a process. Whereas in concurrent execution, the same block of code is executed by many threads simultaneously; thereby you get several outputs at the same time. When your application is multithreaded, it will make your application running slow because of several threads executing simultaneously.

Developing a multithreaded application is tricky and needs alternative thinking because of the complexity of threading. This chapter aims to explain all the necessary basics of concurrency so that the readers will be able to develop reasonably good multithread applications.

12.2 MULTITHREADING USING THREAD CLASS

Before moving on to the creation of threads in Java, let us look at an example of single thread and multithreads. A thread is not a program, it cannot run on its own; but it is a single sequential flow of control within a program. A normal Java program is a single-threaded application as shown in Figure 12.1.

There is nothing special in this single-threaded program. But the interesting part is with multiple threads within a single program as depicted in Figure 12.1.

A concurrent program can be created in two ways; you can create threads using either *java.lang.Thread* class or *java.lang.Runnable* interface. In this section, the readers will learn how to use Thread class to create a multithreaded application. The **Runnable interface** will be introduced in section 12.9.

An easy way to create a thread is to extend the **Thread class**. The Thread class contains all those features required for concurrent execution of the program. Also, you need to override run() method inside your application. The body of the **run** method will be executed concurrently by many threads.

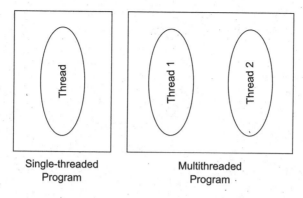

Single-threaded
Program

Multithreaded
Program

Figure 12.1. Single Thread and Multithreads

Therefore, each thread will execute run() method independently giving many outputs. Figure 12.2 explains this Thread behaviour.

Figure 12.2. Extending Thread Class

```
class MyThread extends Thread
{
    pubic void run()
    {
        // block of statements, simultaneously executed by many
        threads
    }
}
```

With this basic understanding of Thread class and how to override run() method, we will now develop an application that will count numbers. As a multithreaded program, we allow several threads to count numbers independently and simultaneously. Remember, the counting behaviour should be inserted inside the overridden run() method. Listing 12.1 depicts this multithreaded counter.

Listing 12.1. CounterThread

```
// CounterThread.java

class Counter extends Thread
{
    int number, max;

    public Counter(int n, int end)
    {
        number = n;
        max = end;
```

```
      start();  // start the thread
   }

   public void run()
   {
      for(int i = 0; i < max; i++)
            System.out.println("Inside Thread" + number + " : "
            + i);
   }
}

public class CounterThread
{
   public static void main(String[] args)
   {
      for(int i = 0; i < 5; i++)
            new Counter(i, 6); // count upto 6
   }
}
```

```
Inside Thread4 : 0
Inside Thread3 : 0
Inside Thread0 : 0
Inside Thread2 : 0
Inside Thread1 : 0
Inside Thread2 : 1
Inside Thread0 : 1
Inside Thread3 : 1
Inside Thread4 : 1
Inside Thread3 : 2
Inside Thread0 : 2
Inside Thread2 : 2
Inside Thread2 : 3
Inside Thread2 : 4
Inside Thread2 : 5
Inside Thread1 : 1
Inside Thread1 : 2
Inside Thread1 : 3
Inside Thread1 : 4
Inside Thread1 : 5
Inside Thread0 : 3
Inside Thread0 : 4
Inside Thread0 : 5
Inside Thread3 : 3
```

```
Inside Thread3 : 4
Inside Thread3 : 5
Inside Thread4 : 2
Inside Thread4 : 3
Inside Thread4 : 4
Inside Thread4 : 5
```

Here, Counter is created as a Thread object and thread behaviour is incorporated inside run() method. The thread has to be started and start() method inside constructor does this task. Unless start() method is called, the thread will never be started. The start() should be defined as a last statement inside constructor as control will immediately branch to run() without executing further statements.

Each thread will execute its copy of run() separately and simultaneously, causing all threads to print the value of its variable **i**. Note that even though *for* loop iterates fixed number of times (say up to *max*), displaying value of **i** of one thread will be interrupted by another thread. Therefore, no *for* loop will finish displaying its **i** values in one go.

Inside main(), we create five Counter thread objects with thread number and maximum value for counting. The main() simply instantiates Counter objects and returns to command prompt. In other words, main() is part of main thread so it dies after the instantiation. One interesting behaviour of threads is that every time you run the program you will get different sequence of outputs. Because we cannot predict which thread will display which value of the variable **i**. Different JDK implementations will follow different thread scheduling policies.

12.3 MAKING THREADS TO SLEEP

In the above application, there is always a fair chance that threads will monopolize the CPU time for longer period of time; thereby other threads will not get its CPU time. In order to give access to CPU time for other threads, the current thread should be made to sleep for a period of milliseconds. This way we will force a thread to go for a **sleep** so that CPU will execute other threads. The sleep() will make the thread to sleep. In Listing 12.2, the readers will learn how to rewrite our earlier Counter thread with the support of sleep().

Listing 12.2. Counter Thread Using Sleep()

```
// CounterThread2.java

class Counter extends Thread
{
    int number, max;

    public Counter(int n, int end)
    {
        number = n;
        max = end;
        start();  // start the thread
    }
```

```
   public void run()
   {
      try {
         sleep(100);  // sleep for 100 milliseconds
      }
      catch(InterruptedException e) { }
      for(int i = 0; i < max; i++)
         System.out.println("Inside Thread" + number + " : " + i);
   }
}

public class CounterThread2
{
   public static void main(String[] args)
   {
      for(int i = 0; i < 5; i++)
         new Counter(i, 6); // count upto 6
   }
}
```

```
Inside Thread2 : 0
Inside Thread0 : 0
Inside Thread2 : 1
Inside Thread0 : 1
Inside Thread0 : 2
Inside Thread0 : 3
Inside Thread0 : 4
Inside Thread0 : 5
Inside Thread2 : 2
Inside Thread2 : 3
Inside Thread2 : 4
Inside Thread2 : 5
Inside Thread1 : 0
Inside Thread4 : 0
Inside Thread3 : 0
Inside Thread4 : 1
Inside Thread1 : 1
Inside Thread4 : 2
Inside Thread3 : 1
Inside Thread4 : 3
Inside Thread1 : 2
Inside Thread4 : 4
Inside Thread3 : 2
Inside Thread3 : 3
```

```
Inside Thread3 : 4
Inside Thread3 : 5
Inside Thread4 : 5
Inside Thread1 : 3
Inside Thread1 : 4
Inside Thread1 : 5
```

The sleep() makes the thread to sleep for the specified duration (here 100 ms) and must be kept inside a try-catch block. The sleep() throws InterruptedException when another thread interrupts this current thread which it is sleeping. You are highly advised to play with this program by varying sleep() time to analyze different outputs by the threads.

12.4 YIELDING CONTROL TO OTHER THREADS

A thread will use *yield()* method to indicate that it has finished its execution so CPU can be relinquished to other threads. This is the exact opposite to sleep(). With sleep(), a thread is made compulsorily to go to sleep(), whereas yield() releases CPU time to other threads. Listing 12.3 shows how to rewrite our Counter thread with yield(). All we need to do is to just change sleep() by yield(). Of course we do not have to keep yield() method inside try-catch block.

Listing 12.3. Counter Thread Using Yield()

```java
// CounterThread3.java

class Counter extends Thread
{
    int number, max;

    public Counter(int n, int end)
    {
        number = n;
        max = end;
        start();  // start the thread
    }

    public void run()
    {
        yield();  // voluntarily relinquish control
        for(int i = 0; i < max; i++)
            System.out.println("Inside Thread" + number + " : "
                + i);
}}

public class CounterThread3
```

```
{
   public static void main(String[] args)
   {
      for(int i = 0; i < 5; i++)
         new Counter(i, 6); // count upto 6
   }
}
```

```
Inside Thread0 : 0
Inside Thread0 : 1
Inside Thread0 : 2
Inside Thread2 : 0
Inside Thread1 : 0
Inside Thread2 : 1
Inside Thread2 : 2
Inside Thread0 : 3
Inside Thread3 : 0
Inside Thread4 : 0
Inside Thread3 : 1
Inside Thread0 : 4
Inside Thread0 : 5
Inside Thread2 : 3
Inside Thread2 : 4
Inside Thread1 : 1
Inside Thread2 : 5
Inside Thread3 : 2
Inside Thread4 : 1
Inside Thread3 : 3
Inside Thread1 : 2
Inside Thread1 : 3
Inside Thread1 : 4
Inside Thread1 : 5
Inside Thread3 : 4
Inside Thread3 : 5
Inside Thread4 : 2
Inside Thread4 : 3
Inside Thread4 : 4
Inside Thread4 : 5
```

12.5 PROBLEM: MULTITHREADED ADDER

Let us find the sum of a given array of integers using two threads. The input array is divided into two parts, and each thread will find individual sums and the main thread will collect individual sums and display the final sum. The multithreaded adder is demonstrated in Listing 12.4.

Listing 12.4. Multithreaded Adder

```java
// MultiThreadedAdder.java
import java.util.*;

class Adder extends Thread
{
    int[] arr;
    int sum = 0;

    public Adder(int[] a)
    {
        arr = a;
        start();
    }

    public void run()
    {
        for(int i = 0; i < arr.length; i++)
            sum += arr[i];

        try
        {
            sleep(10);
        }
        catch(InterruptedException e) { }

        System.out.println("\nThread sum = " + sum);
    }
}

public class MultiThreadedAdder
{
    Random r = new Random();
    final int MAX = 100;
    int[] a = new int[MAX];   // 100 numbers

    Adder[] t = new Adder[2];   // two threads

    public void add()
    {
        // create array of numbers
        for(int i = 0; i < MAX; i++)
            a[i] = r.nextInt(10);

        System.out.println("Original array");
```

```
        for(int i : a)
            System.out.print(i + " ");

        // create two subarrays
        int length = a.length/2;
        int[] a1 = new int[length];
        int[] a2 = new int[length];

        // divide a into 2 subarrays
        System.arraycopy(a, 0, a1, 0, a1.length);
        System.arraycopy(a, length, a2, 0, a2.length);

        // hand over arrays to threads
        t[0] = new Adder(a1);
        t[1] = new Adder(a2);

        // wait for some time for threads to finish
        try {
            Thread.sleep(100);
        } catch(InterruptedException e) { }

        // collect sums
        int sum = t[0].sum + t[1].sum;

        // show
        System.out.println("Final Sum: " + sum);
    }

    public static void main(String[] args)
    {
        MultiThreadedAdder m = new MultiThreadedAdder();
        m.add();
    }
}
```

```
Original array
3 0 0 1 3 3 8 3 4 8 8 5 8 3 7 6 4 0 8 0 2 6 1 0 3 4 8 8 6 6
8 1 1 6 8 5 0 4 2 6 3 5 6 6 0 8 6 7 3 9 3 3 6 9 1 1 7 5 0 8
3 8 9 7 3 2 3 1 8 8 6 6 0 4 3 4 5 3 9 2 3 1 5 0 6 2 7 5 7 4
1 9 6 1 6 4 5 5 6 6
Thread sum = 226
Thread sum = 220
Final Sum: 446
```

The Adder class is simply a thread that will receive an array through its arguments, and it calculates the sum inside the *run()*. The public class is bit long and does a lot of things for us. It generates an array of random integers. The constant MAX defines the maximum size for the array, currently 100 elements. Of course you can set any value for MAX, your application will run, no problem! The *System.array-copy()* does the trick of dividing the array into two subarrays. The rest of the code is self-explanatory. The main thread just instantiates two threads and hands over the two subarrays to them. It waits until both threads finish their execution and collects the individual sums and adds them to get the final sum.

12.6 SUSPENDING CALLER THREAD

A thread may call another thread with *join()* method so that it can wait until the called thread completes its execution. For example, a thread **t1** calls **t2.join()**, so **t1** will wait until **t2** completes its execution. Listing 12.5 explains how JoiningThread waits indefinitely using join() until the called thread T2 finishes its execution.

Listing 12.5. Hello World Using Join()

```
// JoiningThread.java

class T2 extends Thread
{
    public T2()
    {
        start();
    }

    public void run()
    {
        for(int i = 0; i < 10; i++)
            System.out.println("Hello");
    }
}
public class JoiningThread extends Thread
{
    T2 t = new T2();

    public JoiningThread()
    {
        start();
    }

    public void run()
    {
        try {
            t.join(); // suspend JoiningThread until t finishes
```

```
            System.out.println("World");
        }catch(InterruptedException e) { }
    }

    public static void main(String[] args)
    {
        new JoiningThread();
    }
}
```

```
Hello
Hello
Hello
Hello
Hello
Hello
Hello
Hello
Hello
Hello
World
```

Now let us revisit our earlier multithreaded adder application (section 12.5) which calculates the sum of integers in an array. The main thread was made to wait for 100 ms so that the two adder threads will finish its calculation. After this waiting period, the main thread collects the individual sums and prints the final sum. The main drawback with this application is the waiting time. As a developer, we need to make a wild guess. The waiting time we guessed may be too long or too short we never know. So the better solution will be to suspend the main thread's execution until both adder threads complete their execution. Listing 12.6 rewrites our multithreaded adder with join() method.

Listing 12.6. Multithreaded Adder Using Join()

```
// MultiThreadedAdder2.java
import java.util.*;

class Adder extends Thread
{
    int[] arr;
    int sum = 0;

    public Adder(int[] a)
    {
        arr = a;
```

```
      start();
   }

   public void run()
   {
      for(int i = 0; i < arr.length; i++)
          sum += arr[i];

      try
      {
          sleep(10);
      }
      catch(InterruptedException e) { }

      System.out.println("\nThread sum = " + sum);
   }
}

public class MultiThreadedAdder2
{
   Random r = new Random();
   final int MAX = 100;
   int[] a = new int[MAX];  // 100 numbers

   Adder[] t = new Adder[2];  // two threads

   public void add()
   {
      // create array of numbers
      for(int i = 0; i < MAX; i++)
          a[i] = r.nextInt(10);

      System.out.println("Original array");
      for(int i : a)
          System.out.print(i + " ");

      // create two subarrays
      int length = a.length/2;
      int[] a1 = new int[length];
      int[] a2 = new int[length];

      // divide into 2 subarrays
      System.arraycopy(a, 0, a1, 0, a1.length);
      System.arraycopy(a, length, a2, 0, a2.length);
```

```
        // hand over arrays to threads
        t[0] = new Adder(a1);
        t[1] = new Adder(a2);


        try
        {
            t[0].join();  // suspend until t[0] finishes
            t[1].join();  // suspend until t[1] finishes
        }
        catch(InterruptedException e){}


        // collect sums
        int sum = t[0].sum + t[1].sum;


        // show
        System.out.println("Final Sum:  " + sum);
    }


    public static void main(String[] args)
    {
        MultiThreadedAdder2 m = new MultiThreadedAdder2();
        m.add();
    }
}
```

```
Original array
2 2 3 8 3 6 4 2 6 6 0 4 1 1 7 5 2 8 0 2 8 9 6 4 1 1 8 8 9 7
2 6 6 3 1 0 0 8 2 9 6 0 6 3 6 4 5 3 4 1 6 1 4 8 6 3 0 2 1 7
2 1 3 9 8 7 9 2 8 3 7 2 1 4 0 5 3 6 2 0 9 0 3 0 5 8 0 3 7 7
6 8 3 3 5 0 8 6 7 5
Thread sum = 208
Thread sum = 213
Final Sum: 421
```

The Thread.main() waits indefinitely until both threads t[0] and t[1] complete their execution by calling join() methods of t[0] and t[1].

12.7 DAEMON THREADS

Daemon threads are supporting service threads for other threads running in the background as long as all non-daemon threads are running. Daemon thread will terminate when all non-daemon threads terminate. A thread will be called daemon thread if it sets *setDaemon()* to true. The setDaemon()

should appear before *start()* method, failing which the thread will be assumed normal thread and control branches to run(). In Listing 12.7, the readers will know how daemon threads are created in order to say *Good Morning*.

Listing 12.7. Good Morning Daemon Thread1

```
// GoodDaemon.java
public class GoodDaemon extends Thread
{
    int number;

    public GoodDaemon(int i)
    {
        number = i;
        setDaemon(true);
        start();
    }

    public void run()
    {
        while(true)
        {
            try {
                sleep(1000000);
                System.out.println("Daemon " + number + " says
                Good morning");
            } catch (InterruptedException e) { }
        }
    }
    public static void main(String[] args)
    {
        for(int i = 0; i < 10; i++)
            new GoodDaemon(i);
        System.out.println("Thread.main() terminates");
    }
}
```

```
Thread.main() terminates
```

Once setDaemon() is called, thread will be identified as daemon thread. In run(), the daemon thread goes for a long sleep and then it will have to display a string *good morning* indefinitely. The main() simply creates 10 daemon threads and terminates immediately; by the time all daemon threads are still sleeping. Since main() thread is terminated before all daemon threads return from their sleep, all daemon threads eventually terminate along with main() thread without displaying the string *good morning*.

So how to make all daemons say *good morning*. You will have to do two things. First reduce waiting time for all daemons. Second allow Thread.main() to sleep for a while so that all daemons complete their greetings as shown in Listing 12.8.

Listing 12.8. Good Morning Daemon Thread2

```java
// GoodDaemon2.java
public class GoodDaemon2 extends Thread
{
    int number;

    public GoodDaemon2(int i)
    {
        number = i;
        setDaemon(true);
        start();
    }

    public void run()
    {
        while(true)
        {
            try
            {
                sleep(10);
                System.out.println(
                "Daemon " + number + " says Good morning");
            }
            catch (InterruptedException e) { }
        }
    }
    public static void main(String[] args)
    {
        for(int i = 0; i < 5; i++)
                new GoodDaemon2(i);

        // wait for some time so that all daemons greet
        try
        {
            Thread.sleep(10);
        }
        catch(InterruptedException e) { }
        System.out.println("Thread.main() terminates");
    }
}
```

```
Daemon 2 says Good morning
Daemon 4 says Good morning
Daemon 0 says Good morning
Daemon 1 says Good morning
Daemon 3 says Good morning
Daemon 1 says Good morning
Daemon 3 says Good morning
Daemon 2 says Good morning
Daemon 4 says Good morning
Daemon 0 says Good morning
Daemon 3 says Good morning
Daemon 1 says Good morning
Daemon 0 says Good morning
Thread.main() terminates
Daemon 4 says Good morning
Daemon 2 says Good morning
Daemon 2 says Good morning
```

12.8 THREAD PRIORITY

Java Thread class supports different **priority** levels for threads ranging from 1 to 10. Priority of a thread indicates how important this thread is. JVM uses priority of a particular thread to give preference for execution. This is necessary when there are a lot of threads waiting for their CPU time at the same time. The JVM will ensure the execution of all threads even though it will execute the thread with higher priority first.

The *setPriority()* and *getPriority()* methods can be used to assign priority levels to threads and retrieve the current priority level of a thread. Further, Thread class contains three static constants to set priorities: *MAX_PRIORITY* (maximum priority), *MIN_PRIORITY* (minimum priority) and *NORM_PRIORITY* (normal priority). Listing 12.9 explains how to set priorities to threads using setPriority().

Listing 12.9. Expensive Arithmetic and Thread Priorities

```java
// FloorThread.java

class Flooring extends Thread
{
    final int MAX = 100000000;
    int number;
    volatile double d = 0;

    public Flooring(int n, int priority)
    {
        number = n;
```

```
        setPriority(priority);
        start();  // start the thread
    }

    public void run()
    {
        for(int i = 1; i < MAX; i++)
            d = d + (Math.PI + Math.E + Math.floor(i)) /
            (double)i;
        System.out.println("Inside Thread" + number + " : " + d);
    }
}

public class FloorThread
{
    public static void main(String[] args)
    {
        for(int i = 1; i < 11; i++)
            new Flooring(i, 11-i); // priority decreases

    }
}
```

```
Inside Thread2 : 1.000001103154488E8
Inside Thread1 : 1.000001103154488E8
Inside Thread3 : 1.000001103154488E8
Inside Thread4 : 1.000001103154488E8
Inside Thread5 : 1.000001103154488E8
Inside Thread6 : 1.000001103154488E8
Inside Thread8 : 1.000001103154488E8
Inside Thread7 : 1.000001103154488E8
Inside Thread10 : 1.000001103154488E8
Inside Thread9 : 1.000001103154488E8
```

In this example, the Flooring thread performs an expensive arithmetic operation by adding PI value, E value and floor value and a division. This expression is iteratively added many times. This will sufficiently allow a thread to spend longer time in calculation. Suppose if one thread begins its calculation with CPU, other high-priority thread will grab CPU time, thereby the first thread will wait. Here, thread 1 enjoys a highest priority of 10 and priority decreases with other threads. Also note that variable **i** is declared as volatile.

When multiple threads use the same variable, each thread will receive its copy of the local cache for this variable. So, when a thread updates the value of this variable, it is actually updating in the local cache not in the main memory. The other thread which is using the same variable doesn't know anything about the values changed by another thread. By declaring this variable as *volatile*, variable will not be stored in local cache. Whenever a thread updates the values, it is updated directly to the main memory. So that other threads will use the updated value from main memory.

Thus *volatile* keyword is used with a variable declaration to indicate JVM that a thread accessing the variable must always merge its own private copy of the variable with the master copy in the main memory. Accessing a volatile variable synchronizes all cached copies of the variables in the main memory. Volatile should be applied to instance data members and not static data members.

12.9 MULTITHREADING USING RUNNABLE

You have been developing so far multithreaded applications using Thread class. You have developed thread objects by extending Thread class. Suppose your class is already inheriting another class. In this case, you will not be able to inherit Thread class as Java does not support a multiple inheritance. The other alternative to a Thread class is Runnable interface. So your class will implement Runnable interface and override run(). Note that Thread class also implements Runnable. Figure 12.3 clearly explains Runnable interface.

Figure 12.3. Runnable Interface

```
class Countable implements Runnable
{
    public void run()
    {
        // your thread behaviour goes here
    }
}
```

The Runnable interface simply provides run() method. Rather it does not provide any thread behaviour. So you will have to create a Thread inside your class to provide thread behaviour and call start() method of the thread to perform usual thread initialization and to call run() as shown in Example 12.1.

Example 12.1. Runnable Interface with Thread

```
class Countable implements Runnable
{
    Thread t = new Thread(this);

    public Countable()
    {
        t.start();
    }

    public void run()
    {
```

```
        // your thread behaviour goes here
    }
}
```

With this basic understanding of Runnable interface, we all now can rewrite a counter thread using Runnable interface. Listing 12.10 illustrates this countable thread.

Listing 12.10. Countable Thread Using Runnable

```
// CountableThread.java

class Countable implements Runnable
{
    Thread t = new Thread(this);
    int number, max;

    public Countable(int n, int end)
    {
        number = n;
        max = end;
        t.start();  // start the thread
    }

    public void run()
    {
        try {
                t.sleep(100);
        }catch (InterruptedException e) { }

        for(int i = 0; i < max; i++)
            System.out.println("Inside Thread" + number + " : "
            + i);
    }
}

public class CountableThread
{
    public static void main(String[] args)
    {
        for(int i = 0; i < 5; i++)
            new Countable(i, 6); // count upto 6
    }
}
```

```
Inside Thread1 : 0
Inside Thread0 : 0
Inside Thread2 : 0
Inside Thread4 : 0
Inside Thread3 : 0
Inside Thread4 : 1
Inside Thread2 : 1
Inside Thread0 : 1
Inside Thread1 : 1
Inside Thread0 : 2
Inside Thread2 : 2
Inside Thread4 : 2
Inside Thread3 : 1
Inside Thread4 : 3
Inside Thread2 : 3
Inside Thread0 : 3
Inside Thread1 : 2
Inside Thread0 : 4
Inside Thread2 : 4
Inside Thread2 : 5
Inside Thread4 : 4
Inside Thread4 : 5
Inside Thread3 : 2
Inside Thread3 : 3
Inside Thread3 : 4
Inside Thread3 : 5
Inside Thread0 : 5
Inside Thread1 : 3
Inside Thread1 : 4
Inside Thread1 : 5
```

Inside Countable class, you simply implement Runnable interface, instantiate a thread within this current object, start the thread inside constructor and override run() method. Once start() is called inside constructor, then flow of control begins executing run() method. With run(), the thread simply sleeps for a while (using *t.sleep()* instead of sleep()), performs counting, displays thread number and count value and terminates itself. The main() initializes five threads and terminates.

12.10 THREAD SYNCHRONIZATION FOR RESOURCE SHARING

As long as your program is single threaded, all available resources are used by this single thread and execution of your program will be normal. Here a resource can be simply a data member or member functions. But when there are several threads trying to access a common resource at the same time then the system will be in trouble. For instance, two threads may try to access a bank account at the same time, to print their document to the printer at the same and to access a database record one for reading and another for writing data to this record. These are the examples of resource sharing problem. Communication among threads will result into two types of errors as shown in the following scenarios:

- Two threads are trying to update common resource via different methods
- Two sequential statements about a common resource are executed by two different threads

In order to understand scenario-1, let us start with an example as shown in Example 12.2.

Example 12.2. Two Threads Updating Common Resource Via Different Method Calls

```
Step1: count = 0;
Step2: incrementCount() { ++count; }
Step3: decrementCount() { --count; }
Step4: print count
```

Suppose a single thread executes the statements as shown in Figure 12.4. It will not be any problem and the thread will print its count value 0 correctly.

Assume now that there are two threads t1 and t2. Thread t1 executes step2 and t2 executes step3 almost simultaneously (as we have only one CPU) with its own local copy of count (i.e. count = 0 for both t1 and t2). The t1 will have its count value incremented to 1 and t2 will have its count value decremented to −1. Both t1 and t2 will store their values to count; thereby one thread's value will be overwritten by another thread. It is generally unpredictable which thread will overwrite the value of which thread. There might be two overwriting cases for both threads as shown in Figure 12.5 Case 1 and Case 2.

Let us explain scenario-2 with another example as depicted in Example 12.3.

Figure 12.4. Flow of Execution for Single Thread

Single Thread	Master copy of count
Count = 0;	0
incrementCount()	1
incrementCount()	0
print count	0

Figure 12.5. Case1: Master Copy of Count will have Value −1

Thread1	Thread2	Master copy of count
		Initial value = 0
incrementCount()		Thread1 stores 1
	decrementCount()	Thread2 overwrites −1
print count		Thread1 displays −1
	print count	Thread2 displays −1

Figure 12.5. Case2: Master Copy of Count will have Value 1

Thread1	Thread2	Master copy of count
		Initial value = 0
	decrementCount()	Thread2 stores –1
incrementCount()		Thread1 overwrites 1
print count		Thread1 displays 1
	print count	Thread2 displays 1

Example 12.3. Threads Executing Sequential Steps

```
Step1: count = 0
Step2: count = count + 1
Step3: print count
```

If a single thread executes these steps, it starts with step1, executes it and continues with step2 and step3 printing count value 1 correctly. In contrast, assume *count* is shared by two threads t1 and t2. The t1 executes step2 and t2 executes step3 simultaneously. The count value printed by t2 could be 0 instead of 1. The count value incremented by t1 may not be visible to t2; unless t1 completes updating count with a new value before t2 accesses it. Therefore operations done by t1 and t2 should be properly communicated among themselves.

In order to solve resource sharing problem, the requests to access a common resource should be serialized. Assume there is something like a lock available. Whenever a thread wants to access this resource, it gets a lock, locks the resource and uses it. Once it is finished, it releases the lock so that other threads that are waiting for will access it. Of course, there will be a race among all blocked threads to get hold of the resource just released. In this case, priority of threads will play a vital role and high-priority threads will enjoy the resource.

12.11 SYNCHRONIZED METHODS

In order to serialize the requests for common resources, Java supports two types of synchronizations namely **synchronized methods** and **synchronized blocks**. To define a method synchronized, you will have to just add the word *synchronized* as a first word in the method signature. Now let us create a BankAccount class containing a resource *balance* and three synchronized methods to *credit()*, *debit()* and *get()* account balances as shown in Example 12.4.

Example 12.4. Bank Account Class

```
// BankAccount.java

class BankAccount
```

```
{
    private int balance = 0;

    public synchronized void credit(int amt)
    {
        balance += amt;
    }

    public synchronized void debit(int amt)
    {
        balance -= amt;
    }
    public synchronized int get()
    {
        return balance;
    }
}
```

The *credit()*, *debit()* and *get()* methods are declared as *synchronized* methods. By declaring synchronized, access to balance by these methods is streamlined. Synchronized method streamlines requests for common resources by several threads. When one thread currently executes a synchronized method, all other threads will be blocked until the first one finishes. The updates to resource done by the first thread will be made visible to all other threads. All subsequent invocations by other threads will use the updated value only. This way synchronized method handles both errors as discussed earlier.

Having created BankAccount class, now it is easy for us to create Credit and Debit threads to perform deposits and withdrawal of money from account as depicted in Listing 12.11.

Listing 12.11. Threaded Bank Application

```
// ThreadedBank.java
import java.util.*;

class BankAccount
{
    private int balance = 0;

    public synchronized void credit(int amt)
    {
        balance += amt;
    }

    public synchronized void debit(int amt)
    {
        balance -= amt;
```

```
    }
    public synchronized int get()
    {
        return balance;
    }
}

class CreditThread extends Thread
{
    int number;
    BankAccount acc;
    Random r = new Random();

    public CreditThread(int n, BankAccount a)
    {
        number = n;
        acc = a;
        start();
    }

    public void run()
    {
        while (true)
        {
            try {
                sleep(1000);
            }catch(InterruptedException e) { }

            acc.credit(r.nextInt(20));
            System.out.println("Balance after Thread " + number +
            " credit: " + acc.get());
        }
    }
}

class DebitThread extends Thread
{
    int number;
    BankAccount acc;
    Random r = new Random();

    public DebitThread(int n, BankAccount a)
    {
        number = n;
        acc = a;
        start();
```

```
    }
    public void run()
    {
        while (true)
        {
            try {
                sleep(1000);
            }catch(InterruptedException e) { }

            acc.debit(r.nextInt(10));
            System.out.println("Balance after Thread " + number +
            " debit: " + acc.get());
        }
    }
}
public class ThreadedBank
{
    public static void main(String[] args)
    {
        BankAccount b = new BankAccount();
        for(int i = 0; i < 5; i++)
        {
            new CreditThread(i, b);  // thread number i
            new DebitThread(i, b);
        }
    }
}
```

```
Balance after Thread 0 debit: 6
Balance after Thread 3 debit: 6
Balance after Thread 0 credit: 6
Balance after Thread 1 credit: 6
Balance after Thread 2 debit: 6
Balance after Thread 2 credit: 6
Balance after Thread 3 credit: 6
Balance after Thread 1 debit: 6
Balance after Thread 4 debit: 17
Balance after Thread 4 credit: 17
Balance after Thread 0 debit: 29
Balance after Thread 1 debit: 46
Balance after Thread 3 debit: 49
Balance after Thread 2 debit: 54
Balance after Thread 2 credit: 56
Balance after Thread 1 credit: 46
```

```
Balance after Thread 3 credit: 37
Balance after Thread 0 credit: 29
Balance after Thread 4 credit: 59
```

The CreateThread simply deposits money (as a random integer) to bank account after sleeping for a while and shows the current balance after this deposit. Similarly DebitThread after sleeping for a while withdraws money from the same account and displays the current balance of this account. Both threads will loop indefinitely until you break the execution. The main() thread just creates credit and debit threads and terminates.

12.12 SYNCHRONIZED BLOCK

Java synchronization is built around an entity called *monitor lock*. Every object has a monitor lock. The thread will acquire the lock before accessing shared resource and release it when it finished the operation. If a thread owns a lock, then no other thread can acquire this lock and will be blocked when it attempts. When a thread calls a synchronized method, it will automatically acquire the lock for the method's object and releases the lock when the method returns.

Suppose we want several threads to access only part of the code of synchronized method instead of entire method. Then this part of the code can be declared as synchronized block. Further, synchronized block should specify the object that provides the lock as an argument as shown in Example 12.5.

Example 12.5. Negative Credit for Bank Account

```
class BankAccount
{
    private int balance = 0;

    public void credit(int amt)
    {
        if (amt < 0)
        {
            System.out.println( "Negative amount cannot be
            deposited");
            return;
        }

        synchronized(this)
        {
            balance += amt;
        }
    }
}
```

In this example, credit() method should synchronize the changes to balance only. The *if* statement that checks whether amount to be deposited is negative is very specific to this thread only and need not be

part other threads. So *if* statement is safely excluded from synchronization. In the same way, debit()
method can also be rewritten using synchronized block as illustrated in Example 12.6.

Example 12.6. Withdrawing Negative Amount

```
class BankAccount
{
    public void debit(int amt)
    {
        if (amt < 0)
        {
            System.out.println( "Negative amount cannot be
            withdrawn too");
            return;
        }

        synchronized(this)
        {
            balance -= amt;
        }
    }
}
```

Very similar to previous example, if the amount to be withdrawn is negative, then it cannot be withdrawn too. So this checking is not part of common resource and can be ignored and need not be
included in the synchronized block.

12.13 COORDINATION AMONG THREADS

There are situations where the timing of a thread accessing a common resource affects other threads
that need to access the same resource. By timing, we think of the order of thread execution. We just
want to specify which thread should execute the common resource first and which thread should
execute next. These situations compel us to coordinate access timings of threads.

The *java.lang.Object* class provides three interesting methods that are useful for coordinating
threads that access the same resource. All these methods should be called inside synchronized methods or synchronized blocks.

- The **wait()** method causes the current thread to wait (indefinitely or specified time) and release
  its lock until another thread invokes notify() or notifyAll() methods. The wait() should be defined
  inside synchronized method or synchronized block. Also remember that sleep() also causes the
  current thread to sleep for a while; but the difference is sleep() does not release the lock.

- The **notify()** method awakes the first thread that went on sleep using wait() method. For example if you want to **notify** a thread object **x**, then you will have to call notify as *x.notify()* inside
  synchronized block with **x** as an argument.

- The **notifyAll()** method awakes all wait() threads which are currently sleeping.

12.14 PROBLEM: CAR DEALER APPLICATION

In order to appreciate the power of wait() and notify() methods to coordinate threads timings, let us now develop an application for a car company as depicted in Listing 12.12. A car company has a *demo car*, one *marketing manager* and one *engineer*. When potential customers wish to buy a car, they opt for test drive. The engineer will wait for the marketing manager to assign a customer for test drive.

When a customer arrives for test drive, marketing manager notifies the engineer who takes a demo car and customer for test drive. Once test drive is over, engineer waits for a call from marketing manager. The car dealer can serve only 10 customers a day for test drive. This is another interesting problem for thread coordination; here marketing manager is a producer and the engineer is a consumer.

Listing 12.12. Thread Coordination for Car Dealer Application

```
// CarDealer.java

class Engineer extends Thread
{
    public Engineer()
    {
        start();
    }
    public void run()
    {
        while(true)
        {
            synchronized(this)
            {
                try
                {
                    wait();
                }catch(InterruptedException e) { }
            }
            System.out.println("Engineer currently takes customer
            for test drive");
        }
    }
}

class MarketingManager extends Thread
{
    private CarDealer c;
    private Engineer e;
    private int nCustomer = 0;

    public MarketingManager(CarDealer c, Engineer e)
```

```
    {
        this.c = c;
        this.e = e;
        start();
    }

    public void run()
    {
        while(true)
        {
            if(++nCustomer <= c.max)
            {
                System.out.println ("Assign customer" +
                nCustomer + "to engineer for test drive");
                synchronized(e)
                {
                    e.notify();
                }

                try {
                    sleep(100);
                } catch(InterruptedException e) { }
            }
            else
                System.exit(0);
        }
    }
}

public class CarDealer
{
    final int max = 10;  // customers per day for test drive

    public static void main(String[] args)
    {
        CarDealer d = new CarDealer();
        Engineer e = new Engineer();
        MarketingManager m = new MarketingManager(d,e);
    }
}
```

```
Assign customer 1 to engineer for test drive
Engineer currently takes customer for test drive
Assign customer 2 to engineer for test drive
```

```
Engineer currently takes customer for test drive
Assign customer 3 to engineer for test drive
Engineer currently takes customer for test drive
Assign customer 4 to engineer for test drive
Engineer currently takes customer for test drive
Assign customer 5 to engineer for test drive
Engineer currently takes customer for test drive
Assign customer 6 to engineer for test drive
Engineer currently takes customer for test drive
Assign customer 7 to engineer for test drive
Engineer currently takes customer for test drive
Assign customer 8 to engineer for test drive
Engineer currently takes customer for test drive
Assign customer 9 to engineer for test drive
Engineer currently takes customer for test drive
Assign customer 10 to engineer for test drive
Engineer currently takes customer for test drive
```

In this example, *engineer* thread object currently waits for a call from marketing manager thread object. This is accomplished by a wait() method inside a synchronized block of Engineer thread. Once it is awaken by marketing manager thread, it takes the customer for a test drive and goes back to sleep.

The marketing manager object simply assigns customer to an engineer object for test drive. It will also keep track of total number of customers currently served. The car dealer instructs the marketing manager object through **max** the maximum number of customers it can schedule for test drive. Once customer arrives, marketing manager thread notifies engineer thread so that engineer object can perform test drive. Marketing manager thread calls exit() to terminate the application once it reaches the maximum customers to be taken for test drive.

12.15 THREADS LIFE

A thread moves through various states in its life time. For instance, a thread is born, starts, runs and finally dies. A newly created thread exists in any one of the following states:

- **New:** When a thread object is first created, thread is born and it is in newborn state.
- **Runnable:** When we call **start()** method on the thread, it moves to runnable state. That means, it is ready for execution and is waiting for its CPU time from the scheduler.
- **Running:** Now the scheduler has given CPU time to this runnable thread. So it enters into running state and is executing **run()** method.
- **Blocked:** While a thread is waiting or sleeping, it enters into the blocked state. So, scheduler will not give CPU time until it becomes runnable again.
- **Dead:** When a thread reaches end of run() method, it dies naturally.

Figure 12.6 depicts the various life cycle states of a thread from birth to death.

Java 1.2 has few deprecated methods namely *suspend()*, *destroy()*, *stop()* and *resume()*, and we will not examine those methods in this book and ignore them.

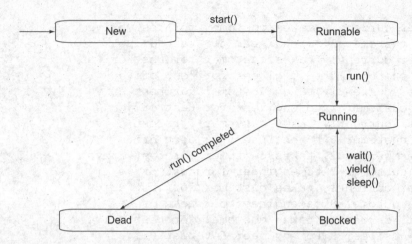

Figure 12.6. Thread Life Cycle

12.16 CONCURRENT PROGRAMMING PACKAGES

The *util.concurrent* package is the new addition to J2SE 1.5 and contains a rich set of classes (locks, condition variables, semaphores, blocking queues, atomic, etc.) that are suitable for concurrent programming in a real-world environment. The following are the three important subpackages:

- **java.util.concurrent:** it provides necessary classes that are useful for concurrent programming
- **java.util.concurrent.atomic:** it is a small subpackage containing classes that support thread safety on a single-resource variable without any locks
- **java.util.concurrent.locks:** it contains interfaces and classes for locking and waiting for conditions. It is a replacement for synchronized methods and synchronized blocks

12.17 THE CONCURRENT PACKAGE

The *java.util.concurrent* package contains some important classes such as Semaphore, Executor and concurrent Collections such as ConcurrentHashMap, ConcurrentLinkedQueue and PriorityBlocking-Queue.

For instance, ConcurrentHashMap is a lock-free thread-safe hash map that will store key-value pairs. It allows several threads to access this hash map and does not need any locks while accessing its contents. In Listing 12.13, let us explore this hash map by creating several threads and making them to insert key-value pairs of user login information simultaneously.

Listing 12.13. Multithreaded Login Generator

```
// ConcurrentHMTest.java
import java.io.*;
import java.util.*;
import java.util.concurrent.*;
```

```
import java.math.*;

class LoginThread extends Thread
{
    ConcurrentHashMap map;
    int max; // maximum updates
    int no;  // thread number

    public LoginThread(int i, ConcurrentHashMap m, int n)
    {
        no = i;
        map = m;
        max = n;
        start();
    }

    public String getString()
    {
        Random r = new Random();
        String rand = new BigInteger(8, r).toString(32);
        // radix 32
        return rand;
    }

    public void run()
    {
        try
        {
            sleep(100);
        }
        catch(InterruptedException e) { }

        for(int i = 0; i < max; i++)
            map.put(getString(), getString());

        System.out.println("By Thread " + no + ": " + map.
        toString());
    }
}

public class ConcurrentHMTest
{
    public static void main(String[] args)
    {
```

```
        ConcurrentHashMap map = new ConcurrentHashMap();

        for(int i = 0; i < 5; i++)
                new LoginThread(i, map, 3);  // maximum 3 insertions
                by each thread
     }
}
```

```
By Thread 2: {6o=56, 3p=7g, 52=c, 5k=6v, 2o=3j, 43=5t, 5i=38,
t=4h, v=6p, 3h=7f, 12=c, 7h=4e, 17=35, 56=3q, 7v=15}
By Thread 4: {6o=56, 3p=7g, 52=c, 5k=6v, 2o=3j, 43=5t, 5i=38,
t=4h, v=6p, 3h=7f, 12=c, 7h=4e, 17=35, 56=3q, 7v=15}
By Thread 3: {6o=56, 3p=7g, 52=c, 5k=6v, 2o=3j, 43=5t, 5i=38,
t=4h, v=6p, 3h=7f, 12=c, 7h=4e, 17=35, 56=3q, 7v=15}
By Thread 1: {6o=56, 3p=7g, 52=c, 5k=6v, 2o=3j, 43=5t, 5i=38,
t=4h, v=6p, 3h=7f, 12=c, 7h=4e, 17=35, 56=3q, 7v=15}
By Thread 0: {6o=56, 3p=7g, 52=c, 5k=6v, 2o=3j, 43=5t, 5i=38,
t=4h, v=6p, 3h=7f, 12=c, 7h=4e, 17=35, 56=3q, 7v=15}
```

Here all 5 threads concurrently insert key-value pairs to concurrent hash map. In the getString(), a BigInteger is created with $2^8 - 1$ bits and a Random object. This number is then converted into a string with radix 32. This random string is used as keys and values by threads. The run() simply inserts random strings into the concurrent hash map and prints the contents of the updated map. The main() instantiates thread objects and terminates.

12.18 THE CONCURRENT.ATOMIC PACKAGE

The *concurrent.atomic* subpackage supports few interesting classes that are lock-free thread-safe classes and can be suitable replacement to volatile variables and array elements. Some important classes are AtomicBoolean, AtomicInteger, AtomicIntegerArray, AtomicLong and AtomicLong-Array. These classes are thread-safe and eliminate the need for synchronized methods and blocks. The get() and set() are the important methods these classes support to get and set a value. The get() method gives an effect of reading a volatile variable directly from main memory. Similarly set() method gives an effect of writing to a volatile variable directly to main memory.

Now let us create a Counter with a single-resource variable of AtomicInteger type as depicted in Listing 12.14.

Listing 12.14. AtomicCounter

```
// AtomicCounter.java

import java.util.concurrent.atomic.*;
import java.util.concurrent.*;
```

```java
class Counter
{
    AtomicInteger c = new AtomicInteger(0);

    public void increment()
    {
        c.getAndIncrement();
    }
    public int get()
    {
        return c.get();
    }
}

public class AtomicCounter extends Thread
{
    int number; // thread number
    Counter counter;

    public AtomicCounter(int no, Counter c)
    {
        number = no;
        counter = c;
        start();
    }

    public void run()
    {
        try
        {
            sleep(10000);
        }
        catch(InterruptedException e) { }

        counter.increment();
        System.out.println("By Thread " + number + ": " + "current
        value " + counter.get());
    }

    public static void main(String[] args)
    {
        Counter c = new Counter();
        final int n = 10;
        AtomicCounter[] t = new AtomicCounter[n];
```

```
        for(int i = 0; i < n; i++)
            t[i] = new AtomicCounter(i, c);

        try
        {
            for(int i = 0; i < n; i++)
                t[i].join();
        }catch(InterruptedException e) { }

        System.out.println("Final count value: " + c.get());
    }
}
```

```
By Thread 0: current value 1
By Thread 1: current value 3
By Thread 6: current value 9
By Thread 5: current value 7
By Thread 4: current value 7
By Thread 7: current value 6
By Thread 3: current value 5
By Thread 2: current value 3
By Thread 8: current value 10
By Thread 9: current value 8
Final count value: 10
```

The getAndIncrement() gets and increments the resource while get() returns the contents of the resource variable. The AtomicCounter is a thread object and we create threads that will call methods from Counter object in order to increment and retrieve the contents of the resource variable. The Thread.main() thread will wait for all threads to finish their execution so that it will finally show the contents of the resource variable.

12.19 PROBLEM: RANDOM STRINGS GENERATOR

Random strings generation is another interesting problem everywhere. Let us now develop a string generator thread that will generate strings only with lowercase and uppercase characters without digits. Listing 12.15 illustrates the method of how to generate strings using AtomicIntegerArray.

Listing 12.15. Random Strings Generator

```
import java.util.concurrent.atomic.*;
import java.util.concurrent.*;
import java.util.*;
```

```java
class Strings
{
    AtomicIntegerArray array;
    Random r = new Random();

    public void init()
    {
        int[] a = new int[52];

        for(int i = 0; i < 26; i++)  // ascii for uppercase alphabets
            a[i] = i+65;
        for(int i = 26; i < 52; i++)  // ascii for lowercase alphabets
            a[i] = i+71;

        array = new AtomicIntegerArray(a);
    }
    public int get()
    {
        return array.get(r.nextInt(51));  // index range 1 to 51
    }
}

public class StringGenerator extends Thread
{
    int number; // thread number
    Strings str;

    public StringGenerator(int no, Strings s)
    {
        number = no;
        str = s;
        start();
    }

    public void run()
    {
        while(true)
        {
            try
            {
                sleep(100);
            }
```

```
            catch(InterruptedException e) { }

            StringBuffer sb = new StringBuffer();
            for( int i = 0; i < 5; i++)
                    sb.append((char)str.get());

            System.out.println("By Thread " + number + ": " +
            sb.toString());
        }
    }

    public static void main(String[] args)
    {
        Strings s = new Strings();
        s.init();

        final int n = 1000;
        for(int i = 0; i < n; i++)
                new StringGenerator(i, s);
    }
}
```

```
By Thread 780: fbuAX
By Thread 778: BHTRn
By Thread 774: hBUZX
By Thread 822: DbbfC
By Thread 820: RgnqN
By Thread 818: iOepa
By Thread 816: rpNkf
By Thread 64: TelBe
By Thread 812: ynyfp
By Thread 810: tMHDS
By Thread 808: gPdfG
By Thread 806: NNfRj
By Thread 804: oICgp
By Thread 802: VYBUU
By Thread 800: SNRdY
By Thread 798: UfEgp
// output manually edited
```

The init() of Strings class instantiates an instance of AtomicIntegerArray that keeps ASCII values of uppercase and lowercase alphabets. The get() returns any one of the ASCII values from the lock-free thread-safe array. The run() simply creates a string of five characters using string buffer and displays the generated string. The main() calls init() and initializes threads (here 1000 threads) that will generate and display strings.

12.20 THE CONCURRENT.LOCKS PACKAGE

The *concurrent.locks* subpackage contains an interface **Lock** and a class **ReentrantLock** that implements the Lock interface. Locks can be used in place of synchronized blocks and to implement synchronized methods. Locks are more flexible than synchronized blocks in a sense that a thread can unlock multiple locks it holds in a different order other than the order in which locks were obtained. This cannot be done with synchronized blocks as synchronized blocks must be lexically nested.

In section 12.11, we have created a BankAccount with synchronized methods to credit and debit account balance. Now let us rewrite BankAccount class with Locks as depicted in Listing 12.16.

Listing 12.16. BankAccount Class with Lock

```java
// BankAccountLock.java

import java.util.concurrent.locks.*;

public class BankAccountLock
{
    Lock mylock = new ReentrantLock();
    private int balance = 0;

    public void credit(int amt)
    {
        mylock.lock();
        try
        {
            balance += amt;
        }
        finally
        {
            mylock.unlock();
        }
    }

    public void debit(int amt)
    {
        mylock.lock();
        try
        {
            balance -= amt;
        }
        finally
```

```
    {
            mylock.unlock();
    }
}


    public int get()
    {
        mylock.lock();
        try
        {
                return balance;
        }
        finally
        {
                mylock.unlock();
        }
    }
}
```

First we obtain a lock as an instance of ReentrantLock. With this lock object, we can lock all resource variables by calling *lock()*. Try block will contain all resources that are to be locked. Once finished its execution, *unlock()* is called to release the lock inside finally block.

Now our revised ThreadedBank will use the above BankAccountLock object so that its credit and debit threads will perform transactions as depicted in Listing 12.17.

Listing 12.17. Threaded Bank with Lock

```
// ThreadedBankLock.java

import java.util.concurrent.locks.*;
import java.util.*;

class CreditThread extends Thread
{
    int number;
    BankAccountLock acc;
    Random r = new Random();

    public CreditThread(int n, BankAccountLock a)
    {
        number = n;
        acc = a;
        start();
    }
```

```java
    public void run()
    {
       while (true)
       {
            try {
                 sleep(1000);
            }catch(InterruptedException e) { }

            acc.credit(r.nextInt(20));
            System.out.println("Balance after Thread " + number +
            " credit: " + acc.get());
       }
    }
}

class DebitThread extends Thread
{
   int number;
   BankAccountLock acc;
   Random r = new Random();

   public DebitThread(int n, BankAccountLock a)
   {
      number = n;
      acc = a;
      start();
   }

   public void run()
   {
      while (true)
      {
            try {
                 sleep(1000);
            }catch(InterruptedException e) { }

            acc.debit(r.nextInt(10));
            System.out.println("Balance after Thread " + number
            + " debit: " + acc.get());
      }
   }
}
public class ThreadedBankLock
{
   public static void main(String[] args)
```

```
    {
        BankAccountLock b = new BankAccountLock();
        for(int i = 0; i < 5; i++)
        {
            new CreditThread(i, b);
            new DebitThread(i, b);
        }
    }
}
```

```
Balance after Thread 0 debit: 2
Balance after Thread 0 credit: 2
Balance after Thread 1 credit: 2
Balance after Thread 2 credit: 2
Balance after Thread 1 debit: 2
Balance after Thread 2 debit: -6
Balance after Thread 3 debit: -3
Balance after Thread 3 credit: 4
Balance after Thread 4 credit: 4
Balance after Thread 4 debit: -6
Balance after Thread 0 credit: 19
Balance after Thread 1 debit: 16
Balance after Thread 0 debit: 25
Balance after Thread 1 credit: 31
```

This revised ThreadedBankLock is a straightforward implementation similar to our earlier ThreadedBank only with a difference; we instantiate BankAccountLock object instead of BankAccount object.

12.21 SUMMARY

1. A process is a program in execution
2. Thread is a lightweight process and it will have its own address space
3. Thread is a single sequential flow of control within a process
4. A thread is created with Thread class or Runnable interface
5. The body of the run() method will be executed concurrently by many threads
6. A thread must be started explicitly
7. The sleep() makes thread to release CPU to other threads
8. The yield() voluntarily relinquishes CPU to other threads
9. Java program starts its execution with main Thread
10. A thread will go on sleeping by calling join() method of another thread
11. Daemon threads are service threads for other threads running in the background
12. Daemon threads will terminate when all non-daemon threads terminate

13. Priority of thread varies from 1 to 10 where 10 is the highest priority

14. There are three constants for thread priority

15. When a class already extends another class, then Runnable interface can be implemented to specify thread behaviour

16. When a common resource is accessed by many threads, then their sequence of access should be synchronized

17. The synchronized method and synchronized blocks handle threads synchronization issues.

18. Synchronized block is more useful when we want to synchronize only part of the method

19. The timing of thread access to a sharable resource is controlled by thread coordination

20. The wait(), notify() and notifyAll() methods coordinate the thread access timing among several threads

21. A thread moves through various states in its life time from birth, running, blocked and dead

22. The *util.concurrent* package is the new addition to J2SE 1.5 and contains a rich set of classes for real-world environments

23. The *util.concurrent.atomic* ensures atomic access to single-resource variable by many threads

24. The *util.concurrent.locks* contains features for synchronized access with Locks

KEY TERMS

Concurrent programming, 360
Daemon threads, 372
Join, 369
Main thread, 360
Monitor lock, 385
Notify, 386

Priority, 375
Process, 360
Resource sharing, 360
Run, 360
Runnable interface, 360
Sleep, 363

Synchronized blocks, 381
Synchronized methods, 381
Thread class, 360
Thread, 360
Volatile, 376
Yield, 365

REVIEW QUESTIONS

Multiple-choice Questions

1. For the following class, choose the correct thread class:

```
public class Test12
{
    public static void main(String[] args)
    {
        Thread1 t = new Thread1();
        t.start();
    }
}
```

a. ```
   class Thread1 extends Thread {
       public void run() {}}
   ```
b. ```
   class Thread1 implements Thread {
       public void run() {}}
   ```
c. ```
   class Thread1 implements Runnable {
       public void run() {}}
   ```
d. ```
   class Thread1 extends Runnable {
       public static void run() {}}
   ```

2. What is the output when you instantiate A?

```
class A extends Thread
{
    public A()
    {
        System.out.println("1");
    }
    public void run()
    {
        System.out.println("2");
    }
}
```

a. 1   b. 2
c. 12   d. 21
e. Unpredictable

3. What is the output if you create an object as *new A().run("3")* ?

```
class A extends Thread
{
    public A()
    {
        System.out.print("1");
    }
    public void run()
    {
        System.out.print("2");
    }
    public void run(String s)
    {
        System.out.print(s);
    }
}
```

a. 12

b. 123

c. 13

d. 23

e. None of the above

4. What is the output?

```
class A implements Runnable
{
    public void run()
    {
        System.out.print("2");
    }
}
public class Test12
{
    public static void main(String[] args)
    {
        A a = new A();
        for(int i=0; i<2; i++)
            new Thread(a).start();
    }
}
```

a. 2

b. 22

c. 222

d. None of the above

5. What is the output?

```
class A implements Runnable
{
    public void run()
    {
        try { Thread.sleep(1000);
        }catch(InterruptedException e){}

        System.out.println(
        Thread.currentThread().getName() + " hello");
    }
}
public class Test12.
{
    public static void main(String[] args)
    {
        A a = new A();
```

```
      Thread t1 = new Thread(a); t1.setName("Jane");
      Thread t2 = new Thread(a); t2.setName("Jose");
      t1.start(); t2.start();
   }
}
```

a. Jane hello Jose hello   b. Jose hello Jane hello

c. Jane Jose hello hello   d. unpredictable in-determinant result

6. What is the output?

```
public class Test12 extends Thread
{
   public static void main(String[] args)
   {
      Test12 t = new Test12();
      t.start();
   }
   public void run()
   {
      while(true)
           System.out.println(" hello");
   }
}
```

a. hello   b. hello hello

c. prints hello indefinitely   d. Unpredictable output

7. What is the output?

```
public class Test12 extends Thread
{
   public static void main(String[] args)
   {
      Test12 t = new Test12();
      t.start(); t.start();
   }
   public void run()
   {
           System.out.println(" hello");
   }
}
```

a. hello
b. hello hello
c. hello followed by IllegalThreadStateException
d. hello hello followed by IllegalThreadStateException
e. None of the above

8. What is the output?

```java
public class Test12 implements Runnable
{
    public static void main(String[] args)
    {
        Test12 t = new Test12();
        Thread th = new Thread();
        th.start();
    }
    public void run()
    {
        System.out.println("hello");
    }
}
```

a. hello   b. hello indefinitely
c. No output   d. llegalThreadStateException

9. What is the output?

```java
public class Test12 extends Thread
{
    public static void main(String[] args)
    {
        Test12 t = new Test12();
        Thread t1 = new Thread(t);
        Thread t2 = new Thread(t);
        t1.start(); t2.start();
    }
    public void run()
    {
        try { Thread.sleep(100);
        }catch(InterruptedException e){}

        System.out.println(" hello");
    }
}
```

    a. hello

    b. hello hello

    c. hello hello indefinitely

    d. None of the above

10. What is the output?

```
public class Test12
{
    public static void main(String[] args)
    throws Exception
    {
        for(int i = 0; i < 5; i++)
        {
        Thread.currentThread().sleep(1000);
        System.out.print(i);
        }
    }
}
```

    a. Prints 0 to 4 at 1-s time gap

    b. Compilation error

    c. Compilation error as InterruptedException is not catched

    d. None of the above

11. Which of the following about sleep() and yield() are true?

    a. sleep() forces the current thread to go for sleep for specified period

    b. yield() voluntarily relinquishes CPU to other threads

    c. sleep() and yield() are static methods in Thread class

    d. All of the above

12. Assume two threads t1 and t2. If t1 calls join() method of t2 as t2.join(), then which of the following is true?

    a. t1 goes to indefinite wait until t2 finishes

    b. t2 goes to indefinite wait until t1 finishes

    c. t1 goes to indefinite wait until t2 calls notify()

    d. t2 goes to indefinite wait until t1 calls notify()

13. Which of the following are true about daemon threads?

    a. Daemon thread will terminate when all non-daemon threads terminate

    b. setDaemon() should appear before *start()* method

    c. Daemon threads are background threads

    d. All of the above

14. How will you make a thread to merge its own private copy of the variable with the master copy in the main memory?
    a. Create this variable as synchronized
    b. Create this variable as volatile
    c. Create this variable with high priority
    d. None of the above

15. How to prevent two threads accessing a shared resource?
    a. Use synchronized method
    b. Use synchronized block
    c. Use volatile variable
    d. All of the above

16. Which of the statements are true considering class Account?

```
class Account
{
    private int balance = 10000;
    public void debit(int amt)
    {
        if (amt < 0)
            return;
        synchronized(this)
        {
            balance -= amt;
        }
    }
}
```

    a. Two threads cannot access *amt*
    b. Two threads cannot access *balance*
    c. Two threads cannot access *amt* as well as *balance*
    d. None of the above

17. Which of the statements are true considering class Account?

```
class Account
{
    private int balance = 10000;
    public synchronized void debit(int amt)
    {
        if (amt < 0)
            return;
        synchronized(this)
        {
            balance -= amt;
        }
    }
}
```

a. Two threads cannot access *amt*

b. Two threads cannot access *balance*

c. Two threads cannot access
amt as well as *balance*

d. None of the above

18. Which of the following is true about sleep() and wait()?
   a. sleep() does not release the lock while the thread is sleeping
   b. wait() does not release the lock while the thread is waiting
   c. sleep() releases the lock while the thread is sleeping
   d. wait() releases the lock while the thread is waiting

19. Which of the following are true?
   a. The wait(), notify() and notifyAll() belong to java.lang.Thread class
   b. The notify() can awake any specific thread of its choice from all waiting threads
   c. The notifyAll() awakes all wait() and yield() threads from sleeping
   d. None of the above

20. What is the output when a thread of type A is started?

```
class A extends Thread
{
   public void run()
   {
      System.out.print("1");
      try { wait(); }
      catch(InterruptedException e){}
      System.out.print("2");
   }
}
```

a. 1

b. 12

c. Indefinite wait

d. None of the above

21. Which of the following is true with respect to Account?

```
class Account
{
   synchronized int balance = 10000;
   public void debit(int amt)
   {
      balance -= amt;
   }
}
```

a. Two threads can access balance

b. Only one thread can access balance

c. Any number of threads can access balance

d. Synchronized cannot be applied to balance

22. Assume a class A has two synchronized methods m1() and m2(). Then which of the following is true?

   a. The m1() and m2() cannot be called by two different threads

   b. The m1() and m2() can be called by two different threads

   c. There cannot be two synchronized methods in a class

   d. None of the above

23. Assume a class A has two synchronized methods m1() and m2() and one non-synchronized method m3(). Then which of the following is true?

   a. The m1() and m2() cannot be called by two different threads

   b. The m1() and m2() can be called by two different threads

   c. There cannot be two synchronized methods in a class

   d. The m3() can be called by many threads

24. What is the output?

```
class A extends Thread {

    public void run() {
        System.out.print("1");
        show();
    }
    public void show() {
    System.out.print("2");
    }
}

public class Test12 {
    public static synchronized void
    main(String[] args) throws Exception{
        A a = new A();
        synchronized(a){
            a.start();
        }

    }
}
```

   a. 1

   b. 2

   c. 12

   d. No output

25. What is the output?

```
public class Test12
{
    public static void
    main(String[] args) throws Exception
    {
        String s = "a";
        System.out.print(s);
        synchronized(s) {
            s.wait(1000);}
        System.out.print(s);
    }
}
```

a. a

b. aa

c. a followed by a after 1 sec

d. a followed by a after 1 min

26. Which of the following are true about Stringbuilder class?

```
class Stringbuilder implements Runnable
{
    private StringBuffer sb = new StringBuffer();
    public synchronized void add(char c) {
        sb.append(c);
    }
    public synchronized void show() {
        System.out.println(sb.length() + ":" + sb);
    }
    public void run()
    {
        while(true)
        {
        try { Thread.sleep(100);
        }catch(InterruptedException e) {}
        int c = (int)(Math.random() * (90-65+1))+65;
        add((char)c); show();
        }
    }
}
public class Test12
{
    public static void main(String[] args)
    {
```

```
    Stringbuilder sb = new Stringbuilder();
    for(int i = 0; i < 100; i++)
        new Thread(sb).start();
}
}
```

a. One hundred threads insert characters to string buffer simultaneously
b. Threads insert only uppercase alphabets
c. The content of string buffer is displayed when an alphabet is inserted
d. All of the above

27. What is the output?

```
class A implements Runnable
{
    char c;
    public A(char c) {this.c = c;}
    public synchronized void m() {
        System.out.print(c);
    }
    public void run(){
        while(true)
        {
            m();
            Thread.yield();
        }.
    }
}
public class Test12 {
    public static void main(String[] args)        {
        A a = new A('x');
        Thread t1 = new Thread(a);
        Thread t2 = new Thread(a);
        t1.start(); t2.start();
    }
}
```

a. Prints x indefinitely by thread1
b. Prints x indefinitely by thread2
c. Prints x indefinitely by thread1 and thread2
d. Prints x two times only because of yield()
e. None of the above

28. What is the output?

```
class A extends Thread
{
    public A(){start();}
    public void run() {
    while(true)
    {
        try {Thread.sleep(1000);
        }catch(InterruptedException e) { }
        System.out.print("Hello ");
    }
    }
}
public class Test12 extends Thread
{
    A t = new A();
    public Test12() {start();}
    public void run() {
        try { t.join();
        System.out.println("Java");
        }catch(InterruptedException e) { }
    }
    public static void main(String[] args) {
        new Test12();
    }
}
```

   a. Prints Java first Hello indefinitely
   b. Prints Hello Java then Hello indefinitely
   c. Prints few times Hello then Java then Hello indefinitely
   d. Prints Hello indefinitely
   e. None of the above

Answers

1. a	2. a	3. c	4. b	5. d	6. c	7. c	8. c	9. b	10. a
11. d	12. a	13. d	14. b	15. a, b	16. b	17. c	18. a, d	19. d	20. d
21. d	22. a	23. a	24. c	25. c	26. d	27. c	28. d		

Short-answer Questions

1. Explain process, multitasking, thread and multithreading.
2. What are the ways of creating threads?

3. How to force thread to wait?
4. How will thread voluntarily wait?
5. Explain the difference between yield and join methods.
6. How will you create daemon threads?
7. Explain thread priority levels.
8. How to handle resource sharing issues?
9. Explain thread coordination with wait and notify methods.
10. Explain life cycle of a thread.
11. Explain file locking briefly.

EXERCISES

12.1 For CounterThread.java, instantiate 10 threads and observe the output. Then instantiate 100 threads, 1000 threads and 10000 threads and observe the output.

12.2 For CounterThread2.java, instantiate 10 threads and observe the output. Then instantiate 100 threads, 1000 threads and 10000 threads and observe the output. Now compare this output with the output of the previous exercise.

12.3 For CounterThread.java, vary sleep time from 100ms to 1000ms and instantiate 100 threads and observe the output. Now again increase sleep time to 10000ms and 10000 threads and observe the output. What is your perception?

12.4 Create a 10-D array with random digits (0-9) populated by 10 threads simultaneously. Scale the dimension and number of threads to 100 and check your output.

12.5 Design MultiThreadedNDAdder application that will sum all element values of an N-D array. Scale N from 3 onwards.

12.6 Modify ThreadedBank.java application by increasing the number of CreditThread and DebitThread from 5 to 50 and observe the credit and debit operations. Now increase threads to 1000 and then to 10000 and observe the credit and debit operations.

13

Processing Byte and Object Streams

OBJECTIVES

- To create File object to obtain the details of files and directories such as length, date created, date modified, its name and many others
- To filter file names in a directory using FileNameFilter
- To filter absolute path names using FileFilter
- To introduce input stream types
- To read file contents using FileInputStream
- To read strings into byte array using ByteArrayInputStream
- To write bytes to file using FileOutputStream
- To copy files as bytes
- To process primitive data type values using DataInputStream and DataOutputStream
- To generate students mark list using Data IO
- To create Serializable objects
- To write Serializable objects to files using ObjectOuputStream
- To read Serializable objects from files using ObjectInputStream
- To write students marks as Serializable objects to file
- To read students Serializable objects and generate mark list
- To prevent a variable from serialization by declaring it as transient

13.1 INTRODUCTION

So far all of your data you created would have been lost and would not be persistently available once you close the application. Files allow you to store your data in a persistent way in disk. Java file processing is centred on streams. Streams can represent different sources and destinations such as disk files, source programs and devices. For instance, streams are interfaces between two entities; input source and output destination where source could be a program and destination could be a disk and vice versa.

Streams support several types of data such as bytes, characters, primitive data types and objects. Streams help us to communicate with files by many ways such as sequentially, randomly, using buffering, byte by byte, character by character, word by word, line by line and many others.

There are two stream types: one for reading from source (**input streams**) and the other for writing to destination (**output streams**). Our program will use input streams to read data from data source and output streams to write data to destination. The earlier Java 1.0 supported byte streams while Java 1.1 added character streams and the recent Java 1.4 included **nio** (new IO) for better performance.

Java IO stream classes are archived in **java.io** and **java.nio** packages that you will import inside your application. There are many classes, each having its own purpose that you should clearly identify. In this chapter, the readers will be introduced to the variety of byte and object stream classes with which you will be able to develop applications, apart from File class. The readers will explore all character-oriented stream classes, random access files and NIO features in Chapter 14.

13.2 THE FILE CLASS

The **File class** represents the path name of a file or a set of files in a directory. Here path name could be absolute or relative path name. Absolute path name starts from the drive and defines a complete path name whereas relative path name defines a file path relative to current directory.

The **File object** can be created with **file path** as a string or url. The File class provides many methods that are straightforward to use. The methods can be classified as shown below:

- access rights: canRead(), canWrite()
- names: getName(), getParent(), getPath()
- checking: isFile(), isDirectory(), compareTo(), equals()
- properties: length(), file(), lastModified() and exists()
- directories: mkdir(), mkdirs(), delete(), renameTo()

All these methods are self-explanatory except mkdirs(). The mkdir() creates a directory in the current directory with absolute path name. The mkdirs() will also create a directory with absolute path name including its parent directory. Listing 13.1 illustrates various methods of File object.

Listing 13.1. The File Class Methods

```
// File1.java
import java.io.*;

public class File1
{
```

```java
public static void main(String[] args) throws IOException
{
    File f = new File("e:\\rajkumar\\javacourse\\io");
    System.out.println("getName: " + f.getName());
    System.out.println("getParent: " + f.getParent());
    System.out.println("getPath: " + f.getPath());
    System.out.println("isDirectory: " + f.isDirectory());
    System.out.println("isFile: " + f.isFile());
    System.out.println("length: " + f.length());
    System.out.println("canRead: " + f.canRead());
    System.out.println("canWrite: " + f.canWrite());
    System.out.println("lastModified:" + f.lastModified());

    String[] list = f.list(); // list of all files
    System.out.println("Listing of all files:");
    for(int i = 0; i < list.length; i++)
            System.out.println(list[i]);

    // create new file in current directory
    File f1 = new File("data.txt");
    System.out.println("creating new file: data.txt");
    if( !f1.exists())
            f1.createNewFile();

    // rename
    System.out.println("Renaming data.txt as datanew.txt");
    File fnew = new File("datanew.txt");
    f1.renameTo(fnew);

    // create dir
    System.out.println("creating new directory: test");
    File f2 = new File("test2");
    f2.mkdir();

    // create directory iotest, parent directory test also
    created
    System.out.println("creating new directory: \\test\\
    iotest");
    File f3 = new File("e:\\rajkumar\\javacourse\\io\\test\\
    iotest");
    f3.mkdirs();

    // delete() deletes file or dir
}
}
```

```
getName: io
getParent: e:\rajkumar\javacourse
getPath: e:\rajkumar\javacourse\io
isDirectory: true
isFile: false
length: 65536
canRead: true
canWrite: true
lastModified:1350711948468


Listing of all files
Adder.class
AtomicCounter.class
AtomicCounter.java
// output edited
```

13.3 FILTERING FILE NAMES

FilenameFilter is an interface that is used to filter file names based on some condition on file names, such *as show me all files with extension ".txt"*. The condition (i.e. *.txt)* is specified by overriding *accept()* method. If a file satisfies this condition then accept() returns true. So *list()* method of File class will include this file as part of the output files. Let us now filter all file names in a given directory based on its extension as depicted in Listing 13.2.

Listing 13.2. Show File Names on Condition

```java
// FilterFiles.java

import java.io.*;

class FilterName implements FilenameFilter
{
    String extn;

    public FilterName(String ext)
    {
        extn = "." + ext;
    }

    public boolean accept(File dir, String name)
    {
        return name.endsWith(extn);
    }
}
```

```
}

public class FilterFiles
{
    public static void main(String[] args)
    {
        File f = new File(args[0]);
        FilenameFilter only = new FilterName(args[1]);
        String[] names = f.list(only);

        for (String s : names)
                System.out.println(s);
    }
}
```

```
E:\Rajkumar\javacourse\io>java FilterFiles.txt
data.txt
data1.txt
datanew.txt
dummy.txt
dummy2.txt
dummy2copy.txt
dummynew.txt
fish.txt
news.txt
news2.txt
student.txt


E:\Rajkumar\javacourse\io>java FilterFiles e:\rajkumar\
javacourse\io dat
baccount.dat
dummyisr.dat
employee.dat
marks.dat
marksobj.dat
pwdata.dat
```

The FilterName implements FilenameFilter interface and overrides accept(). The accept() returns true if a file ends with the required extension. In main(), you create a file object and FilenameFilter for the required extension. The list() of File object receives FilterName object as argument and collects all file names based on whether a file ends with the required extension. Finally the string array containing all file names that satisfied the condition will be displayed.

13.4 FILTERING ABSOLUTE FILE PATHS

FileFilter allows you to filter files not only based on their names but also based on their properties or attributes. For example, we want to filter all directories in a given directory. The FileFilter interface contains *accept()* that you should override to create a file filter similar to file name filter. Listing 13.3 shows all directories in a given directory.

Listing 13.3. Filtered File Paths

```java
// FilterDirs.java
import java.io.*;

class Dirs implements FileFilter
{
   public boolean accept(File file) {
      return file.isDirectory();
   } // similarly you can check any condition on file properties

}

public class FilterDirs
{
   public static void main(String[] args) throws IOException
   {
      File f = new File(args[0]);
      FileFilter filter = new Dirs();

      File[] files = f.listFiles(filter);
      for (File file : files)
            System.out.println(file.getCanonicalPath());
   }
}
```

E:\Rajkumar\javacourse\io>java FilterDirs .
E:\Rajkumar\javacourse\io\test
E:\Rajkumar\javacourse\io\test2

E:\Rajkumar\javacourse\io>java FilterDirs e:\rajkumar\javacourse
E:\Rajkumar\javacourse\.idea
E:\Rajkumar\javacourse\ACM_course
E:\Rajkumar\javacourse\awt
E:\Rajkumar\javacourse\basics
E:\Rajkumar\javacourse\gui_lecture_ex
E:\Rajkumar\javacourse\introjava9ed

```
E:\Rajkumar\javacourse\io
E:\Rajkumar\javacourse\JavaSample
E:\Rajkumar\javacourse\jblearning_javabook
E:\Rajkumar\javacourse\LabSourcecode
E:\Rajkumar\javacourse\OOP
E:\Rajkumar\javacourse\out
E:\Rajkumar\javacourse\Princeton
E:\Rajkumar\javacourse\src
E:\Rajkumar\javacourse\util
```

Here listing all directory names is very similar to listing all file names satisfying the condition on the file name. The *listFiles()* lists all File objects that are directory names in a given directory by taking filter as argument. The condition is defined in accept() method that checks whether the file object is a directory or not with isDirectory() method.

13.5 TYPES OF INPUT STREAMS

The byte streams are set of classes that will either read data or write data as bytes. The byte streams can be divided into two types: InputStream and OutputStream. InputStream classes are responsible for providing features in order to read data from data sources. Similary OutputStream classes are responsible for supporting features so as to write data from programs to output destinations. These two stream types are abstract classes so we will not create objects directly. But there are many useful subclasses with which we will create streams.

InputStream defines just one important method read() that will read a byte or byte array from any of the input sources. With InputStream, you can read data from various sources such as

- array of byes
- string
- file
- pipe

Each of these input sources has useful subclasses of InputStream and some of them are shown below:

- ByteArrayInputStream
- FileInputStream
- PipedInputStream

13.5.1 Reading Files as Bytes

Generally any file processing involves three important steps such as:

1. opening files for reading or writing
2. reading or writing data from/to files
3. closing files

The FileInputStream is an interesting class that can be used to read the contents of a file. The *read()* will read a byte from the stream. Listing 13.4 explains the process of reading a file.

Listing 13.4. Reading Files as Bytes

```java
// FileRead1.java
import java.io.*;

public class FileRead1
{
    public static void main(String[] args) throws IOException
    {
        FileInputStream fis = new FileInputStream("FileRead1.java");

        while(fis.available() > 0)
            System.out.print((char)fis.read());
        fis.close(); // close stream without fail

        // open again
        fis = new FileInputStream("FileRead1.java");
        // read() returns -1 when EOF reached
        int b;
        while ( (b = fis.read()) != -1)
            System.out.print((char)b);

        fis.close(); // close stream without fail
    }
}
```

```
Hello Java How are you today
Hello Java How are you today
```

The first step in file processing is to open a file for reading. The file to be read has to be given as argument to the constructor as a string or File object. If the specified file is not available in the current directory, then JVM will throw FileNotFoundException. So this exception should be caught. If file is opened successfully, then read() reads a byte from the stream and displays it as a character. The stream keeps reading data until there is no more byte to read with *available()* method. Finally, the opened file should be closed with *close()* without fail. Remember *read()* returns –1 when it reaches end of file.

13.5.2 Reading Files into Byte Array

The file contents can be read in a single read operation as a bulk read of bytes with overloaded read(). In order to know the length of a file, we also need to create File object besides FileInputStream. The bulk reading process is illustrated in Listing 13.5.

Listing 13.5. Reading Bytes into Char Array

```java
// FileRead2.java
import java.io.*;

public class FileRead2
{
    public static void main(String[] args) throws IOException
    {
        File file = new File(args[0]);
        FileInputStream in = new FileInputStream(file);

        // create buffer to hold file contents
        byte[] b = new byte[(int)file.length()];
        // read into buffer
        in.read(b);
        System.out.println("Using byte array: " + new String(b));
        in.close(); // close stream without fail
    }
}
```

```
E:\Rajkumar\javacourse\io>java FileRead2 news.txt
Using byte array: it was a rainy day
it was a cold day
i was delighted by the weather
but i was alone
```

Here, single read(), reads an entire content of the file, which is displayed as a single string.

13.5.3 Reading Strings as Bytes

The ByteArrayInputStream class is an implementation of the input stream that uses a byte array as the source. Once the stream is created then you can read one byte at a time from the stream. Listing 13.6 explains the working of this stream.

Listing 13.6. Reading Bytes from Bytes Array

```java
// BAIStest.java
import java.io.*;

public class BAIStest
{
    public static void main(String[] args) throws IOException
    {
        String str = "Hello Java World !";
        byte[] b = str.getBytes();
        ByteArrayInputStream s = new ByteArrayInputStream(b);
```

```
        while(s.available() > 0)
            System.out.print((char)s.read());
        s.close(); // close stream without fail
    }
}
```

```
Hello Java World !
```

Here getBytes() converts the given string into byte array. The byte array input stream is set to the byte array b and read() easily reads a byte one at a time and it is displayed.

13.6 TYPES OF OUTPUT STREAMS

The OutputStream is an abstract class and the base class of all output stream classes. It defines write() method to write a byte as *int* or *byte[]* to stream as well as *flush()* to flush the buffer contents to stream. Similar to input stream, output stream can be created to files, byte array and pipes so that the output of your program will go to these destinations. The important output stream subclasses for the corresponding input streams are:

- ByteArrayOutputStream
- FileOutputStream
- PipedOutputStream

13.6.1 Writing to Files as Bytes

The FileOutputStream is an important output stream that allows us to write data to the designated file, with *write()* method if the output file is available. If it is not available, the stream will create the file for you. The overloaded constructor allows you to specify whether the file contents have to be appended or overwritten. Listing 13.7 illustrates how to write bytes to the output file through stream.

Listing 13.7. Writing Bytes to Files

```
// FileWrite1.java
import java.io.*;

public class FileWrite1
{
    public static void main(String[] args) throws IOException
    {
        FileOutputStream fos = new FileOutputStream("dummy.txt");
                                    // by default, overwrite contents
        String str = "Rajkumar, how are you";
        fos.write(str.getBytes());
        fos.flush(); // flush buffer contents to file
        fos.close(); // close stream without fail
```

```
        // true = append, false = overwrite
        FileOutputStream fos2 = new FileOutputStream("dummy.txt",
        true);
        String str2 = "Hello Java World";
        byte[] b = str2.getBytes();
        for(int i : b)
               fos2.write(i);
        fos2.close(); // close stream without fail
    }
}
```

```
E:\Rajkumar\javacourse\io>type dummy.txt
Rajkumar, how are youHello Java World
```

The *flush()* transfers the contents of the buffer to the output file immediately. Also note that how you can specify file mode either for append or overwrite its contents.

13.6.2 Writing to Byte Array as Bytes

The ByteArrayOutputStream stores data into a byte array. Its size is unlimited and buffer grows automatically. The contents of byte array can be retrieved using *toByteArray()* and can be stored persistently in a file using *writeTo()* method as depicted in Listing 13.8.

Listing 13.8. Writing Bytes to Byte Array

```
// BAOStest.java

import java.io.*;

public class BAOStest
{
    public static void main(String[] args) throws IOException
    {
        // true = append, false = overwrite
        ByteArrayOutputStream os = new ByteArrayOutputStream();

        String str = "Java is one of the interesting languages";
        os.write(str.getBytes());

        // you can also transfer byte array to file
        FileOutputStream fos = new FileOutputStream("dummy2.txt");
        os.writeTo(fos);
        fos.close(); // close stream without fail
    }
}
```

```
E:\Rajkumar\javacourse\io>type dummy2.txt
Java is one of the interesting languages
```

13.7 PROBLEM: COPY FILES AS BYTES

So far in sections 13.5 and 13.6, the readers were introduced to both input stream and output stream classes. So you will observe that for every input stream class there is a corresponding output stream class. With this understanding, it will be easy for us to develop an application that will combine both streams. For instance, let us now develop an application that will copy the contents of source file into target file as illustrated in Listing 13.9.

Listing 13.9. File Copy as Bytes

```java
// FileCopy.java

import java.io.*;

public class FileCopy
{
    public static void main(String[] args) throws IOException
    {
        FileInputStream fis = new FileInputStream("dummy2.txt");
        FileOutputStream fos = new FileOutputStream("dummy2copy.
        txt");

        int b;
        while ((b = fis.read()) != -1)
                fos.write(b);

        fis.close(); // close stream without fail
        fos.close();
    }
}
```

```
E:\Rajkumar\javacourse\io>java FileCopy
E:\Rajkumar\javacourse\io>type dummy2.txt
Java is one of the interesting languages
E:\Rajkumar\javacourse\io>type dummy2copy.txt
Java is one of the interesting languages
```

Here, file input stream reads one byte at a time and writes to file output stream until the end of file is reached. However, you can also read the entire file contents into a byte array so that you can write the entire byte array in a single step. Listing 13.10 will copy the source file to target file in a single step.

Listing 13.10. File Copy Using Byte Array

```java
// FileCopyByte.java
import java.io.*;

public class FileCopyByte
{
    public static void main(String[] args) throws IOException
    {
        File file = new File(args[0]);
        FileInputStream in = new FileInputStream(args[0]);
        FileOutputStream out = new FileOutputStream(args[1]);

        // create buffer to hold file contents
        byte[] b = new byte[(int)file.length()];

        // read and write
        out.write(in.read(b));

        in.close();
        out.close(); // close stream without fail
    }
}
```

```
E:\Rajkumar\javacourse\io>javac FileCopyByte.java
E:\Rajkumar\javacourse\io>java FileCopyByte dummy.txt dummy3.txt
E:\Rajkumar\javacourse\io>type dummy.txt
Rajkumar, how are youHello Java World
E:\Rajkumar\javacourse\io>type dummy3.txt
%
```

One important point you must understand is the way the program copies byte array. That is write() takes read() as argument directly.

13.8 PROCESSING PRIMITIVE DATA TYPES

All input and output stream classes we studied so far handle only bytes. They do not support us to store java primitive data types such as *int, double, long, float,* etc. including *String.* But there are many occasions where we need to store and retrieve primitive data type values in a file. Java IO library has adequate classes to support these file management tasks with **DataInputStream** and **DataOutputStream** classes. The DataOutputStream allows us to write primitive data types to an output stream so that DataInputStream can read those data back from. There are readXXX() and WriteXXX() methods which will do reading and writing primitive data types where XXX denotes any primitive data types. In Listing 13.11, student's information such as roll number, name, address and marks are stored and retrieved using these streams.

Listing 13.11. Processing Primitive Data Types

```java
// DataIOstream.java

import java.io.*;

public class DataIOstream
{
    public static void main(String[] args) throws IOException
    {
        // write to student.txt file
        DataOutputStream dos = new DataOutputStream(
          new FileOutputStream("student.txt"));

        dos.writeInt(5001);
        dos.writeBytes("Rex\n");
        dos.writeUTF("India");
        dos.writeDouble(75.50);
        dos.flush();
        dos.close();

        // read from student.txt file
        DataInputStream dis = new DataInputStream(
          new FileInputStream("student.txt"));

        // read data in the same order as you write
        System.out.println(dis.readInt());
        System.out.println(dis.readLine());
        System.out.println(dis.readUTF()); // readUTF will recover
        data properly
        System.out.println(dis.readDouble());
        dis.close();
    }
}
```

```
5001
Rex
India
75.5
```

Here we cascade DataOutputStream with FileOutputStream so that data we write will be stored using FileOutputStream. In the same way, we can read primitive type values from a file using FileInput-Stream. To store string values, you can either use *writeBytes()* or *writeUTF()*. You will use *readLine()* to read the string that is stored using *writeBytes()*. Generally, *readUTF()* will recover data properly.

13.9 PROBLEM: GENERATING STUDENTS MARK LIST

Let us now assume a big data file containing several records of students' information. Each student will have values for attributes such as *rollno, name, address, mark1, mark2, mark3* and *mark4*. Figure 13.1 gives you the glimpse of the student table of records.

Figure 13.1. Students' Mark Records

Roll No.	Name	Address	Mark1	Mark2	Mark3	Mark4
5001	Rex	Trichy	76	57	87	91
5002	Peter	Chennai	55	87	98	20
......						

Now the issue is we need to store the values of all students in a file persistently so that we can read the file contents at any time. In order to generate the results of students you will have to perform these tasks:

1. Store students details to the file using DataOuputStream
2. Open the file for reading using DataInputStream
3. Read values of records and calculate result
4. Display mark list

The complete program that performs the above tasks is given in Listing 13.12.

Listing 13.12. Preparing Students Mark List from File Data

```java
// MarkList.java

import java.io.*;
import java.util.*;

public class MarkList
{
    Scanner sc = new Scanner(System.in);
    int n;   // number of students

    public void storeMarks() throws IOException
    {
        // open file for writing
        DataOutputStream dos = new DataOutputStream(
          new FileOutputStream("marks.dat"));

        System.out.println("Storing students marks to file
        now....");
        System.out.print("How many students? : ");
        n = sc.nextInt();
```

```
            for( int i = 0; i < n; i++)
            {
                    System.out.print("Enter roll no: ");
                    dos.writeInt(sc.nextInt());

                    sc.nextLine();   // discard \n

                    System.out.print("Enter name: ");
                    dos.writeUTF(sc.nextLine());

                    System.out.print("Enter address: ");
                    dos.writeUTF(sc.nextLine());

                    System.out.print("Enter mark1 ");
                    dos.writeFloat(sc.nextFloat());

                    System.out.print("Enter mark2 ");
                    dos.writeFloat(sc.nextFloat());

                    System.out.print("Enter mark3 ");
                    dos.writeFloat(sc.nextFloat());

                    System.out.print("Enter mark4 ");
                    dos.writeFloat(sc.nextFloat());
            }

    // close stream
    dos.flush();
    dos.close();
}

public void processMarks() throws IOException
{
    // open marks.dat for processing
    DataInputStream dis = new DataInputStream(
      new FileInputStream("marks.dat"));

    System.out.println("Preparing marks from file now....");

    System.out.println("\nStudents Mark List");
    for( int i = 0; i < n; i++)
    {
            System.out.println("Roll no: " + dis.readInt());
            System.out.println("Name: " + dis.readUTF());
            System.out.println("Address: " + dis.readUTF());
```

```
            float m1 = dis.readFloat();
            float m2 = dis.readFloat();
            float m3 = dis.readFloat();
            float m4 = dis.readFloat();

            System.out.print("Marks: ");
            System.out.print("Mark1 " + m1 + " ");
            System.out.print("Mark2 " + m2 + " ");
            System.out.print("Mark3 " + m3 + " ");
            System.out.print("Mark4 " + m4);

            // calculate result
            String result = "fail";
            if (m1 >= 40 && m2 >= 40 && m3 >= 40 && m4 >= 40)
                    result = "pass";

            System.out.println("\nResult: " + result);
        }

        // close stream
        dis.close();
    }

    public static void main(String[] args) throws IOException
    {
        MarkList m = new MarkList();
        m.storeMarks();
        m.processMarks();
    }
}
```

```
Storing students marks to file now....
How many students? : 2
Enter roll no: 5001
Enter name: Rex
Enter address: Trichy
Enter mark1 95
Enter mark2 76
Enter mark3 87
Enter mark4 70
Enter roll no: 5002
Enter name: Rita
Enter address: Chennai
Enter mark1 98
```

```
Enter mark2 78
Enter mark3 85
Enter mark4 35

Preparing marks from file now....
Students Mark List

Roll no: 5001
Name: Rex
Address: Trichy
Marks: Mark1 95.0 Mark2 76.0 Mark3 87.0 Mark4 70.0
Result: pass

Roll no: 5002
Name: Rita
Address: Chennai
Marks: Mark1 98.0 Mark2 78.0 Mark3 85.0 Mark4 35.0
Result: fail
```

This MarkList application has two methods. First *storeMarks()* receives values for students from user and stores those students' information in a file. It will ask first the maximum number of students whose values are to be stored. Based on this value, it will collect all information about each student and store them in the file using writeXXX() methods of DataOutputStream.

The second method *processMarks()* simply opens the file using DataInputStream and iterates through the file and retrieves values using readXXX() methods. Result is calculated based on students' marks and is displayed.

13.10 SERIALIZING OBJECTS

Serialization of objects is another interesting feature of Java. It allows us to create serializable objects so that it can be transmitted over a network to another machine which can even run on different Operating System. The machine in the other side of the network will deserialize the object in order to get the original object. Another important feature of **object serialization** is persistence. All serializable objects can be persistently stored into a disk as a file. The Java Remote Method Invocation (RMI) and Java Beans heavily use object serialization. Of course, RMI and Beans are out of scope for this book.

The object to be serialized needs to first implement Serializable interface. Since Serializable does not have any methods, we need not override anything and just we tag this object as serializable one, that's it.

Once we create serializable object, we can use *writeObject()* from ObjectOutputStream class to serialize the object and send to any OutputStream. Similarly we can use *readObject()* from ObjectInputStream to reverse the process. Since deserialized object is of type java.lang.Object, we need to downcast it to our original object type. In this book, we focus on how to write objects to files using ObjectOutputStream and read file data using ObjectInputStream classes.

In Listing 13.13, you might see how to store objects of type **Fish** to files and read those **Fish** objects.

Listing 13.13. Streaming Fish Objects

```java
// StreamingFish.java

import java.io.*;

class Fish implements Serializable
{
    int id;

    public Fish(int i)
    {
        id = i;
    }
    public String toString()
    {
        return Integer.toString(id);
    }
}

public class StreamingFish
{
    public static void main(String[] args)
        throws IOException, ClassNotFoundException
    {
        // store fishes to file
        ObjectOutputStream out = new ObjectOutputStream(
            new FileOutputStream("fish.txt"));

        for(int i = 0; i < 5; i++)
            out.writeObject(new Fish(i));

        // close it without fail
        out.close();

        // read fishes from file
        ObjectInputStream in = new ObjectInputStream(
            new FileInputStream("fish.txt"));

        for(int i = 0; i < 5; i++)
            System.out.println((Fish)in.readObject());
        // close
        in.close();
    }
}
```

```
E:\Rajkumar\javacourse\io>java StreamingFish
0
1
2
3
4
```

The Fish object is simply made Serializable object and rest of the code in Fish class is normal. We just assign number to each fish and override toString() that will return fish number as a String. In main(), we create object output stream that will allow us to write our serializable objects to file using writeObject() method. The *writeObject()* stores Fish objects to file and then the stream is closed. As a reverse process, we read serialized objects back from the same file using *readObject()* method. The retrieved object should be downcasted to Fish type and must be caught for a possible exception of type ClassNotFoundException without fail.

13.11 PROBLEM: GENERATING STUDENTS' MARK LIST – REVISITED

In section 13.9, you have learnt how to store and retrieve students' details to file using DataInputStream and DataOutputStream. Though data IO, classes allow us to store primitive data types, it will store details as a sequence of bytes, not as student objects themselves. So we will lose information that these bytes constitute a particular students' details. Therefore the solution is to use Object IO. Listing 13.14 illustrates you how to store and retrieve array of student objects to and from file.

Listing 13.14. Serializing Student Objects to File

```java
// StreamingStudents.java

import java.io.*;
import java.util.*;

class Student implements Serializable
{
    int rollno;
    String name;
    String address;
    float m1, m2, m3, m4;

    public void getResult()
    {
        System.out.println("Roll no: " + rollno);
        System.out.println("Name: " + name);
        System.out.println("Address: " + address);
        System.out.println("Marks: " + m1 + " " + m2 + " " + m3
        + " " + m4);
```

```java
        // calculate result
        String result = "fail";
        if (m1 >= 40 && m2 >= 40 && m3 >= 40 && m4 >= 40)
            result = "pass";
        System.out.println("\nResult: " + result);
    }
}


public class StreamingStudents
{
    Scanner sc = new Scanner(System.in);
    int n;  // number of students

    public void storeMarks() throws IOException
    {
        // write to student.txt file
        ObjectOutputStream out = new ObjectOutputStream(
            new FileOutputStream("marksobj.dat"));

        System.out.println("Storing student objects to file now....");
        System.out.print("How many students? : ");
        n = sc.nextInt();

        // create student object array
        Student[] stud = new Student[n];

        for( int i = 0; i < n; i++)
        {
            // instantiate student
            stud[i] = new Student();

            System.out.print("Enter roll no: ");
            stud[i].rollno = sc.nextInt();

            sc.nextLine();  // discard \n

            System.out.print("Enter name: ");
            stud[i].name = sc.nextLine();

            System.out.print("Enter address: ");
            stud[i].address = sc.nextLine();

            System.out.print("Enter mark1 ");
            stud[i].m1 = sc.nextFloat();

            System.out.print("Enter mark2 ");
```

```
            stud[i].m2 = sc.nextFloat();

            System.out.print("Enter mark3 ");
            stud[i].m3 = sc.nextFloat();

            System.out.print("Enter mark4 ");
            stud[i].m4 = sc.nextFloat();
        }

    // write objects to file
    for( int i = 0; i < n; i++)
        out.writeObject(stud[i]);
    // close stream
    out.close();
    }

public void processMarks() throws
    IOException, ClassNotFoundException
    {
    // read data from file and process
    ObjectInputStream in = new ObjectInputStream(
        new FileInputStream("marksobj.dat"));

    System.out.println("Preparing mark list from file now....");
    System.out.println("\nStudents Mark List");

    for( int i = 0; i < n; i++)
        {
        // read object
        Student s = (Student)in.readObject();
        // show details and result
        s.getResult();
        }
    // close stream
    in.close();
    }

    public static void main(String[] args)
        throws IOException, ClassNotFoundException
    {
        StreamingStudents m = new StreamingStudents();
        m.storeMarks();
        m.processMarks();
    }
}
```

```
Storing student objects to file now....
How many students? : 1
Enter roll no: 2001
Enter name: Ramya
Enter address: Bangalore
Enter mark1 85
Enter mark2 87
Enter mark3 67
Enter mark4 90
Preparing mark list from file now....

Students Mark List
Roll no: 2001
Name: Ramya
Address: Bangalore
Marks: 85.0 87.0 67.0 90.0
Result: pass
```

13.12 TRANSIENT VARIABLES

One final point about object serialization; suppose if you have some sensitive data that should not be serialized, then you need to declare those data as **transient** variables. By declaring a variable transient, you instruct your JVM not to serialize it.

To illustrate transient variables, let us create a BankAccount class with *accno* and *balance*. Suppose we do not want *balance* to be visible to other classes even over the network, but we want accno to be visible to all other objects over the network. So we create balance as a transient variable as depicted in Listing 13.15.

Listing 13.15. Transient Variables

```java
// SerializableAccount.java
import java.io.*;

class BankAccount implements Serializable
{
    int accno;
    transient double balance;

    public BankAccount(int a, double d)
    {
        accno = a;
        balance = d;
    }
}
```

```java
public class SerializableAccount
{
    public static void main(String[] args)
        throws IOException, ClassNotFoundException
    {
        // store fishes to file
        ObjectOutputStream out = new ObjectOutputStream(
            new FileOutputStream("baccount.dat"));

        for(int i = 0; i < 5; i++)
            out.writeObject(new BankAccount(i, i * 10000.0));
        // close it without fail
        out.close();

        // read fishes from file
        ObjectInputStream in = new ObjectInputStream(
            new FileInputStream("baccount.dat"));

        for(int i = 0; i < 5; i++)
        {
            BankAccount b = (BankAccount)in.readObject();
            System.out.println("Account number: " + b.accno);
            System.out.println("Balance: " + b.balance);
        }

        // close
        in.close();
    }
}
```

```
Account number: 0
Balance: 0.0
Account number: 1
Balance: 0.0
Account number: 2
Balance: 0.0
Account number: 3
Balance: 0.0
Account number: 4
Balance: 0.0
```

All five bank accounts with *accno* and *balance* are stored as objects in a file. However, while you retrieve them you will notice balance amounts are not visible. Only a default value of 0.0 will be displayed. This way we can prohibit the visibility of sensitive and nonsharable information during object serialization.

13.13 SUMMARY

1. A stream is a group of bytes or characters that can be associated with physical objects such as disks and devices

2. Streams help us to communicate with files by many ways such as sequentially, randomly, using buffering, byte by byte, character by character, word by word and line by line

3. Each stream has a unique purpose and should be used accordingly

4. The File class represents the path name of a file or a set of files in a directory

5. The mkdir() creates a directory whereas mkdirs() creates a directory including its parent directories

6. FilenameFilter is an interface that is used to filter file names based on some condition

7. FileFilter allows you to filter files not only based on their names but also based on their properties or attributes.

8. InputStream classes are responsible for providing features in order to read data from data sources

9. OutputStream classes are responsible for supporting features so as to write data from programs to output destinations

10. FileInputStream allows us to read files as bytes using its read() method

11. FileOutputStream contains write() method in order to write bytes to files

12. The ByteArrayInputStream class uses a byte array as the source

13. The FileOutputStream writes data to the designated file, if the output file is available. If it is not available, the stream will create the file and write data

14. The flush() transfers the contents of the buffer to the output file immediately

15. The readXXX() of DataInputStream and WriteXXX() of DataOutputStream will do reading and writing primitive data types, where XXX denotes any primitive data type

16. Serializable objects can be transmitted over a network to another machine which can even run on different Operating System

17. The writeObject() and readObject() methods of Object IO transmit serializable objects over network

18. Transient variables will be not serialized

KEY TERMS

REVIEW QUESTIONS

Multiple-choice Questions

1. Assume foo does not exist already. Which of the following is true?

```
File file = new File("foo");
```

    a. It creates a file foo
                       b. It creates a file object foo
    c. It creates a subdirectory under foo
      d. None of the above

2. Which of the following is true?

```
File file = new File("foo");
file.createNewFile();
```

    a. A new file object is created by createNewFile()
    b. A new file is created by createNewFile()
    c. Reference file points to the file foo
    d. None of the above

3. Which of the following is true?

```
File file = new File("foo");
file.createNewDirectory();
```

    a. A new directory object is created
    b. A new directory is created
    c. Reference file points to the directory foo
    d. None of the above

4. Which of the following is true?

```
File file = new File("foo");
file.mkdir();
```

    a. A new directory object is created
    b. A new directory is created
    c. Reference file points to the directory foo
    d. None of the above

5. Which of the following is true?
   a. The flush() transfers file to disk
   b. The flush() transfers file to disk immediately
   c. The flush() transfers buffer to disk
   d. The flush() transfers buffer to disk immediately
   e. None of the above

6. What is the output?

```
File file = new File("tools");
File myfile = new File(tools, "pr.dat");
myfile.createNewFile();
```

   a. Creates a directory tools   b. Creates a file pr.dat
   c. Creates a file pr.dat in the directory tools   d. Compilation error
   e. throws IOException

7. Which of the following is true?

```
BufferedReader in = new BufferedReader(
   new FileReader("test13.txt"));
String s;
while((s = in.readLine()) != null)
   System.out.println(s);
in.close();
```

   a. Displays the contents of test13.txt if it exists
   b. Throws FileNotFoundException if test13.txt does not exist
   c. The readLine() returns null if end of file reached
   d. All of the above

8. Choose all correct statements:

```
File f1 = new File("test13.txt");
File f2 = new File("test131.txt");
f1.renameTo(f2);
```

   a. The test13.txt is renamed to test131.txt, if test13.txt exists
   b. The test131.txt is renamed to test13.txt
   c. After renaming test13.txt will not exist
   d. After renaming test13.txt will also exist
   e. After renaming test13.txt will not exist

9. What is true about f3?

```
File f3 = new File("test\\iotest");
f3.mkdirs();
```

    a. It creates the directory iotest if it does not exist

    b. It creates the directory iotest and parent directory test if it does not exist

    c. It creates the directory test and parent directory iotest if it does not exist

    d. If the directory iotest already exists, throws IOException

10. What is true about file?

```
File file = new File("test");
System.out.println(file.length());
```

    a. Displays length in bytes if file abstracts already existing file

    b. Displays length in bytes if file abstracts already existing directory

    c. Displays total number of files if file abstracts already existing directory

    d. Displays unspecified value if file abstracts already existing directory

11. Choose all correct statements:

```
FileOutputStream out = new FileOutputStream("a.txt");
out.write();
```

    a. It will throw IOException if a.txt does not exist

    b. A new file will be created if a.txt not exists

    c. String file name cannot be given to FileOutputStream

    d. Only File object can be given to FileOuputStream

12. What is the output?

```
class A implements Serializable {
    int i = 100; }

public class Test13 {
    public static void main(String[] args) throws Exception {
        A a = new A();
        ObjectOutputStream out = new ObjectOutputStream (
            new FileOutputStream("test13.txt"));
        out.writeObject(a);
        out.close();
```

```
        ObjectInputStream in = new ObjectInputStream (
            new FileInputStream("test13.txt"));
        A a1 = (A)in.readObject();
        System.out.println(a1.i); in.close();
    }
}
```

a. 0   b. Null

c. 100   d. Exception

13. Assume class Test13 as in Example 12. What is the output?

```
class A implements Serializable
{
    int i = 1;
    public A() {System.out.print("2");}
}
```

a. 12   b. 21

c. 11   d. 22

e. None of the above

14. What is the output?

```
class A
{
    int i = 1;
    public A() {System.out.print("2");}
}

public class Test13 extends A implements Serializable
{
    public static void main(String[] args) throws Exception
    {
        Test13 t1 = new Test13();
        // Test13 is serialized
        // Test13 is de-serialized as Test13 t2
        System.out.println(t2.i); in.close();
    }
}
```

a. 112   b. 122

c. 221   d. None of the above

15. What is the output?

```
class A implements Serializable
{
    transient int i = 1;
    public A() {System.out.print("2");}
}

public class Test13 extends A implements Serializable
{
    int j = 3;
    public Test13() {System.out.print("4");}

    public static void main(String[] args) throws Exception
    {
        // Test13 is serialized
        // Test13 is deserialized as usual
        System.out.println(t2.i + "" + t2.j); in.close();
    }
}
```

   a. 2403   b. 1234

   c. 1324   d. 1243

   e. None of the above

16. Assume class Test13 as in Example 15. What is the output?

```
class A implements Serializable
{
    int i = 1;
    public A() {System.out.print("2");}
}
```

   a. 1234   b. 2413

   c. 1324   d. 1423

   e. None of the above

17. What is the output?

```
class A {}
class B implements Serializable
{
```

```
   A a = new A();
   int i = 1;
   public B() {System.out.print("2");}
}
public class Test13 extends B
{
   int j = 3;
   public Test13() {System.out.print("4");}

   public static void main(String[] args)
   {
      try {
      // Test13 is serialized
      // Test13 is deserialized as usual
      System.out.println(t2.i + "" + t2.j);
      in.close();
      }catch(Exception e) {
      System.out.print("0");}
   }
}
```

a. 240   b. 2413
c. 2410   d. 2430

18. What is the output?

```
class A implements Serializable
{
   static int i = 1;
   public A() {System.out.print("2");}
}
public class Test13 extends A
implements Serializable
{
   int j = 3;
   public Test13() {System.out.print("4");}

   public static void main(String[] args)
   throws Exception
   {
      // Test13 is serialized
      i++;
      // Test13 is de-serialized as usual
      System.out.println(t2.i + "" + t2.j);
```

```
        in.close();
    }
}
```

    a. 2234   b. 2423

    c. 2324   d. 4232

    e. None of the above

19. What is the output?

```
class A implements Serializable
{.
    static int i = 1;
    int j = 2;
    public A() {System.out.print("3");}
}
public class Test13 extends A
{
    int k = 4;
    public Test13() {System.out.print("5");}

    public static void main(String[] args)
    throws Exception
    {
        Test13 t = new Test13();
        //Test13 serialized
        i++;
        //Test13 de-serialized
        System.out.println(
        t2.i + "" + t2.j + "" + t2.k);
        in.close();
    }
}
```

    a. 23425

    b. 35224

    c. 22335

    d. None of the above

Answers

1. b	2. b	3. d	4. b	5. d	6. e	7. d	8. c	9. b	10. a
11. b	12. c	13. b	14. c	15. a	16. b	17. a	18. b	19. b	

Short-answer Questions

1. How to display properties of a file?
2. What are the file comparison methods?
3. Explain all methods related to directories.
4. Explain reading and writing bytes from files.
5. Explain all DataInputStream methods.
6. Explain all DataOutputStream methods.
7. Explain the process of serializing objects.
8. Explain the process of deserializing objects.
9. How will you prevent data from serialization?

EXERCISES

13.1. Count the number of characters in a given file.

13.2. Count the number of words in a file.

13.3. Print the frequency (i.e. number of times it occurs) of each character from a given file.

13.4. Print the frequency of words in a given file.

13.5. [File Encryption] Caesar cipher (with k=2) replaces A by C, B by D, .., Y by A and Z by B. Now read characters of a file, encrypt and store it in a new file. Just ignore when you encounter lowercase letters or other characters. Display both source and destination files.

13.6. [File Decryption] Read an already encrypted file, perform the reverse replacement of characters and recover the original file.

14

Processing Character Streams and NIO

OBJECTIVES

- To introduce Reader and Writer abstract classes
- To introduce all Reader types such as FileReader, BufferedReader and PipedReader
- To read files as characters using FileReader
- To read files as lines of text using BufferedReader
- To count word frequencies of a given file
- To generate index for the given text file
- To write characters to file using FileWriter
- To copy file contents using FileReader and FileWriter
- To write lines of text to files using BufferedWriter
- To write bytes to PipedWriter and to read from PiperReader
- To design alphabet generator application using Piped IO and threads
- To format output strings using PrintWriter
- To create RandomAccessFile for direct access for reading and writing
- To convert bytes to characters using InputStreamReader
- To create channels and buffers using NIO
- To read bytes from FileChannel using ByteBuffer
- To write bytes to FileChannel using ByteBuffer
- To write characters to FileChannel using CharBuffer
- To lock files for atomic write operations to FileChannel

14.1 INTRODUCTION

Java 1.1 has provided significant improvements with its character-oriented streams over the earlier Java 1.0 which supported only byte-oriented streams. In Java 1.1 characters are represented with a 16-bit Unicode character representation. The main advantage of character streams is its support for internationalization. Though **character streams** have definite advantages, they are not meant to replace byte streams. This is why many byte streams are still retained so far and have a lot of applications. Moreover character streams are represented internally over byte streams.

In this chapter, the readers are exposed first to all important character stream classes that are available in Java, so that you will be able to develop efficient applications. Then, the readers are introduced to buffered streams classes that will improve the performance of your applications. Further, the readers learn how to bridge input streams and character streams so that byte streams can be converted to character streams. Then the readers create streams that will allow you to open file for both reading and writing and move through the file randomly with file pointers using random access file. Finally, the readers are introduced to the features of *java.nio* package.

14.2 TYPES OF READERS

All character streams are subclasses of either **Reader** or **Writer**. The Reader and Writer are abstract classes. The Reader provides overloaded *read()* method that will read a character from stream or read characters to char array. In Figure 14.1, you will see the correspondence between input streams and readers.

Figure 14.1. Java 1.0 Streams vs. Java 1.1 Readers

InputStream	Reader
FileInputStream	FileReader
ByteArrayInputStream	CharArrayReader
PipedInputStream	PipedReader
BufferedInputStream	BufferedReader

14.2.1 Reading Files as Characters

The FileReader class allows us to read the stream of characters, very similar to reading streams of bytes using FileInputStream. Given a file name as File object or a string, the file reader opens the mentioned file for reading. The *read()* reads a character as int from the stream and returns –1 when end of file is reached. If the declared file is not available, then FileNotFoundException will be thrown. Now let us display the contents of a file using FileReader as depicted in Listing 14.1.

Listing 14.1. Displaying the Contents of File Using FileReader

```
// FileReader1.java
import java.io.*;

public class FileReader1
```

```
{
    public static void main(String[] args) throws
    IOException
    {
        if (args.length != 1)
        {
            System.out.println("Enter file name for
            reading...");
            System.exit(0);
        }


        FileReader fr = new FileReader(args[0]);
        // to read one char at a time
        int c;
        while((c=fr.read()) != -1)
          System.out.print((char)c);
        fr.close();


        // let us concatenate all char into a string
        StringBuffer sb = new StringBuffer();
        fr = new FileReader(args[0]);

        while((c=fr.read()) != -1)
          sb.append((char)c);


        System.out.println("Stringbuffer: " + sb.toString());
        fr.close();
    }
}
```

```
it was a rainy day
it was a cold day
i was delighted by the weather
but i was alone
Stringbuffer: it was a rainy day
it was a cold day
i was delighted by the weather
but i was alone
```

You can also read the file contents into a char array in a single bulk read instead of reading character by character. In this way, your scheduler can minimize the number of disk read. Listing 14.2 tells you all those details about reading characters into char array.

Listing 14.2. Reading File Contents into Char Array

```java
// FileReader2.java
import java.io.*;

public class FileReader2
{
    public static void main(String[] args) throws IOException
    {
        if (args.length != 1)
        {
            System.out.println("Enter file name for reading...");
            System.exit(0);
        }

        // let us use char[]
        File file = new File(args[0]);
        FileReader fr = new FileReader(file);
        char[] b = new char[(int)file.length()];

        fr.read(b);
        System.out.println("Using char array: " + String.
        valueOf(b));
        fr.close();
    }
}
```

```
Using char array: it was a rainy day
it was a cold day
i was delighted by the weather
but i was alone
```

14.2.2 Problem: Word Counting Using FileReader

Let us now rewrite Word counter application that we solved in section 9.3. The only change we make here is the way we input values. Instead of a simple string we now count words of the given file as depicted in Listing 14.3.

Listing 14.3. Counting Words of a File

```java
/ FileWordCounter.java

import java.io.*;
import java.util.*;

public class FileWordCounter
```

```
{
    public static void main(String[] args) throws IOException
    {
        if (args.length != 1)
        {
            System.out.println("Enter file name for word
            counting...");
            System.exit(0);
        }

        // read file contents into sb
        FileReader fr = new FileReader(args[0]);
        StringBuffer sb = new StringBuffer();
        int c;
        while((c=fr.read()) != -1)
            sb.append((char)c);

        // Hashtable to hold words as string and their
        counts as int
        Hashtable<String,Integer> ht = new
        Hashtable<String,Integer>();

        // parse file for different words by stringTokenizer
        StringTokenizer st = new StringTokenizer
        (sb.toString());
        while (st.hasMoreTokens())
        {
            // get next token
            String word = st.nextToken();
            // check if word already present in ht
            if(ht.containsKey(word))
            {
                // System.out.println("HT contains " + word);
                // increment it's count
                int count = ht.get(word);
                // System.out.println("count of " + word + ":" +
                count);
                // increment
                count++;
                // put this new value
                ht.put(word, count);
            }
            else
            {
                // new key to be added in ht with count 1
```

```
                    ht.put(word, 1);
            }
        }

        // display ht
        System.out.println(ht.toString());

    }
}
```

```
Input:
it was a rainy day
it was a cold day
i was delighted by the weather
but i was alone

Output:
{rainy=1, was=4, weather=1, cold=1, it=2, i=2, delighted=1,
but=1, the=1, by=1, day=2, a=2, alone=1}
```

The main() first ensures if user has sent the file name as a command line argument. If not, the application will report a message asking users to type file name for counting and terminates. If an input file name is specified correctly, then FileReader reads one character at a time from file and appends to string buffer. This way a long input string is created from string buffer, so that StringTokenizer generates tokens from string buffer and the frequencies of unique words are stored in the Hashtable.

14.2.3 Reading Files as Lines

Reading character by character from a file is tedious, and most of our file reading happens at the level of line by line. Every line in a text is terminated with **carriage-return** or new-line. The BufferedReader has an interesting method readLine() that will allow us to read line by line terminated by carriage-return or new-line in a given text file. The readLine() method is not new for us. You have been using this method from Chapter 1 onwards. So far, you have connected BufferedReader to standard input (System.in) instead of a file. The application that counts the number of lines in a file is given in Listing 14.4.

Listing 14.4. Counting Lines in a File

```
// bufferedReader1.java
import java.io.*;

public class BufferedReader1
{
    public static void main(String[] args) throws IOException
```

```
{
    if (args.length != 1)
    {
        System.out.println("Enter file name for
        processing...");
        System.exit(0);
    }

    // to read one line at a time
    BufferedReader br = new BufferedReader(new
    FileReader(args[0]));

    String s;
    int count = 0;
    while (( s = br.readLine()) != null)
    {
        System.out.println(s);
        count++;
    }

    // display total number of lines in this file
    System.out.println("No. of lines: " + count);

    br.close();
    }
}
```

```
Input File: news.txt
it was a rainy day
it was a cold day
i was delighted by the weather
but i was alone

Output:
it was a rainy day
it was a cold day
i was delighted by the weather
but i was alone
No. of lines: 4
```

The given input file *news.txt* contains four lines of text. The readLine() will read one line at a time from the file that is connected to FileReader. The while loop terminates when readLine() returns *null*, indicating there is no more a line of text.

14.2.4 Problem: Text Index Generator

Building an index file for the given input file is another important task that many applications use every day. The index file simply records a word and the set of line numbers where this word appears. Listing 14.5 uses Hashtable to store the word and its line numbers indicating where this word appears.

In order to store line numbers, you need an instance of LinkedList so that it will append line numbers as integers. If a word appears even twice in the same line, then linkedlist will also add a node with the same line number. To avoid this duplicate line numbers, you can use *set* behaviour that will suppress duplicates. Therefore, we use HashSet instead of LinkedList to store all values for the given word in the Hashtable. Of course, you can also use Java 1.2 HashMap instead of Hashtable. The complete application is shown in Listing 14.5.

Listing 14.5. Generating Index for a Text File

```java
// TextIndexGenerator.java

import java.io.*;
import java.util.*;

public class TextIndexGenerator
{
    public static void main(String[] args) throws
    IOException
    {
        // check command line
        if (args.length != 1)
        {
            System.out.println("Enter file name for
            processing...");
            System.exit(0);
        }

        // vector will hold all the lines
        Vector<String> lines = new Vector<String>();

        // to read one line at a time
        BufferedReader br = new BufferedReader(new
        FileReader(args[0]));
        String s;
        while (( s = br.readLine()) != null)
            lines.add(s);

        // hashtable to store words and corresponding
        line numbers
```

```
Hashtable<String, HashSet> ht = new Hashtable<String,
HashSet>();

for(int i = 0; i < lines.size(); i++)
{
        // take one line
        StringTokenizer st = new StringTokenizer(lines.
        get(i));
        // separate into words
        while(st.hasMoreTokens())
        {
                // get a word
                String word = st.nextToken();
                // if word not available in ht, add
                if (!ht.containsKey(word))
                ht.put(word, new HashSet());
                // if available, add line number to set
                ht.get(word).add(i);
        }
}

// display
System.out.println(ht.toString());
}
}
```

Input: news.txt
it was a rainy day
it was a cold day
i was delighted by the weather
but i was alone

Output:

```
{rainy=[0], was=[0, 1, 2, 3], weather=[2], cold=[1], it=[0, 1],
i=[2, 3], delighted=[2], but=[3], the=[2], by=[2], day=[0, 1],
a=[0, 1], alone=[3]}
```

The input file *news.txt* contains four lines (assume: line 0 to line 3). The Hashtable maps each word to a set of line numbers as int using HashSet. For instance, the word *rainy* appears in line number 0 only. Similarly, the word *was* appears in all lines.

In Chapter 1, the readers were introduced to Scanner class which can read a file and generate tokens. So, in the above example, instead of BufferedReader you can also use Scanner with a delimiter "*\n*" so that it will return all tokens delimited by new-line as shown in Example 14.1.

Example 14.1. Using Scanner for Reading File

```
// read file
Scanner sc = new Scanner(new File(args[0]));
sc.useDelimiter("\n");

// add lines of text to vector
Vector<String> lines = new Vector<String>();
while(sc.hasNext())
    lines.add(sc.next());
```

14.3 TYPES OF WRITERS

The Writer is an abstract class that provides *append()* to append a char to the stream and *write()* to write a single character or even a string to stream. Figure 14.2 gives you the correspondence between output streams and writers.

Figure 14.2. Java 1.0 Outputstreams vs Java 1.1 Writers

OutputStream	Writer
FileOutputStream	FileWriter
BufferedOutputStream	BufferedWriter
PipedOutputStream	PipedWriter
PrintStream	PrintWriter

14.3.1 Writing Characters to File

The FileWriter class allows you to connect a stream to a file so that characters and strings can be written to file. The file name can be given as File object or a String. The second argument can be used to specify whether file contents are to be overwritten or to be appended. The inherited *append()* and *write()* methods allow us to append or write characters or strings to file. Listing 14.6 demonstrates how we can write a character or string to the file.

Listing 14.6. Writing Strings Using Filewriter

```
// FileWriter1.java
import java.io.*;

public class FileWriter1
{
    public static void main(String[] args) throws IOException
    {
        FileWriter fr = new FileWriter("dummy.txt");
```

```
        String s = "Hello Java, how are you";
        fr.write(s);
        fr.write('!');
        fr.flush();
        fr.close();

        FileWriter fr2 = new FileWriter("dummy.txt", true); //
        append mode
        String s2 = "\nThis is another appended line";
        fr2.write(s2);
        fr2.append('?');
        fr2.flush();
        fr2.close();
    }
}
```

```
Hello Java, how are you!
This is another appended line?
```

For writing characters to file, you can either use write() or append(). To prevent overwriting, you will have to create FileWriter with append mode to be *true*.

14.3.2 Problem: Copy Files Using FileWriter

Thus far you were using streams for either reading or writing characters using character streams. Now let us combine reading and writing processes into a single copy operation as illustrated in Listing 14.7.

Listing 14.7. Copy Files Using FileWriter and BufferedWriter

```java
// FileCopy2.java
import java.io.*;

public class FileCopy2
{
    public static void main(String[] args) throws IOException
    {
        // check command line arguments
        if( args.length != 2)
        {
            System.out.println("Syntax: java FileCopy2 file1
            file2");
            System.exit(0);
        }
    }
```

```
        // create streams
        FileReader in = new FileReader(args[0]);
        FileWriter out = new FileWriter(args[1]);

        // copy char by char
        int c;
        while((c = in.read()) != -1)
             out.write((char)c);

        // close files
        in.close();
        out.close();
    }
}
```

```
E:\Rajkumar\javacourse\io>java FileCopy2 dummy.txt dummynew.txt

E:\Rajkumar\javacourse\io>type dummy.txt
Hello Java, how are you!
This is another appended line?

E:\Rajkumar\javacourse\io>type dummynew.txt
Hello Java, how are you!
This is another appended line?
```

Once user supplies two file names representing source file and destination file, copying files is straightforward. Just you need to read a character from source file with *read()* and write that character to destination file using *write()* until you reach the end of file. The read() returns –1 when end of file is reached.

14.3.3 Writing Lines to Files

In order to write characters line by line, BufferedWriter class should be used. The same inherited write() will store a string onto the file through its stream. Now let us rewrite the above file copy application so that the file is copied line by line instead of char by char. As we use *readLine()* of BufferedReader to read a line of text, it ignores new-line while reading text. So you need to append a new-line with *newLine()* method to the output stream while writing using *write()*. Listing 14.8 explains you the revised file copy application.

Listing 14.8. Copy Lines to Files

```
// FileCopy3.java
import java.io.*;
public class FileCopy3
```

```
{
   public static void main(String[] args) throws
   IOException
   {
      // check command line arguments
      if( args.length != 2)
      {
            System.out.println("Syntax: java FileCopy2 file1
            file2");
            System.exit(0);
      }

      // now copy line by line
      BufferedReader in2 = new BufferedReader(new
      FileReader(args[0]));
      BufferedWriter out2 = new BufferedWriter(new
      FileWriter(args[1]));

      String s;
      while (( s = in2.readLine()) != null)
      {
            out2.write(s);
            out2.newLine();   // you need to add \n
      }

      // close files
      in2.close();
      out2.close();
   }
}
```

```
E:\Rajkumar\javacourse\io>java FileCopy3 dummy.txt dummy3.txt

E:\Rajkumar\javacourse\io>type dummy.txt
Hello Java, how are you!
This is another appended line?

E:\Rajkumar\javacourse\io>type dummy3.txt
Hello Java, how are you!
This is another appended line?
```

The users are expected to supply two files in the command prompt. They denote source and destination file names. The copying process is trivial; the program reads a line from stream and writes to output file along with the new-line character.

14.4 WRITING TO AND READING FROM PIPES

Pipe is an abstraction of another stream with which output of one pipe is fed as input to another pipe. The concept of pipe is not new to you. You know the power of pipe operation in *unix* operating system which redirects output of one command to another command. PipedReader and PipedWriter will do the same. You will have to first write some data to pipe using PipedWriter. Once data are ready, PipedReader can read data from the pipe. The *connect()* method available in both character streams connects one pipe to another pipe. Figure 14.3 depicts how piped character streams are connected together.

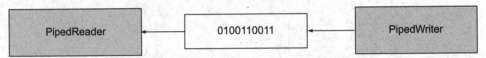

Figure 14.3. Reading and Writing Pipes

Now let us create PipedWriter that will write a string to pipe and PipedReader reads from the pipe if pipe has some available data. Listing 14.9 illustrates the use of piped character streams.

Listing 14.9. Reading and Writing Pipes

```java
// PipeReadWrite.java
import java.io.*;

public class PipeReadWrite
{
    public static void main(String[] args)
    {
        try
        {
            // Create PipedWriter object
            PipedWriter writer = new PipedWriter();
            // Create PipeReader object
            PipedReader reader = new PipedReader();
            // now connect one pipe to another
            reader.connect(writer);
            // also same: writer.connect(reader);

            // Read from the PipedWriter.
            writer.write("Hello Java Good Morning!");

            while (reader.ready())  // check pipe has some data
            {
                System.out.print((char)reader.read());
            }

            // Close pipes
```

```
                reader.close();
                writer.close();
        }
        catch (IOException e)
        {
                System.err.println(e.toString());
        }
    }
}
```

```
Hello Java Good Morning!
```

The *connect()* connects both pipes together. You can use *connect()* that is available in both pipe types. The *ready()* checks whether some data are available.

Problem: Alphabets Generator Pipe

With the understanding of pipe IO character streams, we are now ready to solve slightly bigger problem using threads. Assume we have two threads. One thread converts the given lowercase characters into uppercase and writes them one at a time to PipedWriter object. The other thread reads those characters one at a time from PipedReader object. Listing 14.10 demonstrates both writing and reading threads.

Listing 14.10. Uppercase Letters Generator Pipe

```
// CapitalizingPipe.java
import java.io.*;

class Capitalizer extends Thread
{
    PipedWriter writer;
    char[] c;

    public Capitalizer(PipedWriter w, String s)
    {
        writer = w;
        c = s.toCharArray();
        start();   // start writer thread
    }

    public void run()
    {
        int count = 0;
        while(count < c.length)
        {
                try
```

```
                {
                        sleep(200);  // sleep for 100 milliseconds
                        char upper = Character.toUpperCase(c[count++]);
                        System.out.println("Written uppercase letter to
                        pipe: " + upper);
                        writer.write(upper);
                }
            catch(InterruptedException e) { }
            catch(IOException e) { }
        }
    }
}

class ReadCapitals extends Thread
{
    PipedReader reader;
    public ReadCapitals(PipedReader r)
    {
        reader = r;
        start();  // start reader thread
    }

    public void run()
    {
        while(true)
        {
            try
            {
                    sleep(100);  // sleep for 100 milliseconds

                    char c = (char)reader.read();
                    System.out.println("Read uppercase letter from
                    pipe: " + c);

                    if(c == 'Z')
                            break;
            }
            catch(InterruptedException e) { }
            catch(IOException e) { }
        }
    }
}

public class CapitalizingPipe
{
```

```
    public static void main(String args[]) throws IOException
    {
        PipedWriter writer = new PipedWriter();
        PipedReader reader = new PipedReader(writer);

        String s = "abcdefghijklmnopqrstuvwxyz";
        new Capitalizer(writer, s);
        new ReadCapitals(reader);
    }
}
```

```
Written uppercase letter to pipe: A
Written uppercase letter to pipe: B
Written uppercase letter to pipe: C
Written uppercase letter to pipe: D
Written uppercase letter to pipe: E
Read uppercase letter from pipe: A
Written uppercase letter to pipe: F
Read uppercase letter from pipe: B
Read uppercase letter from pipe: C
Written uppercase letter to pipe: G
Read uppercase letter from pipe: D
Read uppercase letter from pipe: E
Written uppercase letter to pipe: H
Read uppercase letter from pipe: F
Read uppercase letter from pipe: G
Written uppercase letter to pipe: I
Read uppercase letter from pipe: H
Read uppercase letter from pipe: I
Written uppercase letter to pipe: J
Read uppercase letter from pipe: J
Written uppercase letter to pipe: K
Written uppercase letter to pipe: L
Written uppercase letter to pipe: M
Written uppercase letter to pipe: N
Written uppercase letter to pipe: O
Read uppercase letter from pipe: K
Written uppercase letter to pipe: P
Read uppercase letter from pipe: L
Read uppercase letter from pipe: M
Written uppercase letter to pipe: Q
Read uppercase letter from pipe: N
Read uppercase letter from pipe: O
Written uppercase letter to pipe: R
```

```
Read uppercase letter from pipe: P
Read uppercase letter from pipe: Q
Written uppercase letter to pipe: S
Read uppercase letter from pipe: R
Read uppercase letter from pipe: S
Written uppercase letter to pipe: T
Read uppercase letter from pipe: T
Written uppercase letter to pipe: U
Written uppercase letter to pipe: V
Written uppercase letter to pipe: W
Written uppercase letter to pipe: X
Written uppercase letter to pipe: Y
Read uppercase letter from pipe: U
Written uppercase letter to pipe: Z
Read uppercase letter from pipe: V
Read uppercase letter from pipe: W
Read uppercase letter from pipe: X
Read uppercase letter from pipe: Y
Read uppercase letter from pipe: Z
```

The Capitalizer thread receives PipedWriter object and the string as inputs. The *toCharArray()* converts the given string into a series of characters. We do this conversion because we want to write to pipe one character at a time. The *write()* inside *run()* writes this character to the pipe. The thread terminates when it has finished sending all 26 lowercase alphabets to stream.

The ReadCapitals thread simply reads characters from the pipe using PipedReader using *read()*. The thread terminates if the last character read is *z*. Inside *main()*, we create a string of all lowercase alphabets and instantiate both threads.

14.5 FORMATTED PRINTING

Before discussing formatting features available in Java, the readers first learn how to use **PrintWriter**. The PrintWriter class supports methods to store primitive data type values to files, very similar to DataOutputStream. However, remember there is no corresponding PrintReader class in Java. The *print()* and *println()* can write any type of primitive data to the associated stream. Besides inherited methods *append()* and *write()* can be used to store char, char array and string to the stream. In Listing 14.11, you will see *println()* writing some primitive values to the file.

Listing 14.11. PrintWriter Writing Primitive Values to Files

```java
// PrintWriter1.java

import java.io.*;

public class PrintWriter1
```

```
{
    public static void main(String[] args) throws
    IOException
    {
        PrintWriter out = new PrintWriter("dummy.txt");
        PrintWriter out2 = new PrintWriter (
                new FileOutputStream( "dummy2.txt"));

        out.print(100);
        out.println("rex");
        out.print(new Integer(10));

        out2.print(200);
        out2.println("peter");

        out.close();
        out2.close();

        PrintWriter out3 = new PrintWriter(System.out);
        out3.println("To command prompt: Hello !");
        out3.close();
    }
}
```

```
To command prompt: Hello !
```

Java supports C-style features to format the output string. Though its features are very similar to C, it supports more features such as Locale and Date formatting. However, if the formatting specification for Locale or Date formats is incompatible to input data, then JVM will through an exception. The *format()* formats multiple arguments based on a format string. The format specifiers are used to design the format string. Figure 14.4 depicts some frequently used **format specifiers**.

Figure 14.4. Format Specifiers

Format Specifier	Purpose
d	To format an integer value as a decimal value
f	To format a float value as a decimal value
n	To output a platform-specific line terminator
x	To format an integer as a hexadecimal value
s	To format any value as a string

In Listing 14.12, you will see some of the format specifiers in use.

Listing 14.12. Formatting Output Strings

```java
// FormatSpecifiers.java
import java.io.*;

public class FormatSpecifiers
{
    public static void main(String[] args)
    {
        int i = 2;
        System.out.format("The square root of 2 is %f\n", Math.
        sqrt(i));
        System.out.format("The square root of 2 is %5.2f\n", Math.
        sqrt(i));
        System.out.format("PI is %f\n", Math.PI);
        i = 10;
        System.out.format("The hex value of " + i + " is %x", i);
    }
}
```

```
The square root of 2 is 1.414214
The square root of 2 is  1.41
PI is 3.141593
The hex value of 10 is a
```

The PrintWriter can write the formatted output string to the connected stream. For example, if PrintWriter is connected to FileWriter then the formatted output will be written to file as illustrated in Listing 14.13.

Listing 14.13. Formatting Strings Using PrintWriter

```java
// PWFormatting.java
import java.io.*;

public class PWFormatting
{
    public static void main(String[] args) throws IOException
    {
        PrintWriter out = new PrintWriter(new FileWriter("pwdata.
        dat"));
        out.format("%f", Math.sqrt(8));
        out.close();
    }
}
```

PrintWriter can also be used as a replacement for *System.out* so that the outputs will be transferred to command prompt. Let us now develop an application as shown in Listing 14.14 to write data to screen.

Listing 14.14. PrintWriter Writing Data to Command Prompt

```
// PWprompt.java
import java.io.*;

public class PWprompt
{    )
   public static void main(String[] args) throws IOException
   {
       PrintWriter out = new PrintWriter(System.out, true); //
       flush now itself
       out.println("Hello Java !");
       out.println(100000);
       out.close();
   }
}
```

```
Hello Java ! ,
100000
```

In the constructor, *System.out* is an output stream (in our case command prompt) and *true* flushes the buffer contents to the stream immediately, without which you will not be able to see the output in the command prompt immediately.

14.6 RANDOM ACCESS FILE

All byte and character streams we have learnt so far can either read or write to streams. The same file cannot be opened for reading and writing simultaneously. Java supports this sort of functionality with RandomAccessFile class.

A RandomAccessFile is a byte-oriented file that can be thought of as an array of bytes. It can be traversed randomly from the beginning to end of file. The main advantage of random access file is its ability to read or write at the same time. Very similar to DataInputStream and DataOutputStream, you can write and read primitive data types at the same time with random access file. RandomAccessFile can be instantiated with File object or file name as string. Also you will have to specify the access mode. The access mode can be *"r"* denoting read mode and *"rw"* denoting read and write mode. There is no mode for just writing to the file.

The *getFilePointer()* returns the position of the file pointer and *seek()* moves the file pointer to the specified position. Besides, there are readXXX() and writeXXX() methods where XXX denotes any of the primitive data types in order to read from or write to the file. Attempting to read beyond end of file will raise *EOFException*. The *readLine()* and *writeBytes()* are complementary methods for each other. You can also read byte by byte using *readByte()* as well as you can store byte by byte using writeByte() methods. The *length()* determines the length of the file. Listing 14.15 explains all important methods of random access file.

Listing 14.15. Writing to and Reading from RandomAccessFile

```java
// RAF.java
import java.io.*;

public class RAF
{
    public static void main(String[] args) throws IOException
    {
        RandomAccessFile file = new RandomAccessFile("employee.
        dat","rw");
        // RandomAccessFile file = new RandomAccessFile(
        //          new File("employee.dat"), "rw");

        file.writeInt(1001); // int 4 byes
        file.writeChars("Rex\n"); // each char 2 bytes
        file.writeUTF("Trichy"); // each char 1 byte + 2 bytes
        extra, for length information
        file.writeInt(1002);
        file.writeChars("Ria\n"); // 8 bytes
        file.writeUTF("Chennai");   //   each char 1 byte + 2 bytes
        for length information
        file.writeInt(1003);
        file.writeChars("Mia\n");
        file.writeUTF("Mumbai");   // 6 bytes + 2 bytes

        System.out.println("Length: " + file.length());
        System.out.println("current file pointer: " + file.
        getFilePointer());
        file.close();

        // open in read mode
        file = new RandomAccessFile("employee.dat","r");
        for(int i = 0; i < 3; i++)
        {
            System.out.println("At byte " + file.getFilePointer()
            + ": " + file.readInt());
            System.out.println("At byte " + file.getFilePointer()
            + ": " + file.readLine());
            System.out.println("At byte " + file.getFilePointer()
            + ": " + file.readUTF());
        }
```

```
file.seek(12); // position file pointer to byte 12
System.out.println("Ar byte 12 " + file.readUTF());
file.seek(32); // byte 32, starting from byte 0
System.out.println("At byte " + file.getFilePointer() +
": " + file.readUTF());

file.skipBytes(12); // 41 + 12 = 53
System.out.println("Skip 12 bytes: " + file.
getFilePointer());
file.close();

// go to end of file
file = new RandomAccessFile("employee.dat","rw");
file.seek(file.length()); // advance file pointer to the
length of the file
file.writeDouble(12345.6789);
file.close();
    }
}
```

```
Length: 93
current file pointer: 61
At byte 0: 1001
At byte 4:  R e x
At byte 12: Trichy
At byte 20: 1002
At byte 24:  R i a
At byte 32: Chennai
At byte 41: 1003
At byte 45:  M i a
At byte 53: Mumbai
Ar byte 12 Trichy
At byte 32: Chennai
Skip 12 bytes: 53
```

14.7 CONVERTING BYTES TO CHARACTERS

Having learnt how to store data to file using an output stream or writer and read data from that file using the corresponding input stream or reader, an obvious question is, can we store data using output stream and read the same data using reader. Of course yes, Java supports us a bridge with which we can do this sort of conversion namely InputStreamReader. We will try out this exclusive class now with reading data using reader where those data had been earlier stored using output stream as illustrated in Listing 14.16.

Listing 14.16. Converting Bytes of a File to Characters

```java
// FileReadISR.java
import java.io.*;

public class FileReadISR
{
    public static void main(String[] args)throws IOException
    {
        // store fishes to file
        FileOutputStream out = new FileOutputStream(
          "dummyisr.dat");

        byte[] b =
        "This string is stored as bytes and read with reader".
        getBytes();
        // store bytes
        out.write(b);
        // close it without fail
        out.close();

        // use reader
        BufferedReader in = new BufferedReader(new InputStreamReader(
            new FileInputStream("dummyisr.dat")));
        // show
        String s;
        while ((s = in.readLine()) != null)
            System.out.println(s);
        // close
        in.close();
    }
}
```

```
This string is stored as bytes and read with reader
```

14.8 FILE PROCESSING USING NIO

The New Input/Output (NIO) package provides us high-speed block-oriented IO without having to write custom native code. Until now *java.io* package uses only stream-oriented IO to transfer stream of bytes one way either for reading or writing. Stream IO is slower as it deals with one byte at a time. As block-oriented IO handles data as blocks, processing data by blocks will be much faster than processing data by bytes.

The cornerstone of NIO are two objects: *Channel* and *Buffer* (see Figure 14.5). A channel represents a connection to a physical IO device such as file, network socket or even another program.

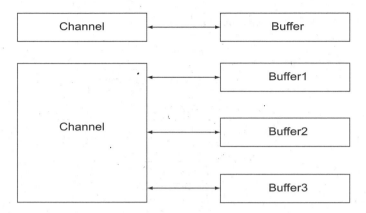

Figure 14.5. Single and Multiple Buffers Connected to a Channel

Channels are similar to standard IO streams, but they are platform-independent version of a stream. Channels are same as normal streams. But there is a difference; streams are unidirectional whereas Channels are bidirectional. FileChannel is one of the implementations of Channel that is used for reading, writing and manipulating files. The getChannel() returns FileChannel that is connected to FileInputStream, FileOutputStream and RandomAccessFile. Example 14.2 obtains you a FileChannel.

Example 14.2. FileChannel Object

```
FileInputStream fis = new FileInputStream("file1.dat");
FileChannel fc = fis.getChannel();
// or directly as below
FileChannel fc = new FileInputStream("in.dat").getChannel();
```

A Buffer is a container that will hold all data that are either to be stored or just now read from Channel. Buffer is an interface between our program and Channel. Whenever data are read, they are read directly into a buffer. Similarly whenever data are written, they are written to buffer only. Buffer is implemented as a byte array with necessary features for structured access to data. The *allocate()* creates a buffer with a required size given as argument as shown in Example 14.3.

Example 14.3. Creating ByteBuffer

```
ByteBuffer buff = ByteBuffer.allocate(1024);
```

There are several types of buffers (as depicted in Figure 14.6) to deal with different primitive data types and all buffers are instances of Buffer interface such as

- ByteBuffer
- CharBuffer
- ShortBuffer
- IntBuffer

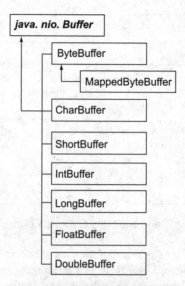

Figure 14.6. NIO Buffers

- LongBuffer
- FloatBuffer
- DoubleBuffer

14.9 READING DATA FROM BUFFER

When we want to read data, we would ask channel to read data into buffer so that we will collect that data from buffer. In the same way, when we have some data to be written, we just transfer them into buffer and ask channel to write from buffer.

We will now develop an application for reading the contents of a file. We need to perform the following tasks:

1. Create a FileInputStream to the required file
2. Get a FileChannel by calling getChannel() of FileInputStream
3. Create a buffer of byte type by calling allocate()
4. Clear the buffer so that we will read data into it
5. Read data from channel into buffer
6. Display the buffer contents

Listing 14.17 demonstrates this file reading tasks using FileChannel.

Listing 14.17. Reading Files onto Buffer

```
// FileReadNIO.java

import java.io.*;
```

```
import java.nio.*;
import java.nio.channels.*;

public class FileReadNIO
{
   public static void main(String args[]) throws Exception
   {
      ByteBuffer buff = ByteBuffer.allocate(1024);
      FileInputStream in = new FileInputStream(args[0]);
      FileChannel fc = in.getChannel();

      buff.clear();
      fc.read(buff);

      buff.flip();   // now buffer read mode
      while(buff.hasRemaining())
            System.out.print((char) buff.get());

      buff.rewind();  // rewind to beginning

      // bulk read
      File f = new File(args[0]);
      byte[] b = new byte[(int)f.length()];
      buff.get(b);
      System.out.println(new String(b));

   }
}
```

```
E:\Rajkumar\javacourse\io>java FileReadNIO news.txt
it was a rainy day
it was a cold day
i was delighted by the weather
but i was alone
it was a rainy day
it was a cold day
i was delighted by the weather
but i was alone
```

The *flip()* is an interesting method with which you can flip a buffer from read mode to write mode and vice versa. That is, the same buffer is used for reading and writing. The *hasRemaining()* checks if buffer has some more bytes for reading. The *rewind()* resets the position of pointer to the beginning of the buffer. The *get()* reads one byte at a time from buffer. The bulk read into byte[] is also possible with the overloaded get().

14.10 WRITING DATA TO BUFFER

Suppose if you have some bytes to be stored onto a file. Then you need an instance of FileChannel along with ByteBuffer so that you can write data to FileOuputStream. This is simply a reverse process of reading data from file. Listing 14.18 illustrates the process of storing bytes to files using FileChannel and ByteBuffer.

Listing 14.18. Writing Data to Buffer

```java
// FileWriteNIO.java

import java.io.*;
import java.nio.*;
import java.nio.channels.*;

public class FileWriteNIO
{
    public static void main(String args[]) throws Exception
    {
        ByteBuffer buff = ByteBuffer.allocate(1024);
        FileOutputStream out = new FileOutputStream(args[0]);
        FileChannel fc = out.getChannel();

        byte[] b = "Hello Java How are you".getBytes();
        buff.put(b); // buff write mode now
        buff.flip(); // flip buff to read mode
        fc.write(buff);
        fc.close();
    }
}
```

```
E:\Rajkumar\javacourse\io>java FileWriteNIO nio.txt
E:\Rajkumar\javacourse\io>type nio.txt
Hello Java How are you
```

In the beginning, you saw the different kinds of buffer. But so far we have been using only Byte-Buffer. Now let us see how to create other types of buffers. Unfortunately, Java does not provide us ways to directly instantiate buffer types. So you need to use methods from ByteBuffer that will give you different perceptions of other buffers. In Listing 14.19, you will notice how a CharBuffer is created and a string is stored using put().

Listing 14.19. Storing String Using CharBuffer

```java
// CharBuffer1.java

import java.io.*;
```

```
import java.nio.*;
import java.nio.channels.*;

public class CharBuffer1
{
    public static void main(String args[]) throws Exception
    {
        ByteBuffer buff = ByteBuffer.allocate(1024);
        FileOutputStream out = new FileOutputStream(args[0]);
        FileChannel fc = out.getChannel();

        String s = "Hello Java How are you";
        buff.asCharBuffer().put(s);
        fc.write(buff);
        fc.close();
    }
}
```

```
E:\Rajkumar\javacourse\io>java CharBuffer1 nio.txt
E:\Rajkumar\javacourse\io>type nio.txt
Hello Java How are you
```

The *asCharBuffer()* gives us the perception of CharBuffer, so that we will be able to store strings.

14.11 COPYING FILES

Copying files using FileChannel is straightforward. We need two channels, one for reading and another for writing. We can simply read data from a channel into a buffer, so that the other channel will write those data in the same buffer to the destination. Since the same buffer is used for reading as well as writing, we need to call *flip()* to change mode. Listing 14.20 depicts file copy application.

Listing 14.20. File Copy Using FileChannel

```
// FileCopyNIO.java

import java.io.*;
import java.nio.*;
import java.nio.channels.*;

public class FileCopyNIO
{
    public static void main(String args[]) throws Exception
```

```
    {
        if(args.length != 2)
        {
            System.out.println( "Usage: java FileCopyNIO file1
            file2");
            System.exit(1);
        }

        FileInputStream in = new FileInputStream(args[0]);
        FileOutputStream out = new FileOutputStream(args[1]);
        FileChannel fcin = in.getChannel();
        FileChannel fcout = out.getChannel();
        ByteBuffer buff = ByteBuffer.allocate(1024);

        buff.clear();
        fcin.read(buff);
        buff.flip(); // now read mode
        fcout.write(buff);
    }
}
```

```
E:\Rajkumar\javacourse\io>java FileCopyNIO nio.txt
Usage: java FileCopyNIO file1 file2

E:\Rajkumar\javacourse\io>java FileCopyNIO nio.txt nio2.txt

E:\Rajkumar\javacourse\io>type nio.txt
Hello Java How are you

E:\Rajkumar\javacourse\io>type nio2.txt
Hello Java How are you
```

14.12 LOCKING FILES

We have already introduced to the readers how a set of statements can be locked for thread synchronization. File lock is a kind of lock-on output files. File locks allow you to lock the entire file or portion of a file temporarily to ensure that a particular write operation is made atomically, without interference from other programs. Remember FileChannel should have been opened on output file for writing. The *lock()* method of FileChannel will return the FileLock object. Once the file is locked, all sensitive operations of the output file can be done. The *unlock()* method can be used to release the file lock after writing operation is completed.

Until now you have used FileInputStream and FileOuputStream to get an instance of FileChannel. You can also obtain a file channel with RandomAccessFile as illustrated in Listing 14.21.

Listing 14.21. Locking Files While Writing

```java
//FileLocking.java

import java.io.*;
import java.nio.*;
import java.nio.channels.*;

public class FileLocking
{
    public static void main(String[] args) throws IOException
    {
        RandomAccessFile raf = new RandomAccessFile( "data.txt",
        "rw" );
        //FileOutputStream out = new FileOutputStream("data.txt");
        FileChannel fc = raf.getChannel();

        ByteBuffer buff = ByteBuffer.allocate(1024);
        byte[] b = "Hello Java How are you today".getBytes();

        //FileLock lock = fc.lock();
        FileLock lock = fc.lock(0, (int)raf.length(), false );
                                    // false - not shared lock

        buff.put(b); // buff write mode now
        buff.flip(); // flip buff to read mode
        fc.write(buff);
        lock.release();

        raf = new RandomAccessFile( "data.txt", "r" );
        fc = raf.getChannel();
        buff.clear();
        fc.read(buff);
        buff.flip();
        while(buff.hasRemaining())
            System.out.print((char)buff.get());
    }
}
```

```
Hello Java How are you today
```

This FileLocking application connects FileChannel to random access file. Once you have created file channel and buffer, you can call overloaded lock() to lock entire file or parts of a file so that you will perform atomic operations on the file. Later the random access file is opened in read mode so that *read()* will fill up buffer with the contents of the file and buffer contents are displayed.

14.13 SUMMARY

1. Java 1.1 supports character streams and Java 1.4 supports NIO
2. Each character is represented using 16-bit Unicode representation
3. All character streams are subclasses of either Reader or Writer, both are abstract classes
4. FileReader allows us to read characters from files
5. FileNotFoundException will be thrown if file is not assigned for reading or writing
6. BufferedReader allows us to read files line by line
7. Characters can be written to file using FileWriter
8. PipedWriter can write bytes to pipes
9. PipedReader can read data from pipes if pipe is ready
10. The connect() method connects both input pipes and output pipes
11. With PrintWriter, we can format output strings
12. PrintWriter can also be used instead of System.out to send data to command promt
13. PrintWriter is another way of storing primitive data types to files
14. A RandomAccessFile behaves as both input file and output file
15. InputStreamReader converts bytes to characters
16. The channels and buffers are cornerstone of NIO
17. The allocate() method creates buffer
18. FileChannel allows us to read or write to files by using buffers
19. You can get FileChannel by calling getChannel() available in FileInputStream, FileOutputStream or RandomAccessFile
20. The flip() flips buffer from read mode to write mode and vice versa
21. Locks can be obtained on files so that atomic write operations can be performed

KEY TERMS

Buffer, 470	Character streams, 448	Pipe, 460	Reader, 448
Channel, 470	Format specifiers, 465	PrintWriter, 464	Writer, 448

REVIEW QUESTIONS

Multiple-choice Questions

1. How many bytes can you read?

```
DataOutputStream out = new DataOutputStream(
    new FileOutputStream("test1.txt"));
out.writeInt(10000);
```

```
out.writeInt(20000);
out.close();
```

a. 32   b. 16

c. 8   d. 4

e. None of the above

2. What is the output?

```
DataOutputStream out = new DataOutputStream(
    new FileOutputStream("test1.txt"));
out.writeInt(10000);
out.writeInt(20000);
out.close();
DataInputStream in = new DataInputStream(
    new FileInputStream("test1.txt"));
System.out.println(in.available());
in.close();
```

a. 32   b. 16

c. 8   d. 4

e. None of the above

3. How many bytes are stored to file?

```
DataOutputStream out = new DataOutputStream(
    new FileOutputStream("test1.txt"));
out.writeChar('a');
out.writeChars("b");
out.writeUTF("d");
out.close();
```

a. 3   b. 4

c. 6   d. 7

e. None of the above

4. Which of the following is an abstract class?

   a. Reader

   b. InputStream

   c. Writer

   d. OutputStream

   e. All of the above

5. What is the output?

```
FileReader fr = new FileReader(file);
char[] b = new char[(int)file.length()];
fr.read(b);
```

    a. Reads contents of file into char array

    b. Reads contents of file as bytes into char array

    c. Reads contents of file as Byte object into char array

    d. None of the above

6. How will you detect end of file while reading using FileReader?

    a. The read() returns null   b. The read() returns –1

    c. The read() returns 0   d. None of the above

7. What is the output?

```
BufferedReader br = new BufferedReader(new FileReader(args[0]));
String s;
while (( s = br.readLine()) != null)
    System.out.println(s);
```

    a. Displays file contents into a single array

    b. Displays file contents line by line

    c. Displays file contents into a single array as readLine() skips \n

    d. None of the above

8. Which of the following is true?

    a. FileWriter fr2 = new FileWriter("dummy.txt", true);

    b. FileWriter opens dummy.txt

    c. FileWriter creates dummy.txt if it does not exist for append mode

    d. FileWriter opens dummy.txt for append mode if it already exists

    e. None of the above

9. How will you read bytes as characters?

    a. using BufferedReader   b. using InputStreamReader

    c. using PipedReader   d. None of the above

10. Which of the following are the valid file modes for random access file?

    a. r   b. w

    c. rw   d. r+w+

    e. None of the above

11. DataInput and DataOutput are
    a. classes used to process primitive datatypes
    b. abstract classes to process primitive datatypes
    c. interfaces to process primitive datatypes
    d. None of the above

12. Unicode characters in Java are
    a. 8 bits   b. 16 bits
    c. 3 bits   d. None of the above

13. Choose all correct declarations about DataInputStream
    a. new DataInputStream();
    b. new DataInputStream("test.txt", "rw");
    c. new DataInputStream(System.in);
    d. new DataInputStream(new FileInputStream("test.txt"));
    e. All of the above

14. Which of the following is true about read() of the abstract class InputStream?
    a. It returns any int value in the range of 0 to 127
    b. It returns any int value in the range of 0 to 255
    c. It can also return −1
    d. All of the above

15. Which of the following classes accept string name as filename?
    a. FileInputStream   b. FileReader
    c. RandomAccessFile   d. All of the above

16. How will you create Reader from InputStream?
    a. use InputStreamReader   b. use OutputStreamReader
    c. use create() of InputStream   d. use create() of OutputStream
    e. None of the above

17. What is the equivalent Reader for ByteArrayInputStream?
    a. ByteArrayReader   b. CharArrayReader
    c. CharacterArrayReader   d. ByteArrayInputReader
    e. None of the above

18. BufferedReader throws IllegalArgumentException when buffer size is
    a. +ve number   b. −ve number
    c. 0   d. None of the above

19. Which of the following is correct?

```
FileReader in = new FileReader("tools");
where tools is the name of a directory
```

a. IllegalArgumentException   b. FileNotFoundException

c. IOException   d. None of the above

20. Which of the following is correct?

```
FileWriter out = new FileWriter("tools", true);
where tools is the name of a directory
```

a. FileNotFoundException   b. IOException

c. Opens in append mode   d. None of the above

21. What is the output?

```
FileWriter out = new FileWriter(FileDescriptor.out);
out.write("a");out.close();
```

a. Compilation error   b. IOException

c. a   d. None of the above

22. Which of the following is true about PrintWriter?

a. It can write to file   b. It can write to any OutputStream

c. It can write to any Writer   d. All of the above

23. Which of the following is true?

```
PrintWriter out = new PrintWriter(new FileWriter("test14.txt",
true));
out.write("A");
```

a. A is automatically flushed to file

b. flush() has to be called manually for immediate flushing

c. IOException

d. None of the above

24. Which of the following methods need flush() to be manually called?

a. printf()   b. println()

c. format()   d. None of the above

25. What is the output?

```
RandomAccessFile file = new RandomAccessFile("employee.dat","rw");
file.writeInt(1001);
```

```
file.writeChars("Rex\n");
file.writeUTF("Trichy");
System.out.println(file.getFilePointer());
```

a. 13

b. 14

c. 20

d. 24

e. None of the above

26. What is the output?

```
RandomAccessFile file = new
    RandomAccessFile("employee.dat","rw");
file.writeInt(1001);
file.writeChars("Rex\n");
file.writeUTF("Trichy");
file.seek(4);
System.out.println(file.readChar());
```

a. R

b. h

c. T

d. None of the above

27. A file can be locked using
    a. lock() from FileChannel class
    b. fileLock() method from FileChannel
    c. fileLock() from Lock class
    d. None of the above

28. Which of the following classes supports getChannel()?
    a. FileInputStream
    b. FileOutputStream
    c. RandomAccessFile
    d. All of the above

29. How will you change ByteBuffer from read mode to write mode and vice versa?
    a. flip()
    b. swap()
    c. exchange()
    d. None of the above

Answers

1. c   2. c   3. d   4. e   5. a   6. b   7. b   8. c, d   9. b   10. a, c
11. c   12. d   13. c, d   14. b, c   15. d   16. a   17. b   18. b, c   19. b   20. b
21. a   22. d   23. b   24. d   25. c   26. a   27. a   28. d   29. a

Short-answer Questions

1. Differentiate read() and readLine() methods.
2. Differentiate append() and write().

3. How to write strings to files?

4. Explain reading and writing from/to pipes.

5. What are the features of PrintWriter?

6. Explain reading and writing methods of RandomAccessFile.

7. Explain seek(), getFilePointer() and skipBytes() of RandomAccessFile.

8. How to convert bytes to characters?

9. Explain the steps to read the contents of a file in NIO.

10. Explain lock() and unlock() methods in NIO.

EXERCISES

14.1. [*File Tokenizer*] Design an application that will read file from command line and print the frequency of words excluding stop words. For example, words like *a, an, the, that, of* and others are stop words. Prepare at least 20 stop words and use them for your filtering. Hint: you can reduce the amount of computation by representing stop words as a set.

14.2. [*File Translator*] Read a source file containing English text and property file containing translation words from user and display its translated content to a target language such as *Tamil, Hindi, French, Spanish, German* or others. Prepare a property file containing at least 10 words that are used for translation.

14.3. [*Sport News Service*] Download few news articles about sports from Google or Yahoo sports and save them in your local disk. Develop an application that reads a topic from user such as *cricket* and displays those lines in files where this topic appears.

14.4. [*Business News Service*] Modify the above application for business news articles.

14.5. [*Dictionary Lookup*] Download some free dictionary data from internet and save it in your local disk. Then read a word from user and display its meaning by consulting the dictionary.

14.6. [*Login Manager*] Modify Exercise 9.7 so that you can prepare a property file containing few usernames and passwords. Receive username and password from keyboard and check his credentials. If there is a match, give him a message *Login successful*. If username does not exist, collect username and password from user and insert a new entry. Hint: you need Hashtable or HashMap to manipulate these key-value pairs.

14.7. [*Spam Detector*] Modify Exercise 9.8, so that all spam words are stored in a file and consulted for checking your input email files whether they are spam or not.

14.8. [*Stock Quote Service*] Download stock prices of Indian companies from Yahoo! finance or Google finance and save them into a file in your local disk. Read a company name from user and display its current stock price from the file.

14.9. [*Address Book Manager*] Create a class *Address* that represents name, mobile number and email details as strings. Design a public class *AddresBookManager* that supports the following operations

1. *Add new address*

2. *Edit address*

3. *Remove address*

4. *Show address book*

5. *Exit*

   Select your option:

Use ArrayList<Address> to manipulate the addresses. Finally, when Exit option is selected store all Address objects to a file using ObjectOutputStream.

14.10. Modify the above exercise so that Address objects were retrieved from file using ObjectInput-Stream first and all Address objects are loaded onto the ArrayList before you display options to users.

PART V Java GUI Programming

OBJECTIVES

- To explain class hierarchy of swing components and containers
- To introduce three containers: JFrame, JPanel and JApplet
- To draw geometric shapes such as *lines, arcs, ovals, rectangles, polygons and polylines* using methods from *Graphics* class
- To generate random multilines
- To draw random rectangles
- To load images using Toolkit and ImageIcon and display them
- To design multithreaded blinking balls
- To paint random circles using JApplet
- To use Graphics2D class methods for painting geometric shapes such as lines, curves, rectangles, ellipses and arcs
- To introduce Colors, GradientPaint and TexturePaint classes
- To draw arbitrary shapes using GeneralPath class
- To apply *translation, rotation, scaling* and *shear* transformations to coordinate system
- To clip a shape or image against another shape
- To introduce affine transformations on images

15.1 INTRODUCTION

In part 1–4, the readers were introduced to Java basics, Object-oriented programming, all Java containers to hold objects and Java threads and IO streams. Part 5 of this book introduces you to Graphics programming, GUI development using **JFrames** and GUI development using **JApplets**. Swing is an efficient Java Platform, which is a part of Java Foundation Classes (JFC), for graphical user interface (GUI) programming. So here is a word UI. What is word UI for? It stands for user interface. Still not clear! UI is any object that allows interaction between users and the computer. For example, you might think of mouse, keyboard, music, video, button, combo box and window; all are UIs. We separate all graphical objects such as button, combo box and windows and call them as GUIs. So swing is a piece of software package that handles all interactions between a user and computer. So far, we have used only one UI for our computations namely *command window* and it gives us textual view of the inputs and outputs and Swing takes us to the next level of user interaction with its graphical UI components.

Java's journey with GUI started with Abstract Windowing Toolkit (AWT) introduced in Java 1.0. The set of classes and interfaces available in Java 1.0 was very limited and mostly not suitable for large-scale GUI projects. Besides, AWT was very much prone to platform-specific bugs and not fully based on object-oriented design principles. Then came Java 1.1 with object-oriented design support. Java's journey ended with its well-matured GUI tool kit with Java 1.2 or Java 2. This robust, versatile and flexible library is called Swing. Swing is considered to be lightweight components as it depends less on the target platform and uses less native GUI resources.

Swing GUI components are prefixed with J. Even though all AWT components are still supported in Java, those components are deprecated and will fade away very slowly. Hence this book will attempt to base GUI design on top of Swing instead of AWT components. Therefore you will learn all GUI programming principles, tricks and techniques using Swing instead of AWT. In this chapter, the readers will be led to the understanding of the Swing GUI basics, in particular an overview of components and containers that are necessary to develop graphics applications using Java 2D graphics API. In chapters 16 and 17, the readers will be introduced to all components that are required to develop GUI using JFrame (Chapter 16) and JApplet (Chapter 17).

As part of Java 2D graphics, *java.awt.geom* package defines all shapes such as *point, line, curve, rectangle, arc, ellipse*, etc. and performs operations related to 2D geometry. You will be using *Graphics2D* class from AWT package to draw various shapes that are defined in *geom* package. One final note: readers are expected to be able to read Javadoc of Swing classes (in Sun's API) to learn about the structure and use of various methods. Note that some of these methods are static methods and variables (mostly constants).

15.2 SWING COMPONENTS AND CONTAINERS: OVERVIEW

The Java GUI API classes can be classified into two groups: **containers** and **components**. There are some more supportive helping classes related to those components such as Colors and Fonts.

The java.awt.*Component* is the base class of all Java components including all AWT and Swing components. The javax.swing.*JComponent* is the base class of all Swing components (see class hierarchy in Figure 15.2). Both are abstract classes, so you cannot instantiate these classes. JComponent class contains hundreds of methods every swing component can use. JComponent provides important functionalities as discussed below:

- It provides painting or drawing infrastructure for all components
- It knows how to handle keyboard presses
- It contains *add()* that will add other components. That is you can add any swing component to any other swing component
- Multiple look and feel for each component
- Support for tool tips and others

Java containers will hold all components. The AWT package provides Applet, Frame, Panel and Window containers. These containers are extended in Swing package and we will be using JFrame, JPanel, JApplet and JDialog in order to hold swing components as depicted in Figure 15.1.

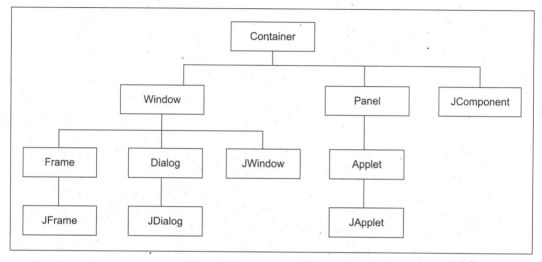

Figure 15.1. Swing Containers

The *javax.swing* package contains a wealth of components with which you will be able to feed input values and display outputs in GUI applications. Figure 15.2 depicts a subset of the class hierarchy of swing components. The java.awt.Container is the base class for javax.swing.Jcomponent which in turn is the base class for all swing components such as JButton, JLabel and so on.

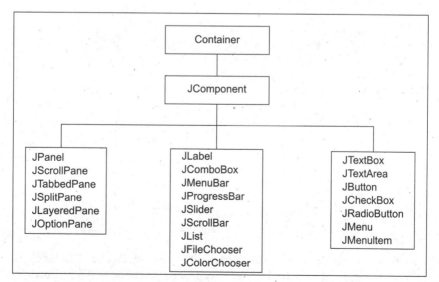

Figure 15.2. Swing Components

15.3 FRAMES AND PANELS

In order to create a UI, you need to create a container such as JFrame or JApplet that will hold all swing components that properly organized and presented to users. You can set title and size to the frame using *setTitle()* and *setSize()* methods. The *setVisible()* method makes the frame visible without which you will not be able to see the frame. The JPanel is another subcontainer that can hold swing components. It can be added to JFrame as any other component. The JPanel has another distinct advantage; it can be used as a canvas on which you can draw any shape. With this understanding, let us now develop a simple frame as depicted in Listing 15.1.

Listing 15.1. Simple Swing JFrame

```
// FirstFrame.java
import javax.swing.*;

public class FirstFrame
{
   public static void main(String[] args)
   {
      JFrame f = new JFrame();
      f.setTitle("First Frame");
      f.setSize(300,200);
      f.setLocationRelativeTo(null);   // centres to screen
      f.setDefaultCloseOperation(JFrame.EXIT_ON_CLOSE); // closes
      frame
      f.setVisible(true);
   }
}
```

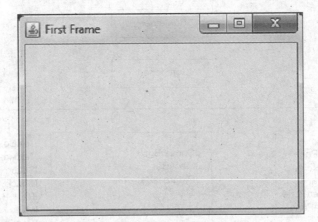

The setSize(300,200) creates this frame with 300 pixels width and 200 pixels height. The setLocationRelativeTo(null) centres the frame to screen while the setDefaultCloseOperation() method with a constant closes the frame; otherwise you need to press Cntl-C to break the execution.

Instead of creating a JFrame inside public class, we can convert the public class itself as a frame and the constructor can be used for initializing the frame properties as shown in Listing 15.2.

Listing 15.2. MyFrame Application

```java
// MyFrame.java
import javax.swing.*;
import java.awt.*;

public class MyFrame extends JFrame
{
    public MyFrame()
    {
        setTitle("First Frame");
        setSize(300,200);
        getContentPane().setBackground(Color.magenta);
        setLocationRelativeTo(null);   // centres frame to screen
        setDefaultCloseOperation(JFrame.EXIT_ON_CLOSE); // closes
        frame
        setVisible(true);
    }

    public static void main(String[] args)
    {
        MyFrame f = new MyFrame();
    }
}
```

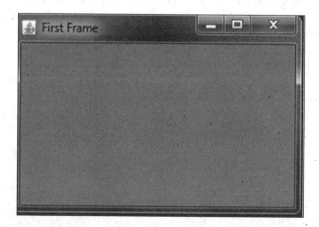

The background colour for the frame can be painted using *setBackground()* method that takes **colour** value as a static constant. Instead of directly calling setBackground(), you can also call it from getContentPane(). The getContentPanel() of JFrame returns something called **ContentPane** and you set the required colour to the ContentPane instead of JFrame. In fact, whatever component you add

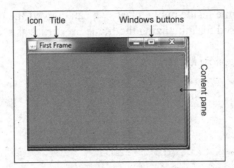

Figure 15.3. Content Pane

to JFrame is simply added to only ContentPane and not directly to JFrame. But for certain methods like setBackground(), you need to add to ContentPane. Basically, a frame has two parts – header and content pane – as shown in Figure 15.3. So all java components are only added to content pane even though we say we add components to frame.

15.4 DRAWING SHAPES USING GRAPHICS CONTEXT

The Graphics class provides us methods to draw geometric objects such as lines, rectangles, polygons, arcs and ellipses. With these methods, we can draw any shapes and figures as we like. In order to draw graphical objects, we need a canvas onto which we can draw these graphics.

Elegantly there is a container named JPanel which is a lightweight container that can hold swing components and also helps us to paint the required graphics. What we need to do is to extend this JPanel container and to override its *paintComponent()* method. The paintComponent() takes an argument of type *Graphics* object. As Graphics class is an abstract class, this way we will obtain Graphics object and use all those methods that are available in Graphics class to draw geometric objects, strings, images and fonts. Figure 15.4 shows some important methods of *Graphics* class that you will use inside paintComponent() method.

Figure 15.4. Some Important Methods of Graphics Class

```
public void paintcomponent(Graphics g)
{
   // Set colour
   g.setColor(Color);
   // set font
   g.setFont(Font);
   // Draw a geometric shape
   g.drawString();
   g.drawLine()
   g.drawRect(); // outline
   g.fillRect(); // solid
   g.drawRoundRect()   // outline
   g.fillRoundRect()   // solid colour
```

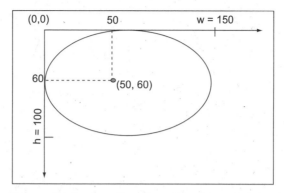

Figure 15.5. Java Drawing Coordinate System

```
    g.drawPolygon(); // outline
    g.fillPolygon(); // solid
    g.drawOval(); // outline
    g.fillOval(); // solid
}
```

One more final point you need to observe before moving on to learning all those methods for drawing graphical primitives. That is about the painting coordinate system. Conventionally we assume an origin (0, 0) at the centre of a paper and plot all graphics. But Java follows a different painting origin. The origin (0, 0) indicates the pixel at the top-left corner of the painting canvas. The x axis goes horizontally and y axis goes vertically downwards. The lower right pixel will hold upper coordinate for the screen as depicted in Figure 15.5. Generally all shapes will be painted just below the starting coordinate and enlarges to its width and height. Also in Figure 15.5, an ellipse is painted from (0, 0) with a width of 150 and height of 100 pixels.

15.5 DRAWING STRINGS AND LINES

The drawString(s, x, y) paints a string s starting at the specified coordinate (x, y). The drawLine(x1, y1, x2, y2) takes four values representing the starting point (x1, y1) and ending point (x2, y2) of the straight line. Listing 15.3 demonstrates you the ways of drawing strings and straight lines.

Listing 15.3. Drawing String and Lines

```
// LinesFrame.java
import javax.swing.*;
import java.awt.*;

class Lines extends JPanel
{
    public void paintComponent(Graphics g)
    {
```

```
        //super.paintComponent(g);
        g.setColor(Color.RED);
        g.setFont(new Font("Times", Font.BOLD, 24));
        g.drawString("Hello Java Frame", 100, 100); // at (100,10)
        g.drawLine(100,150, 300, 150); // (100,150) to (300,150)
        g.drawLine(150,200, 300, 250);
        g.drawLine(350,100, 350, 200);
    }
}

public class LinesFrame extends JFrame
{
    Lines panel = new Lines();

    public LinesFrame()
    {
        add(panel);

        setTitle("Drawing Lines");
        setSize(400,400);
        setLocationRelativeTo(null);   // centres to screen
        setDefaultCloseOperation(JFrame.EXIT_ON_CLOSE); // closes
        frame
        setVisible(true);
    }

    public static void main(String[] args)
    {
        LinesFrame f = new LinesFrame();
    }
}
```

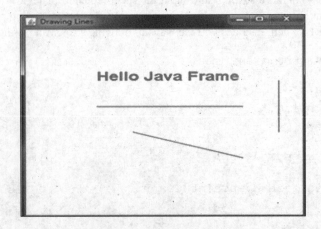

The *setFont()* method uses Font object as argument. The java.awt.Font object is created with three arguments: the font name, whether PLAIN, BOLD or ITALIC and size in points such as 20 points. You can have different font names such as *Times, Courier* and *SansSerif.*

15.6 PROBLEM: MULTILINE GENERATION

Let us now develop an application that will generate random straight lines from the centre of the panel of course with different colours and different lengths, but within the size of the panel. We might use *nextInt()* method from util.Random class to generate colour values for *rgb* colours, any value from 0 to 255. Also we should generate a random point where our rectangles will begin painting. Remember a random location should be within the size of the frame. So our *nextInt()* should generate appropriate point considering the width and height of the frame. The complete application is depicted in Listing 15.4.

Listing 15.4. Multiline Generator

```
// MultilinesFrame.java
import javax.swing.*;
import java.awt.*;
import java.util.*;

class Lines extends JPanel
{
    Random r = new Random();
    public void paintComponent(Graphics g)
    {
        int w = getWidth();
        int h = getHeight();
        int x = 0, y = 0;

        for (int i = 0; i < 500; i++)
        {
            int red = r.nextInt(255);
            int green = r.nextInt(255);
            int blue = r.nextInt(255);
            g.setColor(new Color(red, green, blue));

            x = r.nextInt(w);
            y = r.nextInt(h);
            g.drawLine(w/2, h/2, x, y);
        }
    }
}

public class MultilinesFrame extends JFrame
{
    Lines panel = new Lines();
```

```
    public MultilinesFrame()
    {
       add(panel);

       setTitle("Drawing Multi Lines");
       setSize(250,250);
       setLocationRelativeTo(null);  // centres to screen
       setDefaultCloseOperation(JFrame.EXIT_ON_CLOSE); // closes
       frame
       setVisible(true);
    }

    public static void main(String[] args)
    {
       MultilinesFrame f = new MultilinesFrame();
    }
}
```

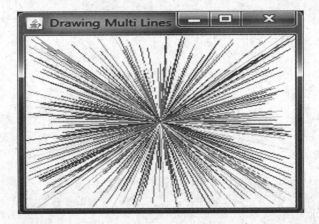

Here we use JPanel as a canvas for painting. The *paintComponent()* method is automatically invoked by JVM in order to draw the graphics. The *setColor()* defines colour for the graphics objects. The Color object will be created with random values for red, green and blue. All lines are drawn from the origin to a random point. The origin is the centre point of the frame, which is nothing but half of its width and height. The random point is generated using nextInt() method from util.Random class. Rest of the code is self-explanatory.

15.7 DRAWING RECTANGLES

There are different types of rectangles – normal, round rectangle, 3D rectangle. Each of these three types can be drawn as outline or filled in with colour. The Graphics class offers six methods for drawing all these rectangle types.

■ The *drawRect(x, y, w, h)* paints a rectangle at the specified location with its width and height.

■ The *fillRect(x, y, w, h)* is similar to drawRect() but it fills it with the defined colour.

- The *drawRoundRect(x, y, w, h, aw, ah)* paints a round rectangle where aw and ah specifies the width and height of the arc.
- The *fillRoundRect()* fills the round rectangle with the predefined colour.
- The *draw3DRect(x, y, w, h, raised)* paints 3D rectangle. Also you should specify a boolean value mentioning you want your rectangle *raised* or *lowered*
- The *fill3DRect()* is same as 3D rectangle with a predefined colour

Now let us develop a simple application that will generate all these six rectangles with different colours as depicted in Listing 15.5.

Listing 15.5. Painting Rectangles

```java
// RectangleFrame.java
import javax.swing.*;
import java.awt.*;

class Rect extends JPanel
{
    public void paintComponent(Graphics g)
    {
        super.paintComponent(g);
        g.setColor(Color.RED);
        g.drawString("Rectangles", 100, 50);
        g.drawRect(100, 100, 75, 50);   // width = 75, height = 50
        g.setColor(Color.YELLOW);
        g.fillRect(200, 100, 75, 50);
        g.setColor(Color.BLUE);
        g.drawRoundRect(300, 100, 75, 50, 30, 30); // aw = 30, ah = 30
        g.setColor(Color.MAGENTA);
        g.fillRoundRect(100, 200, 75, 50, 30, 30);
        g.setColor(Color.GREEN);
        g.draw3DRect(200, 200, 75, 50, true);
        g.setColor(Color.CYAN);
        g.fill3DRect(300, 200, 75, 50, false);

        g.setColor(new Color(159, 182, 210));
        g.fillRect(100, 300, 75, 50);
        g.setXORMode(new Color(25, 32, 250));
        g.fillRect(150, 325, 75, 50);
        g.setPaintMode(); // restores to original colour mode
        g.fillRect(200, 350, 75, 50);
    }
}

public class RectangleFrame extends JFrame
{
```

```
Rect panel = new Rect();

public RectangleFrame()
{
    add(panel);
    setTitle("Drawing Rectangles");
    setSize(500,500);
    setLocationRelativeTo(null);
    setDefaultCloseOperation(JFrame.EXIT_ON_CLOSE);
    setVisible(true);
}

public static void main(String[] args)
{
    RectangleFrame f = new RectangleFrame();
}
}
```

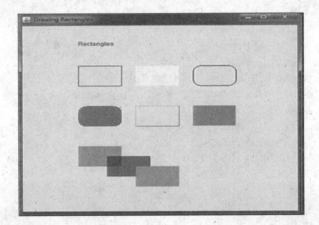

The *setColor()* defines colour for the graphics with colour specified as constants such as *Color.red, Color.RED, Color.pink* and so on. Note that your colour constants support both lowercase and upper-case static variables. The Color can be specified with its colour constant or its *rgb* values which can take any value from 0 to 255. The *setXORMode()* performs *XOR* on two colour values. The intersection of the two objects will be painted with the XOR colour. The setPaintMode() restores the drawing back to the original colour. Also we call base class' super.paintComponent(g) method to clear the contents of the paint buffer. Further round rectangles assume half of the diameter of the arc's width and height to all four corners of the rectangle.

15.8 PROBLEM: RANDOM RECTANGLE GENERATOR

Similar to drawing lines of random sizes, now let us develop an application that generates rectangles of fixed size and displays them at random locations. We might use util.Random class to generate colour values for *rgb* colours. For these three primary colours, we need to generate any value from 0 to 255.

Also we should generate a random point where our rectangles will begin painting. Remember a random location should be within the size of the frame. So our *nextInt()* should generate appropriate point considering the width and height of the frame. Listing 15.6 illustrates random rectangle generator.

Listing 15.6. Generating Random Rectangles

```
// RandomRectangle.java
import javax.swing.*;
import java.awt.*;
import java.util.*;

class Rect extends JPanel
{
    Random r = new Random();

    public void paintComponent(Graphics g)
    {
        for (int i = 0; i < 100; i++)
        {
            int red = r.nextInt(255);
            int green = r.nextInt(255);
            int blue = r.nextInt(255);
            g.setColor(new Color(red, green, blue));
            int w = getWidth();
            int h = getHeight();
            int x = r.nextInt(w);
            int y = r.nextInt(h);
            g.fillRect(x, y, 30,15);
        }
    }
}

public class RandomRectangle extends JFrame
{

    Rect panel = new Rect();
    public RandomRectangle()
    {
        add(panel);
        setTitle("Random Rectangles");
        setSize(500,400);
        setLocationRelativeTo(null);
        setDefaultCloseOperation(JFrame.EXIT_ON_CLOSE);
        setVisible(true);
    }

    public static void main(String[] args)
```

```
    {
        RandomRectangle f = new RandomRectangle();
    }
}
```

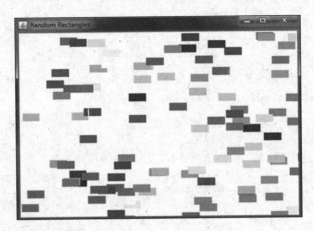

15.9 DRAWING CIRCLES AND ELLIPSES

Drawing circles and ellipse is slightly different in swing as it does not provide direct methods using exclusive names. To draw circles and ellipse, you will have to use *drawOval(x,y,w,h)* method. The appropriate values for height (h) and width (w) will result into a circle or ellipse. For example, if height and width values are same then the oval is a circle; otherwise it will be a horizontal ellipse (if width > height) or vertical ellipse, otherwise. The *fillOval()* method fills the circle or ellipse with the predefined colour. In Listing 15.7, you will see these methods in practice.

Listing 15.7. Drawing Circles and Ellipses

```
// OvalFrame.java

import javax.swing.*;
import java.awt.*;

class Oval extends JPanel
{
    public void paintComponent(Graphics g)
    {
        super.paintComponent(g);
        g.setColor(Color.RED);
        g.drawOval(50, 50, 60, 60);   // circle
        g.setColor(Color.YELLOW);
        g.fillOval(150, 50, 60, 60);    // filled circles
```

```
      g.setColor(Color.BLUE);
      g.drawOval(50, 150, 100, 50);     // horizontal ellipse,
      width > height
      g.setColor(Color.MAGENTA);
      g.fillOval(200, 150, 100, 50); // filled horizontal ellipse
      g.setColor(Color.GREEN);
      g.drawOval(50, 250, 50, 100);     // vertical ellipse, width <
      height
      g.setColor(Color.CYAN);
      g.fillOval(150, 250, 50, 100);    // filled vertical ellipse
   }
}

public class OvalFrame extends JFrame
{
   Oval panel = new Oval();

   public OvalFrame()
   {
      add(panel);
      setTitle("Drawing Circles and Ellipses");
      setSize(350,400);
      setLocationRelativeTo(null);
      setDefaultCloseOperation(JFrame.EXIT_ON_CLOSE);
      setVisible(true);
   }

   public static void main(String[] args)
   {
      OvalFrame f = new OvalFrame();
   }
}
```

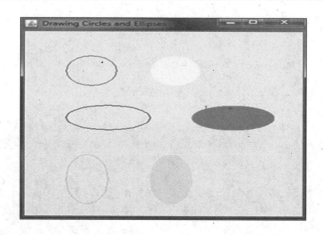

15.10 DRAWING ARCS

The *drawArc(x, y, w, h, sa, aa)* and *fillArc()* methods are used to paint arcs within the bounding rectangle either only outline or filled with colour. This is similar to drawOval() method, but with two more arguments specifying start angle (*sa*) and arc angle (*aa*) values in degrees (Figure 15.6). A positive value indicates a counter clockwise rotation angle. Similarly a negative angle values indicates a clockwise rotation angle.

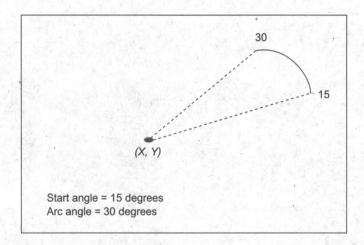

Figure 15.6. Arc Example

Listing 15.8 demonstrates painting of few arcs both outline and filled with colours.

Listing 15.8. Drawing Arcs and Filled Arcs

```
// ArcFrame.java
import javax.swing.*;
import java.awt.*;

class Arc extends JPanel
{
    public void paintComponent(Graphics g)
    {
        super.paintComponent(g);
        g.setColor(Color.RED);
        g.fillArc(0, 0, getWidth(), getHeight(), 0, 45);
        g.drawArc(0, 0, getWidth(), getHeight(), 45, 45);

        g.setColor(Color.YELLOW);
        g.fillArc(0, 0, getWidth(), getHeight(), 90, 45);
        g.drawArc(0, 0, getWidth(), getHeight(), 135, 45);
```

```
        g.setColor(Color.MAGENTA);
        g.fillArc(0, 0, getWidth(), getHeight(), 180, 45);
        g.drawArc(0, 0, getWidth(), getHeight(), 225, 45);

        g.setColor(Color.GREEN);
        g.fillArc(0, 0, getWidth(), getHeight(), 270, 45);
        g.drawArc(0, 0, getWidth(), getHeight(), 315, 45);
    }
}

public class ArcFrame extends JFrame
{
    Arc panel = new Arc();

    public ArcFrame()
    {
        add(panel);
        setTitle("Drawing Arcs");
        setSize(300, 300);
        setLocationR elativeTo(null);
        setDefaultCloseOperation(JFrame.EXIT_ON_CLOSE);
        setVisible(true);
    }

    public static void main(String[] args)
    {
        ArcFrame f = new ArcFrame();
    }
}
```

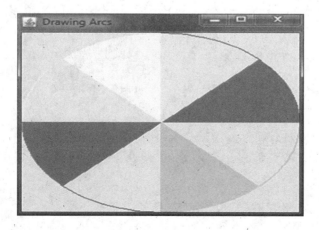

This application generates four arcs and four filled-in arcs one after another starting from angle 0 degree to 360 degrees. The arcs are drawn inside the enclosed frame whose dimension can be obtained with getWidth() and getHeight() methods. We assume start angles for the arcs start at 0 and continues in steps of 45. The arc angle for all arcs and filled arcs is always 45.

15.11 DRAWING POLYGONS AND POLYLINES

The *drawPolygon(x[], y[], n)* method takes arrays of x and y values along with number of points n and paints a Polygon object to the panel. Alternatively it can also take an array of values for x and y coordinates and draws outline of the polygon. There is also *fillPolygon()* method to paint a polygon with the specified colour. The drawPolyline(*x[], y[], n*) creates a sequence of connected lines with the array of coordinate values. However, the difference is that polygon is closed with line segments whereas polyline is open connected line segments. Listing 15.9 paints polygons and polylines as depicted.

Listing 15.9. Painting Polygons and Polylines

```java
// PolygonFrame.java
import javax.swing.*;
import java.awt.*;
import java.util.*;

class Polygons extends JPanel
{
    public void paintComponent(Graphics g)
    {
        int[] x = {30, 100, 20, 50, 150};
        int[] y = {20,100, 80, 150, 120};
        g.setColor(Color.pink);
        g.fillPolygon(x, y, 5);   // 5 points

        int[] x2 = {100, 300, 150, 175, 150};
        int[] y2 = {50,100, 80, 150, 120};
        g.setColor(Color.gray);
        g.drawPolygon(x2, y2, 5); // 5 points

        int[] x3 = {150, 200, 240, 170};
        int[] y3 = {150, 210, 175, 120};
        g.setColor(Color.orange);
        g.drawPolyline(x3, y3, 4);
    }
}

public class PolygonFrame extends JFrame
```

```
{
    Polygons panel = new Polygons();

    public PolygonFrame()
    {
        add(panel);

        setTitle("Drawing Polygons");
        setSize(350, 275);
        setLocationRelativeTo(null);  // centres to screen
        setDefaultCloseOperation(JFrame.EXIT_ON_CLOSE); // closes
        frame
        setVisible(true);
    }

    public static void main(String[] args)
    {
        PolygonFrame f = new PolygonFrame();
    }
}
```

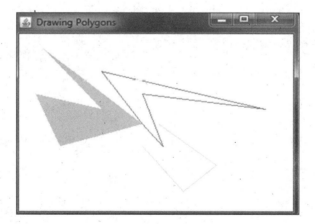

15.12 DISPLAYING IMAGES

A bitmap image is a 2D rectangular array of *pixels*. Each pixel has a *color* value (typically in RGB). The dimension of the image is represented by its *width* and *length* in pixels. In Java, the origin (0, 0) of an image is positioned at the top-left corner, like all other shapes.

The *drawImage()* method paints an image onto JPanel. In order to display an image, the image has to be first constructed from the image file. The *ImageObserver* will track the loading of the image into the application. Image can be loaded into the program using *getImage()* from *Toolkit* or *ImageIcon* classes. Example 15.1 illustrates the process of loading image files.

Example 15.1. Loading Images

```
Toolkit toolkit = Toolkit.getDefaultToolkit();
Image img = toolkit.getImage("rk_pic_red.jpg");

// you can also use ImageIcon to construct image
ImageIcon icon = new ImageIcon("rk_pic_red.jpg");
Image img = icon.getImage();
```

The static *getDefaultToolkit()* returns an object of *Toolkit*, and with this instance you can call getImage() with the filename as String. The getImage() returns the corresponding Image object. Alternatively, you can use getImage() from ImageIcon class to load the image. Listing 15.10 displays the image onto the canvas.

Listing 15.10. Painting Images

```
// ImageFrame.java
import javax.swing.*;
import java.awt.*;
class Img extends JPanel
{
    public void paintComponent(Graphics g)
    {
        super.paintComponent(g);

        Toolkit toolkit = Toolkit.getDefaultToolkit();
        Image img = toolkit.getImage("chappel.png");
        g.drawImage(img, 50, 50, this);

        // use can also use ImageIcon to construct image
        ImageIcon icon = new ImageIcon("rangoli.png");
        Image img2 = icon.getImage();

        // width and height can also be specified
        g.drawImage(img2, 50, 250, getWidth(), getHeight(),
        this);
    }
}
public class ImageFrame extends JFrame
{
    Img panel = new Img();

    public ImageFrame()
    {
```

```
        add(panel);

        setTitle("Displaying Images");
        setSize(500, 400);
        setLocationRelativeTo(null);   // centres to screen
        setDefaultCloseOperation(JFrame.EXIT_ON_CLOSE); // closes
        frame
        setVisible(true);
    }

    public static void main(String[] args)
    {
        ImageFrame f = new ImageFrame();
    }
}
```

15.13 PROBLEM: THREADED BLINKING BALLS

So far JPanel canvas was used by only main() and you generated shape objects iteratively inside paintComponent() method. Suppose we allow several threads to collectively use the canvas and paint colour-filled circles. Also each thread will generate circles at different locations within the panel indefinitely. The main() inside JFrame simply creates as many threads as required. It gives an appearance of blinking as every time a new Graphics context is created. The program shown in Listing 15.11 illustrates the generation of threaded blinking balls.

Listing 15.11. Threaded Blinking Balls

```
// BlinkingBall.java
import java.awt.*;
import javax.swing.*;
```

```java
import java.util.*;

class Ball extends Thread
{
    Random r = new Random();
    // panel for drawing circles
    private JPanel p;

    public Ball(JPanel p1)
    {
        p = p1;
        // start this thread
        start();
    }

    public void run()
    {
        while(true)
        {
            // get graphics instance
            Graphics g = p.getGraphics();
            // generate rgb values
            int red = r.nextInt(255);
            int green = r.nextInt(255);
            int blue = r.nextInt(255);
            // set the colour
            g.setColor(new Color(red, green, blue));

            // get random coord values
            int x = r.nextInt(p.getWidth());
            int y = r.nextInt(p.getHeight());
            // draw circle
            g.fillOval(x, y, 25, 25);

            // current thread to sleep
            try
            {
                sleep(10);
            }catch(InterruptedException e) { }

            // paint updates
            p.update(g);
        }
    }
}
```

```
}

public class BlinkingBall extends JFrame
{
    public BlinkingBall(JPanel panel)
    {
        add(panel);
        setTitle("Blinking Balls");
        setSize(350,350);
        setLocationRelativeTo(null);
        setDefaultCloseOperation(JFrame.EXIT_ON_CLOSE);
        setVisible(true);
    }

    public static void main(String[] args)
    {
        JPanel panel = new JPanel();
        // add panel to frame
        BlinkingBall bb = new BlinkingBall(panel);
        // create 50 threads to paint on this panel
        for(int i = 0; i < 50; i++)
                new Ball(panel);
    }
}
```

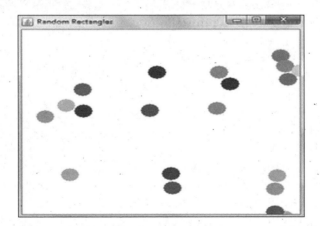

15.14 PAINTING USING JAPPLET

So far we have been using JPanel as a canvas for painting all graphical objects. Now let us use another container JApplet as a canvas for printing graphics. The JApplet is a small program that can be embedded onto an application. We will embed JApplet inside a frame. As we override paintComponent() inside JPanel, we need to override paint() inside JApplet. The applet receives graphics context through the Graphics object as an argument of paint().

Listing 15.12. CircleApplet

```java
// CircleApplet.java
import javax.swing.*;
import java.awt.*;
import java.util.*;

public class CircleApplet extends JApplet
{
    Random r = new Random();

    public void paint(Graphics g)
    {
        for (int i = 0; i < 200; i++)
        {
            int red = r.nextInt(255);
            int green = r.nextInt(255);
            int blue = r.nextInt(255);
            g.setColor(new Color(red, green, blue));
            int w = getWidth();
            int h = getHeight();
            int x = r.nextInt(w);
            int y = r.nextInt(h);
            g.fillOval(x, y, 25,25);
        }
    }

    public static void main(String[] args)
    {
        JFrame f = new JFrame();
        f.add(new CircleApplet());
        f.setTitle("Random Rectangles");
        f.setSize(400,400);
        f.setLocationRelativeTo(null);
        f.setDefaultCloseOperation(JFrame.EXIT_ON_CLOSE);
        f.setVisible(true);
    }
}
```

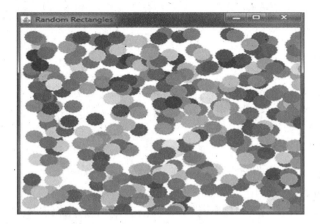

Inside main(), JFrame instance is created and JApplet instance is added to frame. Since we define main() inside the applet, we can execute this applet as a normal Java application. The aim of this application is to just introduce JApplet as a container for swing components and to override paint() so that we will be able to draw graphical objects and display images. The JApplet architecture, functionality and applications are huge and we will differ the discussions to Chapter 17.

15.15 JAVA 2D GRAPHICS

You have been working with Graphics class so far developing different geometric shapes. You might have observed the limitations of Graphics class: shapes are drawn with single pixel width, filling with only solid colours and inability to scale objects properly. The Java 2D API supports us with rich set of classes to develop intuitive and high-quality applications.

The *awt.Graphics2D* class, which extends *awt.Graphics* class, allows us to draw and fill simple shape objects such as lines, arcs, curves and ellipses; change their appearance with different outline and fill colours and apply transformations to move objects from one location to another, to rotate them and to enlarge or reduce their shapes. It also helps us to reduce the shape object according to the required size with clip operation and to shear horizontally or vertically when they are rendered.

Further in order to make a compatibility with Swing in Java 1.1, the Graphics class has to be type-casted to Graphics2D class. This will allow us to use methods from Graphics2D class to create basic shapes and transform them into more complex images.

Before drawing any shape object, we will have to create the shape first. All shape objects support both float precision and double precisions. Once we create shape object then we can draw them using *draw()* method and *fill()* them with colour or gradient paint or texture paint. Figure 15.7 presents you some of the methods of Graphics2D class that you will use inside *paintComponent()* method.

Figure 15.7. Summary of Some Graphics2D Methods

```
public void paintComponent(Graphics g)
{
    // Clear canvas
    super.paintComponent(g);
```

```
    // Typecast Graphics to Graphics2D
    Graphics2D g2 = (Graphics2D)g;

    // Create a shapes such as lines, arcs, ellipses
    // Draw those shapes
    g2.draw(); // outline
    // Fill those shapes
    g2.fill(); // solid

    // set the colour
    g2.setPaint(color);
    // apply transformations to coordinate system
    g2.translate();
    g2.rotate();
    g2.scale();
    g2.shear();
}
```

15.16 DRAWING LINES AND CURVES

The Line2D class defines a line shape that we can instantiate with starting and end points. With this object we can either draw this line or fill this line with the required colour. Each Shape object such as Line2D comes with two versions Shape.Float and Shape.Double. The Float stores object coordinates as a float precision number whereas Double version stores as a double precision number. Generally manipulating single precision number using float is slightly faster. Figure 15.8 illustrates a Line2D object.

Figure 15.8. Drawing Lines

```
Graphics2D g2 = (Graphics2D)g;
Line2D.Double line = new Line2D.Double(x1, y1, x2, y2);
And then draw as
g2.draw(line);
Alternatively you can just use constructor itself to instantiate
object as
g2.draw(new Line2D.Double(x1, y1, x2, y2));
```

The QuadCurve2D.Float and QuadCurve2D.Double classes create us quadratic (bezier) curves given both end points of the curve as well as control point. The control point (namely (cx, cy) in Figure 15.9) specifies the impact for the curvature between the two end points.

Similarly CubicCurve2D.Double and CubicCurve2D.Float classes create us cubic (spline) curves from starting point to ending point with the two control points that define the curvature as depicted in Figure 15.10.

Figure 15.11 depicts the process of instantiation of quad curves and cubic curves.

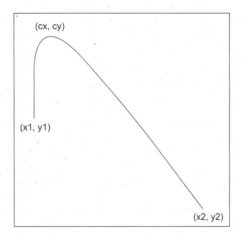

Figure 15.9. Quadratic Curves

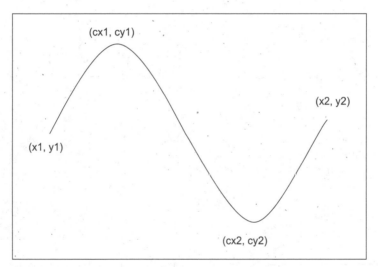

Figure 15.10. Cubic Curves

Figure 15.11. Creating Quad and Cubic Curves

```
QuadCurve2D.Float qc = new QuadCurve2D.Float(x1, y1, cx, cy, x2,
y2);
QuadCurve2D.Double qc = new QuadCurve2D.Double(x1, y1, cx, cy,
x2, y2);
CubicCurve2D.Double cc = new CubicCurve2D.Double(x1,y1,cx1,cy1,
cx2,cy2,x2,y2);
CubicCurve2D.Float cc = new CubicCurve2D.Float(x1,y1,cx1,cy1,cx2,
cy2,x2,y2);
```

The program depicted in Listing 15.13 paints Lines, QuadCurves and CubicCurves. Also, you will observe how *setPaint()* paints the panel with a colour. You can also use setCurve() method to define coordinates for quad curve and cubic curve instead of using constructor for initialization.

Listing 15.13. Drawing Lines and Curves

```
// GeometricPrimitives2D.java

import javax.swing.*;
import java.awt.*;
import java.awt.geom.*;

class Panel2D extends JPanel
{
    public void paint(Graphics g)
    {
        // cast
        Graphics2D g2 = (Graphics2D)g;

        //Create Point2D.Double
        Point2D.Double point = new Point2D.Double(20,20);
        //setLocation(point);

        g2.setPaint(Color.red);
        // draw horizontal line
        g2.draw(new Line2D.Double(50,50,150, 50));
        // draw vertical line
        g2.draw(new Line2D.Float(50, 50, 50, 200));

        g2.setPaint(Color.magenta);
        // create curve from (150,200) to (250, 100)
        // control point (175, 25) specified in between end points
        QuadCurve2D.Float q =
                new QuadCurve2D.Float(150, 100, 175, 25, 250, 100);
        g2.draw(q);
        q.setCurve(175, 150, 225, 275, 250, 150);
        g2.draw(q);

        g2.setPaint(Color.green);
        // create new CubicCurve2D.Double
        CubicCurve2D.Double c = new CubicCurve2D.Double();
        // curve from (250,250) to (320,225)
        // two control points: (275, 200) and (300, 275) in between
        end points
        c.setCurve(250, 250, 275, 200, 300, 275, 320, 225);
        g2.draw(c);
```

```
    }
}

public class GeometricPrimitives2D extends JFrame
{

    Panel2D panel = new Panel2D();    public
GeometricPrimitives2D()
    {
        add(panel);
        setTitle("Geometric Primitives");
        setSize(350,350);
        setLocationRelativeTo(null);
        setDefaultCloseOperation(JFrame.EXIT_ON_CLOSE);
        setVisible(true);
    }

    public static void main(String[] args)
    {
        GeometricPrimitives2D gp = new GeometricPrimitives2D();
    }
}
```

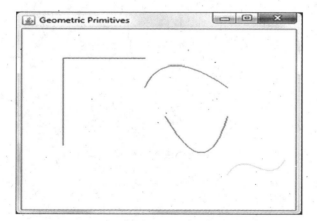

15.17 DRAWING RECTANGLE, ELLIPSES AND ARCS

The Rectangle2D.Double and Rectangle2D.Float classes define rectangle objects given a point and the dimension as width by height. Similarly RoundRectangle2D.Double and RoundRectangle2D. Float define round rectangle objects. Very similar to drawRect() of Graphics class, these two classes need x and y values representing corner arc besides the other four values.

The Ellipse2D.Double and Ellipse2D.Float classes create ellipses taking four argument values (even as float and double) similar to rectangle class so that draw() of fill() methods can paint ellipses.

The Arc2D.Double and Arc2D.Float classes define arcs. Besides the usual origin from top-left corner, dimension in terms of width and height and both angle values representing start angle and arc angle, you need to specify arc closure. There are three types of arc closures: Arc2D.CHORD, Arc2D.OPEN and Arc2D.PIE as depicted in Figure 15.12.

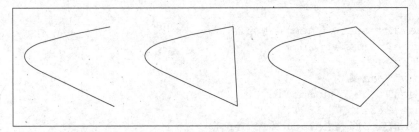

Figure 15.12. Arc Closures: OPEN, PIE and CHORD

In the example shown in Listing 15.14, you will notice rectangles, ellipses and arcs drawn with different colours. Hope you will remember circles are nothing but ellipses with equal height and width. Also, the program paints all three arc types.

Listing 15.14. Drawing Rectangles, Ellipses and Arcs

```java
// GeomPrim2.java

import javax.swing.*;
import java.awt.*;
import java.awt.geom.*;

class Panel2D extends JPanel
{
    public void paint(Graphics g)
    {
        // cast
        Graphics2D g2 = (Graphics2D)g;

        g2.setPaint(Color.red);
        // draw Rectangle2D.Double
        g2.draw(new Rectangle2D.Double(20, 20, 100, 50));

        g2.setPaint(Color.green);
        // draw RoundRectangle2D.Double
        g2.draw(new RoundRectangle2D.Double(20, 100, 100, 50,
        20, 20));

        g2.setPaint(Color.blue);
        g2.draw(new Ellipse2D.Double(150, 20, 100, 50));
        g2.draw(new Ellipse2D.Double(150, 100, 50, 50));
```

```
      g2.setPaint(Color.magenta);
      g2.draw(new Arc2D.Double(20, 175, 100, 50, 90, 135, Arc2D.
      OPEN));
      g2.draw(new Arc2D.Double(150, 175, 100, 50, 90, 135,
      Arc2D.CHORD));
      g2.draw(new Arc2D.Double(75, 175, 100, 50, 90, 135,
      Arc2D.PIE));
   }
}

public class GeomPrim2 extends JFrame
{
   Panel2D panel = new Panel2D();

   public GeomPrim2()
   {
      add(panel);
      setTitle("Rect Ellipse Arcs");
      setSize(350,350);
      setLocationRelativeTo(null);
      setDefaultCloseOperation(JFrame.EXIT_ON_CLOSE);
      setVisible(true);
   }

   public static void main(String[] args)
   {
      GeomPrim2 gp = new GeomPrim2();
   }
}
```

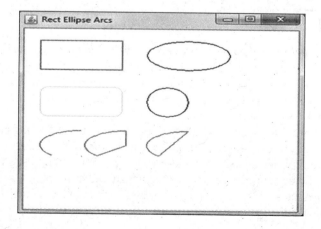

15.18 FILLING WITH COLOR, GRADIENTPAINT AND TEXTUREPAINT

The *awt.Graphics* class just supports solid colour with which you will paint the shape. But, solid filling is not appealing; the entire surface is painted with a single colour. Also you will have to use only limited colour choices either with predefined colour constants or with *rgb* values from 0 to 255 representing colour values. The Color class in 2D graphics apart from colour constants allows us to specify float values for *rgb* in the range of *0.0f* to *1.0f*. Internally the corresponding *float* value is converted to *int* value by multiplying 255 and rounding up. For example, let us define a colour with float type for *rgb* as shown in Figure 15.13.

Figure 15.13. Creating Color Object

```
Color c = new Color(float r, float g, float b);
```

Once colour object is created, then you can use *setPaint()* method to paint Graphics2D context with new colour. Remember colour object can also be instantiated as an argument inside setPaint().

The **GradientPaint** class blends two colours with a smooth transition from one colour to the second colour. So to fill a shape with a gradient paint, you will have to first create a GradientPaint object, invoke *setPaint()* method with this GradientPaint object and finally *fill()* will fill the shape with this gradient paint. Figure 15.14 explains you how to create GradientPaint object and Figure 15.15 depicts the blending of two colours.

Figure 15.14. GradientPaint for Blending Two Colours

```
GradientPaint gcolor = new GradientPaint(x1, y1, c1, x2, y2, c2);
g2.setPaint(gcolor);
g2.fill(s);
Where c1 and c2 are colour objects, s is a shape object and
smooth transition from one colour to second colour happens in
between (x1, y1) and (x2, y2)
```

As depicted in Figure 15.15, the area in between gradient line (also delimited within dotted lines) will be painted with the blended colours. The area covered by c1 will be painted with colour c1. Similarly area covered by c2 will be painted with colour c2. Therefore, horizontal gradient line results into blending left to right; diagonal gradient line results into blending of colours diagonally and vertical line results into blending of colours vertically.

Besides colour filling and gradient filling, there is one more type of filling possible with shapes, known as texture filling. A texture should be created using a BufferedImage first. Then this texture will be painted repeatedly like laying floor with tiles. The **TexturePaint** class represents a texture. Then a rectangle should be defined using this texture image, and this rectangle will be replicated over the shape. The texture image will be automatically scaled to fit into the rectangle. For example, let us create a texture as shown in Figure 15.16.

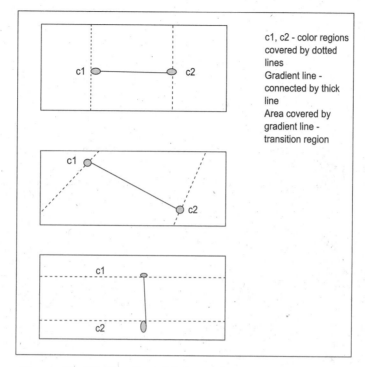

c1, c2 - color regions
covered by dotted
lines
Gradient line -
connected by thick
line
Area covered by
gradient line -
transition region

Figure 15.15. Blending of Colours Between Gradient Line

Figure 15.16. A Texture Rectangle

Here our texture image consists of a rectangle with red and an ellipse filled in with magenta. This texture rectangle can be repeated over and over again on the shape. In Listing 15.15, you will find all these three types of filling in use.

Listing 15.15. Colour, Gradient and Texture Filling

```java
// FillRect2D.java

import javax.swing.*;
import java.awt.*;
import java.awt.geom.*;
import java.awt.image.BufferedImage;
```

```java
class Panel2D extends JPanel
{
    public void paint(Graphics g)
    {
        // typecast
        Graphics2D g2 = (Graphics2D)g;

        // some random float values for rgb
        Color c = new Color(0.3587398f, 0.98276653f, 0.81728922f);
        g2.setPaint(c);
        g2.fill(new Rectangle2D.Double(20, 20, 100, 50));

        // Paint with two colours
        Color c1 = new Color(0.222222f, 0.111113232953f,
        0.888888888f);
        Color c2 = new Color(
          0.3023825898f, 0.9898093283223f, 0.11839328722f);
        Color c3 = new  Color(
          0.778890232825898f, 0.9898093283223f, 0.5333339328722f);
        GradientPaint gcolor = new GradientPaint(70, 110, c1, 90,
        130, c2);
        g2.setPaint(gcolor);
        g2.fill(new RoundRectangle2D.Double(20, 100, 100, 50, 10,
        10));

        // paint with two colours, repeat pattern
        gcolor = new GradientPaint(220, 110, c3, 235, 140, c,
        true);
        g2.setPaint(gcolor);
        g2.fill(new Ellipse2D.Double(210, 100, 50, 50));

        g2.setPaint(c3);
        g2.fill(new Ellipse2D.Double(150, 20, 100, 50));
        g2.setPaint(Color.pink);
        g2.fill(new Arc2D.Double(150, 100, 100, 50, 90, 135, Arc2D.
        OPEN));
        BufferedImage bi =
          new BufferedImage(5, 5, BufferedImage.TYPE_INT_RGB);
        Graphics2D gg = bi.createGraphics();
        gg.setColor(Color.green);
        gg.drawRect(0, 0, 5, 5);
        gg.setColor(Color.pink);
        gg.fillOval(0, 0, 5, 5);
        Rectangle r = new Rectangle(0, 0, 5, 5);
        g2.setPaint(new TexturePaint(bi, r));
```

```
        Rectangle rect = new Rectangle(20, 175, 200, 50);
        g2.fill(rect);
    }
}

public class FillRect2D extends JFrame
{
    Panel2D panel = new Panel2D();

    public FillRect2D()
    {
        add(panel);
        setTitle("Geometric Primitives");
        setSize(300,275);
        setLocationRelativeTo(null);
        setDefaultCloseOperation(JFrame.EXIT_ON_CLOSE);
        setVisible(true);
    }

    public static void main(String[] args)
    {
        FillRect2D gp = new FillRect2D();
    }
}
```

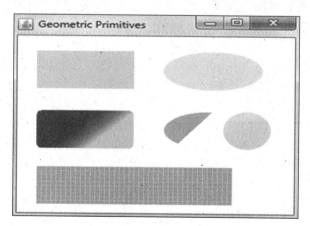

15.19 DRAWING ARBITRARY SHAPES

Java 2D allows you to create your own shapes with an interesting class *GeneralPath*. This class allows us to create a shape using lines, curves and cubic curves. To begin creating a shape, you need to first position the starting point using moveTo() method. Then you can use *lineTo(), curveTo()* and *quadTo()* methods to continue drawing the shape. Finally *closePath()* completes the shape object. If *moveTo()*

is not invoked first, then JVM will generate *IllegalPathStateException*. Listing 15.16 draws two arbitrary shapes: one diamond and one random figure using lines and quad curve. Also *setStroke()* defines thickness in points for lines.

Listing 15.16. User-defined Shapes

```java
// GeneralPath2D.java

import java.awt.*;
import javax.swing.*;
import java.awt.geom.*;

class Panel2D extends JPanel
{
    public void paint(Graphics g)
    {
        Graphics2D g2 = (Graphics2D)g;
        GeneralPath path = new GeneralPath();

        // define a rectangle
        path.moveTo(50,50);
        path.lineTo(75, 75);
        path.lineTo(50, 100);
        path.lineTo(25, 75);
        path.lineTo(50,50);

        // define two lines and quadratic curve
        path.moveTo(125, 125);
        path.lineTo(300,175);
        path.quadTo(200,250,275,275);
        path.lineTo(275, 275);

        // close shape definition
        path.closePath();
        g2.setPaint(Color.magenta);
        g2.setStroke(new BasicStroke(8));   // 8-pixels
        g2.draw(path);
    }
}

public class GeneralPath2D extends JFrame
{
    Panel2D panel = new Panel2D();
    public GeneralPath2D()
    {
        add(panel);
```

```
        setTitle("General Path Drawing");
        setSize(400, 400);
        setLocationRelativeTo(null);
        setDefaultCloseOperation(JFrame.EXIT_ON_CLOSE);
        setVisible(true);
    }

    public static void main(String[] args)
    {
        GeneralPath2D gp = new GeneralPath2D();
    }
}
```

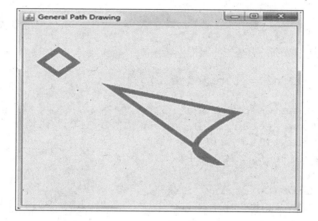

15.20 COORDINATE TRANSFORMATIONS

Java 2D allows us to translate, rotate, scale and shear the coordinate system instead of calculating new coordinates for each point in the shape. Translation allows the coordinate system to move to a position instead of moving the shape. Similarly rotation performs spinning, scale either reduces or enlarges coordinate system and shear stretches unevenly in either x-direction or y-direction, called x-shear and y-shear.

The Graphics2D class contains methods to perform these transformations. The translate(), rotate(), scale() and shear() methods perform translation, rotation, scaling and shear respectively. One final important note, transformations are additive. That is, every transformation is continued with the result of previous transformation. The example shown in Figure 15.17 explains you how to use these methods and Listing 15.17 illustrates coordinate transformations.

Figure 15.17. Applying Transformations

```
Graphics2D g2 = (Graphics2D)g
g2.translate(100,100); // move to (100,100)
g2.rotate(180); // rotate coordinate system 180 degrees
```

```
g2.scale(2.0, 3.0); // scale width 2 times and height 3 times
g2.scale(0.5, 0.5); // reduce both 50%
g2.shear(0.3, 0.0);  // stretch x 30%
g2.shear(0.0, 0.2); // stretch y 20%
```

Listing 15.17. Coordinate Transformations

```java
// Transformation2D.java

import java.awt.*;
import javax.swing.*;
import java.awt.geom.*;

class Panel2D extends JPanel
{
   public void paint(Graphics g)
   {
      Graphics2D g2 = (Graphics2D)g;

      g2.setPaint(Color.green);
      g2.fill(new Rectangle2D.Double(0, 0, 50, 50));
      g2.translate(100, 100);
      g2.rotate(30.0 * Math.PI/180.0);
      g2.scale(2.0, 2.0);
      g2.setColor(Color.red);
      g2.fill(new Rectangle2D.Double(0, 0, 50, 50));
   }
}

public class Transformation2D extends JFrame
{
   Panel2D panel = new Panel2D();

   public Transformation2D()
   {
      add(panel);
      setTitle("2D Transformations");
      setSize(350,350);
      setLocationRelativeTo(null);
      setDefaultCloseOperation(JFrame.EXIT_ON_CLOSE);
      setVisible(true);
   }

   public static void main(String[] args)
   {
```

```
Transformation2D gp = new Transformation2D();
    }
}
```

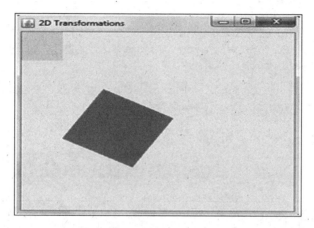

We will develop another application that will apply *shear* transformation for the coordinate system as depicted in Listing 15.18.

Listing 15.18. Shear Transformations

```
// Shear2D.java

import java.awt.*;
import javax.swing.*;
import java.awt.geom.*;

class Panel2D extends JPanel
{
    public void paint(Graphics g)
    {
        Graphics2D g2 = (Graphics2D)g;

        g2.setPaint(Color.green);
        g2.fill(new Rectangle2D.Double(50, 50, 75, 75));

        g2.shear(0.3, 0); // x-shear = 30%
        g2.fill(new Rectangle2D.Double(150, 50, 75, 75));
    }
}

public class Shear2D extends JFrame
{
    Panel2D panel = new Panel2D();
```

```
    public Shear2D()
    {
        add(panel);
        setTitle("Shear Transformations");
        setSize(350,200);
        setLocationRelativeTo(null);
        setDefaultCloseOperation(JFrame.EXIT_ON_CLOSE);
        setVisible(true);
    }

    public static void main(String[] args)
    {
        Shear2D gp = new Shear2D();
    }
}
```

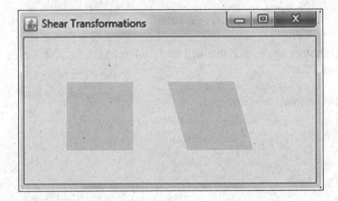

15.21 2D CLIPPING

Clipping is another interesting feature in Graphics2D class. Clipping is a process of removing all uninterested portions of the given image or shape by rendering only the interested portion of the shape or image. In order to perform clipping, you need to first define clip boundary within the panel by using setClip() method. Then clip() will render the portion of the shape that is common to clip boundary and the given shape. In Listing 15.19, a rectangle is clipped against an ellipse.

Listing 15.19. Clipping Shapes

```
// Clip2D.java

import java.awt.*;
import javax.swing.*;
import java.awt.geom.*;

class Panel2D extends JPanel
{
```

```java
    public void paint(Graphics g)
    {
        Graphics2D g2 = (Graphics2D)g;

        g2.setPaint(Color.green);

        Ellipse2D.Double e = new Ellipse2D.Double(50, 50, 100, 50);
        Rectangle2D.Double r = new Rectangle2D.Double(50, 50, 200,
        200);
        g2.setClip(e);
        g2.clip(r);
        g2.fill(r);
    }
}

public class Clip2D extends JFrame
{
    Panel2D panel = new Panel2D();

    public Clip2D()
    {
        add(panel);
        setTitle("Clipping");
        setSize(400, 400);
        setLocationRelativeTo(null);
        setDefaultCloseOperation(JFrame.EXIT_ON_CLOSE);
        setVisible(true);
    }

    public static void main(String[] args)
    {
        Clip2D gp = new Clip2D();
    }
}
```

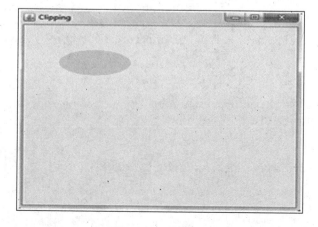

15.22 AFFINE TRANSFORMATIONS ON IMAGES

Graphics2D supports affine transformations such as rotation and scaling and image filtering operations on images. Java 2D's affine transform works on bitmap image as well as on vector graphics. However, instead of manipulating the Graphics2D's current transform context (which operates on vector-graphics only via rendering methods draw() and fill()), you need to allocate an AffineTransform object to perform transformation on images. Listing 15.20 illustrates transformations performed on images.

Listing 15.20. Affine Transformations on Image

```java
// ImageTrans2D.java
import javax.swing.*;
import java.awt.*;
import java.awt.geom.*;

class Img extends JPanel
{
    public void paintComponent(Graphics g)
    {
        super.paintComponent(g);
        Graphics2D g2 = (Graphics2D)g;
        setBackground(Color.white);

        ImageIcon icon = new ImageIcon("rose.png");
        Image img = icon.getImage();

        int w = img.getWidth(this);
        int h = img.getHeight(this);
        g2.drawImage(img, 0, 0, this);

        // drawImage() does not use the current transform of
        // the Graphics2D context
        // Need to create a AffineTransform and pass into
        drawImage()
        AffineTransform t = new AffineTransform();  // identity
        transform
        t.translate(200, 200);
        t.scale(0.8, 0.8);
        t.rotate(Math.toRadians(15), w/2, h/2);
        g2.drawImage(img, t, this);
    }
}
public class ImageTrans2D extends JFrame
{
```

```
Img panel = new Img();

public ImageTrans2D()
{
    add(panel);

    setTitle("Transformation on Images");
    setSize(500, 400);
    setLocationRelativeTo(null);  // centres to screen
    setDefaultCloseOperation(JFrame.EXIT_ON_CLOSE); // closes
    frame
    setVisible(true);
}

public static void main(String[] args)
{
    ImageTrans2D f = new ImageTrans2D();
}
}
```

15.23 SUMMARY

1. Swing toolkit is part of JFC for designing GUI applications
2. Swing components and containers start with a letter J to distinguish AWT components and containers
3. The geom package defines all geometrical shapes
4. The JFrame, JPanel and JApplet are some important swing containers
5. To draw a shape, paintComponent() is overridden inside JPanel
6. The paintComponent() receives Graphics context as an argument, so that all of its drawXXX() and fillXXX() can be used to paint outline and filled shapes

7. The drawing panel starts at top-left corner, *x* axis denotes its width and *y* axis denotes its height
8. The add() adds a component into container directly instead of adding them to content pane
9. The drawImage() paints an image that is loaded with Toolkit or ImageIcon class
10. The JApplet can be used as a container to create shapes
11. The Graphics2D class extends Graphics class and contains draw() and fill() methods for painting shapes
12. The shapes are defined in geom package
13. The shapes can be created with Float precision or Double precision in contrast to int precision of Graphics context
14. The Color object can take innumerable colour choices with float values for rgb
15. The GradientPaint blends two colours together by specifying blending region
16. The TexturePaint allows us to create a paint pattern so that it will be repeatedly painted like floor tiles
17. Arbitrary shapes can be drawn using GeneralPath
18. The translation, rotation, scaling and shear are important transformations that can be applied to coordinate plane instead of shapes
19. The clip() from Graphics2D class removes uninteresting portions of a shape against a clipping shape
20. The AffineTransform object performs transformations such as translation, rotation, scaling and filtering on images

KEY TERMS

Colour, 493	GradientPaint, 520	JFrames, 489
Components, 490	Graphics, 494	TexturePaint, 520
Containers, 490	Graphics2D, 490	
ContentPane, 493	JApplets, 489	

REVIEW QUESTIONS

Multiple-choice Questions

1. Which of the following are true about Swing and AWT?
   a. AWT components are heavy-weight components
   b. Swing components are lightweight components
   c. Look and feel of the GUI can be changed in Swing, but not in AWT
   d. For drawing, AWT uses screen rendering where Swing uses double buffering
   e. All of the above

2. Which of the following are true about JComponent?
   a. Abstract class
   b. Supports look-and-feel
   c. Supports keystroke handling
   d. All of the above

3. What method you override to draw graphics primitives such as lines and circles?
   a. paint()
   b. paintComponent()
   c. draw()
   d. All of the above

4. What method controls the visibility of swing components?
   a. visible()
   b. setVisible()
   c. show()
   d. None of the above

5. What is the base class of swing.JComponent?
   a. swing.Component
   b. awt.Component
   c. awt.Container
   d. swing.JWindow
   e. None of the above

6. The setOpaque(true) sets component to
   a. paint every pixel within its rectangular bounds
   b. hide all pixels to the default colour palette
   c. convert all foreground objects to background colour palette
   d. None of the above

7. Choose all correct statements about JFrame:
   a. The add() adds components to JFrame
   b. The add() can add JPanel to JFrame
   c. The add() adds components to content pane of JFrame
   d. None of the above

8. What method makes JFrame visible?
   a. setVisible()
   b. setVisible(true)
   c. JFrame is visible by default
   d. None of the above

9. The setBackground(colour) paints
   a. The background color JFrame with the required colour
   b. The background colour of the content pane with the required colour
   c. The background colour of the screen with full resolution
   d. None of the above

10. What is the origin (0,0) of the painting coordinate system?
    a. Centre of the painting coordinate system
    b. Top-left of the painting coordinate system
    c. Bottom-left of the painting coordinate system
    d. It depends of the Java look-and-feel
    e. None of the above

11. What method displays a string hello at location (50,50)?
    a. drawString(50,50,"hello");
    b. Graphics.drawString(50,50,"hello");
    c. drawString("hello", 50, 50);
    d. None of the above

12. What is the output?

```
drawLine(100,100,200,100)
```

    a. It draws a horizontal line   b. It draws a vertical line

    c. It draws a left diagonal line   d. It draws a right diagonal line

    e. None of the above

13. What is the output?

```
drawLine(100,100,300,300)
```

    a. It draws a horizontal line   b. It draws a vertical line

    c. It draws a left diagonal line   d. It draws a right diagonal line

    e. None of the above

14. How to get the dimension of a component/container?

    a. Using getWidth() and getHeight()   b. Using getX() and getY()

    c. getSize()   d. None of the above

15. How to draw rectangle at (50,50) with height 20 and width 30?

    a. drawRect(50,50,20,30);   b. drawRect(50,50,30,20);

    c. drawRect(20,30,50,50);   d. drawRect(30,20,50,50);

    e. None of the above

16. How to paint a rectangle at (x,y) with a colour?

    a. fillRect(x,y,20,20);   b. fillRect(color, x,y,20,20);

    c. fillRect x,y,20,20, color);   d. None of the above

17. The *draw3DRect(50,100,20,30,false)* displays

    a. a lowered 3D rectangle   b. a raised 3D rectangle

    c. a opaque 3D rectangle   d. None of the above

18. The setXORMode()

    a. returns an intersection of two circles

    b. returns an intersection of two rectangles

    c. returns an intersection of two ellipses

    d. None of the above

19. How to clear the content of the paint buffer?

    a. repaint()   b. setPaintMode(color);

    c. super.paintComponent(g);   d. None of the above

20. What method draws a horizontal ellipse?
    a. drawEllipse(20,20,50,30)
    b. drawOval(20,20,50,30)
    c. drawEllipse(20,20,30,50)
    d. drawOval(20,20,30,50)
    e. None of the above

21. What method draws a vertical ellipse?
    a. drawEllipse(20,20,50,30)
    b. drawOval(20,20,50,30)
    c. drawEllipse(20,20,30,50)
    d. drawOval(20,20,30,50)
    e. None of the above

22. What is the output?

```
g.fillArc(0, 0, 50, 50, 0, 45)
```

    a. Displays a coloured arc from 0 to 45 degrees within a rectangle of size(50,50)
    b. Displays a coloured arc from 0 to 45 degrees within a circle of size(50,50)
    c. Displays a coloured arc from 45 to 0 degrees within a rectangle of size(50,50)
    d. None of the above

23. What is the output?

```
g.drawArc(0, 0, 50, 50, 10, 45)
```

    a. Displays an outline arc from 10 to 55 degrees within a rectangle of size(50,50)
    b. Displays an outline arc from 45 to 10 degrees within a circle of size(50,50)
    c. Displays an outline arc from 10 to 45 degrees within a rectangle of size(50,50)
    d. None of the above

24. What is the output?

```
draw(new Line2D.Double(100,100,300,100));
```

    a. Draws a horizontal line
    b. Draws a vertical line
    c. Draws a left diagonal line
    d. Draws a right diagonal line
    e. None of the above

25. What method draws a bezier curve?
    a. draw(new QuadCurve2D.Float(150, 100, 175, 25, 250, 100));
    b. draw(new QuadCurve2D.Double(150, 100, 175, 25, 250, 100));
    c. draw(new QuadCurve2D.Long(150, 100, 175, 25, 250, 100));
    d. None of the above

26. What method draws a spline curve?
    a. draw(new CubicCurve2D.Double(250, 250, 275, 200, 300, 275, 320, 225));
    b. draw(new CubicCurve2D.Float(250, 250, 275, 200, 300, 275, 320, 225));
    c. draw(new CubicCurve2D.Long(250, 250, 275, 200, 300, 275, 320, 225));
    d. None of the above

27. What are arc closures?
    a. Arc2D.CHORD   b. Arc2D.OPEN
    c. Arc2D.PIE   d. All of the above

28. Which class blends two colours with a smooth transition from one colour to another?
    a. TexturePaint   b. GradientPaint
    c. BlendedPaint   d. None of the above

29. In Graphics2D, arbitrary shapes can be drawn using
    a. ArbitraryShape class   b. GeneralPath class
    c. ArbitraryPath class   d. None of the above

30. A geometric object can be tilted horizontally using
    a. shear()   b. translate()
    c. rotate()   d. scale()
    e. None of the above

31. The method shear(0.4,0) results the object
    a. to tilt horizontally 4 times   b. to tilt horizontally 40 percent
    c. to tilt vertically 4 times   d. None of the above

32. Which of the following is true?
    a. Java 2D's affine transform works on bitmap image
    b. Java 2D's affine transform works on vector graphics
    c. Affine transformations allow rotation and scaling and image filtering operations on images
    d. All of the above

Answers

1. e	2. d	3. b	4. b	5. c	6. b	7. c	8. b	9. b	10. b
11. c	12. a	13. c	14. a	15. b	16. a	17. a	18. d	19. c	20. a
21. d	22. a	23. a	24. a	25. a,b	26. a	27. d	28. b	29. b	30. a
31. b	32. d								

Short-answer Questions

1. Write an overview of swing containers.
2. What is content pane?
3. How to draw lines and strings?

4. How to draw outline and colour-filled rectangles?
5. How to draw outline and colour-filled circles?
6. How to draw outline and colour-filled arcs?
7. Explain the process of drawing polygons and polylines.
8. Explain 2D curve drawing methods.
9. Explain 2D arc drawing methods.
10. Explain 2D ellipse drawing methods.
11. Explain Color, GradientPaint and TexturePaint classes.
12. Explain 2D transformations and clipping methods.
13. What is affine transformation?

EXERCISES

15.1. Display at least five smileys (smiling humaniod face) with multiple colours.
15.2. Display the following graphical objects: cube, prism, cylinder, sphere and cone.
15.3. Display a chess board (8×8 squares) with red and black colours.
15.4. Draw various ellipses of same size so that it appears like a flower.
15.5. Draw diamond inside another diamond recursively (upto N levels).
15.6. Draw the image of the coloured heart.
15.7. Simulate the sine, cosine and tan waves with different colours.
15.8. Draw few fractal images as you like. Hint: refer any graphics book on fractal geometry.
15.9. Display the animated analog clock.
15.10. Draw few random art images. Basically x and y coordinate values range from −1 to +1 along with sin() and cos() values for rgb values. (Good reference at http://www.random-art.org/.)
15.11. Generate large random numbers (say 1000 numbers) and sort them using bubble sort. Display the progress of sorting by various lines.

16

GUI Development Using JFrame

OBJECTIVES

- To explain the general structure of any GUI application
- To create JLabel and JButton using swing package
- To develop a digital clock as a JLabel
- To introduce event handling, ActionEvent and ActionListener
- To explain different layout managers such as FlowLayout, BorderLayout, GridLayout, BoxLayout and Box
- To use JPanel to design multiple layouts for the frame
- To explain the three fillers for Box namely *strut, glue* and *rigid area*
- To introduce event types, their listeners, adapters and all methods
- To paint JLabel with random colours whenever a button is pressed
- To move a filled circle to random locations whenever a button is pressed
- To create textfield, password textfield and text area
- To display the contents of a file in text area
- To develop a textfield that accepts only digits
- To develop text copy cat application
- To create checkboxes, radiobuttons, comboboxes and lists
- To create dialog windows
- To create file choosers and colour choosers
- To create message dialogs, confirm dialogs, option dialogs and input dialogs
- To design course registration form using JFrames

- To create editor pane and text pane
- To display images in text pane
- To create sliders and handling ChangeEvent
- To create tabbed pane
- To create menubar, menus and menu items
- To create tables using array of objects and vectors
- To create custom swing components

16.1 INTRODUCTION

In Chapter 15, the readers were introduced to the art of developing graphics applications and the class hierarchy for Swing Components and Containers. To just recall, an instance of a component can be displayed on the screen and similarly an instance of a container will hold an instance of a component. The readers have learnt how to use the instances of containers such as JApplet, JFrame and JPanel. Though you have come across some of the components such as JButton, JLabel and others, you never had an opportunity to develop applications utilizing swing components so far. In this chapter, you will be exposed to all interesting swing components with which you can development efficient GUI applications using JFrame. Chapter 17 focuses on GUI development using JApplet. One final thought, you might also wonder whether it is possible to automatically generate GUI forms by dragging and dropping very similar to .NET framework. Though Java GUI API needs simple hard coding of components, you might also leverage automatic GUI builders (aka, IDE) for Java such as Eclipse and NetBeans, especially if your GUI becomes very large.

16.2 CREATING LABELS AND BUTTONS

Before creating a button and a label, let us first see the general structure of a GUI program. Assume that you have a JFrame as a container and you create a lot of components such as buttons, labels, checkboxes, radio buttons, etc. and assemble them inside the frame according to your prefered arrangement or order of the components. Also you want to perform actions on the components such as *click a button, select an item from list, select an item from combobox* or *select an item from radio button* or *press a key* or *press mouse*. Based on the actions, you will carry out certain operations such as *open a file, do a calculation, change a color* or *save data to file*. To put it otherwise, here is an example of action-operation sequence. If a user clicks a button, then open a file for reading. Figure 16.1 explains the general structure of a GUI application.

Figure 16.1. Skeleton of a GUI Application

```
public class ClassName extends JFrame
{
    // create all components

    public ClassName()
    {
        // instantiate all components
```

```
        // set properties for components if any
        // set the required layout using setLayout()
        // add all components to JFrame using add()
        // register all required listeners (ie actions)
    }

    // create nested classes for all registered listeners (ie
    operations)

    public static void main(String[] args)
    {
        // set frame properties for the public class
    }
}
```

Creating a label in swing will be very simple. Just you need to instantiate **JLabel** class with the required text as an argument. Labels can also be created with an image as an argument. The *setText()* assigns the given text to label at runtime. You can also create a border to label with *setBorder()* method for which you need to create a border first and assign it to label. Remember all swing borders are available in swing.border package that should be first imported.

Buttons are created in swing using **JButton** class. Similar to JLabel you should instantiate it with a text so that you can push the button. Just as JLabel you can instantiate a button with an image. The *setMnemonic()* allows you to set a keyboard character for button so that you can select it along with *Alt* key. The *setToolTipText()* sets a text to button that will be displayed when mouse is hovered on it.

When you create a button with an image and text, *setHorizontalAlignment()* and *setVerticalAlignment()* methods can be used to align the image and text horizontally or vertically. In the same way, *setHorizontalTextPosition()* and *setVerticalTextPosition()* methods control the position of the text with respect to the image. Listing 16.1 explains to us how to create a label and button in swing.

Listing 16.1. Creating Labels and Buttons

```
// Buttons.java
import javax.swing.*;
import java.awt.*;

public class Buttons extends JFrame
{
    // create components
    JLabel lblLogin;
    JButton btnExit;

    public Buttons()
    {
        // instantiate components
```

```
        lblLogin = new JLabel("Login Frame", JLabel.CENTER);
        btnExit = new JButton("Exit");

        // set component properties, if any
        btnExit.setMnemonic('b');
        btnExit.setToolTipText("Closes frame");

        // set required layout
        // here we use default layout of JFrame

        // add components to JFrame
        // add label to north
        add(lblLogin, BorderLayout.NORTH);   // method 1
        // add button to south
        add("South", btnExit);   // method 2
    }

    public static void main(String[] args)
    {
        Buttons f = new Buttons();
        // frame properties
        f.setTitle("User Login");
        f.setSize(300,200);
        f.setLocationRelativeTo(null);   // centres to screen
        f.setDefaultCloseOperation(JFrame.EXIT_ON_CLOSE); // closes
        frame
        f.setVisible(true);
    }
}
```

Label can be aligned to frame with the static constants LEFT, RIGHT or CENTER. When a label is created with an image some more alignments such as BOTTOM, TOP, etc. can be specified. The swing components are added to frame according to the specified layout. Here we use the default layout of frame which is BorderLayout. We add label to north and button to south. Remember there are two ways for adding components – with constants such as NORTH and string such as "South". You will learn further details of various layouts and their applications in section 16.5. The main() simply instantiates the frame and sets frame properties such as title, size, closing and visibility.

When you run this application you might see how the label and button are placed in north and south of the frame. However when you press the button or press Alt-b you will observe the frame is not closing. That is the button does not recognize the *action* of the user, the button press using mouse or keyboard key. In Java terminology, these actions are called events and the program should handle these events. This process is refered to as **event handling**, which is discussed in section 16.4.

16.3 PROBLEM: DIGITAL CLOCK AS JLABEL

This ClockLabel application is a JLabel thread that is painted with the current time. It can be added to any component as it is just a JLabel. We will instantiate this clock label into a frame when we discuss Color Label application. Here is the complete program depicted in Listing 16.2.

Listing 16.2. Clock Label Thread

```
// ClockLabel.java

import java.awt.*;
import javax.swing.*;
import java.awt.event.*;
import java.util.*;

class ClockLabel extends JLabel implements Runnable
{
    private Thread clockThread;
    String text;

    public ClockLabel(String text)
    {
        super(text, JLabel.CENTER);
        this.text = text;
        clockThread  = new Thread(this);
        clockThread.start();
    }

    public void run()
    {
        while(true)
        {
            Calendar calendar = Calendar.getInstance();
            calendar.setTime(new Date());
```

```
          int hours   = calendar.get(Calendar.HOUR_OF_DAY);
          int minutes = calendar.get(Calendar.MINUTE);
          int seconds = calendar.get(Calendar.SECOND);
          setText(text + ": " + hours + " : " + minutes + " : "
          + seconds);

          try
          {
                Thread.sleep(1000);
          }
          catch(InterruptedException e) {
                System.out.println("Clock Interrupted..");
          }
     }
  }
}
```

16.4 BASICS OF EVENT HANDLING

All interfaces, classes and methods that are required for handling events are defined in *awt.event* package, and you need to first import it before using them. Each component in swing will report (or fire) all events that may happen to it. It is left to us whether you are interested in an event. If you are interested in a particular event, then you will register a **listener** for this event that will perform the necessary operations through its implementation. Therefore event handling has two parts: register listeners for all interested events of a component and provide implementations for the listeners that will do the task for you.

For instance in the previous example shown in Listing 16.2, we have created a button. We are interested in an action or event namely button press. The button reports to us using an event **ActionEvent**. So we need to register a listener to this button using addActionListener() method. This method will take an argument that is an object that implements the **ActionListener** interface. The ActionListener interface has a method *actionPerformed()* that takes ActionEvent as an argument. Therefore the operation you want to do while the button is pressed should be nested inside this *actionPerformed()* method. That is, *actionPerformed()* method will be called when the button is pressed. In other words, you are overriding *actionPerformed()* with the functionality you want while implementing Action-Listener interface. So all we want from the button of Listing 16.2 is just close the frame when it is clicked. We will now rewrite this program with the required functionality as shown in Listing 16.3.

Listing 16.3. Buttons2 with Event Handling

```
// Buttons2.java
import javax.swing.*;
import java.awt.*;
import java.awt.event.*;

public class Buttons2 extends JFrame
```

```java
{
    // create components
    JLabel lblLogin;
    JButton btnExit;

    public Buttons2()
    {
        // instantiate components
        lblLogin = new JLabel("Login Frame", JLabel.CENTER);
        btnExit = new JButton("Exit");

        // set component properties, if any
        btnExit.setMnemonic('b');
        btnExit.setToolTipText("Closes frame");

        // set required layout
        // here we use default layout of JFrame

        // add components to JFrame
        // add label to north
        add(lblLogin, BorderLayout.NORTH);   // method 1
        // add button to south
        add("South", btnExit);   // method 2

        //register listener for button
        btnExit.addActionListener(new BtnExitL());
    }

    class BtnExitL implements ActionListener
    {
        public void actionPerformed(ActionEvent e)
        {
            System.exit(0);
        }
    }

    public static void main(String[] args)
    {
        Buttons2 f = new Buttons2();
        // frame properties
        f.setTitle("User Login");
        f.setSize(300,200);
        f.setLocationRelativeTo(null);   // centres to screen
        f.setDefaultCloseOperation(JFrame.EXIT_ON_CLOSE); // closes
        frame
```

```
        f.setVisible(true);
    }
}
```

The JLabel does not define any events and we are of course not interested in it. The major update of this program from the earlier one is the final part of the constructor. For each event of the components we are interested in, we should register listener with an instance of an implementation class for the ActionListener interface. The implementation class must be defined as an inner class. So there will be as many inner classes as that of components. Also you must remember, all listeners should be registered at the end of the constructor as a last statement.

The BtnExitL inner class simply implements ActionListener and overriddes *actionPerformed()* method. The *System.exit()* simply closes the frame. This is in addition to *setDefaultCloseOperation (JFrame.EXIT_ON_CLOSE)* method that will close the window by its window closing button. The Java 1.1 event handling is an elegant way of handling events. Here the user interface is clearly separated from its implementation. The implementations of user interface components are defined as inner classes effectively supporting excellent object-oriented design. We need not bother about the number of components, the inner classes scale up very well. You will learn more about different types of events that are generated by components and how to handle them in section 16.6.

16.5 LAYOUT MANAGERS

When there are several user interface components, it will be very difficult for the developers to place them in appropriate locations inside the container, as one needs to calculate the location for each component. Java eliminates the manual positioning of components with layout managers. The **layout managers** are classes that will arrange the components according to the predefined format. The *add()* method is used to add a component to frame. The following are the important layout managers in Java that we will discuss in this book:

- FlowLayout
- GridLayout
- BorderLayout
- Multiple Layouts using JPanel
- BoxLayout and Box

16.5.1 FlowLayout

The FlowLayout is the simplest of all layouts where components are placed left to right in the order they appear. When the end of line is reached, the flowing continues in the next line. By default, FlowLayout aligns each component to FlowLayout.CENTER. However you can also align components to LEFT as well as to RIGHT. Also the space between two components is 5 pixels horizontally and vertically by default. But you can customize as you wish when you instantiate FlowLayout. All components are compacted according to their size. Figure 16.2 illustrates the creation of flow layout.

Figure 16.2. Flow Layout

```
FlowLayout()
FlowLayout(FlowLayout.LEFT)
FlowLayout(FlowLayout.RIGHT, 10, 20) // hspace = 10, vspace = 20
pixels
```

Now let us create a frame that will display a label and button using flow layout as depicted in Listing 16.4.

Listing 16.4. Login Frame Using FlowLayout

```java
// FlowLayout1.java
import javax.swing.*;
import java.awt.*;
import java.awt.event.*;

public class FlowLayout1 extends JFrame
{
    // create components
    JLabel lblLogin;
    JButton btnExit;

    public FlowLayout1()
    {
        // instantiate components
        lblLogin = new JLabel("Login Frame", JLabel.CENTER);
        btnExit = new JButton("Exit");

        // set component properties, if any
        btnExit.setMnemonic('b');
        btnExit.setToolTipText("Closes frame");

        // set required layout
        setLayout(new FlowLayout());

        // add components to JFrame
```

```
        add(lblLogin);
        add(btnExit);

        //register listener for button
        btnExit.addActionListener(new BtnExitL());
    }

    class BtnExitL implements ActionListener
    {
        public void actionPerformed(ActionEvent e)
        {
            System.exit(0);
        }
    }

    public static void main(String[] args)
    {
        FlowLayout1 f = new FlowLayout1();
        // frame properties
        f.setTitle("User Login");
        f.setSize(300,200);
        f.setLocationRelativeTo(null);   // centres to screen
        f.setDefaultCloseOperation(JFrame.EXIT_ON_CLOSE); // closes
        frame
        f.setVisible(true);
    }
}
```

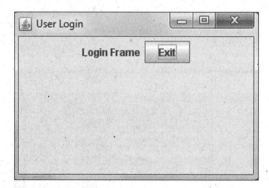

Here you can set mnemonic for button so that button can also be clicked with keyboard keys apart from mouse clicks. Further, text for toop tip defines a popup text when mouse is hovered on the button.

We will now play with an application shown in Listing 16.5 where let us try different constructors of flow layout. This program displays series of buttons with different alignments such as left, right and centre apart from horizontal and vertical gaps between buttons.

Listing 16.5. Buttons Using FlowLayout

```java
// FlowButtons.java
import javax.swing.*;
import java.awt.*;

public class FlowButtons extends JFrame
{
    public FlowButtons()
    {
        // set required layout
        setLayout(new FlowLayout());   // by default, centre
        alignment
        //setLayout(new FlowLayout(FlowLayout.LEFT));
        //setLayout(new FlowLayout(FlowLayout.RIGHT, 10,20));
        // instantiate and add buttons
        for(int i = 0; i < 10; i++)
            add(new JButton("Button" + i));
    }

    public static void main(String[] args)
    {
        FlowButtons f = new FlowButtons();
        // frame properties
        f.setTitle("Flowing of buttons");
        f.setSize(300,200);
        f.setLocationRelativeTo(null);   // centres to screen
        f.setDefaultCloseOperation(JFrame.EXIT_ON_CLOSE); // closes
        frame
        f.setVisible(true);
    }
}
```

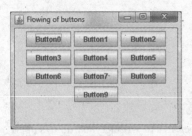
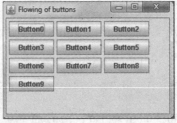
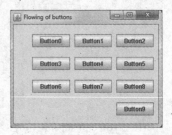

In this program, apart from alignments of button components, you might observe gaps between two components in which 10 and 20 indicate horizontal and vertical gaps between buttons. Though flow layout appears to be very simple, it will not be always suitable when components are arranged unevenly. Readers are advised to manually resize the frame and appreciate how flow layout changes the position of components. This is possible only with flow layout, but not with other layout managers.

16.5.2 BorderLayout

BorderLayout manager adds components in five regions: NORTH, SOUTH, EAST, WEST and CEN-TER. If you do not specify the region to which a component is to be placed, then by default it will be placed in the centre. Also a component placed in the centre region will occupy neighboring regions if that region does not contain any component. So it is always necessary that you add component to centre only after adding components to all other regions. By default, frame uses border layout. Some examples of creating border layout is shown in Figure 16.3.

Figure 16.3. Border Layout

```
BorderLayout()
BorderLayout(10,20)   // use this constructor if you initialize
hspace and vspace
```

We will now place 5 buttons inside all 5 regions of the frame using borderlayout as depicted in Listing 16.6.

Listing 16.6. Buttons in Border Layout

```
// BorderLayout1.java
import javax.swing.*;
import java.awt.*;

public class BorderLayout1 extends JFrame
{
    public BorderLayout1()
    {
        // instantiate and add buttons
        add(BorderLayout.NORTH, new JButton("NORTH"));
        add(BorderLayout.SOUTH, new JButton("SOUTH"));
        add(BorderLayout.EAST, new JButton("EAST"));
        add(BorderLayout.WEST, new JButton("WEST"));
        add(BorderLayout.CENTER, new JButton("CENTER"));

    }
    public static void main(String[] args)
    {
        BorderLayout1 f = new BorderLayout1();
        // frame properties
        f.setTitle("Buttons using BorderLayout");
        f.setSize(300,200);
        f.setLocationRelativeTo(null);   // centres to screen
```

```
        f.setDefaultCloseOperation(JFrame.EXIT_ON_CLOSE); // closes
        frame
        f.setVisible(true);
    }
}
```

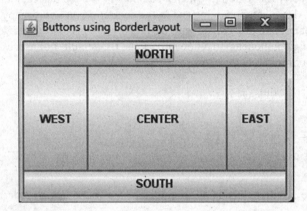

If you do not have a component to be placed in east or west, do not worry, the centre component will occupy those regions and the GUI will look cleaner too.

16.5.3 GridLayout

The GridLayout manager adds components to frame in a matrix (grid) format. The components are added left to right, top to bottom in the order in which they are added using add() method. You need to specify the values for *rows* and *columns* for the grid. Figure 16.4 illustrates the grid layout.

Figure 16.4. Creating Grid Layout

```
GridLayout(row, col)
GridLayout(col)  // rows are determined automatically during
runtime
GridLayout(row) // cols are determined automatically during
runtime
GridLayout(row, col, hspace, vspace)
```

Now let us add buttons to frame using gridlayout as depicted in Listing 16.7.

Listing 16.7. Buttons Using Grid Layout

```
// GridLayout1.java
import javax.swing.*;
import java.awt.*;
```

```
public class GridLayout1 extends JFrame
{
    public GridLayout1()
    {
        // set required layout
        setLayout(new GridLayout(2,4));
        // instantiate and add buttons
        for(int i = 1; i < 9; i++)
            add(new JButton("Button" + i));
    }

    public static void main(String[] args)
    {
        GridLayout1 f = new GridLayout1();
        // frame properties
        f.setTitle("Flowing of buttons");
        f.setSize(400,100);
        f.setLocationRelativeTo(null);  // centres to screen
        f.setDefaultCloseOperation(JFrame.EXIT_ON_CLOSE); // closes
        frame
        f.setVisible(true);
    }
}
```

The above application creates a grid layout of two rows and four columns and eight buttons are added to frame according to grid layout. GridLayout manager is another interesting layout manager besides BorderLayout.

16.5.4 Multiple Layouts Using JPanel

Suppose you want to group several components into a single cell in gridlayout or region in borderlayout; JPanel is a nice container that can group components together. For instance, you have two buttons that have to be placed in south. So all you need to do is to put them inside JPanel and add this panel to south as shown in Listing 16.8.

Listing 16.8. Buttons Inside Panel

```
// Buttons3.java
import javax.swing.*;
import java.awt.*;
```

```
public class Buttons3 extends JFrame
{
    JLabel lblLogin = new JLabel("Login Frame", JLabel.CENTER);
    JButton btnCancel = new JButton("Cancel");
    JButton btnExit = new JButton("Exit");

    public Buttons3()
    {
        add(lblLogin, BorderLayout.NORTH);
        // add buttons to south
        JPanel p = new JPanel();   // by default, flow layout
        p.add(btnCancel);
        p.add(btnExit);
        add("South", p);
    }

    public static void main(String[] args)
    {
        Buttons3 f = new Buttons3();
        // frame properties
        f.setTitle("Buttons inside panel");
        f.setSize(300,200);
        f.setLocationRelativeTo(null);   // centres to screen
        f.setDefaultCloseOperation(JFrame.EXIT_ON_CLOSE); // closes
        frame
        f.setVisible(true);
    }
}
```

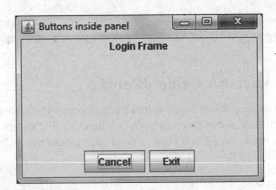

By default, JPanel uses flow layout and centre alignment. So buttons are added one after another and the panel is added to the south of the frame. The setLayout() helps us to specify the required layout for the panel. You might also observe how panel preserves the size of the components and sizes are different according to the text of the buttons. The JPanel is the extensively used container in swing because it behaves like a frame and you can do all things whatever you do with frames. Suppose you have a main frame that consists of 20–30 different modules to be integrated. Then all you will have to do is to create each module as a JPanel and insert them inside frame. If necessary, integrate panel into another panel, no worry!

16.5.5 BoxLayout and Box

The swing package includes another interesting general-purpose layout manager namely **BoxLayout** that arranges the components either horizontally or vertically. The main advantage of BoxLayout is its ability to preserve the width and height of the components. That is, the components will not wrap when the frame is resized too. The syntax of BoxLayout is shown in Figure 16.5.

Figure 16.5. Syntax of BoxLayout

```
BoxLayout(container, BoxLayout.X_AXIS)    // left to right
placement
BoxLayout(container, BoxLayout.Y_AXIS)    // top to bottom
placement
```

In the program depicted in Listing 16.9, we will display three buttons of different sizes horizontally and vertically using BoxLayout.

Listing 16.9. Buttons Using BoxLayout

```java
// BoxLayout1.java
import java.awt.*;
import javax.swing.*;

public class BoxLayout1 extends JFrame
{
    public BoxLayout1()
    {
        JPanel jp = new JPanel();
        jp.setLayout(new BoxLayout(jp, BoxLayout.X_AXIS));
        jp.add(new JButton("Button 1"));
        jp.add(new JButton("2"));
        jp.add(new JButton("Button Three"));
        add("North", jp);

        jp = new JPanel();
        jp.setLayout(new BoxLayout(jp, BoxLayout.Y_AXIS));
        jp.add(new JButton("Button 1"));
        jp.add(new JButton("2"));
        jp.add(new JButton("Button Three"));
        add("South", jp);
    }
```

```
    public static void main(String[] args)
    {
        BoxLayout1 f = new BoxLayout1();
        // frame properties
        f.setTitle("Buttons using Box Layout");
        f.setSize(300,200);
        f.setLocationRelativeTo(null);   // centres to screen
        f.setDefaultCloseOperation(JFrame.EXIT_ON_CLOSE); // closes
        frame
        f.setVisible(true);
    }
}
```

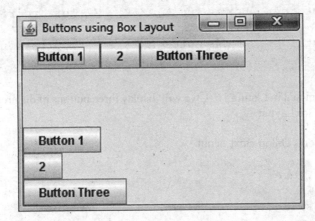

In this program, all three buttons are of different sizes and box layout manager preserves the sizes of the buttons. If you have added these buttons to grid layout, you will see all buttons are placed in equal sizes.

The BoxLayout is set to JPanel and all swing components are added to JPanel either horizontally or vertically. Generally, BoxLayout does not use gaps in between components. If you want to control spacing between components, you should use Box container that uses in turn BoxLayout as its layout manager.

Box is another lightweight container that uses internally BoxLayout manager to arrange components left to right horizontally using *static createHorizontalBox()* method or top to bottom vertically using *static createVerticalBox()* method. The add() method inserts a component to box. Let us now create three buttons and store them inside horizontal box and vertical box containers as illustrated in Listing 16.10.

Listing 16.10. Buttons Inside Box

```
// Box1.java
import java.awt.*;
import javax.swing.*;
```

```java
public class Box1 extends JFrame
{
    public Box1()
    {
        Box box = Box.createHorizontalBox();
        box.add(new JButton("Button 1"));
        box.add(new JButton("2"));
        box.add(new JButton("Button Three"));
        add("North", box);

        box = Box.createVerticalBox();
        box.add(new JButton("Button 1"));
        box.add(new JButton("2"));
        box.add(new JButton("Button Three"));
        add("South", box);
    }
    public static void main(String[] args)
    {
        Box1 f = new Box1();
        // frame properties
        f.setTitle("Buttons using Box");
        f.setSize(300,200);
        f.setLocationRelativeTo(null);    // centres to screen
        f.setDefaultCloseOperation(JFrame.EXIT_ON_CLOSE); // closes
        frame
        f.setVisible(true);
    }
}
```

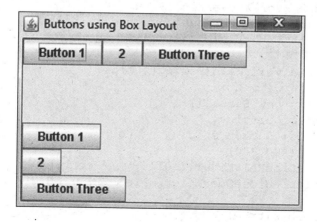

If you want to leave some space in between components, then Box provides three types of fillers namely **strut**, *glue* and *rigid area*. There are couple of methods to create these fillers with which you can create gaps. Remember these gaps are also identified as components and so you need to add them to Box as a normal component.

If you need fixed amount of space (in pixels) in between two components, then you should use either horizontal strut or vertical strut. The *createHorizontalStrut()* gives gap between two horizontal components whereas *createVerticalStrut()* gives gap between two vertical components. Listing 16.11 explains the application of struts.

Listing 16.11. Buttons Using Strut Gap

```java
// Strut1.java
import java.awt.*;
import javax.swing.*;

public class Strut1 extends JFrame
{
    public Strut1()
    {
        Box box = Box.createHorizontalBox();
        box.add(new JButton("Button 1"));
        box.add(box.createHorizontalStrut(20));
        box.add(new JButton("2"));
        box.add(box.createHorizontalStrut(20));
        box.add(new JButton("Button Three"));
        add("North", box);

        box = Box.createVerticalBox();
        box.add(new JButton("Button 1"));
        box.add(box.createVerticalStrut(20));
        box.add(new JButton("2"));
        box.add(box.createVerticalStrut(20));
        box.add(new JButton("Button Three"));
        add("South", box);
    }
    public static void main(String[] args)
    {
        Strut1 f = new Strut1();
        // frame properties
        f.setTitle("Button spacing using strut");
        f.setSize(400,300);
        f.setLocationRelativeTo(null);  // centres to screen
        f.setDefaultCloseOperation(JFrame.EXIT_ON_CLOSE); // closes
        frame
        f.setVisible(true);
    }
}
```

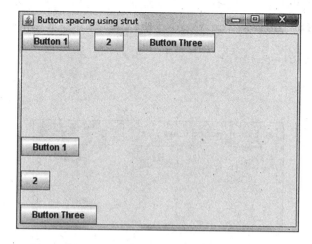

Suppose you have fixed-sized components that are to be placed either horizontally or vertically with gaps that can stretch to the edges of the frame. Then, you should use either horizontal glue (with createHorizontalGlue() method) or vertical glue (with createVerticalGlue() method) which controls gaps between components evenly as illustrated in Listing 16.12.

Listing 16.12. Buttons with Glue Gap

```
// Glue1.java
import java.awt.*;
import javax.swing.*;

public class Glue1 extends JFrame
{
    public Glue1()
    {
        Box box = Box.createHorizontalBox();
        box.add(new JButton("B1"));
        box.add(box.createHorizontalGlue());
        box.add(new JButton("B2"));
        box.add(box.createHorizontalGlue());
        box.add(new JButton("B3"));
        add("North", box);
    }
    public static void main(String[] args)
    {
        Glue1 f = new Glue1();
        // frame properties
        f.setTitle("Button spacing using Glue");
        f.setSize(300,200);
        f.setLocationRelativeTo(null);   // centres to screen
```

```
        f.setDefaultCloseOperation(JFrame.EXIT_ON_CLOSE); // closes
        frame
        f.setVisible(true);
    }
}
```

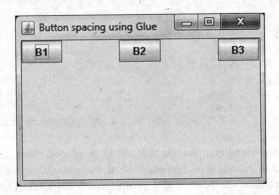

Here in this program, you will see the gaps between B1, B2 and B3 are stretched equally with respect to the edges of the frame.

Finally if you need gap both horizontally and vertically between two components, then *createRigidArea()* gives us gaps horizontally as well as vertically. To create gap component, you will have to instantiate *Dimension(w,h)* object with necessary pixels for width and height. For instance, Example 16.1 creates rigid area of size 10 by 15 between two buttons.

Example 16.1. Rigid Area

```
Box box = Box.createHorizontalBox();
box.add(new JButton("B1"));
box.add(box.createRigidArea(new Dimension(10,15)));
box.add(new JButton("B2"));
```

16.6 EVENT HANDLING REVISITED

Generally components will fire events and the registered listener for an event will act upon it. The event listener is an object of an event type. So all you need to do is to register listeners (using *addXXXListener()* methods where XXX denotes event name such as *Action, Key, Text, Mouse, MouseMotion, Item, Adjustment, Window* or *Focus*) for the events that are fired by components and supply event logic which specifies what is to be done when a particular event is fired. Remember your listener object should implement appropriate interface and override the methods that are available for the event listener.

In Figure 16.6, you will observe event names, its corresponding listerer interface name and a list of components that will fire these events. Though you have been introduced to only label and button components so far, you will also encounter some more names of the components you have never seen in Figure 16.6.

Figure 16.6. Event, Listeners and Firing Components

Name of the Event	Corresponding Listener Interface	Components Firing this Event
ActionEvent	ActionListener	JButton, JTextField, JMenuItem, JMenu, JPopupMenu
DocumentEvent	DocumentListener	JTextArea, JTextField
ItemEvent	ItemListener	JCheckBox, JCheckBoxMenuItem, JComboBox
ListSelectionEvent	ListSelectionListener	JList
KeyEvent	KeyListener	Any component
MouseEvent	MouseListener	Any component
MouseEvent	MouseMotionListener	Any component
AdjustmentEvent	AdjustmentListener	JScrollbar
WindowEvent	WindowListener	Any subclass of window such as JFrame, JDialog, JFileDialog
FocusEvent	FocusListener	Any component
ChangeEvent	ChangeListener	JSlider, JTabbedPane
HyperlinkEvent	HyperlinkListener	JEditorPane

Here each component supports only few types of events. Further each listener in Figure 16.6 has a collection of methods that can be overridden. In Figure 16.7, you will learn all methods that are part of each listener interfaces.

In Figure 16.7, you might see there are some listeners that have more than one interface methods. Since your listener object will implement these listener interfaces, overridding more than one method

Figure 16.7. Listeners and their Methods

Listener Interface	Listener Methods
ActionListener	actionPerformed(ActionEvent)
ItemListener	itemStateChanged(ItemEvent)
DocumentListener	changedUpdate(DocumentEvent) insertUpdate(DocumentEvent) removeUpdate(DocumentEvent)
ListSelectionListener	valueChanged(ListSelectionEvent)
KeyListener	keyPressed(KeyEvent) keyReleased(KeyEvent) keyTyped(KeyEvent)
AdjustmentListener	adjustmentValueChanged(AdjustmentEvent)
MouseListener	mouseClicked(MouseEvent) mouseEntered(MouseEvent) mouseExited(MouseEvent) mousePressed(MouseEvent) mouseReleased(MouseEvent)

MouseMotionListener	mouseDragged(MouseEvent) mouseMoved(MouseEvent)
WindowListener	windowOpened(WindowEvent) windowClosed(WindowEvent) windowClosing(WindowEvent) windowActivated(WindowEvent) windowDeactivated(WindowEvent) windowIconified(WindowEvent) windowDeiconified(WindowEvent)
FocusListener	focusGained(FocusEvent) focusLost(FocusEvent)
ChangeListener	stateChanged(ChangeEvent)
HyperlinkListener	hyperlinkUpdate(HyperlinkEvent)

Figure 16.8. Listeners and their Adapters

Listener	Equivalent Adapter
KeyListener	KeyAdapter
MouseListener	MouseAdapter
MouseMotionListener	MouseMotionAdapter
WindowListener	WindowAdapter
FocusListener	FocusAdapter

is combersome as we are interested to override only one method and not all methods. To solve this issue, Java provides **Adapter** classes with which it is enough to override only the method you are interested in. Figure 16.8 depicts listeners and its adapter equivalent.

So all you have to do is to just extend an Adapter class and override the respective method you are interested in to override. For example, let us now override windowClosing() method of Window-Adapter class in BoxFrame application as shown in Figure 16.9.

Figure 16.9. BoxFrame with WindowClosing()

```
// BoxFrame2.java
import java.awt.*;
import javax.swing.*;
import java.awt.event.*;

public class BoxFrame2 extends JFrame
{
    public BoxFrame2()
    {
        JPanel jp = new JPanel();
        jp.setLayout(new BoxLayout(jp, BoxLayout.Y_AXIS));
```

```
       jp.add(new JButton("Button 1"));
       jp.add(new JButton("2"));
       jp.add(new JButton("Button Three"));
       add("North", jp);
       addWindowListener(new MyWindowA());
    }

    class MyWindowA extends WindowAdapter
    {
       public void windowClosing(WindowEvent e)
       {
            System.exit(0);
       }
    }

    public static void main(String[] args)
    {
       BoxFrame2 f = new BoxFrame2();
       // frame properties
       f.setTitle("BoxLayout with Window Adapter");
       f.setSize(300,200);
       f.setLocationRelativeTo(null);   // centres to screen
       f.setVisible(true);
    }
}
```

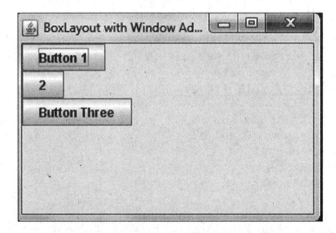

In the above code, as usual, three buttons are added to panel according to box layout. The interesting part in the program is how we handle clicking of close button of the window. The windowClosing() method is overridden by extending WindowAdapter class. Inside the method, we simply call exit() method.

16.7 PROBLEM: COLOR LABEL APPLICATION

The ColorLabel application will create a label and a button. Whenever this button is clicked, the foreground colour of the label should be updated with a new colour. Also, ClockLabel class (that we created in section 16.3) should be instantiated so that it will display current time. The complete source code is depicted in Listing 16.13.

Listing 16.13. Colour Label Application

```java
// ColorLabel.java
import javax.swing.*;
import java.awt.*;
import java.awt.event.*;
import java.util.*;

public class ColorLabel extends JFrame
{
    // create components
    JLabel lblHello = new JLabel("Hello", JLabel.CENTER);;
    JButton btnChange = new JButton("Change Color");
    JButton btnExit = new JButton("Exit");

    // also display clock
    ClockLabel clock = new ClockLabel("Current Time: ");

    public ColorLabel()
    {
        // add clock north
        add("North", clock);
        lblHello.setFont(new Font("Serif", Font.BOLD, 36));
        // add label to north
        add("Center", lblHello);

        // add buttons to south
        JPanel p = new JPanel();
        p.add(btnChange);
        p.add(btnExit);
        add("South", p);

        //register listener for button
        btnChange.addActionListener(new BtnChangeL());
        btnExit.addActionListener(new BtnExitL());
    }

    class BtnChangeL implements ActionListener
```

```
{
    public void actionPerformed(ActionEvent e)
    {
        Random ra = new Random();
        int r = ra.nextInt(255);
        int g = ra.nextInt(255);
        int b = ra.nextInt(255);
        lblHello.setForeground(new Color(r,g,b));
    }
}

class BtnExitL implements ActionListener
{
    public void actionPerformed(ActionEvent e)
    {
        System.exit(0);
    }
}

public static void main(String[] args)
{
    ColorLabel f = new ColorLabel();
    // frame properties
    f.setTitle("Color Label");
    f.setSize(300,200);
    f.setLocationRelativeTo(null);  // centres to screen
    f.setDefaultCloseOperation(JFrame.EXIT_ON_CLOSE); // closes
    frame
    f.setVisible(true);
}
}
```

Inside actionPerformed(), three random numbers from 0 to 255 are created representing colour values for red, green and blue and the label is set with this new colour. The ColorLabel object, being a thread, displays current time continuously.

16.8 PROBLEM: THROW BALL APPLICATION

The ThrowBall application moves a random-coloured circle to random locations whenever a button is pressed. A coloured circle is drawn using fillOval() method onto JPanel. When a button is clicked, you need to simply repaint() the panel. That is it. Listing 16.14 illustrates throw ball application.

Listing 16.14. Throw Ball Application

```java
// ThrowBall.java
import javax.swing.*;
import java.awt.*;
import java.awt.event.*;
import java.util.*;

class BallPanel extends JPanel
{
    Random r = new Random();

    public void paintComponent(Graphics g)
    {
        super.paintComponent(g);
        // generate rgb values
        int red = r.nextInt(255);
        int green = r.nextInt(255);
        int blue = r.nextInt(255);
        // set the colour
        g.setColor(new Color(red, green, blue));

        // get random coord values
        int x = r.nextInt(getWidth());
        int y = r.nextInt(getHeight());
        // draw circle
        g.fillOval(x, y, 25, 25);
    }
}

public class ThrowBall extends JFrame
{
    // create components
    JButton btnThrow = new JButton("Throw");
    JButton btnExit = new JButton("Exit");
    // create ball panel
```

```java
    BallPanel bpanel = new BallPanel();
    public ThrowBall()
    {
        // add ball panel to centre
        add("Center", bpanel);

        // add buttons to south
        JPanel p = new JPanel();
        p.add(btnThrow);
        p.add(btnExit);
        add("South", p);

        //register listener for button
        btnThrow.addActionListener(new BtnThrowL());
        btnExit.addActionListener(new BtnExitL());
    }

    class BtnThrowL implements ActionListener
    {
        public void actionPerformed(ActionEvent e)
        {
            bpanel.repaint();
        }
    }

    class BtnExitL implements ActionListener
    {
        public void actionPerformed(ActionEvent e)
        {
            System.exit(0);
        }
    }

    public static void main(String[] args)
    {
        ThrowBall f = new ThrowBall();
        // frame properties
        f.setTitle("Throwing Ball");
        f.setSize(400,350);
        f.setLocationRelativeTo(null);  // centres to screen
        f.setDefaultCloseOperation(JFrame.EXIT_ON_CLOSE); // closes
        frame
        f.setVisible(true);
    }
}
```

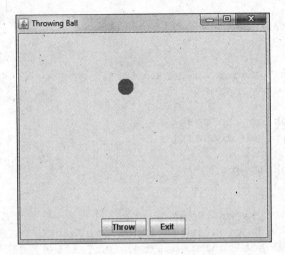

16.9 CREATING TEXT FIELD AND TEXT AREA

The JTextField holds one line of text and inherits from JTextComponent, which in turn inherits from JComponent. You can specify the size of the textfield while creating an instance of JTextField as depicted in Example 16.2.

Example 16.2. JTextField

```
JTextField tf = new JTextField()
JTextField tf = new JTextField(25)
```

The setText() and getText() methods are used to store and retrieve text from textfield. In order to pro-vide password like behaviors you can use its subclass **JPasswordField** so that the characters entered will not be visible and will be echoed with *. With an another interesting subclass **JFormattedText-Field**, you can specify a valid set of characters that can be typed in a textfield.

When you press ENTER key while typing, JTextField object fires ActionEvent. Further you can register TextListener to the textfield so that you can handle the associated TextEvent. Since all com-ponents fire KeyEvent and also JTextField, you can handle KeyEvent too. Here is an example shown in Listing 16.15 that receives username in textfield and password in passwordfield. When submit button is clicked, both username and password details are displayed in the command prompt for verification.

Listing 16.15. User Login Frame

```
// LoginFrame.java
import javax.swing.*;
import java.awt.*;
import java.awt.event.*;
```

```java
public class LoginFrame extends JFrame
{
    JLabel lblTitle = new JLabel("User Login", JLabel.CENTER);
    JLabel lblUser = new JLabel("Enter User name");
    JLabel lblPwd = new JLabel("Enter Password");

    JTextField tfUser = new JTextField(25);
    JPasswordField tfPwd = new JPasswordField(25);

    JButton btnSubmit = new JButton("Submit");

    public LoginFrame()
    {
        // add title to north
        add("North", lblTitle);

        JPanel p = new JPanel();
        p.setLayout(new GridLayout(2,2));
        p.add(lblUser);
        p.add(tfUser);
        p.add(lblPwd);
        p.add(tfPwd);

        // add lbl and tf to centre
        add("Center", p);

        // add btn to south
        p = new JPanel();
        p.add(btnSubmit);
        add("South", p);

        // register listeners to handle events
        btnSubmit.addActionListener(new bsubmitL());
    }

    class bsubmitL implements ActionListener
    {
        public void actionPerformed(ActionEvent e)
        {
            System.out.println(tfUser.getText() + " : " + tfPwd.
            getText());
        }
    }
}
```

```
    public static void main(String[] args)
    {
        LoginFrame f = new LoginFrame();
        // frame properties
        f.setTitle("User Login");
        f.setSize(300,150);
        f.setLocationRelativeTo(null);  // centres to screen
        f.setDefaultCloseOperation(JFrame.EXIT_ON_CLOSE); // closes
        frame
        f.setVisible(true);
    }
}
```

In this program, JPasswordField component echoes a * character for each password character we type. You can also change this echo character with your own echo character using setEchoChar() method.

The JTextArea component holds multiline text, and its size is determined by its row and column values. Similar to JTextField, it supports setText() and getText() methods to store and retrieve its contents. The append() method appends a string to the end of the text. The setEditable() method enables (by default) or disables editing the text. This is especially useful when you want to treat text area only as a display device. The setLineWrap() enables wrapping of lines if set to true. The setWrapStyle-Word() supports wrapping of words if set to true. The JTextArea class does not provide scroll bars in contrast to awt.TextArea. So if you need scrolling behavior, you need to insert JTextArea inside JScrollPane component. Now let us create a simple text area as shown in Example 16.3.

Example 16.3. Creating a JTextArea

```
JTextArea ta = new JTextArea(5, 25);   // 5 rows, 25 columns
ta.setLineWrap(true);
ta.setWrapStyleWord(true)
ta.setEditable(false);
ta.setFont(new Font("Courier", Font.BOLD, 14));
JScrollPane spane = new JScrollPane(ta);
```

16.10 PROBLEM: FILE LISTER

We want to revise our earlier file lister application (section 14.2.3) so that it will display the contents of a text file inside a text area instead of a command prompt. Once the user types the file name in textfield and presses a button, the file contents should be appended to text area. Ofcourse, we need an instance of FileReader that will open a text file and read line by line. The complete program is illustrated in Listing 16.16.

Listing 16.16. File Lister Application

```java
// FileLister.java
import javax.swing.*;
import java.awt.*;
import java.awt.event.*;
import java.io.*;

public class FileLister extends JFrame
{
    JLabel lblMsg = new JLabel("Type file: ");
    JTextField tf = new JTextField(25);
    JTextArea ta = new JTextArea(10,50);
    JButton btnShow = new JButton("Show File");

    public FileLister()
    {
        // set properties of ta
        ta.setEditable(false);
        ta.setFont(new Font("Courier", Font.ITALIC, 12));

        Box box = Box.createHorizontalBox();
        box.add(lblMsg);
        box.add(tf);
        box.add(btnShow);
        add("North", box);

        JScrollPane pane = new JScrollPane(ta);
        add("Center", pane);

        // register listerners
        btnShow.addActionListener(new bselectL());
        tf.addActionListener(new tfL());
    }

    class tfL implements ActionListener
    {
            public void actionPerformed(ActionEvent e)
```

```java
                    {
                        showFile();
                    }
        }
    class bselectL implements ActionListener
    {
        public void actionPerformed(ActionEvent e)
        {
                showFile();
        }
    }

    public void showFile()
    {
                String fileName;
                // if file name not typed, show current file
                if((fileName = tf.getText()).equals(""))
                    fileName = "FileLister.java";

                // display contents
                String s;
                try
                {
                BufferedReader in = new BufferedReader(
                        new FileReader(fileName));
                while ((s = in.readLine()) != null)
                        ta.setText(ta.getText() + s + "\n");
                // close stream
                in.close();
                }catch (IOException e1) { }
    }

    public static void main(String[] args)
    {
        FileLister f = new FileLister();
        // frame properties
        f.setTitle("File Lister");
        f.setSize(400,500);
        f.setLocationRelativeTo(null);  // centres to screen
        f.setDefaultCloseOperation(JFrame.EXIT_ON_CLOSE); // closes
        frame
        f.setVisible(true);
    }
}
```

When a user types file name and presses ShowFile button, the text area is inserted with the contents of the selected file. Another interesting part of this program is that action listener is also registered for textfield so that users can also press ENTER key once they type file name in the textfield. You might feel typing file name is boring. So do not worry, you will be introduced to a UI component that will allow you to choose file name directly from Windows dialogs in section 16.15. The rest of the source code is self-explanatory.

16.11 PROBLEM: NUMERIC TEXT FIELD

In many applications, users should enter only numeric values in a text field. For example, users should enter only digits for amount and not any other characters. Even if they enter other characters, the program should not accept those characters. Listing 16.17 displays a text field that accepts only digits.

Listing 16.17. Numeric Textfield

```
// NumericTF.java
import javax.swing.*;
import javax.swing.event.*;
import javax.swing.text.*;
import java.awt.*;
import java.awt.event.*;

public class NumericTF extends JFrame
{
    JTextField tf = new JTextField(30);
    JLabel lbl = new JLabel(" ");

    public NumericTF()
    {
```

```java
        Box box = Box.createVerticalBox();
        box.add(tf);
        box.add(lbl);
        add(box);

        tf.addKeyListener(new TFL());
    }

    class TFL extends KeyAdapter
    {
        public void keyPressed(KeyEvent e)
        {
            String value = tf.getText();
            if (e.getKeyChar() >= '0' && e.getKeyChar() <= '9')
            {
                tf.setEditable(true);
                lbl.setText(" ");
            }
            else
            {
                tf.setEditable(false);
                lbl.setText("Type only digits(0-9)");
            }
        }

    }

    public static void main(String[] args)
    {
        NumericTF f = new NumericTF();
        f.setTitle("Numeric Textfield");
        f.setSize(300,100);
        f.setLocationRelativeTo(null);
        f.setDefaultCloseOperation(JFrame.EXIT_ON_CLOSE);
        f.setVisible(true);
    }
}
```

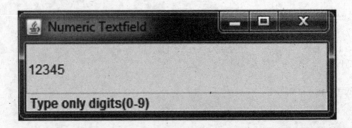

16.12 PROBLEM: TEXT COPY CAT

Let us develop a funny application that echoes whatever you type in a text field to another text field an illustrated in Listing 16.18.

Listing 16.18. Text Copy Cat

```java
// TextCopyCat.java
import javax.swing.*;
import javax.swing.event.*;
import javax.swing.text.*;
import java.awt.*;
import java.awt.event.*;

public class TextCopyCat extends JFrame
{
    JTextField tf1 = new JTextField(30);
    JTextField tf2 = new JTextField(30);

    public TextCopyCat()
    {
        Box box = Box.createVerticalBox();
        box.add(tf1);
        box.add(tf2);
        add(box);

        tf1.getDocument().addDocumentListener(new TF1L());
    }

    class TF1L implements DocumentListener
    {
        public void changedUpdate(DocumentEvent e) { }
        public void insertUpdate(DocumentEvent e)
        {
            tf2.setText(tf1.getText());
        }
        public void removeUpdate(DocumentEvent e)
        {
            tf2.setText(tf1.getText());
        }
    }

    public static void main(String[] args)
    {
        TextCopyCat f = new TextCopyCat();
        f.setTitle("Text CopyCat");
        f.setSize(200,100);
```

```
        f.setLocationRelativeTo(null);
        f.setDefaultCloseOperation(JFrame.EXIT_ON_CLOSE);
        f.setVisible(true);
    }
}
```

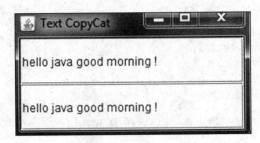

16.13 CREATING CHECKBOX, RADIOBUTTON, COMBOBOX AND LIST

16.13.1 CheckBoxes

You can create a checkbox using JCheckBox class that is nothing but an item which can be selected or deselected. A checkbox generates one ItemEvent and one ActionEvent when it is clicked (selected or deselected). It is generally enough you handle any one of these two events. You can check whether a checkbox is selected or not using isSelected() method. The getText() returns the label of a checkbox. A checkbox can also have an image icon apart from its title string. Now let us define few checkboxes representing names of some programming languages as shown in Figure 16.10.

Figure 16.10. Checkboxes

```
JCheckBox cbRuby = new JCheckBox("Ruby");
JCheckBox cbJava = new JCheckBox("Java");
JCheckBox cbPython = new JCheckiBox("Python");
```

In Listing 16.19, we create a panel that will include three checkboxes and a textfield. Whenever a checkbox is clicked, the name of the checkbox is displayed in the textfield.

Listing 16.19. Handling Checkbox Clicks

```
// CheckBox1.java
import javax.swing.*;
import java.awt.*;
import java.awt.event.*;

class CheckBoxPanel extends JPanel
```

```
{
    JCheckBox cbRuby = new JCheckBox("Ruby");
    JCheckBox cbJava = new JCheckBox("Java");
    JCheckBox cbPython = new JCheckBox("Python");
    JTextField status = new JTextField(20);

    public CheckBoxPanel()
    {
        // set grid layout
        setLayout(new GridLayout(2,1));

        // add cb to box
        Box box = Box.createHorizontalBox();
        box.add(cbRuby);
        box.add(box.createHorizontalGlue());
        box.add(cbJava);
        box.add(box.createHorizontalGlue());
        box.add(cbPython);

        // add them to frame
        add(box);
        add(status);

        // register listeners
        cbRuby.addItemListener(new cbRubyL());
        cbJava.addItemListener(new cbJavaL());
        cbPython.addItemListener(new cbPythonL());
    }

    // inner class for cbRuby
    class cbRubyL implements ItemListener
    {
        public void itemStateChanged(ItemEvent e)
        {
            status.setText("Check box " + cbRuby.getText() + " is
            clicked");
        }
    }

    class cbJavaL implements ItemListener
    {
        public void itemStateChanged(ItemEvent e)
        {
            status.setText("Check box " + cbJava.getText() + " is
            clicked");
```

```
      }
   }

   class cbPythonL implements ItemListener
   {
      public void itemStateChanged(ItemEvent e)
      {
          status.setText("Check box " + cbPython.getText()
          + " is clicked");
      }
   }
}

public class CheckBox1 extends JFrame
{
   public static void main(String[] args)
   {
      CheckBox1 f = new CheckBox1();
      CheckBoxPanel cbp = new CheckBoxPanel();
      f.add("Center", cbp);

      // frame properties
      f.setTitle("CheckBox Demo");
      f.setSize(300,100);
      f.setLocationRelativeTo(null);  // centres to screen
      f.setDefaultCloseOperation(JFrame.EXIT_ON_CLOSE); // closes
      frame
      f.setVisible(true);
   }
}
```

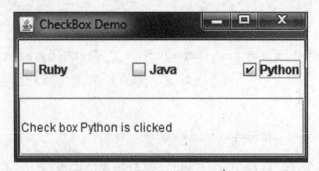

For each checkbox, we need to register ItemListener and override itemStateChanged() method. Inside this method, we simply extract the name of the checkbox using getText() method and update the textfield accordingly. We create a public class and add this checkbox panel to this frame.

16.13.2 Radio Buttons

Radio buttons are created using JRadioButton class. Radiobuttons allow us to select any one of the buttons from a group of buttons. Radio buttons are similar to checkboxes but with a difference. At any point of time, you can select only one radio button whereas you can select multiple checkboxes. To have a group behavior, all radio buttons are added to ButtonGroup object. Radio buttons fire ItemEvent and ActionEvent when it gets clicked. Figure 16.11 illustrates the creation of radio buttons.

Figure 16.11. Creating Radio Buttons

```
JRadioButton rbMale = new JRadioButton("Male");
JRadioButton rbFemale = new JRadioButton("Female");

ButtonGroup bg = new ButtonGroup();
bg.add(rbMale);
bg.add(rbFemale);
```

To illustrate the functioning of radio buttons, let us now develop an application that will add three radio buttons in a panel and displays its name onto the textfield of CheckBoxPanel class as explained in Listing 16.20.

Listing 16.20. Handling Radio Button Selection

```
// Radiobutton1.java
import javax.swing.*;
import java.awt.*;
import java.awt.event.*;

class RadioPanel extends JPanel
{
    JRadioButton rbSlow = new JRadioButton("SlowTrack");
    JRadioButton rbMedium = new JRadioButton("MediumTrack");
    JRadioButton rbFast = new JRadioButton("FastTrack");

    // RadioPanel is added to this CheckBoxPanel
    CheckBoxPanel cbp;

    public RadioPanel(CheckBoxPanel p)
    {
        // receive handle to update cbp
        cbp = p;

        ButtonGroup bg = new ButtonGroup();
        bg.add(rbSlow);
        bg.add(rbMedium);
```

```java
        bg.add(rbFast);

    // add cb to box
    Box box = Box.createVerticalBox();
    box.add(rbSlow);
    box.add(box.createVerticalGlue());
    box.add(rbMedium);
    box.add(box.createVerticalGlue());
    box.add(rbFast);

    // add
    setLayout(new BorderLayout());
    add("Center", box);

    // register listeners
    rbSlow.addItemListener(new rbSlowL());
    rbMedium.addItemListener(new rbMediumL());
    rbFast.addItemListener(new rbFastL());
}

// inner class
class rbSlowL implements ItemListener
{
    public void itemStateChanged(ItemEvent e)
    {
        cbp.status.setText("Radio button " + rbSlow.getText()
        + " is clicked");
    }
}


class rbMediumL implements ItemListener
{
    public void itemStateChanged(ItemEvent e)
    {
        cbp.status.setText("Radio button " + rbMedium.
        getText() + " is clicked");
    }
}


class rbFastL implements ItemListener
{
    public void itemStateChanged(ItemEvent e)
    {
```

```
                    cbp.status.setText("Radio button " + rbFast.getText()
                    + " is clicked");
            }
        }
}


public class Radiobutton1 extends JFrame
{
    public static void main(String[] args)
    {
        Radiobutton1 f = new Radiobutton1();
        CheckBoxPanel cbp = new CheckBoxPanel();
        f.add("Center", cbp);
        f.add("East", new RadioPanel(cbp));

        // frame properties
        f.setTitle("RadioButton Demo");
        f.setSize(300,100);
        f.setLocationRelativeTo(null);   // centres to screen
        f.setDefaultCloseOperation(JFrame.EXIT_ON_CLOSE); // closes
        frame
        f.setVisible(true);
    }
}
```

In this example, we try to combine the user interface of radiobutton panel with CheckBoxPanel. We instantiate CheckBoxPanel here and add it to the centre of the frame and radio button panel is added to the east of the frame.

16.13.3 Combo Boxes

JComboBox allows us to select any one of the set of items. It is also called dropdown list as the full list will be displayed when the down arrow button is clicked. The JComboBox will fire ItemEvent and ActionEvent when an item is selected. The getSelectedItem() returns a currently selected item as String while addItem() adds an Object to combo box. You can populate combo box using array of objects or a Vector directly. Here is an example shown in Figure 16.12 that creates a combo box.

Figure 16.12. Creating a Combo Box

```
String[] Mstatus = {"Single", "Married", "Engaged"};
JComboBox cb = new JComboBox(Mstatus);
```

Let us display a combo box containing information about marital status. The textfield should be updated with the text of the selected item when a user clicks an item in the combo box as shown in Listing 16.21.

Listing 16.21. Selecting Item from Combo Box

```java
// ComboBox1.java
import javax.swing.*;
import java.awt.*;
import java.awt.event.*;

public class ComboBox1 extends JFrame
{
    String[] Mstatus = {"Single", "Married", "Engaged"};
    JComboBox cb = new JComboBox(Mstatus);
    JTextField status = new JTextField(20);

    public ComboBox1()
    {
        // make status non editable
        status.setEditable(false);

        // add cb to box
        Box box = Box.createVerticalBox();
        box.add(cb);
        box.add(status);
        // add them to frame
        add(box);

        // register listeners
        cb.addItemListener(new cbL());
    }

    class cbL implements ItemListener
    {
        public void itemStateChanged(ItemEvent e)
        {
            status.setText(cb.getSelectedItem() + " is
            selected");
        }
    }
```

```
    }

    public static void main(String[] args)
    {
        ComboBox1 f = new ComboBox1();
        // frame properties
        f.setTitle("CheckBox Demo");
        f.setSize(300,150);
        f.setLocationRelativeTo(null);  // centres to screen
        f.setDefaultCloseOperation(JFrame.EXIT_ON_CLOSE); // closes
        frame
        f.setVisible(true);Li
    }
}
```

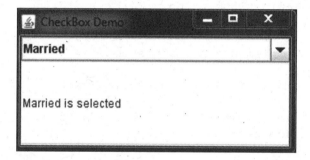

The getSelectedItem() returns the name of the selected item from the combo box and is displayed in the textfield. In the previous example, combo box has been populated with item names while it was instantiated first. No items were added when the program was running or at runtime. It is also possible to add an item to combo box at runtime. The addItem() appends an item to combobox at runtime as shown in Listing 16.22.

Listing 16.22. Adding Item to Combo Box at Runtime

```
// DynamicComboBox.java
import javax.swing.*;
import java.awt.*;
import java.awt.event.*;

public class DynamicComboBox extends JFrame
{
    String[] Mstatus = {"Single", "Married", "Engaged"};
    JComboBox cb = new JComboBox(Mstatus);
    JTextField item = new JTextField(20);
    JTextField status = new JTextField(20);
```

```java
public DynamicComboBox()
{
    // make status non editable
    status.setEditable(false);

    // add cb to box
    Box box = Box.createVerticalBox();
    box.add(cb);
    box.add(item);
    box.add(status);
    // add them to frame
    add(box);

    // register listeners
    cb.addItemListener(new cbL());
    item.addActionListener(new itemL());
}

class itemL implements ActionListener
{
    public void actionPerformed(ActionEvent e)
    {
        // if a text entered, then add to cb
        cb.addItem(item.getText());
        // clear item
        item.setText("");
    }
}

class cbL implements ItemListener
{
    public void itemStateChanged(ItemEvent e)
    {
        status.setText(cb.getSelectedItem() + " is
        selected");
    }
}

public static void main(String[] args)
{
    DynamicComboBox f = new DynamicComboBox();
    // frame properties
    f.setTitle("Dynamic ComboBox Demo");
    f.setSize(300,150);
    f.setLocationRelativeTo(null);   // centres to screen
```

```
        f.setDefaultCloseOperation(JFrame.EXIT_ON_CLOSE); // closes
        frame
        f.setVisible(true);
    }
}
```

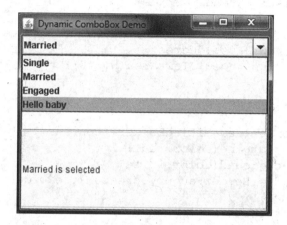

In this example, a combo box, textfield and uneditable textfield are added to frame using vertical box. The combo box was initialized with few items when it was created. Users are allowed to type item names to combo box in the textfield. Whenever a new item name is entered in the textfield, it gets appended to combobox immediately. The uneditable textfield behaves as a status which displays every change in the combo box.

16.13.4 Lists

A list can be created with JList and is another interesting JComponent that is very similar to JCombo-Box. From JList you can select one item, or multiple items. A list can be initialized using an array or vector of objects and displayed in one or more columns. The items from list can be selected in three ways: single click, multiple click (by holding Ctrl-key and clicking) and range click (by holding Shift-key and clicking).

The JList fires ListSelectionEvent when a single item or multiple items are selected. In order to process list clicks, ListSelectionListener interface should be implemented by overridding valueChanged() method with the handling behavior you want to include for the selection. The getSelectedValuesList() returns a List containing all selected items from JList. The getValueIsAdjusting() method from ListSelectionEvent helps us to ignore the same item being added to the list of selected items because of more than one event being fired. Listing 16.23 demonstrates the functioning of JList.

Listing 16.23. JList Handling

```
// List1.java
import javax.swing.*;
import java.awt.*;
```

```java
import java.awt.event.*;
import javax.swing.event.*;
import javax.swing.border.*;
import java.util.*;

public class List1 extends JFrame
{
    String[] degree = {"Bachelors", "Masters", "Doctoral"};
    JList lst = new JList(degree);
    JTextArea status = new JTextArea(5, 20);

    public List1()
    {
        lst.setBorder(new TitledBorder("Courses"));
        lst.setForeground(Color.red);
        lst.setBackground(Color.white);
        Border brd = BorderFactory.createMatteBorder(1, 1, 2, 2,
        Color.blue);
        status.setBorder(brd);

        // make status non editable
        status.setEditable(false);

        // add cb to box
        Box box = Box.createHorizontalBox();
        box.add(new JScrollPane(lst));
        box.add(new JScrollPane(status));
        // add them to frame
        add(box);

        // register listeners
        lst.addListSelectionListener(new lstL());
    }

    class lstL implements ListSelectionListener
    {
        public void valueChanged(ListSelectionEvent e)
        {
            if(e.getValueIsAdjusting())
                return;
            status.setText("");
            List list = lst.getSelectedValuesList();
            ListIterator it = list.listIterator();
            while (it.hasNext())
```

```
                         status.setText(status.getText() + it.next());
        }
    }

    public static void main(String[] args)
    {
        List1 f = new List1();
        // frame properties
        f.setTitle("JList handling");
        f.setSize(325,200);
        f.setLocationRelativeTo(null);   // centres to screen
        f.setDefaultCloseOperation(JFrame.EXIT_ON_CLOSE); // closes
        frame
        f.setVisible(true);
    }
}
```

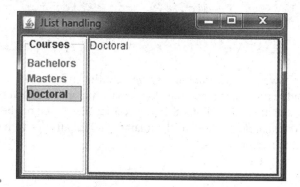

The JList is instantiated with an array of string items. The horizontal box contains the list and a text area. The list is surrounded by title border and the text area by matte border. Both list and text area are added to scrollpane that will allow us to view their contents with automatically added scrollbars if the contents do not fit into the components. As JList fires ListSelectionEvent, ListSelectedListener is registered that will handle list operations such as selecting an item from the list. The getValueIsAdjusting() returns true if the user is still manipulating the selection. Otherwise, getSelectedValuesList() returns a util.List instance that is iterated with ListIterator interface and text area updates each selected item.

16.14 DIALOG WINDOWS

Dialog windows are one of the important types of communication between the user and the application. The dialog windows are classified into two types: custom dialog windows and standard dialog windows. The JDialog class is used to create custom dialogs, where you will have to just extend JDialog class very similar to extending JFrame and you are done. The standard dialog windows are custom built-in swing and you need to instantiate them in order to include them inside your applications. Some of the standard dialog windows are **JOptionPane**, **JFileChooser** and **JColorChooser**. The dialog windows are also classified based on modality. While JDialog is nonmodal, then all standard dialog windows including JOptionPane, JFileChooser and JColorChooser are modal. In sections 16.15 to 16.17, let us explore these dialog windows with illustrative examples.

16.15 CHOOSING FILE NAMES

The swing.filechooser.JFileChooser class provides a graphical window for us to select a file or a directory from the list. You can select a file for either reading or storing data. The showOpenDialog() method displays a dialog window to select a file for reading data. Similarly showSaveDialog() displays file list to select a file for storing data. The getSelectedFile() returns the currently selected file as File object while getName() returns the string name of File object. Figure 16.13 illustrates the creation of JFileChooser.

Figure 16.13. JFileChooser

```
JFileChooser fc = new JFileChooser(); // sets fc to the current
working directory
fc.showOpenDialog();  // displays open dialog for reading
String fileName = fc.getSelectedFile().getName()  // returns
selected file name
```

The setFileFilter() allows us to set FileFilter so that the file chooser will display only files based on the selected type and restricts unwanted files from appearing in the directory listing. The FileNameExtensionFilter is a subclass of FileFilter that will restrict files based on the list of file extensions given as arguments. For example, Figure 16.14 explains filtering all files with extension ".java" and ".class" from the current directory.

Figure 16.14. Filter .Java Files

```
JFileChooser fc = new JFileChooser();
fc.setFileFilter(new FileNameExtensionFilter("Filtering Java
files", "java", "class");
```

The JFileChooser by default displays only files in the current directory. But setFileSelectionMode(int) method can be used to set file modes to directories as well as files and directories where int value 0, 1 or 2 indicate its file only, directory only or both types. Now in Listing 16.24, we will develop a GUI that will receive a file name from JFileChooser and display its name and directory in a textfield. The JFileChooser has been designed for both open and save mode.

Listing 16.24. Selecting File Names for Open and Save Modes

```
// FileChooser.java
import javax.swing.*;
import javax.swing.filechooser.*;
```

```java
import java.awt.*;
import java.awt.event.*;
import java.io.*;

public class FileChooser extends JFrame
{
    JTextField tfFile = new JTextField(25);
    JTextField tfDir = new JTextField(25);
    JLabel lblFile = new JLabel("Selected File: ");
    JLabel lblDir = new JLabel("Current Dir: ");

    JButton btnOpen = new JButton("Open");
    JButton btnSave = new JButton("Save");
    JButton btnExit = new JButton("Exit");

    String[] list = {".java", ".c", ".cpp", ".txt", ".class"};
    JComboBox cbMode = new JComboBox(list);

    String extn = ".java"; //  filter extension, by default java
    files

    public FileChooser()
    {
        Box box = Box.createVerticalBox();

        Box box1 = Box.createHorizontalBox();
        // first row
        box1.add(lblFile);
        box1.add(tfFile);
        // second row
        Box box11 = Box.createHorizontalBox();
        box11.add(lblDir);
        box11.add(tfDir);

        box.add(box1);
        box.add(box11);

        // third row
        Box box2 = Box.createHorizontalBox();
        box2.add(cbMode);
        box2.add(btnOpen);
        box2.add(btnSave);
        box2.add(btnExit);
        box.add(box2);
        add(box);
```

```java
        // register listerner for button
        cbMode.addItemListener(new ModeL());
        btnOpen.addActionListener(new OpenL());
        btnSave.addActionListener(new SaveL());
        btnExit.addActionListener(new ExitL());
}

class ModeL implements ItemListener
{
    public void itemStateChanged(ItemEvent e)
    {
        extn = (String)cbMode.getSelectedItem();
    }
}

class OpenL implements ActionListener
{
    public void actionPerformed(ActionEvent e)
    {
        // create file chooser
        JFileChooser fc = new JFileChooser();
        // set filter
        fc.setFileFilter(new FileNameExtensionFilter
        ("Opening files", extn));
        // show both files and directories
        fc.setFileSelectionMode(2);
        int val = fc.showOpenDialog(FileChooser.this);   //
        show it in this class
        // check if file name selected
        if(val == JFileChooser.APPROVE_OPTION)
        {
            // display selected file
            tfFile.setText(fc.getSelectedFile().getName());
            // display current directory
            tfDir.setText(fc.getCurrentDirectory().
            toString());
        }
        // you can also check for APPROVE_CANCEL option
    }
}

class SaveL implements ActionListener
{
    public void actionPerformed(ActionEvent e)
```

```
        {
            // create file chooser
            JFileChooser fc = new JFileChooser();
            // set filter
            fc.setFileFilter(new FileNameExtensionFilter("Saving
            files", extn));
            // show both files and directories
            fc.setFileSelectionMode(2);
            int val = fc.showSaveDialog(FileChooser.this);   //
            show it in this class
            // check if file name selected and display
            if(val == JFileChooser.APPROVE_OPTION)
            {
                // display selected file
                tfFile.setText(fc.getSelectedFile().getName());
                // display current directory
                tfDir.setText(fc.getCurrentDirectory().
                toString());
            }
            // you can also check for APPROVE_CANCEL option
        }
    }


class ExitL implements ActionListener
{
    public void actionPerformed(ActionEvent e)
    {
        System.exit(0);
    }
}


public static void main(String[] args)
{
    FileChooser f = new FileChooser();
    // frame properties
    f.setTitle("File Chooser");
    f.setSize(400,150);
    f.setLocationRelativeTo(null);   // centres to screen
    f.setDefaultCloseOperation(JFrame.EXIT_ON_CLOSE); // closes
    frame
    f.setVisible(true);
}
}
```

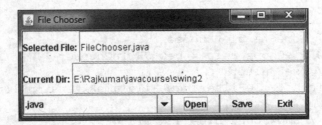

This application is yet another classic example of box layout manager. The user interface is divided into three rows. In the first row and second row, a label and textfield are added. The third row contains a combo box and three buttons. The combo box has been populated with five file extensions such as .java, .txt and others.

On clicking Open button, showOpenDialog() of FileChooser displays files and directories for user selection for open mode. The showOpenDialog() returns a value and you can check whether this value is same as JFileChooser.APPROVE_OPTION. If it is the same, then a file name is selected by user. Therefore file name and directory name are displayed in the respective textfields.

Similarly showSaveDialog() displays a dialog box so that users can choose a file name for writing. Once users select a file name, it will be displayed in the textfield along with its path name in another textfield.

16.16 CHOOSING COLORS

So far in this book, we have been setting colours to different objects by defining Color object. Instead of defining a colour, you can also choose colours directly from the colour palette. The *swing.color-chooser.JColorChooser* is an interesting class that will allow applications to choose colours from its palette. Once you instantiate JColorChooser object, you can just call ***showDialog(parent, title, initial-color)*** method that will display the colour chooser as a pop-up modal window from where you can select a colour from palette and return the selected colour. Here is an example depicted in Listing 16.25 that paints a JLabel with the colour selected from colour chooser.

Listing 16.25. Choosing Colours

```
// ColorChooser.java
import javax.swing.*;
import javax.swing.colorchooser.*;
import javax.swing.event.*;
import java.awt.*;
import java.awt.event.*;

public class ColorChooser extends JFrame
{
    JLabel lblTitle = new JLabel("Paint Me", JLabel.CENTER);
    JButton btnPaint = new JButton("Paint");

    public ColorChooser()
```

```
    {
        lblTitle.setFont(new Font("Serif", Font.BOLD, 48));
        add("Center", lblTitle);
        add("South", btnPaint);
        btnPaint.addActionListener(new PaintL());
    }

    class PaintL implements ActionListener
    {
        public void actionPerformed(ActionEvent e)
        {
            // create file chooser
            JColorChooser cc = new JColorChooser();
            Color c = cc.showDialog(ColorChooser.this,
                    "Select color", Color.white);
            lblTitle.setForeground(c);
        }
    }

    public static void main(String[] args)
    {
        ColorChooser f = new ColorChooser();
        // frame properties
        f.setTitle("Color Chooser");
        f.setSize(400,150);
        f.setLocationRelativeTo(null);
        f.setDefaultCloseOperation(JFrame.EXIT_ON_CLOSE);
        f.setVisible(true);
    }
}
```

Here, the showDialog() displays a colour chooser dialog box inside the parent container with a title and initial colour and returns the selected Color object. The setForeground() sets the selected colour of the label.

Unusually, you can also display JColorChooser object inside a frame like displaying other swing components. In this case, you will have to handle the event associated with colour selection. The

JColorChooser object fires ChangeEvent and so your class can also implement ChangeListener and override stateChanged() method. As JColorChooser is a type of dialog, it also fires ActionEvent. The getColor() returns a Color object as the user selects a colour. Here is an example depicted in Listing 16.26 that displays JColorChooser palette.

Listing 16.26. Displaying JColorChooser Inside Frame

```java
// ColorChooser2.java
import javax.swing.*;
import javax.swing.colorchooser.*;
import javax.swing.event.*;
import java.awt.*;
import java.awt.event.*;

public class ColorChooser2 extends JFrame
{
    JLabel lblTitle = new JLabel("Paint Me", JLabel.CENTER);
    JColorChooser cc = new JColorChooser();

    public ColorChooser2()
    {
        lblTitle.setFont(new Font("Serif", Font.BOLD, 48));
        add("North", lblTitle);

        JPanel p = new JPanel();
        p.add(cc);
        add("Center", p);
        cc.getSelectionModel().addChangeListener(new CCL());
    }

    class CCL implements ChangeListener
    {
        public void stateChanged(ChangeEvent e)
        {
            lblTitle.setForeground(cc.getColor());
        }
    }

    public static void main(String[] args)
    {
        ColorChooser2 f = new ColorChooser2();
        // frame properties
        f.setTitle("Color Chooser");
        f.setSize(450,300);
```

```
        f.setLocationRelativeTo(null);
        f.setDefaultCloseOperation(JFrame.EXIT_ON_CLOSE);
        f.setVisible(true);
    }
}
```

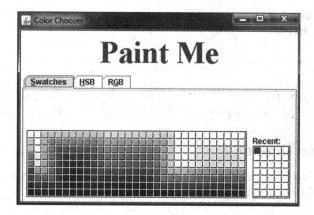

In this example, the default selection model is obtained via getSelectionModel() method as is needed to register ChangeListener for JColorChooser.

16.17 DISPLAYING MESSAGES

A dialog window is an independent subwindow within the frame and is used to display messages to users. The JOptionPane class creates a dialog window. Using JOptionPane you can create different kinds of dialogs as below:

- Message dialog using showMessageDialog()
- Confirmation dialog using showConfirmDialog()
- Option dialog using showOptionDialog()
- Input dialog using showInputDialog()

16.17.1 Message Dialogs

The showMessageDialog() method can be used to create message dialog boxes with different message icons such as message without title, WARNING_MESSAGE, ERROR_MESSAGE, PLAIN_MESSAGE and INFORMATION_MESSAGE as shown in Figure 16.15.

Figure 16.15. Message Dialogs

```
Syntax:
JOptionPane.showMessageDialog(jframe, mesg, title, icon);
```

```
Example:
JOptionPane.showMessageDialog(jframe, "Data Submitted",
"Submission Info", JOptionPane.INFORMATION_MESSAGE);
```

16.17.2 Confirm Dialogs

The showConfirmDialog() displays a confirmation message to users with YES_NO_OPTION buttons as depicted in Figure 16.16.

Figure 16.16. Confirm Dialogs

```
JOptionPane.showOptionDialog(jframe, "Would you prefer red wine
with goose?", "Wine Choice", JOptionPane.YES_NO_OPTION);
```

16.17.3 Option Dialogs

The showOptionDialog() can be used to create option dialogs with message, title, buttons, icons, option_mesgs and initial_option as illustrated in the Figure 16.17.

Figure 16.17. Option Dialogs

```
Syntax:

JOptionPane.showOptionDialog(jframe, mesg, title, button, icon,
null, option_mesgs, intial_option);

Where
    ▪ button can be any of YES_NO_OPTION, YES_NO_CANCEL_OPTION,
      OK_CANCEL_OPTION and DEFAULT_OPTION
    ▪ option_mesgs is an array of objects for button titles
    ▪ intial_option represents the default selection of a button and
    ▪ icon represents message icons as defined in message dialogs

Example:

Object[] options = {"Yes", "No", "Cancel"};
JOptionPane.showOptionDialog(jframe, "Would you prefer red wine
with cake?", "Wine Choice", JOptionPane.YES_NO_CANCEL_OPTION,
    JOptionPane.QUESTION_MESSAGE, null, options, options[1]);
```

16.17.4 Input Dialogs

The input dialog window behaves like a combo box or a textfield. The showInputDialog() allows users either to select an option from combo box or type a string value and returns the string. Figure 16.18 illustrates input dialogs.

Figure 16.18. Input Dialogs

```
Example:
Object[] drinks = {"Red wine", "White wine", "Beer", "Coke",
"Spring water"};
JOptionPane.showInputDialog(jframe, "Chicken and ham with",
"Select drinks", JOptionPane.PLAIN_MESSAGE, null, options,
options[2]);


Example:
JOptionPane.showInputDialog(jframe, "Chicken and ham with", "Type
drinks", JOptionPane.PLAIN_MESSAGE, null, null, null);
```

16.18 PROBLEM: DESIGNING COURSE REGISTRATION FORM

The course registration frame will receive the applicant's details such as name, address, mobile number, sex, marital status, course name and course track from a user and store the details in a text file. Listing 16.27 illustrates this course registration form.

Listing 16.27. Course Registration Form

```
import java.awt.*;
import java.awt.event.*;
import javax.swing.*;
import javax.swing.event.*;
import javax.swing.filechooser.*;
import javax.swing.border.*;
import java.io.*;

class RegistrationForm extends JFrame
{
    // define labels
    JLabel lblFname = new JLabel("Name");
    JLabel lblAddr = new JLabel("Address");
    JLabel lblMobile = new JLabel("Mobile Number");
    JLabel lblDOB = new JLabel("Date of Birth");
    JLabel lblSex = new JLabel("Sex");
    JLabel lblMstatus = new JLabel("Marital Status");
    JLabel lblCourse = new JLabel("Course");
    JLabel lblTrack = new JLabel("Course Track"); //Regular, Fast
    track

    //define TF and TA
    JTextField tfFname = new JTextField(30);
    JTextField tfMobile = new JTextField(30);
```

```java
JTextField tfDOB = new JTextField(30);
JTextArea taAddr = new JTextArea(5,30);

//define RBs
ButtonGroup bgSex = new ButtonGroup();
JRadioButton rbMale = new JRadioButton("Male");
JRadioButton rbFemale = new JRadioButton("Female");

//define CB
JComboBox cbMstatus = new JComboBox();

// add items to list at runtime
DefaultListModel lmodel = new DefaultListModel();
JList lstCourse = new JList(lmodel);
JScrollPane spane = new JScrollPane(lstCourse);

// define CB
JCheckBox cbRegular = new JCheckBox("Regular");
JCheckBox cbFasttrack = new JCheckBox("Fast Track");

//define BTNs
JButton btnSubmit = new JButton("submit");
JButton btnExit = new JButton("Exit");

RegistrationForm()
{
   //layout
   setLayout(new GridLayout(9, 2));
   taAddr.setBorder(new LineBorder(Color.black));

   // add components
   add(lblFname); add(tfFname);
   add(lblAddr); add(taAddr);
   add(lblMobile); add(tfMobile);
   add(lblDOB); add(tfDOB);

   add(lblSex);
   bgSex.add(rbMale);
   bgSex.add(rbFemale);
   JPanel p = new JPanel();
   p.add(rbMale);
   p.add(rbFemale);
   add(p);

   add(lblMstatus);
```

```
        cbMstatus.addItem("Single");
        cbMstatus.addItem("Married");
        add(cbMstatus);

        add(lblCourse);
        lmodel.addElement("HTML");
        lmodel.addElement("Java");
        lmodel.addElement(".NET");
        lmodel.addElement("PHP");
        lmodel.addElement("Python");
        lmodel.addElement("Ruby");
        add(spane);

        add(lblTrack);
        p = new JPanel();
        p.add(cbRegular);
        p.add(cbFasttrack);
        add(p);

        add(btnSubmit);
        add(btnExit);

        // register listeners
        rbMale.addItemListener(new MaleL());
        rbFemale.addItemListener(new FemaleL());
        cbMstatus.addItemListener(new MstatusL());
        lstCourse.addListSelectionListener(new CourseL());
        cbRegular.addItemListener(new RegularL());
        cbFasttrack.addItemListener(new FasttrackL());
        btnSubmit.addActionListener(new SubmitL());
        btnExit.addActionListener(new ExitL());
    }

String sex;
class MaleL implements ItemListener
{
    public void itemStateChanged(ItemEvent e)
    {
        sex = (String)rbMale.getText();
    }
}

class FemaleL implements ItemListener
{
    public void itemStateChanged(ItemEvent e)
```

```java
        {
            sex = (String)rbFemale.getText();
        }
}

String mstatus;
class MstatusL implements ItemListener
{
    public void itemStateChanged(ItemEvent e)
    {
       mstatus = (String)cbMstatus.getSelectedItem();
    }
}

String course;
class CourseL implements ListSelectionListener
{
    public void valueChanged(ListSelectionEvent e)
    {
        course = (String)lstCourse.getSelectedValue();
    }
}

String track;
class RegularL implements ItemListener
{
    public void itemStateChanged(ItemEvent e)
    {
        track = (String)cbRegular.getText();
    }
}

class FasttrackL implements ItemListener
{
    public void itemStateChanged(ItemEvent e)
    {
        track = (String)cbFasttrack.getText();
    }
}

class SubmitL implements ActionListener
{
    public void actionPerformed(ActionEvent e)
    {
        storeInFile();
```

```
    }
}

class ExitL implements ActionListener
{
    public void actionPerformed(ActionEvent e)
    {
        System.exit(0);
    }
}

public void storeInFile()
{
    String data = tfFname.getText() + "-" +
    taAddr.getText() + "-" +
    tfDOB.getText() + "-" +
    sex + "-" +
    mstatus + "-" +
    course + "-" +
    track + "*"; //* - end of file indicator
    try
    {
        // select file name
        JFileChooser fc = new JFileChooser();
        //fc.setFileSelectionMode(2);
        fc.setFileFilter(new FileNameExtensionFilter(
            "Saving files", "txt"));
        int val = fc.showSaveDialog(RegistrationForm.this);

        // check if file name selected and display
        String fileName = "";
        if(val == JFileChooser.APPROVE_OPTION)
            fileName = fc.getSelectedFile().getName();

        PrintWriter pw = new PrintWriter(new
            FileWriter(fileName, true)); //append mode
        pw.println(data);
        pw.flush(); //MUST TO FLUSH

    } catch(IOException e)
    {
        System.out.println("File writing error" + e);
    }

    // show message
```

```
    JOptionPane.showMessageDialog(RegistrationForm.this,
        "Data submitted to file", "Submission Info",
        JOptionPane.INFORMATION_MESSAGE);
}

public static void main(String[] args)
{
    RegistrationForm f = new RegistrationForm();
    // frame properties
    f.setTitle("Course Registration Form");
    f.setSize(500,400);
    f.setLocationRelativeTo(null);
    f.setDefaultCloseOperation(JFrame.EXIT_ON_CLOSE);
    f.setVisible(true);
}
}
```

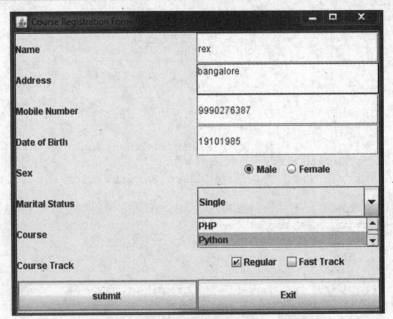

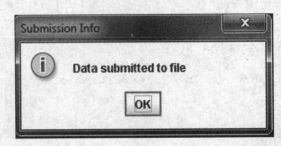

This application instantiates all user interface components labels, textfields, text areas, buttons, radiobuttons, comboboxes, lists and checkboxes. Some components are directly instantiated during declaration phase itself such as labels, buttons, textfields and text areas. Some components are populated inside constructor such as lists and combo boxes using addElement() and addItem() methods. The JList is created with a DefaultListModel and is added inside scroll pane. Event Listeners are registered for radiobuttons, comboboxes, checkboxes, lists and buttons and appropriate inner classes define behaviour for these components. When Submit button is clicked, a FileChooser selects a file name from user and all updated values from these components are stored in a text file using println() of PrintWriter object. A confirmation message is also given to users by way of information box that displays a message *Data submitted to file* with a OK button.

16.19 CREATING EDITOR PANE AND TEXT PANE

The **JEditorPane** and **JTextPane** classes are used to create a editor pane and text pane in swing. In fact, JTextPane is a subclass of JEditorPane class. These two classes allow us to create styled documents such as html and rtf. The JEditorPane can display text documents, whereas JTextPane cannot display plain documents. The JTextPane can embed images and other components, whereas JEditorPane cannot embed directly into it but can embed via html tags. The setPage() mehod loads URL into uneditable editor pane without knowing the type of data and read() displays the information onto the pane. Now let us create two editor panes – one displays a html file and the other renders or loads the output of a html file as depicted in Listing 16.28.

Listing 16.28. Loading URL and Files to Editor Panes

```java
// EditorPane.java
import javax.swing.*;
import javax.swing.border.*;
import javax.swing.filechooser.*;
import java.awt.*;
import java.awt.event.*;
import java.io.*;

public class EditorPane extends JFrame
{
    JEditorPane ep = new JEditorPane();
    JButton btnShow = new JButton("Show File");

    JEditorPane ep2 = new JEditorPane();
    JButton btnShow2 = new JButton("Render File");

    public EditorPane()
    {
        // editor pane properties
        ep.setEditable(false);
        ep.setForeground(Color.magenta);
```

```
        ep.setBackground(Color.yellow);
        ep.setBorder(new BevelBorder(BevelBorder.LOWERED));
        // add ep to panel
        JPanel p = new JPanel();
        p.setLayout(new BorderLayout());
        p.add("Center", ep);
        JPanel p2 = new JPanel();
        p2.add(btnShow);
        p.add("South", p2);

        // editor pane2 properties
        ep2.setEditable(false);
        ep2.setForeground(Color.blue);
        ep2.setBackground(Color.green);
        ep2.setBorder(new BevelBorder(BevelBorder.LOWERED));
        // add ep2 to pane
        JPanel p1 = new JPanel();
        p1.setLayout(new BorderLayout());
        p1.add("Center", ep2);
        p2 = new JPanel();
        p2.add(btnShow2);
        p1.add("South", p2);

        // add p and p2 to frame
        setLayout(new GridLayout(1,2));
        add(p);
        add(p1);

        btnShow.addActionListener(new ShowL());
        btnShow2.addActionListener(new Show2L());
    }

    class ShowL implements ActionListener
    {
        public void actionPerformed(ActionEvent e)
        {
            // select file name
            JFileChooser fc = new JFileChooser();
            fc.setFileFilter(new FileNameExtensionFilter(
                "Opening files", "txt", "html", "htm", "rtf"));
            int val = fc.showOpenDialog(EditorPane.this);

            // check if file name selected and display
            String fileName = "";
```

```java
        if(val == JFileChooser.APPROVE_OPTION)
           fileName = fc.getSelectedFile().getName();


        // set URL
        try
        {
           ep.read(new FileReader(fileName), null);
        }catch(IOException e1) { }
    }
}


class Show2L implements ActionListener
{
    public void actionPerformed(ActionEvent e)
    {
        // select file name
        JFileChooser fc = new JFileChooser();
        fc.setFileFilter(new FileNameExtensionFilter(
           "Opening files", "txt", "html", "htm", "rtf"));
        int val = fc.showOpenDialog(EditorPane.this);


        try
        {
           if(val == JFileChooser.APPROVE_OPTION)
           {
                File file = fc.getSelectedFile();
                ep2.setPage("file:\\" + file.getAbsolutePath());
           }
        }catch(IOException e1) { }
    }
}


public static void main(String[] args)
{
    EditorPane f = new EditorPane();
    // frame properties
    f.setTitle("Editor Panes");
    f.setSize(400,300);
    f.setLocationRelativeTo(null);  // centres to screen
    f.setDefaultCloseOperation(JFrame.EXIT_ON_CLOSE);
    f.setVisible(true);
}
}
```

The JEditorPane has two interesting methods. The read() displays the source file in its display area. The setPage() sets a URL of a page. If URL of the page is html then the output of the html file will be rendered in the display area. From the absolute path name, you can construct a file url by appending file:\\ before the path name.

Though JTextPane extends JEditorPane, it can display images directly using insertIcon() method. Here is an example depicted in Listing 16.29 that will display an image in its display area.

Listing 16.29. Displaying Images in Text Pane

```java
// ImageTextPane.java
import javax.swing.*;
import javax.swing.border.*;
import javax.swing.filechooser.*;
import java.awt.*;
import java.awt.event.*;
import java.io.*;
public class ImageTextPane extends JFrame
{
    JTextPane textPane = new JTextPane();
    JFileChooser fc = new JFileChooser();
    JButton btnShow = new JButton("Show Image");

    public ImageTextPane() throws Exception
    {
        // set text pane non editable
        textPane.setEditable(false);
        add("Center", textPane);
        add("South", btnShow);
        btnShow.addActionListener(new ShowL());
    }

    class ShowL implements ActionListener
    {
```

```
    public void actionPerformed(ActionEvent e)
    {
        fc.setFileFilter(new FileNameExtensionFilter(
            "Opening files", "jpg", "jpeg", "gif", "bmp"));
        int val = fc.showOpenDialog(ImageTextPane.this);

        if(val == JFileChooser.APPROVE_OPTION)
        {
            File file = fc.getSelectedFile();
            Icon icon = new ImageIcon(file.
            getAbsolutePath());
            textPane.insertIcon(icon);
        }
    }
}

public static void main(String[] args) throws Exception
{
    ImageTextPane f = new ImageTextPane();
    // frame properties
    f.setTitle("TextPane Image");
    f.setSize(400,400);
    f.setLocationRelativeTo(null);  // centres to screen
    f.setDefaultCloseOperation(JFrame.EXIT_ON_CLOSE);
    f.setVisible(true);
}
}
```

Here initially the absolute path of the image is selected from file chooser and image icon is created with this path name. The insertIcon() inserts this image icon into the text pane.

16.20 CREATING SLIDER

The JSlider allows users to select, by adjusting its knob, a numeric value from a range of values defined by *setMinimum()* and *setMaximum()* methods. The range of numeric values is divided into ticks. You can define major ticks and minor ticks space with *setMajorTickSpacing()* and *setMinor-TickSpacing()* methods. For example, a slider for a range 0 to 100 with a major tick space of 10 and minor tick space of 2 will divide it into 10 major intervals and each major interval into five minor intervals. The *setPaintLabels(true)* can set numeric values visible and *setPaintTicks(true)* makes tick marks visible. You can display slider vertically or horizontally with *setOrientation()* method that takes the orientation constant as input. The *getValue()* returns the currently selected slider value, while *setValue()* method sets a numeric value for the slider.

In Listing 16.30, we create two sliders representing temperature; one for Centigrade and the other for Fahrenheit.

Listing 16.30. Temperature Converter Using JSlider

```
// TemperatureSlider.java
import javax.swing.*;
import javax.swing.border.*;
import javax.swing.filechooser.*;
import javax.swing.event.*;
import java.awt.*;
import java.awt.event.*;
import java.io.*;

public class TemperatureSlider extends JFrame
{
    JSlider cs = new JSlider();
    JSlider fs = new JSlider();

    public TemperatureSlider()
    {
        // cs properties
        cs.setMajorTickSpacing(5);
        cs.setMaximum(60);
        cs.setMinorTickSpacing(1);
        cs.setOrientation(JSlider.VERTICAL);
        cs.setPaintLabels(true);
        cs.setPaintTicks(true);
        cs.setValue(0);

        // fs properties
```

```
    fs.setMajorTickSpacing(5);
    fs.setMaximum(150);
    fs.setMinorTickSpacing(1);
    fs.setOrientation(JSlider.VERTICAL);
    fs.setPaintLabels(true);
    fs.setPaintTicks(true);
    fs.setValue(0);

    // add components
    Box box = Box.createHorizontalBox();
    box.add(cs);
    box.add(box.createHorizontalGlue());
    box.add(fs);
    add("Center", box);
    // register listeners
    cs.addChangeListener(new CSL());
    fs.addChangeListener(new FSL());
    }

class CSL implements ChangeListener
{
    public void stateChanged(ChangeEvent e)
    {
        if(!cs.getValueIsAdjusting())
        {
            // calc faren and update fs
            int cent = cs.getValue();
            int faren = cent * 9/5 + 32;
            fs.setValue(faren);
        }
    }
}

class FSL implements ChangeListener
{
    public void stateChanged(ChangeEvent e)
    {
        if(!fs.getValueIsAdjusting())
        {
            // calc cent and update cs
            int faren = fs.getValue();
            int cent = (faren - 32) * 5/9;
            cs.setValue(cent);
        }
    }
}
```

```
    }

    public static void main(String[] args)
    {
        TemperatureSlider f = new TemperatureSlider();
        // frame properties
        f.setTitle("Temp Converter using JSlider");
        f.setSize(150,500);
        f.setLocationRelativeTo(null);   // centres to screen
        f.setDefaultCloseOperation(JFrame.EXIT_ON_CLOSE);
        f.setVisible(true);
    }
}
```

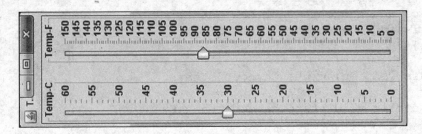

The centigrade slider represents values from 0 to 60 with major ticks 5 and minor ticks 1. The paint labels (i.e. 0, 5, 10, etc.) and paint ticks (small and larger hyphens) are made visible and sliders are displayed vertically. Here, to save space, they are rotated (manually) so that they appear horizontally. The ChangeListeners are registered for each slider. When a slider is adjusted, it fires ChangeEvent and the associated Listener gets executed. Inside stateChanged() method, the sliders value representing a temperature gets converted to the other temperature. For example, Centigrade slider's value is converted to Fahrenheit value and the Fahrenheit slider is set with this value. Similarly, Fahrenheit slider's value gets converted to centigrade value and the centigrade slider is set with this value. You can adjust any slider and the other slider will move automatically to the correct value.

16.21 DESIGNING TABBED PANE

The JTabbedPane class allows you to create a tabbed pane that arranges GUI components into row of elements. Out of this row, only one tab will be visible at any time. Users can access each element or tab by clicking a tab or using arrow keys or also via keyboard shortcuts. When a user clicks a tab, the appropriate component will be displayed. A tab can contain any components such as buttons. It can also contain a container such as panel, so that each panel can have its own set of components with independent layouts.

Here is an example shown in Listing 16.31 that adds multiple tabs and for each tab we add a button. Also, there is a textfield that displays the currently selected tab label.

Listing 16.31. Tabbed Pane Demo

```java
// TabbedPane.java
import javax.swing.*;
import javax.swing.border.*;
import javax.swing.event.*;
import java.awt.*;

public class TabbedPane extends JFrame
{
    String[] tabs = {"Fruits", "Vegetables", "Chocolates",
    "Cookies", "Cakes"};
    JTabbedPane tpane = new JTabbedPane();
    JTextField tf = new JTextField();

    public TabbedPane()
    {
        // add buttons as tabs
        for(int i = 0; i < tabs.length; i++)
            tpane.addTab(tabs[i], new JButton("Tab " + i));

        add(tpane);
        add("South", tf);
        tpane.addChangeListener(new TPL());
    }

    class TPL implements ChangeListener
    {
        public void stateChanged(ChangeEvent e)
        {
            tf.setText("Tab " + tpane.getSelectedIndex());
        }
    }

    public static void main(String[] args)
    {
        TabbedPane f = new TabbedPane();
        // frame properties
        f.setTitle("Tabbed Pane");
        f.setSize(400,200);
        f.setLocationRelativeTo(null);
        f.setDefaultCloseOperation(JFrame.EXIT_ON_CLOSE);
        f.setVisible(true);
    }
}
```

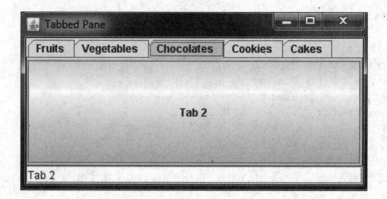

Here, initially a string array defines a set of tabs. Inside constructor, addTab() method adds a string representing a tab and associates a button for this tab. The ChangeListener handles tab selection and getSelectedIndex() returns the index value of the selected tab.

16.22 HANDLING MENU

Menus are yet another important component for any GUI design with which it is easy to bundle a collection of components. In Java, applets and frames (and its descents too such as panel and dialog) can hold menus. Generally, menus are added to menubar, which in turn added to frame or applet. Similarly menu items are added to a menu. Very similar to menu item, checkbox menu item and radio button menu item can be added to a menu.

The corresponding classes that handle menus are JMenuBar, JMenu, JMenuItem, JCheckBox-MenuItem and JRadioButtonMenuItem. The add() method adds a menu item to menu and menu to menubar. The setJMenuBar() adds menubar to frame or applet. The JMenuItem fires ActionEvent and so you need to register ActionListener in order to handle the click of menu item. Also ItemEvent will be fired by JCheckBoxMenuItem and JRadioButtonMenuItem. Let us now create a simple text editor that arranges few menus, and each menu contains menu items as illustrated in Listing 16.32.

Listing 16.32. A Mini Text Editor

```
// TextEditor.java
import javax.swing.*;
import javax.swing.filechooser.*;
import javax.swing.border.*;
import java.awt.*;
import java.awt.event.*;
import java.io.*;

public class TextEditor extends JFrame
{
    JMenuBar mb = new JMenuBar();
```

```java
JMenu mFile = new JMenu("File");
JMenu mEdit = new JMenu("Edit");
JMenu mTools = new JMenu("Tools");
JMenu mHelp = new JMenu("Help");

JMenuItem miNew = new JMenuItem("New");
JMenuItem miOpen = new JMenuItem("Open");
JMenuItem miSaveas = new JMenuItem("SaveAs");
JMenuItem miExit = new JMenuItem("Exit");

JLabel lblTitle = new JLabel(
    "Text Editor v1.0", JLabel.CENTER);
JTextArea taDisplay = new JTextArea();
JTextField tfStatus = new JTextField();

public TextEditor()
{
    // add menu items to menu
    mFile.add(miNew);
    mFile.add(miOpen);
    mFile.add(miSaveas);
    mFile.add(miExit);

    //add menu to menubar
    mb.add(mFile);
    mb.add(mEdit);
    mb.add(mTools);
    mb.add(mHelp);

    //add menubar to frame
    setJMenuBar(mb);

    //add TA and TF
    add(lblTitle, "North");
    add(taDisplay, "Center");
    add(tfStatus, "South");

    // make non editable initially
    tfStatus.setEditable(false);
    taDisplay.setEditable(false);
    taDisplay.setBackground(Color.yellow);

    //add listeners
    miNew.addActionListener(new NewL());
    miOpen.addActionListener(new OpenL());
```

```
        miSaveas.addActionListener(new SaveasL());
        miExit.addActionListener(new ExitL());
}

class SaveasL implements ActionListener
{
    public void actionPerformed(ActionEvent e)
    {
        JFileChooser fc = new JFileChooser();
        // show both files and directories
        fc.setFileSelectionMode(2);
        int val = fc.showSaveDialog(TextEditor.this);
        // check if file name selected
        String fileName = "";
        if(val == JFileChooser.APPROVE_OPTION)
        {
            // display selected file
            fileName = fc.getSelectedFile().getName();
        }

        // store text area
        try
        {
            PrintWriter pw = new PrintWriter(
              new FileWriter(fileName, true));
            pw.println(taDisplay.getText());
              pw.flush();
        }
        catch (IOException e1) { }
    }
}

class OpenL implements ActionListener
{
    public void actionPerformed(ActionEvent e)
    {
        // create file chooser
        JFileChooser fc = new JFileChooser();
        // show both files and directories
        fc.setFileSelectionMode(2);
        int val = fc.showOpenDialog(TextEditor.this);
        // check if file name selected
        String fileName = "";
        if(val == JFileChooser.APPROVE_OPTION)
```

```
                {
                        // display selected file
                        fileName = fc.getSelectedFile().getName();
                }

                taDisplay.setEditable(true);

                // display contents
                String s;
                try
                {
                        BufferedReader in = new BufferedReader(
                                new FileReader(fileName));
                        while ((s = in.readLine()) != null)
                        taDisplay.setText(taDisplay.getText() + s +
                        "\n");
                        // close stream
                        in.close();
                }catch (IOException e1) { }
                // show status
                tfStatus.setText(fileName + " loaded");
        }
}

class NewL implements ActionListener
{
    public void actionPerformed(ActionEvent e)
    {
            taDisplay.setText("");
            taDisplay.setEditable(true);
    }
}
class ExitL implements ActionListener
{
    public void actionPerformed(ActionEvent e)
    {
            System.exit(0);
    }
}

public static void main(String[] args)
{
    TextEditor f = new TextEditor();
    f.setTitle("Text Editor");
    f.setSize(400,300);
```

```
        f.setLocationRelativeTo(null);
        f.setDefaultCloseOperation(JFrame.EXIT_ON_CLOSE);
        f.setVisible(true);
    }
}
```

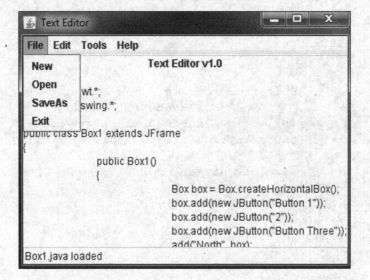

In this application, there are four menus namely File, Edit, Tools and Help. The File menu contains four menu items namely New, Open, SaveAs and Exit. There is also a large text area where text files can be displayed and textfield that acts like a status board. Inside constructor, menu items are first added to menu using add() method. Then menus are added to menubar using the same overloaded add() method. The setJMenuBar() adds menubar to frame.

The ActionListeners are added to menu items. Initially text area is made uneditable and when New is selected, it becomes editable so that text can be entered into the text area. When Open is selected, a FileChooser allows a user to choose a file name and its contents will be displayed inside the text area. Similarly when a SaveAs is clicked, the current contents of the text area are saved to a file that has been selected with file chooser. Finally, Exit menu item closes the frame.

16.23 TABLE HANDLING

Swing supports yet another elegant component to display a grid of values using JTable. The JTable contains many features to show element values and also to edit table cell values. In order to create an instance of JTable, users should create a 2D object array and a 1D header array. With these two arrays, you can instantiate a table as shown in Figure 16.19.

Figure 16.19. Creating JTable

```
JTable table = new JTable(2D data_array, 1D header_array);
```

You can add table to scroll pane so that you will be able to scroll it with horizontal and vertical scroll bars. If you want table to be automatically resized to fit into the frame, then *setFillsViewportHeight(true)* method will resize table to the size of the frame. In Listing 16.33, grade details of students are displayed in JTable.

Listing 16.33. Creating Tables with Object Array

```java
// MarksTable.java
import javax.swing.*;
import javax.swing.event.*;
import java.util.*;
import java.io.*;

public class MarksTable extends JFrame
{
    // heading
    Object[] cols = {"Roll No", "Name", "Year Joined", "Grade"};
    // cell data
    Object[][] data = {
        {"5001", "Rex", "2009", "S"},
        {"5002", "Peter", "2009", "A"},
        {"5003", "Hilda", "2009", "S"},
        {"5004", "Rita", "2009", "B"},
    };
    // jtable
    JTable table = new JTable(data, cols);

    public MarksTable()
    {
        // adjust data to entire container
        table.setFillsViewportHeight(true);

        // put tables to scrollpane
        JScrollPane pane = new JScrollPane(table);

        // add pane to frame
        add(pane);
    }

    public static void main(String[] args)
    {
        MarksTable f = new MarksTable();
        f.setTitle("Students Grade Info");
        f.setSize(500,150);
        f.setLocationRelativeTo(null);
```

```
        f.setDefaultCloseOperation(JFrame.EXIT_ON_CLOSE);
        f.setVisible(true);
    }
}
```

Here, two object arrays *cols* and *data* define table header and cell values for the table. With these object arrays, JTable instance is created and added to frame.

The JTable can also be instantiated with util.Vector of values. As table cell values are 2D, a vector of vector representing rows is needed. Here is a Listing 16.34 that creates two tables, one populated with objects and the other populated with vector of vectors.

Listing 16.34. Creating Tables from Vector and Object Array

```java
// StudentInfo.java
import javax.swing.*;
import javax.swing.event.*;
import java.util.*;
import java.io.*;

public class StudentInfo extends JFrame
{
    Object[] cols = {"Roll No", "Name", "Year Joined", "Grade",
    "Hosteller"};
    Object[][] data = {
        {"5001", "Rex", "2009", "S", new Boolean(false)},
        {"5002", "Peter", "2009", "A", new Boolean(false)},
        {"5003", "Hilda", "2009", "S", new Boolean(true)},
        {"5004", "Rita", "2009", "B", new Boolean(true)},
    };

    JTable table1, table2;
    // to hold table heads
    Vector vhead = new Vector();
    // to hold cell data
```

```java
Vector<Vector> vtable = new Vector<Vector>();

public StudentInfo()
{
    // create table1 with object[][]
    table1 = new JTable(data, cols);

    // load data to vector
    loadVector();
    // create table2 with vectors
    table2 = new JTable(vtable, vhead);

    // adjust data to entire container
    table1.setFillsViewportHeight(true);
    table2.setFillsViewportHeight(true);

    // put tables to scrollpane
    JScrollPane pane1 = new JScrollPane(table1);
    JScrollPane pane2 = new JScrollPane(table2);

    // add scroll panes to box
    Box box = Box.createVerticalBox();
    box.add(pane1);
    box.add(Box.createVerticalGlue());
    box.add(pane2);

    // add box to frame
    add(box);
}

public void loadVector()
{
    // copy head
    for(int i = 0; i < cols.length; i++)
        vhead.add(cols[i]);

    // copy row, col values
    Vector v2;
    for(int i = 0; i < data.length; i++)
    {
        // reset v2 each time
        v2 = new Vector();

        for(int j = 0; j < data[i].length; j++)
            v2.add(data[i][j]);
```

```
                 // add v2 to table vector
                 vtable.add(v2);
         }
    }


    public static void main(String[] args)
    {
        StudentInfo f = new StudentInfo();
        f.setTitle("Students Information");
        f.setSize(500,300);
        f.setLocationRelativeTo(null);
        f.setDefaultCloseOperation(JFrame.EXIT_ON_CLOSE);
        f.setVisible(true);
    }
}
```

Roll No	Name	Year Joined	Grade	Hosteller
5001	Rex	2009	S	false
5002	Peter	2009	A	false
5003	Hilda	2009	S	true
5004	Rita	2009	B	true

Roll No	Name	Year Joined	Grade	Hosteller
5001	Rex	2009	S	false
5002	Peter	2009	A	false
5003	Hilda	2009	S	true
5004	Rita	2009	B	true

In this example, object arrays are created initially. Inside constructor, one table is created with object arrays as in the previous example. Then loadVector() populates vectors with object array values. In order to populate cell values, you will use vector containing vectors where each vector will keep a row of cell values. With these two vectors, the second table is created. Then they are added to scrollpanes and in turn added to frame.

16.24 CREATING CUSTOM SWING COMPONENTS

Creating a custom component is a matter of subclassing an existing component and adding the new functionality you wish for the component. Though adding some minor features is easy, writing a complete custom component from the scratch is relatively complicated. It is always better to refer to J2SE API source code that will help you to create custom components. To illustrate the process of creating new components, let us design a colour button with white foreground and blue background, Serif font, raised BevelBorder and 5 pixel margin all around as shown in Listing 16.35.

Listing 16.35. Creating ColorButton Class

```java
//ColorButton.java
import javax.swing.*;
import java.awt.*;
import javax.swing.border.*;

public class ColorButton extends JButton
{
    public ColorButton(String label)
    {
        super(label);
        setBackground(Color.blue);
        setForeground(Color.white);
        setFont(new Font("Serif", Font.BOLD, 14));
        setBorder(new BevelBorder(BevelBorder.RAISED));
        setMargin(new Insets(5, 5, 5, 5));
    }
}
```

You can add this ColorButton class into a package you have already created so that it can be imported by any required class. Now we will create a testing class that will instantiate ColorButton just like a normal JButton as depicted in the Listing 16.36.

Listing 16.36. Using ColorButton Class

```java
//ColorButtonTest.java
import javax.swing.*;
import java.awt.*;

public class ColorButtonTest extends JFrame
{
    ColorButton bSubmit = new ColorButton("Submit");
    ColorButton bCancel = new ColorButton("Cancel");
    ColorButton bExit = new ColorButton("Exit");

    JLabel lbl = new JLabel("Color Buttons", JLabel.CENTER);

    public ColorButtonTest()
    {
        JPanel p = new JPanel();
        p.add(bSubmit);
        p.add(bCancel);
        p.add(bExit);
        add("Center", lbl);
```

```
        add("South", p);
    }
    public static void main(String[] args)
    {
        ColorButtonTest f = new ColorButtonTest();
        f.setTitle("Color Button");
        f.setSize(300,200);
        f.setLocationRelativeTo(null);
        f.setDefaultCloseOperation(JFrame.EXIT_ON_CLOSE);
        f.setVisible(true);
    }
}
```

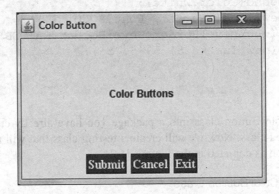

In the same way, you can create any new component as you like by deciding the properties you want your component to support. Since all swing components extend JComponent, you can also extend JComponent and override all necessary methods.

16.25 SUMMARY

1. JLabel can be aligned left (by default), centre and right
2. JButton fires ActionEvent when it is clicked
3. Layout manager arranges components into the container such as JFrame and JPanel
4. The setLayout() sets the necessary layout for the container
5. FlowLayout places components left to right in the order they added
6. BorderLayout places components in five regions; north, south, east, west and centre
7. GridLayout places components in a matrix format
8. BoxLayout arranges components either horizontally or vertically, preserving the dimension of the components
9. Box is another lightweight container that uses internally BoxLayout manager to arrange components left to right horizontally or top to bottom vertically
10. Box uses three types of fillers – *struts, glue* and *rigid area* – to leave space between components

11. JComponents fire various events. In order to handle these events the respective listeners can be registered using addXXXListener() methods
12. Adapter classes can be used when all listener methods need not be overridden
13. Inner classes are excellent ways of representing listener interfaces and adapter classes
14. DocumentLister can be used to handle whether a character is pressed or erased from textfield or text area
15. Checkboxes, comboboxes and radiobuttons fire ItemEvent
16. Some of the standard dialog windows are JOptionPane, JFileChooser and JColorChooser
17. JOptionPane is used to create message dialogs, option dialogs, option dialogs and input dialogs
18. Editor pane and its subclass text pane can display text, html files and images
19. Sliders allow us to select a numeric value from a range of values and fire ChangeEvent
20. GUI components can be arranged in a row using tabbed pane
21. Menus allow us to bundle a collection of components
22. JTable displays a grid of values. Values can be given as object array or a vector of objects
23. New components can be created simply by extending GUI components and overriding necessary methods

KEY TERMS

Adapter, 560
BoxLayout, 553
Event handling, 542
JButton, 540
JColourChooscr, 585

JEditorPane, 601
JFileChooser, 585
JLabel, 540
JOptionPane, 585
JTextPane, 601

Layout managers, 545
Listener, 543
Strut, 555

REVIEW QUESTIONS

Multiple-choice Questions

1. Which layout manager places GUI components in one of five regions: north, south, east, west, and centre?
   a. BoxLayout
   b. GridLayout
   c. BorderLayout
   d. FlowLayout

2. Clicking a mouse button will always generate which event?
   a. MouseButtonEvent
   b. ActionEvent
   c. MouseClickEvent
   d. MouseEvent

3. What is the default layout manager for JFrame?
   a. BoxLayout
   b. GridLayout
   c. BorderLayout
   d. FlowLayout

4. How to assign keyboard character for JButton?

    a. assign(char)

    b. setMnemonic(char)

    c. assignChar(char)

    d. None of the above

5. What is the output?

```
import javax.swing.*;
import java.awt.*;
public class Test16 extends JFrame
{
    JButton b = new JButton("Cancel");
    public Test16()
    {
        add(b, BorderLayout.SOUTH);
        add("North", b);
    }
    public static void main(String[] args)
    {
        Test16 t = new Test16();
        t.setSize(100, 200);
        t.setVisible(true);
    }
}
```

    a. Cancel button is added to only South

    b. Cancel button is added to only North

    c. Cancel button is added to South and North

    d. No output

6. What is the output?

```
public class Test16 extends JFrame
{
    JLabel label = new JLabel("Press Me");
    public Test16()
    {
        label.setText("Dont Disturb");
        add("North", label);
    }
    public static void main(String[] args)
    {
        Test16 t = new Test16();
        t.setSize(100, 200);
        t.setVisible(true);
    }
}
```

    a. Press Me   b. Don't disturb

    c. No output   d. Compilation error

7. What is the default arrangement of components for FlowLayout?
    a. FlowLayout.CENTER   b. FlowLayout.LEFT
    c. FlowLayout.RIGHT   d. None of the above

8. The hspace attribute
    a. defines the gap between adjacent components
    b. defines the gap between components of two rows
    c. controls the size of the components in inches
    d. None of the above

9. Choose all correct statements:

```
setLayout(new FlowLayout(FlowLayout.RIGHT, 10,20));
```

    a. hspace =10   b. vspace =20
    c. Arranges components right justified   d. All of the above

10. Which layout manger arranges components left to right in the order they appear?
    a. BoxLayout   b. GridLayout
    c. BorderLayout   d. FlowLayout

11. What is the output?

```
import javax.swing.*;
import java.awt.*;
public class Test16 extends JFrame
{
   public Test16()
   {
      add("Center", new JButton("2"));
      add("North", new JButton("1"));
      add("South", new JButton("3"));
   }
   public static void main(String[] args)
   {
      Test16 t = new Test16();
      t.setSize(100, 200);
      t.setVisible(true);
   }
}
```

a. 3 rows of buttons   b. 3 columns of buttons

c. 2 occupies the space of west and east   d. No output

12. What is the output?

```java
public class Test16 extends JFrame
{
    public Test16()
    {
        add("Center", new JButton("2"));
    }
    public static void main(String[] args)
    {
        Test16 t = new Test16();
        t.setSize(100, 200);
        t.setVisible(true);
    }
}
```

a. 2 occupies centre   b. 2 occupies centre, west and east regions

c. 2 occupies the entire frame   d. None of the above

13. Which layout manager arranges components in matrix format?

a. BoxLayout   b. GridLayout

c. BorderLayout   d. FlowLayout

14. What is the output?

```java
setLayout(new GridLayout(2,0));
add(new JButton("1"));
add(new JButton("2"));
add(new JButton("3"));
add(new JButton("4"));
add(new JButton("5"));
add(new JButton("6"));
```

a. Buttons are displayed in 6 rows   b. Buttons are displayed in 6 columns

c. Buttons are displayed in 2 rows, 3 columns   d. Buttons are displayed in 3 rows, 2 columns

e. None of the above

15. How to initialize JTable?

a. Object[][]   b. Vector

c. ArrayList   d. All of the above

16. What is the output?

```
setLayout(new GridLayout(0, 2));
add(new JButton("1"));
add(new JButton("2"));
add(new JButton("3"));
add(new JButton("4"));
add(new JButton("5"));
add(new JButton("6"));
```

    a. Buttons are displayed in 6 rows   b. Buttons are displayed in 6 columns
    c. Buttons are displayed in 2 rows, 3 columns   d. Buttons are displayed in 3 rows, 2 columns
    e. None of the above

17. How to create several layouts inside a container?
    a. using JWindow   b. using JFrame
    c. using JPanel   d. None of the above

18. What is the default layout for JPanel?
    a. FlowLayout   b. BoxLayout
    c. BorderLayout   d. GridLayout

19. Which layout manager preserves the width and height of the components?
    a. FlowLayout   b. BoxLayout
    c. BorderLayout   d. GridLayout

20. Which layout manager arranges components either horizontally or vertically?
    a. FlowLayout   b. BoxLayout
    c. BorderLayout   d. GridLayout

21. Which container uses BoxLayout internally?
    a. FlowLayout   b. Box
    c. BorderLayout   d. GridLayout

22. Which layout manager supports createVerticalBox() method?
    a. BoxLayout   b. Box
    c. GridBagLayout   d. None of the above

23. How to leave space between components in Box?
    a. Strut   b. Glue
    c. Rigid area   d. All of the above

24. The strut can be created using
    a. createHorizontalstrut()   b. createVerticalStrut()
    c. Both 1 and 2   d. None of the above

25. How to stretch gaps vertically in between fixed sized components to the edges of the container?
    a. createVerticalStrut()
    b. createVerticalGlue()
    c. createVerticalGap()
    d. None of the above

26. How to stretch gaps horizontally in between fixed sized components to the edges of the container?
    a. createHorizontalStrut()
    b. createHorizontalGlue()
    c. createHorizontalGap()
    d. None of the above

27. Which method gives gaps horizontally and vertically between two components?
    a. createRigidArea()
    b. createGlue()
    c. createStrut()
    d. createGap()
    e. None of the above

28. Which components fire ActionEvent?
    a. JButton
    b. JTextField
    c. JMenuItem, JMenu, JPopupMenu
    d. All of the above

29. Which components fire DocumentEvent?
    a. JTextField
    b. JTextArea
    c. JScrollBar
    d. None of the above

30. Which components fire ListSelectionEvent?
    a. JList
    b. JScrollBar
    c. JComboBox
    d. None of the above

31. Which components fire AdjustmentEvent?
    a. JList
    b. JScrollBar
    c. JComboBox
    d. None of the above

32. Which interface supports actionPerformed()?
    a. ActionListener
    b. ListSelectionListener
    c. AdjustmentListener
    d. DocumentListener
    e. None of the above

33. Which interface supports insertUpdate()?
    a. ActionListener
    b. ListSelectionListener
    c. AdjustmentListener
    d. DocumentListener
    e. None of the above

34. Which interface supports valueChanged()?
    a. ActionListener
    b. ListSelectionListener
    c. AdjustmentListener
    d. DocumentListener
    e. None of the above

35. What events are fired by JTextField?
    a. ActionEvent
    b. KeyEvent
    c. DocumentEvent
    d. All of the above

36. What is the base class for JPasswordField?
    a. JTextField
    b. JTextArea
    c. JTextComponent
    d. None of the above

37. How to wrap text to the level of line and words and make non-editable text?
    a. setLineWrap(true);
    b. setWrapStyleWord(true)
    c. setEditable(false)
    d. All of the above

38. Which event supports getKeyChar() method?
    a. KeyEvent
    b. KeyboardKeyEvent
    c. AsciiKeyEvent
    d. None of the above

39. What events JRadioButton fires?
    a. ActionEvent
    b. ItemEvent
    c. KeyEvent
    d. All of the above

40. How to insert items to JComboBox?
    a. insert()
    b. add()
    c. addItem()
    d. None of the above

41. Which method prevents insertion of same item to JList as a result of multiple events?
    a. getValueIsAdjusting()
    b. isDuplicate()
    c. isDuplicateInsertion()
    d. None of the above

42. The method setFileSelectionMode(1) results
    a. JFileChooser sets only files for selection
    b. JFileChooser sets only directories for selection
    c. JList sets only directories for selection
    d. JList sets only files for selection
    e. All of the above

43. Which method JOptionPane does not support?
    a. showMessageDialog()
    b. showInputDialog()
    c. showConfirmDialog()
    d. showOptionDialog()
    e. None of the above

44. Which component displays html tags?
    a. JTextField
    b. JTextArea
    c. JEditorPane
    d. All of the above

45. How to render html file onto JEditorPane?
    a. read()
    b. getPage()
    c. setPage()
    d. None of the above

46. Which component supports imageIcon()?
    a. JEditorPane
    b. JTextPane
    c. JTextArea
    d. All of the above

47. What method adds menu bar to JFrame?
    a. setMenuBar()
    b. setJMenuBar()
    c. add()
    d. None of the above

48. What is the output?

```java
public class Test16 extends JFrame
{
    public Test16()
    {
        add(new JButton("6"));
    }
    public static void main(String[] args)
    {
        Test16 t = new Test16();
        t.setSize(50, 50);
        t.setVisible(true);
    }
}
```

    a. Compilation error
    b. No output
    c. 6 is added to the entire frame /
    d. None of the above

Answers

1. c	2. d	3. c	4. b	5. b	6. b	7. a	8. a	9. d	10. d
11. a, c	12. c	13. b	14. c	15. a, b	16. d	17. c	18. a	19. b	20. b
21. b	22. b	23. d	24. c	25. b	26. b	27. a	28. d	29. a, b	30. a
31. b	32. a	33. d	34. b	35. d	36. a	37. d	38. a	39. d	40. c
41. a	42. b	43. e	44. c	45. c	46. b	47. b	48. c		

Short-answer Questions

1. What are the three label alignments?
2. Explain FlowLayout with an example.
3. Explain BorderLayout with an example.
4. Explain GridLayout with an example.

5. Explain BoxLayout with an example.
6. Explain strut, glue and rigid area with an example.
7. What is DocumentListener and explain its uses?
8. Explain ChangeListener and its applications.
9. Why do you need HyperlinkListener?
10. How to create a textfield for typing passwords?
11. Explain JFileChooser and JColorChooser.
12. How will you use JOptionPane to display various messages?
13. How will you display HTML files?
14. How will you render HTML files?
15. How do you display images JTextPane?
16. Explain the process of creating custom components.

EXERCISES

16.1. Modify Exercise 14.6 to design a GUI-based Login frame by collecting username and password through text field and password text field.

16.2. [Simple calculator] Collect two integers and an operator from text fields. Create four buttons representing +, −, * and / operations. Display the result in another text field.

16.3. [Arithmetic calculator] Design full-featured arithmetic calculator with buttons representing digits from 0 to 9, operators and text field to collect data and display result.

16.4. [Currency Converter] Create two combo boxes representing source and target currencies (USD, GDP and INR). Create two text fields representing source and target values. Collect source currency code and a value to be converted to target currency. On clicking *Calculate* button, the converted value should appear in target text field.

16.5. Complete TextEditor application with other menu items: *cut, copy, paste, find* and *replace* for Edit menu.

16.6. [GUI calendar] Display calendar for 2013. Use combo box to select month and non-editable text field to display numbers representing day. Hint: you may need Calendar and Gregorian-Calendar classes.

16.7. [Tiny Social Networking Tool] Develop a simple Facebook with which you can add a user, remove him from the list, insert his image, add friend (if he already exists in the list), small chat window with JtextArea and just imagine other features.

17

GUI Development Using JApplet

OBJECTIVES

- To explain applets, its advantages and restrictions
- To introduce applet lifecycle methods
- To run applets with web browser, appletviewer and command prompt
- To use applets as a top-level container
- To design GUI forms using applets
- To explain applet input parameters: param tag and getParameter()
- To display images inside applets using JPanel
- To create Timers for repeated firing of ActionEvent
- To play audio clips in applets
- To create AudioClip object for repeated playing of appets
- To handle mouse events
- To handle hyperlink events
- To build archives using jar tool
- To create digital certificates for signing applets
- To design a web browser that will download website pages from www

17.1 INTRODUCTION

Swing uses three generally useful top-level containers: JFrame, JDialog and **JApplet**. In Chapter 16, the readers were introduced to JFrame and JDialog containers. The readers have learnt how to develop GUI applications using JFrame and to use JDialog to display messages to users. Now the readers will learn the other top-level container *JApplet*, available in swing package.

Similar to JFrame, JApplet can also contain content pane, with which you can add any swing component such as labels, buttons textfields, etc., onto JApplet. Further, it can also include menubar. Like JFrame, JApplet by default uses BorderLayout. However, you can select any layout manager as you like with setLayout(). Since JApplet extends *awt.applet.Applet*, you can also leverage the functionality of Applet class and other interfaces available in *java.applet* package.

Apart from being a top-level container, applets are designed as a client side programming tool. An applet is a small application that can be embedded into another application such as *html* page. A static web page will include applets and so you can run applets inside a web browser. **Applets** can download web pages, display documents and images and play audio clips. Also applet can communicate with other applets. In this chapter, the readers will be introduced to all programming tips and tricks of applets.

17.2 APPLET ADVANTAGES AND RESTRICTIONS

Applets can extend the functionality of a web page. However, programming with applets is restrictive in a sense that applets are always inside a sandbox. This implies that applet has some restrictions in order to be considered safe applet. That is,

- *Applets cannot read or write local files stored in harddisk.* This is a major setback to applets. But this is always necessary because you never know whether a webpage containing applet is safe to download or not. However, applets that are digitally signed can have access to local storage of your machine.
- *Applets will be downloaded every time it is running.* This will take longer time to display the contents of an applet.

Despite all these shortcomings, applets have definite advantages when you build two-tier or three-tier applications. There is no need to really install applets. All you will need to do is simply download applet in any platform. So applets support pure platform independence. Since all applets are digitally signed by either third-party digital signatures such as Verisign or Thwarte or self-signed, you can download it without any worry. Signed applets are always safe to download indeed.

17.3 CREATING AND RUNNING APPLETS

Creating an applet in swing is easy and interesting. All your class needs to do is just extend JApplet class and override necessary methods. The following are the methods that are derived from its superclass *java.applet.Applet* that you might be interested while creating your applets. Figure 17.1 explains applet methods.

With this basic information about applet methods, let us now create a simple applet that displays a string *Hello Applet* as shown in Listing 17.1.

Figure 17.1. Applet Methods

Method Name	Purpose
init()	Applet is instructed to initialize applet
start()	After init(), start() instructs applet that it should start execution
stop()	With stop(), applet is instructed to stop its execution
destroy()	Applet is instructed to destroy any resources currently using

Listing 17.1. HelloApplet Application

```
// HelloApplet.java
import javax.swing.*;
import java.applet.*;

public class HelloApplet extends JApplet
{
    JLabel lbl = new JLabel("Hello Applet !");

    public void init()
    {
        add(lbl); // by default, BorderLayout
    }
}
```

In the above application, we have just created a JLabel and included into init() method using add(). This step is very similar to adding components to JFrame that we discussed in the previous chapter but with a difference. When developing application using JFrame, you have added all swing components to the constructor. But with JApplet, you will add all swing components to init() method. Besides there is also another difference; JApplet does not contain main() method. Therefore, init() will contain all components that are to be instantiated and all listeners for all the required components. You will also call setLayout() inside init() to change default BorderLayout and setJMenuBar() to add menubar to applet. So, now let us get back to running this applet code.

Applets can be executed in any of the three different ways as shown below:

- Running applets inside web browser
- Running applets using **appletviewer**
- Running applets inside JFrame

17.3.1 Running Applets with Web Browser

In order to run applet code inside a web browser, you will have to insert applet code inside a **HTML** file. The HTML source contains a collection of tags. Every HTML tag performs an operation such as displaying text, list, tables, images and others. You can add JApplet code inside HTML with <applet> tag. An example of <applet> tag is shown in Figure 17.2.

Figure 17.2. The <applet> Tag

```
<applet code="class-file" width=size height=size></applet>
```

The applet tag has several attributes; currently we focus only three important attributes: *code, width* and *height*. With *code* attribute, you will assign *class name* where the applet resides, and *width* and *height* represent the size of the JApplet in pixels. With this understanding, let us now create a HTML file with <applet> tag as depicted in Listing 17.2.

Listing 17.2. HelloApplet.html HTML File

```html
<html>
<head>
   <title> MyApplet </title>
</head>
<body>
   <applet code="HelloApplet.class" width=400 height=300></applet>
</body>
</html>
```

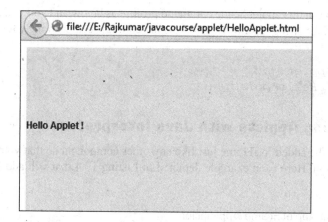

Now, you can run this applet by simply selecting this HTML file with any java enable web browser and you will see the string displaying Hello Applet ! Here the basic assumption is that both applet class file and html file are located in the same directory. In order to make applets accessible at www, you will have to store *html* file and the class file inside the web server. So when you type url of the html file in any web browser, web browser sends a request to web server for this html page and web server returns the corresponding html page back to browser and in turn the browser displays this html page on its window.

17.3.2 Running Applets with Appletviewer

The JDK contains a small utility called appletviewer that has the ability to identify <applet> tag and execute the applet defined in the *code* attribute. So we need not create HTML file containing <applet> tag, rather simply include <applet> tag inside JApplet class as a comment statement. Then, we can just run this applet with appletviewer as *appletviewer HelloApplet.java* after compiling the java file containing the applet using *javac*. Listing 17.3 illustrates how to include <applet> tag inside java file containing applet.

Listing 17.3. The <applet> Tag Inside Java File

```java
// HelloApplet1.java
// <applet code="HelloApplet1.class" width=400 height=300> </applet>

import javax.swing.*;
import java.applet.*;
```

```
public class HelloApplet1 extends JApplet
{
    JLabel lbl = new JLabel("Hello Applet !");

    public void init()
    {
        add(lbl); // by default, BorderLayout
    }
}
```

Now it is easy to run this applet inside command prompt as below and you will see a separate window appearing with the string "Hello Applet !" displayed in the center of the window.

```
javac HelloApplet.java
appletviewer HelloApplet.java
```

17.3.3 Running Applets with Java Interpreter

The applet can also be added to JFrame just like any other component so that you can run JFrame as a window application. Here is an example depicted in Listing 17.4 that will add HelloApplet inside JFrame.

Listing 17.4. HelloAppletFrame Application

```
// HelloAppletFrame.java
import javax.swing.*;
import java.awt.*;
import java.applet.*;

class HelloApplet extends JApplet
{
    JLabel lbl = new JLabel("Hello Applet !");

    public HelloApplet()
    {
        add("Center", lbl);
    }
}

public class HelloAppletFrame extends JFrame
{
    public static void main(String[] args)
    {
        HelloAppletFrame f = new HelloAppletFrame();
        f.add(new HelloApplet());
```

```
      f.setSize(400, 300);
      f.setLocationRelativeTo(null);
      f.setDefaultCloseOperation(JFrame.EXIT_ON_CLOSE);
      f.setVisible(true);
   }
}
```

In this code, JApplet behaves as a JPanel where a JLabel is added to applet inside the constructor itself. Note that init() is not at all used. This is also possible if you want JApplet to function like any other top-level container. However, if your applet needs to stop, then start again, then stop its execution, then you should override applet methods such as start(), stop() as illustrated in Listing 17.5.

Listing 17.5. Applet Overridding Start and Stop Methods

```
// HelloAppletFrame2.java
import javax.swing.*;
import java.awt.*;
import java.applet.*;

class HelloApplet2 extends JApplet
{
    JLabel lbl = new JLabel("Hello Applet !");

    public HelloApplet2()
    {
        add(lbl);
    }

    public void start()
    {
        lbl.setText("Applet restarted");
    }

    public void stop()
    {
        lbl.setText("Applet stopped");
    }
}

public class HelloAppletFrame2 extends JFrame
{
    public static void main(String[] args)
    {
        HelloAppletFrame2 f = new HelloAppletFrame2();
        f.add(new HelloApplet2());
```

```
    f.setSize(400, 300);
    f.setLocationRelativeTo(null);
    f.setDefaultCloseOperation(JFrame.EXIT_ON_CLOSE);
    f.setVisible(true);
  }
}
```

17.4 CREATING GUI COMPONENTS INSIDE APPLETS

The JApplet can contain any GUI component as a top-level container. It is also easy to convert any JFrame containing several user interface components such as buttons, comboboxes, checkboxes, radiobuttons, menus and others into JApplet. There is also another strategy in which you create panels with its own layouts so that you can add these panels to either JFrame or JApplet depending on the need. To give you some intuition of adding components to applets, let us convert a LoginFrame application into an applet. Receiving user's access data with applets is meaningful if your server application has to validate client's credentials at remote client machines. Here is the complete application as illustrated in Listing 17.6.

Listing 17.6. LoginApplet Applet

```java
// LoginApplet.java
import javax.swing.*;
import java.awt.*;
import java.awt.event.*;

public class LoginApplet extends JApplet
{
    JLabel lblUser = new JLabel("Enter User name");
    JLabel lblPwd = new JLabel("Enter Password");

    JTextField tfUser = new JTextField(15);
    JPasswordField tfPwd = new JPasswordField(25);

    JButton btnSubmit = new JButton("Submit");
    JButton btnCancel = new JButton("Cancel");

    public void init()
    {
        JPanel p = new JPanel();
        p.setLayout(new GridLayout(2,2));
        p.add(lblUser);
        p.add(tfUser);
        p.add(lblPwd);
        p.add(tfPwd);

        // add lbl and tf to center
```

```
        add("Center", p);

        // add btn to south
        p = new JPanel();
        p.add(btnSubmit);
        p.add(btnCancel);
        add("South", p);

        // register listeners to handle events
        btnSubmit.addActionListener(new SubmitL());
        btnCancel.addActionListener(new CancelL());
    }

    class SubmitL implements ActionListener
    {
        public void actionPerformed(ActionEvent e)
        {
          JOptionPane.showMessageDialog(null, "Data Submitted",
          "Submission Info", JOptionPane.INFORMATION_MESSAGE);
        }
    }

    class CancelL implements ActionListener
    {
        public void actionPerformed(ActionEvent e)
        {
            tfUser.setText("");
            tfPwd.setText("");
        }
    }
}
```

Here is the HTML file containing LoginApplet class as shown in Listing 17.7.

Listing 17.7. LoginApplet.html

```
<html>
<head>
    <title> User Login </title>
</head>
<body>
    <applet code="LoginApplet.class" height=100 width=300>
    </applet>
</body>
</html>
```

```
file:///E:/Rajkumar/javacourse/applet/LoginApplet.html
```

Enter User name	admin
Enter Password	••••••••
	Submit Cancel

17.5 APPLET INPUT PARAMETERS

A HTML file can transmit strings to applets with a tag named <param>. The **param tag** takes two attri-butes *name* and *value*. Now the applet can receive this *value* for the given *name* through getParameter() method inside applet. There can be any number of <param> tags for the given *name-value* pairs. Just think of *util.properties* file for these name-value pairs! We are now ready to develop an applet that will receive a user name and greets him *Good Morning* with his name as depicted in Listing 17.8.

Listing 17.8. WelcomeApplet.java

```java
// WelcomeApplet.java
import javax.swing.*;
import java.applet.*;
import java.awt.*;
import java.awt.event.*;

public class WelcomeApplet extends JApplet
{
    JLabel lblMesg = new JLabel();
    JPanel p = new JPanel();

    public void init()
    {
        p.add(lblMesg);
        Color color = Color.getHSBColor((float)Math.random(), 1.0F,
        1.0F );
        p.setOpaque(true); // forces painting the component
        p.setBackground(color);
        add(p);

        String s = getParameter("mesg");
        lblMesg.setText("Good morning " + s);
    }
}
```

The *getHSBColor(hue, saturation, brightness)* is a static method that is used to mix our own color with **HSB** color model, similar to **RGB** color model. The argument *hue* indicates hue value from 0.0

to 1.0. The *saturation* indicates how deep the color should be. With value 1, you can make color to be so deep and value 1 will take color out of mixure and make it a shade of gray. The *brightness* defines obviously the brightness of the color. The color becomes light when brightness value is 1 and very dark when it is 0. The setOpaque() forces painting the component immediately. Otherwise you may not see the color effect immediately (Listing 17.9).

Listing 17.9. WelcomeApplet.html

```
<html>
<head>
    <title> Welcome Applet </title>
</head>
<body>
    <p align=center>
    <applet code="WelcomeApplet.class" width=400 height=300>
        <param name="mesg" value="Rajkumar !"/>
    </applet>
    </p>
</body>
</html>
```

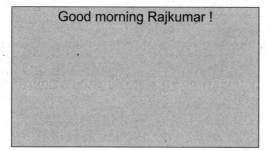

17.6 IMAGES IN APPLETS

Unlike Applets, images should not be directly painted onto JApplets by overriding paint() method. In order to paint an image, you will use JPanel as usual and override paintComponent() method and use drawImage() to paint an image onto panel. Applets will receive image files using getImage() method. The getImage() is a overloaded method where it will take any URL of an image or URL of the applet along with the image file name.

The Applet class defines getCodeBase() and getResource() methods. The getCodeBase() returns URL of the directory which contains this applet. On the other hand, getResource(filename) returns the URL of the filename in the class path. The getClass() returns an instance of java.lang.Class which is created for every class that is loaded by JVM. The java.net.URL class can be used to identify files, images and other files on the internet. Here is an example depicted in Listing 17.10 that illustrates displaying images to applets.

Listing 17.10. Displaying Images

```java
// ImageApplet.java
import javax.swing.*;
import java.awt.*;
import java.io.*;
import java.net.*;

publi c class ImageApplet extends JApplet
{
    String desc;
    Color bgcolor;
    Image image, image2;
    URL url;

    public void init()
    {
        try
        {
        bgcolor = new Color(Integer.parseInt(getParameter("bg"),
        16));
        }
        catch(Exception e) { }

        desc = getParameter("mesg");
        image = getImage(getCodeBase(), getParameter("picture"));

        //url = this.getClass().getResource(getParameter("pict
        ure"));
        //image2 = getImage(url);

        // add to panel
        add(new ImagePanel());
    }

    class ImagePanel extends JPanel
    {
        public ImagePanel()
        {
            setBackground(bgcolor);
        }

        public void paintComponent(Graphics g)
        {
            super.paintComponent(g);
            g.drawImage(image, 0, 0, getWidth(), getHeight()-50,
            this);
```

```
        //g.drawImage(image2, 0, 0, getWidth(),
        getHeight()-50, this);
        g.drawString(desc, 100, 300);
    }
}
}
```

file:///E:/Rajkumar/javacourse/applet/ImageApplet.html

Lovely Nature Image

Here, ImageApplet.html (Listing 17.11) file transmits three name-value pairs to ImageApplet class. The parameters are *bg, mesg* and *picture* whose values are *AAFF55, Lovely Nature Image* and *nature.jpg*, respectively. Here *AAFF55* represents RGB color values in hex for the background color of the panel. Inside init(), getParameter() method receives these values for the given names. The getImage() returns Image object by using either the URL of the applet or the URL of the image file. Once these values are read into applet inside init(), the JPanel will be painted with this color, message and image by overriding paintComponent(). Remember this JPanel is added as an inner class inside applet.

Listing 17.11. ImageApplet.html

```
<HTML>
<BODY>
<APPLET code="ImageApplet.class" width=300 height=325>
<PARAM name="bg" value="AAFF55">
<PARAM name="mesg" value="Lovely Nature Image">
<PARAM name="picture" value="nature.jpg">
```

```
</APPLET>
</BODY>
</HTML>
```

17.7 TIMERS FIRING ACTIONEVENT

The swing.Timer is yet another interesting class that is used to fire ActionEvent repeatedly at periodic time intervals. The swing.Timer is the ideal **timer** for all swing components as all swing timers share the same timer thread. There is also a general purpose timer defined in *util* package. The start() and stop() methods can be used to start and stop the timer, while setRepeats() specifies timer to fire ActionEvent repeatedly or not, by default it is true. The constructure Timer(delay-time, actionlistener) takes delay time in milliseconds and the name of the ActionListener for this timer. You can create timer object as shown in Figure 17.3.

Figure 17.3. Creating Timer Object

```
Timer timer = new Timer(1000, action-listener);
timer.start();
where action-listener is the instance of ActionListener that is
associated for timer
```

In order to appreciate the power of timer, here is an example that displays counter value 1, 2, 3, etc., incremented and displayed every second as depicted in Listing 17.12.

Listing 17.12. Counting Numbers Applet

```
// CounterApplet.java
//<applet code="CounterApplet.class" height=100 width=300></
  applet>

import javax.swing.*;
import java.awt.*;
import java.awt.event.*;

public class CounterApplet extends JApplet
{
    JTextField tfDisplay = new JTextField(20);
    // initial value for timer
    int i = 0;

    public void init()
    {
        Box box = Box.createVerticalBox();
        box.add(tfDisplay);
```

```
        add(box);

        ActionListener timerL = new TimerL();
        //triger timer every 1000 ms
        Timer timer = new Timer(1000, timerL);
        timer.start();
    }

    class TimerL implements ActionListener
    {
        public void actionPerformed(ActionEvent e)
        {
            Color color = Color.getHSBColor(
                (float)Math.random(), 1.0F, 1.0F );
            tfDisplay.setBackground(color);
            tfDisplay.setText("Counting: "+ ++i);
        }
    }
}
```

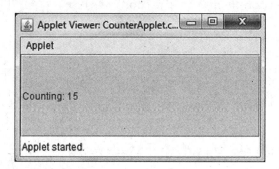

Here, timer fires actionevent every second and the associated ActionListener is executed, displaying the current value of the variable *i* inside the textfield. Also, background color of the text field is changed every time its actionevent is fired with a random HSV color.

17.8 PLAYING AUDIO CLIPS

Audio clips can be played inside applet or frame. Java supports multiple audio file formats such as *wav, aiff, au, mid* and *rmf* formats. The JApplet class contains play() that plays a sound clip only once, given the URL of the file. If you want to play the audio clip repeatedly, then you should create *java. applet.AudioClip* object of the sound file that supports *loop()* for repeated playing and *stop()* to pause the audio clip, besides *play()* for playing audio clip. An AudioClip object can be created with the static Applet.newAudioClip(url) method given the *url* as input. Since you will develop only JApplet, the other instance method of Applet class getAudioClip(url) will not be useful for you. The application shown in Listing 17.13 explains you how to play sound clips inside JApplet.

Listing 17.13. Playing Audio Clips Along with Photo Book

```java
//AudioPlayerApplet.java

//<applet code="AudioPlayerApplet.class" height=200 width=260>
//<param name="sound" value="raj_sound.au">
//</applet>

import javax.swing.*;
import java.awt.*;
import java.awt.event.*;
import java.io.*;
import java.util.*;
import java.net.*;

public class AudioPlayerApplet extends JApplet
{
    // max images inside imagee directory
    int max = 7;
    // to hold images
    ImageIcon[] icon = new ImageIcon[max];
    // to select random image
    Random r = new Random();
    // label painted with image
    JLabel lblImage = new JLabel();

    public void init()
    {
        // play url
        play(getDocumentBase(), getParameter("sound"));

        // add to panel
        JPanel panel = new JPanel();
        panel.setLayout(new BorderLayout());
        panel.add("Center", lblImage);
        add("Center", panel);

        // load all images from images dir into icon array
        loadImages();

        // create timer and start
        ActionListener timerL = new TL();
        javax.swing.Timer timer = new javax.swing.Timer(1000,
        timerL);
        timer.start();
```

```
    }

    public void loadImages()
    {
        for(int i = 0; i < max; i++)
        {
            System.out.println(i);
            icon[i] = new ImageIcon(getClass().getResource(
                "images/flower" + i + ".jpg"));
        }
    }

    class TL implements ActionListener
    {
        public void actionPerformed(ActionEvent e)
        {
            // select new image icon based on random number from 0
            to 6
            lblImage.setIcon(icon[r.nextInt(6)]);
        }
    }
}
```

Here, AudioPlayerApplet does two things. It plays a sound clip that is stored in the current directory where the applet resides. It also displays random images that are stored inside a subdirectory *images*. The subdirectory *images* contains the following images.

Flower0   Flower1   Flower2   Flower3   Flower4   Flower5   Flower6

Inside init() method, play() method of JApplet class plays the sound clip *raj_sound.au* that is sent to applet via <param> tag. The loadImages() method downloads all seven images from *images* subdirectory and images are instantiated as ImageIcons and kept inside an array *icon*.

The timer object fires ActionEvent every second and the registered action listener TL is called. Inside actionPerformed() method, the JLabel is painted with a random ImageIcon from *icon* array by calling setIcon() method of JLabel class. Note that you will call this applet using appletviewer as <applet> tag is inserted as a comment statement inside this java file.

17.9 HANDLING MOUSE EVENT

In Chapter 16, the readers were introduced to various events including MouseEvent. For MouseEvent, there are two listeners that you can register to components – MouseListener and MouseMotionListener. If you are interested to override only one method from the available methods, then your class can extend its corresponding Adapter class. Suppose, if you want to obtain the coordinate of the mouse press, release, click and so on, then you can call MouseEvent's getX() and getY() methods. In Listing 17.14, you will see an implementation of MouseEvent where mouse clicks and mouse dragging on a small rectangle are handled.

Listing 17.14. Moving and Dragging Rectangles

```java
// DragApplet.java
//<applet code="DragApplet" height=400 width=400></applet>

import java.awt.*;
import java.awt.event.*;
import javax.swing.*;

class Square extends JPanel
{
    // origin
    int x, y;
    // offset position
    int offsetX, offsetY;

    public Square()
    {
        // initial position
        x = 10; y = 10;
        setBackground(Color.LIGHT_GRAY);
```

```
         // register ML and MML for this panel
         addMouseListener(new ML());
         addMouseMotionListener(new MML());
    }

    public void paintComponent(Graphics g)
    {
        super.paintComponent(g);
        g.setColor(Color.MAGENTA);
        g.fillRect(x, y, 25, 25);
    }

    class ML extends MouseAdapter
    {
        public void mousePressed(MouseEvent e)
        {
            // new loc
            x = e.getX();
            y = e.getY();
            repaint();
        }
    }


    class MML extends MouseMotionAdapter
    {
        public void mouseDragged(MouseEvent e)
        {
            int x1 = e.getX();
            int y1 = e.getY();

            if(x1 >= x && x1 < x+25 && y1 >= y && y1 < y+25)
            {
                offsetX = x1 - x;
                offsetY = y1 - y;
            }

            // Move
            x = x1 - offsetX;
            y = y1 - offsetY;
            repaint();
        }
    }
}

public class DragApplet extends JApplet
```

```
{
    Square panel = new Square();
    public void init()
    {
        add(panel);
    }
}
```

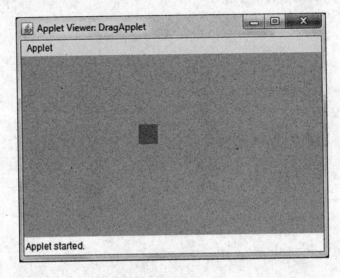

In this application, a small color-filled square of 25 pixels height and width is drawn on JPanel. Inside the overridden mousePressed(), the coordinate values of mouse click is collected using getX() and getY() methods, so that the square will be moved to this new location. Similarly, inside mouseDragged(), a new coordinate value is calculated so that square is moving when mouse is dragged. Also, it is necessary to repaint JPanel whenever there is an update, which is done with repaint() method.

17.10 HANDLING HYPERLINK EVENT

The **HyperlinkEvent** is fired by the components indicating that some action is happened on hypertext link. There are three event types for HyperlinkEvent namely ACTIVATED, ENTERED and EXITED. In the application shown in Listing 17.15, the JEditorPane recognizes the click on hyperlinks and a new html page will be rendered inside the editor pane. Listing 17.16 depicts the corresponding html file for Web Browser applet.

Listing 17.15. Web Browser Recognizing Hyperlinks

```
// WebBrowser.java
import java.awt.*;
import java.awt.event.*;
import javax.swing.*;
```

```
import javax.swing.event.*;
import javax.swing.border.*;
import java.net.URL;

public class WebBrowser extends JApplet
{
    JEditorPane pane = new JEditorPane();
    JLabel lblMesg = new JLabel("Location");
    JTextField tfURL = new JTextField(30);
    JButton btnGo = new JButton("Go");

    public WebBrowser()
    {
        JPanel p = new JPanel();
        p.setBackground(Color.BLACK);
        p.setLayout(new BorderLayout());
        p.setBorder(BorderFactory.createLineBorder(Color.BLACK,1));

        JPanel p1 = new JPanel();
        p1.add(lblMesg);
        p1.add(tfURL);
        p1.add(btnGo);
        p.add("North", p1);

        pane.setEditable(false);
        p.add("Center", new JScrollPane(pane));

        // add entire panel to applet
        add(p);
        // listening to hyperlinks
        pane.addHyperlinkListener(new HyperlinkL());
        btnGo.addActionListener(new GoL());
    }

    class HyperlinkL implements HyperlinkListener
    {
        public void hyperlinkUpdate(HyperlinkEvent e)
        {
            if (e.getEventType() == HyperlinkEvent.EventType.
            ACTIVATED)
            {
                try
                {
                    // show web page
```

```
                 pane.setPage(e.getURL());
                 }
             catch(Exception e1) { }
          }
      }
}

class GoL implements ActionListener
{
    public void actionPerformed(ActionEvent e)
    {
        // construct URL
        URL url = null;;

        try
        {
            String location = tfURL.getText().trim();
            if (location.length() == 0)
                throw new Exception();
            if(location.contains("html") || location.
            contains("htm"))
            url = WebBrowser.this.getClass().
            getResource(location);
            System.out.println(url.toString());
        }
        catch (Exception e1)
        {
            JOptionPane.showMessageDialog(
                WebBrowser.this, "URL Not Exist");
            return;
        }

        try
        {
            // show web page
            pane.setPage(url);
        }
        catch(Exception e1) {
            JOptionPane.showMessageDialog(
                WebBrowser.this, "Unable to set page");
            return;
        }
    }
}
```

```java
    public static void main(String[] args)
    {
        JFrame f = new JFrame();
        f.add(new WebBrowser());
        f.setTitle("Web Browser");
        f.setSize(600,500);
        f.setLocationRelativeTo(null);   // centers to screen
        f.setDefaultCloseOperation(JFrame.EXIT_ON_CLOSE); // closes
        frame
        f.setVisible(true);
    }
}
```

Listing 17.16. WebBrowser.html

```html
<html>
<head>
   <title>Web Browser using jar </title>
</head>
<body>
<applet code="WebBrowser.class"
   width=500 height=400>
</applet>
</body>
</html>
```

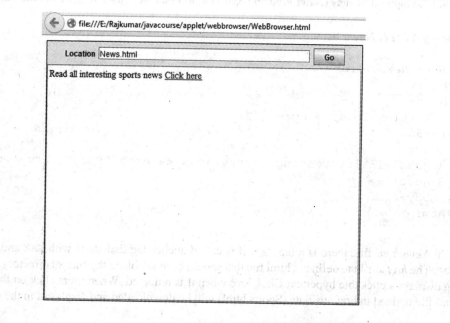

When the user types any html file available in the current directory in the text field and presses *Go* button, the content of the html file will be displayed inside the editor pane. Remember this web browser applet recognizes only files with *.html* and *.htm* extensions. The *setPage()* method takes the *url* of the html file as input and displays its contents. If there is a hyperlink in the html page, then users can click on the hyperlink so that the clicked file will be displayed. Listing 17.17 and Listing 17.18 depict the input html files (*News.html* and *Sports.html*) that were used to generate the output.

Listing 17.17. News.html

```
<! -- News.html -->
<html>
<head>
    <title> Today's News </title>
</head>
<body>
    Read all interesting sports news <a href="Sports.html">Click
    here</a>
</body>
<html>
```

In *News.html* file, there is a tag <a>. It is called anchor tag that starts with <a> and closes with </a>. The *href* attribute defines a html file that should be available in the current directory. The anchor tag displays a clickable hypertext *Click here* when it is rendered. When users click on the hyperlink, html file defined in href attribute (Sports.html) will be downloaded and displayed in the editor pane.

In *Sports.html* (Listing 17.18), an unordered list (defined using <ul> and </ul> tag) with two list items (defined using <li> and </li> tag) is created. The <h1> tag is used to define heading. HTML supports six levels of headings from <h1> to <h6> where <h1> is the biggest in font size. Also, comment is included inside <!-- and -- > tags in html. One final note for you! There are many other features that HTML5 supports. However we do not cover them all in this book because they are outside the scope of this book. Therefore, readers are advised to refer to other books to learn all those necessary features.

Listing 17.18. Sports.html

```
<! -- Sports.html -- >
<html>
<head>
    <title> Sports News </title>
</head>
<body>
    <h1>Sports News </h1>
    <ul>
        <li>Cricket news</li>
        <li>Soccer news</li>
    </ul>
</body>
<html>
```

17.11 BUILDING ARCHIVES USING JAR

The *code* attribute of the <applet> tag defines the Java class file that will be executed when the browser opens the html file. This is fine as long as there is only one class file that is to be included for the *code* attribute. But there may be several class files that are to be included inside the html file. You might have noticed there are several inner classes inside an applet and so there will be several class files for this applet. You can combine these class files into a single archive with the free tool **jar**, available in jdk distributions. You can run *jar* command inside command prompt as shown in Figure 17.4.

Figure 17.4. The Jar File Creation

```
jar cf filename.jar *.class
```

Here all class files that exist in this current directory are bundled as a *jar* file with a name *filename.jar*. Please ensure that the curent directory contains only class files that are part of this applet. Otherwise your jar file will include class files that may be part of other java applets that are not at all required and will unnecessarily increase its size.

The jar command has many options. You can study these options by typing jar in the command prompt. The option *c* creates new archive and *f* specifies archive file name. The archive that is created using jar command should be included inside the html file with *archive* attribute of <applet> tag. For instance, Listing 17.19 illustrates our earlier WebBrowser.html with the additional *archive* attribute.

Listing 17.19. WebBrowser.html

```
<html>
<head>
    <title>Web Browser using jar </title>
</head>
<body>
<applet code="WebBrowser.class"
    archive="WebBrowser.jar"
    width=500 height=400>
</applet>
</body>
</html>
```

17.12 SIGNING APPLETS

Generally all applets are considered to be unsafe applets that might harm the client machine when it is downloaded. To ensure that an applet is safe to be downloaded by client machine, all applets are expected to possess a digital signature. The digital signature can be obtained by any third-party authorities such as Verisign. Also applets can be self-signed by the creator with jdk's free utility named *keytool*. With keytool, you can obtain a certificate or private key that can be used to sign the applet. Then you can use *jarsigner* command to sign the jar file containing the applet so that now applet becomes a safe applet with minimum level of security. Thereby you can access local file contents and download the files. Thus when your applet is downloaded by client computer, it will understand the applet is a trusted applet as it is signed with a certificate. Creating a self-signed applet involves three basic steps:

1. Create a private–public key pair using *–genkey* attribute of *keytool*
2. Create a certificate for this key pair using *–selfcert* attribute of *keytool*
3. Associate this certificate with JAR file representing the applet using *jarsigner*

```
Step1: Type keytool -genkey -keystore mykeystore -alias myalias
Step2: Type keytool -selfcert -keystore mykeystore -alias myalias
Step3: Type jarsigner -keystore mykeystore filename.jar -alias
       myalias
```

In step1, you create a private–public key with genkey attribute. Your key will have an alias named *myalias* and is stored inside a file named *mykeystore*. The keystore file *mykeystore* will be created in the current directory where you typed keytool command. The keytool command will ask you several details that will be attached to the key as below and you will have to supply those details.

```
Enter keystore password: xxxxxx
What is your first and last name?
   [Unknown]:  rajkumar kannan
What is the name of your organizational unit?
   [Unknown]:  CS Department
What is the name of your organization?
   [Unknown]:  Bishop Heber College Autonomous
What is the name of your City or Locality?
   [Unknown]:  Tiruchirappalli
What is the name of your State or Province?
   [Unknown]:  Tamil Nadu
What is the two-letter country code for this unit?
   [Unknown]:  IN
Is CN=rajkumar kannan, OU=CS Department, O=Bishop Heber College
Autonomous, L=Tiruchirappalli, ST=Tamil Nadu, C=IN correct?
   [no]:  yes
Enter key password for <myalias>
        (RETURN if same as keystore password):
```

Then in step2, you will create a digital certificate, again with keytool command but with *selfcert* attribute. The certificate will be stored in the same keystore file that has been created in step1.

Finally in step3 you will sign your JAR file containing the applet with *jarsigner* utility where you will mention keystore name and alias name along with the JAR file name. This will create a hash for each file in the JAR and sign them with the private key created in step1. These hashes, the public key and the certificate are added to the META-INF directory of the JAR file alongside the JAR's manifest.

Assume FilesApplet.jar is your jar filename and it contains three class files:

- FilesApplet$OpenL.class
- FilesApplet$SaveL.class
- FilesApplet.class

Then you can check them with *tf* attributes of *jar*, as shown below:

```
C:\>jar -tf FilesApplet.jar
META-INF/MANIFEST.MF
META-INF/MYKEYNAM.SF
META-INF/MYKEYNAM.DSA
META-INF/
FilesApplet$OpenL.class
FilesApplet$SaveL.class
FilesApplet.class
```

Once a JAR file is signed, its contents cannot be changed. In other words, if you update the java source file, then you need to compile and create JAR file again and sign it digitally with jarsigner. Then the client machine can safely download your applet as it is now digitally signed.

To illustrate applet signing, let us create and sign an applet so that it will access local files as depicted in Listing 17.20. Listing 17.21 depicts the corresponding html file for FilesApplet.java.

Listing 17.20. Accessing Local Files in Hardisk

```java
// FilesApplet.java
import javax.swing.*;
import javax.swing.filechooser.*;
import javax.swing.border.*;
import java.awt.*;
import java.awt.event.*;
import java.io.*;
import java.net.*;

public class FilesApplet extends JApplet
{
    JTextPane taDisplay = new JTextPane();
    JButton btnOpen = new JButton("Open");
    JButton btnSave = new JButton("Save");

    public void init()
    {
        JPanel p = new JPanel();
        p.setBackground(Color.lightGray);
        p.add(btnOpen);
        p.add(btnSave);
        add("South", p);

        taDisplay.setBackground(Color.yellow);
        add("Center", new JScrollPane(taDisplay));

        //add listeners
        btnOpen.addActionListener(new OpenL());
        btnSave.addActionListener(new SaveL());
    }

    class SaveL implements ActionListener
    {
        public void actionPerformed(ActionEvent e)
        {
            JFileChooser fc = new JFileChooser();
            // show both files and directories
            fc.setFileSelectionMode(2);
            int val = fc.showSaveDialog(FilesApplet.this);

            try
            {
                if(val == JFileChooser.APPROVE_OPTION)
```

```
                {
                    FileWriter fw = new FileWriter(
                        fc.getSelectedFile());
                    // write to file
                    taDisplay.write(fw);
                    fw.close();
                }
            }
        catch (IOException e1) {
            taDisplay.setText(e1.toString());
        }
    }
}

class OpenL implements ActionListener
{
    public void actionPerformed(ActionEvent e)
    {
        // create file chooser
        JFileChooser fc = new JFileChooser();

        // show both files and directories
        fc.setFileSelectionMode(2);
        int val = fc.showOpenDialog(FilesApplet.this);

        // display contents
        URL url = null;
        String s;
        try
        {
            if(val == JFileChooser.APPROVE_OPTION)
            {
                // display selected file
                url = fc.getSelectedFile().toURL();
            }

            // read file contents
            BufferedReader in = new BufferedReader(
                new InputStreamReader(url.openStream()));
            // show
            while ((s = in.readLine()) != null)
                taDisplay.setText(taDisplay.getText() + s + "\n");

            // close stream
            in.close();
        }catch (IOException e1) {
```

```
            taDisplay.setText(el.toString());
            }
        }
    }
}
```

Listing 17.21. FilesApplet.html

```html
<html>
    <head>
            <title>Signed Applet</title>
    </head>
    <body>
        <applet
            code="FilesApplet.class"
            archive="FilesApplet.jar"
            width="400"
            height="580">
            Your browser does not support Applets.
        </applet>
    </body>
</html>
```

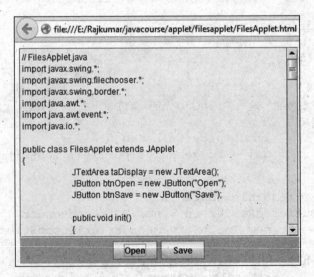

When users click *Open* button, the file chooser collects a file name from the user and url object is constructed and *openStream()* converts *url* into *InputStream* so that *BufferedReader* instance can be created and *readLine()* performs line by line reading of the selected file. The concatenated string is displayed in the text pane.

When users click *Save* button, they will be asked to choose a file name. A FileWriter stream is associated for the selected file and *write()* stores the contents of the text pane onto the stream. This kind of reading and writing with local disk is possible once the applet is digitally signed. Otherwise, all unsigned applets will throw *java.security.AccessControlException* when an attempt is made to access local files.

17.13 PROBLEM: ACCESSING WEBSITES FROM WWW

Suppose we want to design a trivial web browser that can display a web page of a real website such as *http://www.yahoo.com*. When user types a valid url, then setPage() method can receive this url and display its contents inside editor pane or text pane. This is possible only when the applet is digitally signed. The complete application for accessing websites from internet is shown in Listing 17.22. Listing 17.23 depicts the corresponding html file for WebBrowserReal applet.

Listing 17.22. Real Web Browser

```
// WebBrowserReal.java
import java.awt.*;
import java.awt.event.*;
import java.io.*;
import javax.swing.*;
import javax.swing.event.*;
import javax.swing.border.*;
import java.net.*;

public class WebBrowserReal extends JApplet
{
    JEditorPane pane = new JEditorPane();
    JLabel lblMesg = new JLabel("Location");
    JTextField tfURL = new JTextField(30);
    JButton btnGo = new JButton("Go");

    public void init()
    {
        JPanel p = new JPanel();
        p.setBackground(Color.BLACK);
        p.setLayout(new BorderLayout());
        p.setBorder(BorderFactory.createLineBorder(Color.RED,1));

        JPanel p1 = new JPanel();
        p1.add(lblMesg);
        p1.add(tfURL);
        p1.add(btnGo);
        p.add("North", p1);

        pane.setEditable(false);
```

```java
        p.add("Center", new JScrollPane(pane));

    // add entire panel to applet
    add(p);
    // listening to button clicks
    btnGo.addActionListener(new GoL());
    }

class GoL implements ActionListener
{
    public void actionPerformed(ActionEvent e)
    {
        // construct URL
        URL url = null;;

        try
        {
            // eg: http://www.yahoo.com
            String location = tfURL.getText().trim();
            if (location.length() == 0)
                throw new Exception();
            url = new URL(location)

        }
        catch (Exception e1)
        {
            JOptionPane.showMessageDialog(
                WebBrowserReal.this, "URL Not Exist");
            return;
        }

        try
        {
            pane.setPage(url);
        }
        catch(Exception e1) {
            String s = e1.toString();
            JOptionPane.showMessageDialog(
                WebBrowserReal.this, s);
            return;
        }
    }
  }
}
```

Listing 17.23. WebBrowserReal.html

```html
<html>
<head>
   <title>Web Browser Real </title>
<html>
<head>
   <title>Web Browser Real </title>
</head>
<body>
<applet code="WebBrowserReal.class"
   archive="WebBrowserReal.jar"
   width=500 height=400>
</applet>
</body>
</html>
```

In this application, when the user types an url *http://www.yahoo.com* in the text field and presses *Go* button, a web page from *yahoo.com* is displayed.

17.14 SUMMARY

1. An applet is a small application that can be embedded into another application such as html page
2. Unsigned Applets cannot read or write local files stored in hard disk
3. Applets will be downloaded every time it is running

4. There is no need to install applets, just it can be downloaded
5. Applet life cylce includes init(), start(), stop() and destroy() methods
6. The <applet> tag includes the class file of the applet to be executed
7. Applets can be run inside command prompt using appletviewer utility
8. To use appletviewer, <applet> tag should be included as a comment statement inside java code
9. Applet can be added to JFrame just like any other component
10. GUI forms can be created with applets like frames
11. A HTML file can transmit strings to applets with a tag named <param>
12. Applet can collect <param> tag *value* for the given *name* through getParameter() method inside applet
13. To paint image, use JPanel and add JPanel to applet
14. A timer can fire ActionEvent repeatedly at periodic time intervals
15. The play() method of JApplet class will play an audio clip
16. For repeated playing of sound clips, you must create AudioClip object and you can use loop() method of AudioClip object
17. The getX() and getY() returns the location for mouse events
18. A hyperlink inside html file can be handled with HyperlinkEvent
19. The anchor tag <a> is used to create a hyperlink
20. The <ul> tag is used to create unordered list
21. Jar utility is used to build archive containing class files
22. The keytool command is used to generate private key
23. The selfcert attribute of keytool command generates self certificate
24. The jarsigner command can be used to sign jar file with self-certificate
25. The signed applet can download web pages from world wide web

KEY TERMS

Appletviewer, 632
Applets, 631
Audio clips, 643
HSB, 638

HTML, 632
HyperlinkEvent, 648
Jar, 653
JApplet, 630

Param tag, 638
RGB, 638
Timer, 642

REVIEW QUESTIONS

Multiple-choice Questions

1. JApplet has been designed for
   a. Client side programming
   c. Middleware programming
   b. Server side programming
   d. None of the above

2. Which of the following are true about JApplet?
   a. JApplet is a small program that can be embedded into html files
   b. JApplet extends awt.Applet class
   c. JApplet contains content pane to hold swing components
   d. All of the above

3. Which of the following are true about JApplet?
   a. JApplet can run inside a web browser
   b. JApplets can download web pages
   c. JAppets display documents and images and play audio clips
   d. JApplet can communicate with other applets
   e. All of the above

4. Choose all incorrect statements:
   a. JApplets can read and write to local files in hard disk
   b. JApplets will be downloaded every time it is running
   c. JApplets have to be installed in client machines
   d. None of the above

5. Which of the following are JApplet methods?
   a. init()   b. start()
   c. stop()   d. destroy()
   e. All of the above

6. What is the default layout manager for JApplet?
   a. FlowLayout   b. BorderLayout
   c. GridLayout   d. BoxLayout

7. Which container supports FlowLayout manager?
   a. JFrame   b. JApplet
   c. JPanel   d. None of the above

8. What are the ways to run applets?
   a. Web browser   b. Appletviewer
   c. Adding JApplet to JFrame   d. All of the above

9. How to add applet class file to html file?
   a. using <applet> tag   b. using <appletviewer> tag
   c. using <appletstub> tag   d. None of the above

10. What method transmits strings from html file to applet?
    a. <applet>
    b. <param>
    c. <attrib>
    d. None of the above

11. What method applets use to receive strings from html files?
    a. getValue()
    b. getParameter()
    c. get()
    d. None of the above

12. How many param tags can applet tag have?
    a. 1
    b. 2
    c. 3
    d. Any number of tags

13. Which method returns URL of the directory which contains an applet?
    a. getDirectory()
    b. getCodeBase()
    c. getURL()
    d. None of the above

14. Which class fires ActionEvent at periodic intervals?
    a. JButton
    b. JMenu
    c. swing.Timer
    d. util.Timer
    e. None of the above

15. What method plays audio clips?
    a. JApplet.play()
    b. AudioClip.play()
    c. Audio.play()
    d. None of the above

16. Which class supports audio playback facilities?
    a. JApplet
    b. JAudioClip
    c. applet.AudioClip
    d. applet.JAudioClip

17. Which of the following are methods of AudipClip?
    a. play()
    b. loop()
    c. stop()
    d. All of the above

18. Which methods return mouse coordinates?
    a. getX()
    b. getY()
    c. get()
    d. None of the above

19. Which class implements HyperlinkListener interface?
    a. JTextArea
    b. JSlider
    c. JEditorPane
    d. None of the above

20. Which method displays the content of a URL?
    a. setPage()
    b. setURL()
    c. showURL()
    d. None of the above

21. Can your JApplet be compiled using javac?
    a. Yes
    b. No
    c. No – using appletviewer only
    d. None of the above

22. Can applet tag appear inside JApplet class?
    a. Yes
    b. No
    c. Yes–but as a comment statement only
    d. None of the above

23. Which of the following are the attributes of applet tag?
    a. Code
    b. Width
    c. Height
    d. All of the above

24. Which of the following are the attributes of applet tag?
    a. Codebase
    b. Name
    c. Alt
    d. All of the above

25. Which of the following are the attributes of param tag?
    a. Name
    b. Value
    c. Link
    d. All of the above

26. What utility is used to create an archive of class files?
    a. zip
    b. gzip
    c. jar
    d. None of the above

27. What utility is used to create signed applets?
    a. jar
    b. zip
    c. jarsigner
    d. All of the above

28. Choose all correct statements:
    a. Signed applets can access local files
    b. Signed applets are safe to be downloaded by client computer
    c. Unsigned applets will throw AccessControlException when attempt is made to access local files
    d. All of the above

Answers

1. a	2. d	3. e	4. a, c	5. e	6. b	7. c	8. d	9. a	10. b
11. b	12. d	13. b	14. c	15. a,b	16. c	17. d	18. a,b	19. c	20. a
21. a	22. c	23. d	24. d	25. a,b	26. c	27. c	28. d		

Short-answer Questions

1. What is an applet?
2. How applets differ from an application?
3. Explain applet life cycle.
4. What are the ways of running an applet?
5. Can applet access local files in hard disk?
6. How will you make applets to access local files?

7. Can applet be used just like other containers such as panel and frame?

8. Can you add applet onto JFrame?

9. Explain passing parameter values from HTML file to applet.

10. How will you display images inside applet?

11. How will you play audio clips inside applet?

12. Explain the process of signing an applet.

13. How will you handle HyperlinkEvent?

EXERCISES

17.1. [*Analog clock*] Create an analog clock applet.

17.2. [*Tic-Tac-Toe*] Create an applet for Tic-Tac-Toe game. Use 9 (3×3) buttons to represent X and O symbols. Create a text field to collect player name and a button to start a new game.

17.3. [*Arithmetic calculator*] Create an applet based arithmetic calculator.

17.4. [*Tiny social networking*] Design a tiny social networking tool using applet.

17.5. [*Dancing man*] Design a dancing human skeleton using lines and circles with different colours.

17.6. [*Stock Ticker*] Create an applet that will roll stock names horizontally and their prices right-to-left simulating marquee behaviour. Use the stock price file you have downloaded earlier.

17.7. [*Image editor*] Create a simple image editor that will

- create 2D primitives such as lines, rectangles, etc.
- change foreground color, background color of the figure
- change foreground color partially based on mouse selection
- rotate figure vertically or horizontally

17.8. [*Song recommender*] Create a song file that contains song name, name of the actor(s), genre such as *romantic, sorrow, comedy, folk, traditional*, etc. Design a GUI that will collect username and his interests and accordingly show him a set of songs he might like to listen. Also roll horizontally newly arrived song names inside a window like marquee.

17.9. [*Song player*] Improve exercise 17.8 such that when user selects a song from the list, song player applet plays the selected song.

17.10. Design an applet that displays a string at random locations continuously with different colours.

JAVA KEYWORDS (RESERVED WORDS)

abstract	continue	for	new	switch
assert	default	goto	package	synchronized
boolean	do	if	private	this
break	double	implements	protected	throw
byte	else	import	public	throws
case	enum	instanceof	return	transient
catch	extends	int	short	try
char	final	interface	static	void
class	finally	long	strictfp	volatile
const	float	native	super	while

SELECTED JAVA7 PACKAGES

java.applet	java.security	javax.sql
java.awt	java.sql	javax.swing
java.awt.color	java.text	javax.swing.border
java.awt.datatransfer	java.util	javax.swing.colorchooser
java.awt.dnd	java.util.concurrent	javax.swing.event
java.awt.event	java.util.concurrent.atomic	javax.swing.filechooser
java.awt.font	java.util.concurrent.locks	javax.swing.plaf
java.awt.geom	java.util.regex	javax.swing.table
java.awt.print	javax.annotation	javax.swing.text
java.beans	javax.imageio	javax.swing.tree
java.io	javax.jws	javax.tools
java.lang	javax.lang.model.util	javax.xml
java.lang.annotation	javax.management	javax.xml.ws
java.math	javax.naming	javax.xml.xpath
java.net	javax.net	org.omg.CORBA
java.nio	javax.rmi	org.omg.Messaging
java.nio.channels	javax.rmi.CORBA	org.w3c.dom
java.nio.file	javax.rmi.ssl	org.xml.sax
java.rmi	javax.sound.midi	

SYLLABUS FOR ORACLE CERTIFIED ASSOCIATE (OCA), JAVA SE 7 PROGRAMMER-I (EXAM NUMBER 1Z0-803)

Java Basics

- Define the scope of variables
- Define the structure of a Java class
- Create executable Java applications with a main method
- Import other Java packages to make them accessible in your code

Working with Java Data Types

- Declare and initialize variables
- Differentiate between object reference variables and primitive variables
- Read or write to object fields
- Explain an object's lifecycle (creation, "dereference" and garbage collection)
- Call methods on objects
- Manipulate data using the StringBuilder class and its methods
- Creating and manipulating Strings

Using Operators and Decision Constructs

- Use Java operators
- Use parenthesis to override operator precedence
- Test equality between Strings and other objects using == and equals ()
- Create if and if/else constructs
- Use a switch statement

Creating and Using Arrays

- Declare, instantiate, initialize and use a one-dimensional array
- Declare, instantiate, initialize and use multidimensional array
- Declare and use an ArrayList

Using Loop Constructs

- Create and use while loops
- Create and use for loops including the enhanced for loop
- Create and use do/while loops
- Compare loop constructs
- Use break and continue

Working with Methods and Encapsulation

- Create methods with arguments and return values
- Apply the static keyword to methods and fields
- Create an overloaded method
- Differentiate between default and user-defined constructors
- Create and overload constructors
- Apply access modifiers
- Apply encapsulation principles to a class
- Determine the effect upon object references and primitive values when they are passed into methods that change the values

Working with Inheritance

- Implement inheritance
- Develop code that demonstrates the use of polymorphism
- Differentiate between the type of a reference and the type of an object
- Determine when casting is necessary
- Use super and this to access objects and constructors
- Use abstract classes and interfaces

Handling Exceptions

- Differentiate among checked exceptions, RuntimeExceptions and Errors
- Create a try-catch block and determine how exceptions alter normal program flow
- Describe what Exceptions are used for in Java
- Invoke a method that throws an exception
- Recognize common exception classes and categories